'This is an autobiography no fil
Daily Mail

'Enormously enjoyable'

Times Literary Supplement

'Unabashed and discreet'

Sunday Telegraph

'Perceptive and enjoyable'

Total Film

'He writes exactly as he speaks in private or on television – with enthusiasm, humour and honesty . . . a commendably candid and keenly observed journey through an eventful life lived well'

Irish Times

'He is a funny, skilled and perceptive writer . . . he has a wealth of incident to recall and a fund of anecdotes to tell. If he wasn't so wry and self-deprecating, he might be accused of name-dropping'

Tribune

'This is not just a book for movie-lovers, though they will revel in its many entertaining anecdotes, but for a far wider audience; written with sparkle and integrity, it's uninhibited, fair-minded, infinitely quotable and never, ever boring'

Good Book Guide

Barry Norman, CBE, is best known for fronting the BBC's seminal *Film* programme. He has worked as a show business editor for the *Daily Mail*, a satirical columnist for the *Guardian*, a sports interviewer for the *Observer* and has written for *The Times* and the *Radio Times* amongst others. He is the author of ten novels and eight works of non-fiction, most recently *100 Best Films of the Century*. Barry was awarded the BAFTA's Richard Dimbleby Award in 1980, Magazine Columnist of the Year in 1990 and a CBE in 1998. He is married to the historical novelist Diana Norman, has two daughters and is a passionate cricketer.

BARRY NORMAN

and why not?
(as I never did say)

Memoirs of a film lover

POCKET BOOKS

LONDON • SYDNEY • NEW YORK • TOKYO • SINGAPORE • TORONTO

First published in Great Britain by Simon & Schuster UK Ltd, 2002
This edition first published by Pocket Books, 2003
An imprint of Simon & Schuster UK Ltd
A Viacom Company

1 3 5 7 9 10 8 6 4 2

Simon & Schuster UK Ltd
Africa House
64–78 Kingsway
London WC2B 6AH

www.simonsays.co.uk

Simon & Schuster Australia
Sydney

A CIP catalogue record for this book is available from the British Library
ISBN 0-7434-4970-3

Typeset by M Rules
Printed and bound in Great Britain by
Bookmarque Ltd, Croydon, Surrey

PICTURE CREDITS

The publishers have used their best endeavours to contact all
copyright holders. They will be glad to hear from anyone who recognises their
photographs. 1: courtesy of Canal+ Image UK Ltd; 9: David Steen; 11, 27, 12:
BBC; 12, 14: Deborah Beer; 17, 18, 19, 21, 26, 32–38, 42, 46: courtesy of
Bruce Thompson; 20, 22, 23: Pic Photos; 25: Agence Angeli; 28, 31, 41, 43,
47, 49: PA Photos; 29: Echo & Post Ltd; 30: Denis Waugh; 39: *Southern Daily
Echo*; 45: Jane Moore Publicity Associates; 48: BAFTA; 52:
Archant Regional; 54: Alan Olley/Scope

This is for Bertie, Harry and Charlie,
who are quite simply my best mates.

Acknowledgements

My thanks to all those, notably Diana, Rick, Bruce Thompson
and Barry Brown, who helped to jog my memory.
Any mistakes in this book are mine, not theirs.

Preface

SOON AFTER HALF-PAST nine on the night of Friday, 12 March 1971, the Daily Mail did me the most enormous favour – it made me redundant. Mind you, it didn't seem like much of a favour at the time – it seemed more like an insult. What had I done to deserve this? I was thirty-seven years old, had served the paper faithfully and, in my opinion, well for thirteen years and had risen to the rank of show business editor. Admittedly, this was a pretty lowly rank; it gave me a few quid a week more than I had been getting as show business correspondent but it didn't give me entrée to the corridors of power. I wasn't invited to editorial conferences and none of the other executives ever sought my opinion on matters of policy. Indeed, at times all it seemed to mean was that if any of the Mail's team of show business writers missed a story I was held responsible. But even so I was on the executive ladder, wasn't I, and now they were kicking me out.

Actually, they also kicked out 131 other people that night, rather more than half the total editorial staff, because the *Mail* was about to merge with its sister paper, the *Daily Sketch*, where a similar amount of downsizing – and what a weaselly euphemism that is – was going on at exactly the same time.

Maybe I shouldn't have felt quite so hurt because I had volunteered for redundancy. On the other hand, the management couldn't possibly have known that. Originally the list of those to be shown the door was to have been announced on the following Tuesday; the deadline for volunteering to go was noon on that Friday to give the management time to decide which of the volunteers it would retain and which it would cheerfully usher on their way. Together with my friend Julian Holland, later to become the distinguished editor of the *Today* programme on BBC Radio 4, I had done my volunteering about ten minutes before the deadline and it was only a few hours later that we were told the redundancies were to be announced imminently. So unless they had actually been waiting for Julian and me to put our names forward – pretty unlikely, I think – the volunteer list was meaningless.

An excited reporter broke the news early in the evening when a large number of the *Mail* staff had gathered, as was its custom, in the White Swan (or 'Mucky Duck'), the pub next door. 'Redundancies in an hour,' he said. 'It's official.' Julian and I and many others hung around, discussing our possible fates, until about 9.30 when we went back to the office for what became known in Fleet Street lore – until Fleet Street itself ceased to be the newspaper capital of Britain – as 'the Night of the Long Envelopes'.

The procedure was as follows: you lurked around the newsroom – and I'd never seen so many journalists in the *Mail* newsroom as there were that night – until the head of your department called you into his office. And there you were either handed a long white envelope or you were not. If you were you knew, without even opening the thing, that you were redundant. My turn came when Ian Smith, the features editor, beckoned me over and said, 'Will you go in to see Walter?'

Walter Terry, the deputy editor, had been lumbered with the job of overseeing these grisly proceedings, both Arthur Brittenden, editor of the *Mail*, and David English, editor of the *Sketch* and later of the new, combined paper, having, wisely no doubt, made themselves scarce that evening. I liked Walter, though I didn't know him very well. He had a most disconcerting habit: when you were talking to him in his office he would seize a large pair of scissors and stick his tongue between the open blades, so that you sat there fascinated, knowing that any minute now he would cut half his tongue off and spurt you with blood from across the desk. This made it very difficult to concentrate on what he was actually saying.

Tonight, however, was clearly not an occasion for tongues and scissors. Indeed, he looked positively distraught as he handed me my envelope. 'I'm sorry,' he said, 'but I've got to give you one of these.'

'That's all right, Walter,' I said. What else could I say? It wasn't his fault.

'No, it's not all right,' he said. 'You know it's not. It's bloody awful.'

I went out, brandishing my envelope and Sandy Fawkes, the fashion editor, said, 'My God, you look like Chamberlain coming back from Munich.'

All around us our friends and colleagues were coming and going from the executive offices, some looking relieved, some desperately worried, others grinning as bravely as they could manage. There was an awful lot of noise, not the usual noise of the newsroom – typewriters clattering, telephones ringing – but the noise of everyone talking at once. There was a lot of laughter, too, much of it verging on the hysterical, and not a little weeping. The only quiet people there were those still waiting anxiously to be summoned.

And in the midst of all this cacophony and misery a party of visitors was ushered into the newsroom. Tour parties were not uncommon in newspaper offices but the fact that this one was still being conducted around was proof to all of us that the decision to bring the redundancies forward from Tuesday to Friday had been made suddenly and even perhaps on the spur of the moment. God knows what these bemused people made of the scene in front of them or what the tour guide said before he ushered them out again – possibly something on the lines of, 'This is where the famous *Daily Mail* writers work and if you look closely you can just see one of them hanging himself in the corner.'

Bit by bit the room cleared as people, with or without envelopes, went back to the Mucky Duck to get drunk. I went, too, but I didn't get drunk. This seemed to be the sort of occasion you wanted to remember, the sort which with any luck would not be repeated too often in your lifetime. At one point in the evening a television crew turned up to interview us and one of the *Mail* reporters dropped his trousers and mooned at the camera, which seemed to be as pertinent a comment on the events as any.

I was among those interviewed and burbled something upbeat into the microphone, although I wasn't feeling particularly upbeat at the time. In a way this was what I had wanted; I had felt for the last year or so that I had gone about as far as I was likely to go on the *Mail*. Promotion was unlikely and besides I didn't want it. I had no desire to be an executive – I'd only taken the show biz editor's job because of the extra money; I wanted to write. But though I was happy writing about films and theatre, my specialist subjects, I also wanted to write about other things as well and this was proving difficult because it would have meant popping out of the pigeonhole into which I had been placed and invading somebody else's. But I had always lacked both the capital and the nerve to leave and set myself up as a freelance. Now it looked as though that was what I would have to become whether I liked it or not and I was scared. Angry, too. After all, I was one of the *Mail*'s best-known writers – big bylines, picture in the paper. How dare they dispose of me in this cavalier fashion.

In fact, I knew why I and so many of my friends had been cleared out. We'd all been there a long time and were by prevailing standards highly paid. The new paper, the new tabloid *Daily Mail*, would be staffed by younger and cheaper people than us. Although, maybe that wasn't the only reason . . .

Some months later, someone whose job made her well placed to know these things told me that there was never any chance of either Julian Holland or me being kept on. What she said was that a few days before the Night of the Long Envelopes David English consulted Arthur Brittenden to seek his advice on which of the *Mail* people to retain. And when they got to Julian's name and then mine, Arthur said, 'No, don't give him a job.'

The background to this is that until a few months earlier Julian and I had been fringe members of Arthur's inner circle, among the handful of people who were invited to lunch with him at a curry house in the West End every Friday. Arthur wasn't the host, you understand; we all paid our share of the bill but it was still a privilege to be asked. For some reason, however, Arthur and Julian fell out; Julian became *persona non grata* and I, because I was his mate, became just as *non grata* as he was. What caused this state of affairs I never knew but just how out of favour Julian and I were became very clear whenever we were in the Mucky Duck – which I have to admit was often – and the surviving members of the inner circle would gather at the opposite end of the bar and pretend we weren't there.

That much I can vouch for; as to whether Arthur did indeed urge David English not to give us jobs I only have anecdotal evidence. But if he did I would like him to know that I am deeply grateful to him because leaving the *Daily Mail* was, professionally, the best thing that could have happened to me at that time. Had I stayed God knows where I would have ended up.

For a start, I don't think I would have lasted long on the aggressive, ultra-right-wing paper that David English edited. At best, I might have clung on for a year or so, becoming ever more disenchanted and increasingly hanging out in El Vino, the wine bar of choice for cynical Fleet Street hacks, before being booted off the paper as surplus to requirements. To do . . . what? I don't know. I really don't know. Of this, though, I am sure: none of the things that happened to me in the next thirty years would have been possible without that redundancy.

Much of the above I have recounted before in a book called *Tales of the Redundance Kid*, now out of print as, alas, most of my books are. But I repeat it here because that night turned out to be so important for me, the night when my career changed course, had to change course, and went off in directions I had never even contemplated.

Incidentally, there is a small footnote to be added. A few years later Peter Black, the *Mail's* former television critic, was asked to write a history of the newspaper and when he was researching the Night of the Long Envelopes he asked David English why he had not offered employment to people like Julian and myself, who had gone on to do other things rather successfully. By this time I had become quite well known both on television and as a newspaper columnist and Peter asked whether it had been a mistake to let me go.

No, no, said English, presumably anxious that Peter should not think him guilty of an error of judgement. It was not like that, not at all. Before the list of redundancies was drawn up, he said, he had asked me to come and see him because he was keen to have me aboard. But I had said I would rather leave and English, not wishing to stand in my way, reluctantly and selflessly agreed to let me go.

Which was very nice of him except that there wasn't a word of truth in his story. I had neither seen nor spoken to David English for several years before the night my life was so drastically altered.

Introduction

INTERIOR, NIGHT. THE Savoy Hotel, London, a Sunday early in 1981. This was the evening when the British Academy of Film and Television Arts handed out its annual awards. All the great and good of the film and television industries were there and so was I. There was, however, a difference between the great and good and me. They wanted to be there and I didn't. I wanted to be at home; I wanted to be in bed.

For some days I had been suffering agony from a trapped nerve in my neck and walked around like an early prototype of Frankenstein's monster. If I wanted to talk to somebody who wasn't directly in front of me I had to turn from the waist, my neck having pretty well seized up. This caused bemusement and even alarm in those unaware of my condition.

My presence at BAFTA was required because I had been asked to hand out one of the prizes, a music award but . . . 'I don't want to go,' I complained, piteously, to my wife, Diana. 'I'm in pain.'

'Then don't,' she said. 'Phone them. They can find someone else to present the award.'

So I phoned. I phoned the BBC, I phoned the Savoy, I phoned everyone I could think of but as the day wore on I was unable to contact anybody in a position to find a deputy for me. And in the late afternoon . . . 'Sod it, I'll have to bloody go,' I said, 'but I'll hate every minute of it.' Fortitude in moments of suffering is not one of my more prominent attributes.

Diana, of course, was coming with me but our daughters,

Samantha, who was then eighteen, and Emma, who had just turned seventeen, had not been invited. Even so they were excited. The event was to be televised live and they planned to stay up and watch it. Diana and I told them not to bother. My bit would be coming on very late and I'd only be on screen for about ten seconds. Set the recorder and go to bed, we said.

Among the BBC executives with whom Diana and I sat for dinner before the awards ceremony began I was hardly a cheerful presence. Given the choice, I think our companions would have preferred Banquo's ghost. People soon gave up asking me how I felt but I kept telling them anyway and I expect it was a relief to everybody when my moment finally came.

A young assistant led me from the table to the area backstage where make-up was slapped on my face and the award I was to present was put into my hands. Melvyn Bragg was there, too, also charged with handing over a prize.

'I'm always being asked to present these things,' he said, 'but nobody gives one to me. Have you ever won an award?'

'Me?' I said. 'No. Never.'

Melvyn went off to do his stuff and then David Frost, the master of ceremonies, announced my name, I went on stage, the names of the music nominees were flashed on screen, I opened the envelope and revealed the winner, who bounded up to much applause, and swivelling courteously from the waist I handed him his prize.

Thank God that's over, I thought, now I can go home. But as I walked away to rejoin Diana and the others at the dinner table, David called me back.

'Just a minute, Barry,' he said. 'We have something here for you.'

And then to my utter astonishment he revealed that I was to receive the Richard Dimbleby Award for 'outstanding personal contribution to factual television'. I couldn't believe it. The Dimbleby award, named for Britain's most famous broadcaster of the post-war period, is the biggest prize available to television presenters, virtually the only prize available to them because pretty nearly everything else is reserved for producers and the like. And I had won it.

David's announcement was greeted with generous applause, as was my feeble (because totally unprepared) speech of thanks, though not everyone approved wholeheartedly. Clive James, who was commentating on the events for TV, thought I had won it too early, arguing that it should have been an award for overall achievement towards the end of a career. And, as I discovered from the newspapers the following day, Richard Dimbleby's sons, David and Jonathan, were somewhat displeased. They had nothing against me personally, they said, and I believed them because I had not then met either of them, but they felt that the Dimbleby should be reserved, as it always had been in the past, for people involved in hard news and current affairs. Covering the curious goings-on of the film industry (which was what I did) was not, they suggested, strictly speaking factual television.

Did I care? No, I did not. I was sorry – though not very sorry – that the Dimbleby boys were unhappy and I thought Clive was wrong. But I felt, as Shirley Maclaine did when she received her Oscar for *Terms of Endearment*, that I deserved it. And besides, whether I deserved it or not, I'd got it and nobody could take it away from me.

Ecstatically, I bore the trophy back to the table where I discovered that everyone except Diana and me had known all along what was going to happen and where Diana was beating the tabletop with her fists, saying, 'I bet the girls forgot to turn on the recorder, I just bet they did.'

But she was wrong. Ignoring stern parental injunctions they had, bless them, stayed up to watch the show and had turned on the machine in time to preserve if not all then most of the significant events. Even today, somewhere among all the videotapes that infest our house like mice lurks a record of their father's supreme moment of professional glory.

I have never won the Dimbleby award since but, then, nobody is allowed to win it more than once. I have, I may say immodestly, been given other honours – a CBE for services to film and television, a prize for magazine writing, awards for services to film criticism from the London Film Critics' Circle and the Guild of Regional Film Writers, honorary doctorates of letters from the Universities of East Anglia and

Hertford and honorary life membership of the National Union of Journalists and BAFTA itself – but the Dimbleby is the only award I have ever received from the television industry and I value it highly.

As to how that came about, well, thereby – as they used to say – hangs a tale . . .

I come from a film family. At the height of his career – a distinguished one I think – my father, Leslie Norman, was first an editor, then a producer, then a director at Ealing Studios when, under Michael Balcon, they represented the very best of British cinema. My mother, Elizabeth (née Crafford), worked in the cutting rooms of British International Pictures at Elstree in the early 1930s. So did Dad and it was while they were there that they married.

Before the Second World War, and for some time after, working in films was regarded as a somewhat raffish occupation. When around 1943 we moved to Hassocks in Sussex to escape the bombing – not to mention my mother's family, which was just as dangerous – and it was decided to send me to the junior school of Hurstpierpoint College, a ticklish problem arose. Hurstpierpoint did not accept the sons of trades- men and there was much head shaking and sucking of teeth over the question of whether or not film editing was a trade. In the end the school thought it wasn't and I was accepted, although I rather fancy the fact that Dad was an officer in the army at the time had something to do with it. You could hardly accuse an officer of being a tradesman, could you?

In 1946 when I went to my second public school, Highgate, there were no such difficulties. Indeed my contemporaries, sons of solicitors, doctors, bank managers and the like, were rather envious of my father's occupation. Their parents, however, remained uneasy. To the suburban middle class of that generation the cinema was still somewhat vulgar; if their children demanded entertainment (this being before the age of television) there was the wireless or, better still, the the-ay-ter.

Fortunately, my parents were happily unaware of such prejudice. Films were both their livelihood and – for Dad, anyway – their life. They were not theatre people so when, in my middle teens, I would be moping around at home on a wet afternoon, my mates busy with their own families and I much too shy to have a girlfriend, they would say, 'What are you hanging around here for? There's a very good film at the Ritz. Go and see it.'

So I did. There were at least four cinemas within walking distance or a short bus ride of where we lived in Edgware and some weeks, in the school holidays, I would visit all of them. You might think this a mis-spent childhood but for me it was sheer bliss. At their best the movies were, and still are, magic. It could be argued that books, or the radio, are even more magical because the pictures are better: they are *your* pictures, images you have conjured up in your own imagination.

But the movies are different; the movies are special. They are BIG, much, much bigger than life. Everything is big – the people, the build-ings, the landscapes, the explosions, the chases, the guns, the emotions, the heroism and the villainy. And, too, they are populated by the most remarkable people, handsome, macho men and women so beautiful and photographed so cunningly that they look as if you could eat them with a spoon. The archetypal movies, the escapist movies, the movies we all love, present us with the world not as it is but as it ought to be, replete with sights and spectacles that even while they surpass our own imagination also feed it, sending us home with our heads full of roman-tic thoughts and impossible dreams that might, just might, turn out to be not quite so impossible after all.

As I wafted away from these cinemas at which, especially on Sundays, classic movies were revived, I was General Custer (the homogenized Errol Flynn version of *They Died With Their Boots On*), or Robin Hood (Errol Flynn again; I was a big fan of Errol Flynn) or Wyatt Earp (Henry Fonda in *My Darling Clementine*) or Humphrey Bogart as Rick in *Casablanca*. I read, too, of course – voraciously. But movies had a particular appeal of their own. I knew perfectly well that they were just make-believe because my father actually made films, but because he made them, and thereby earned his living, they were more than just entertainment, they were something truly important. And to me they have always remained so.

These things being so, you might wonder why I didn't go into the

film industry myself. My brother did, briefly, so did my sister; even
Diana, my wife, once worked as a unit publicist on a movie and my
elder daughter, Samantha, took a short speaking role in a film as a
favour to a friend. But I never really came close to going into the family
business and I shall explain why later on in the course of what is, I suppose, not so much an autobiography as a memoir, a collection of
reminiscences, as you will discover if you can bring yourself to read
on . . .

Chapter One

WHEN I WAS about eight, or maybe nine, my friend Ron introduced me to a life of crime. He must have been much the
same age, perhaps a year or two older, or he wouldn't have had anything to do with me, but he was way ahead of me in maturity.

We – my mother, my younger brother Rick and I – were living with
my grandparents in Taunton at the time. Wartime it was, and my father
was working in London. Most of my uncles and, I think, Ron's father,
too, were away in the army. Ron was an only child who lived with his
mother a few houses down the street and we became close friends, Ron
always the leader in whatever enterprise we undertook. And one of the
most significant and regular of these enterprises was the robbing of
Woolworths.

Before I came along I suppose he must have done this by himself
but having a willing accomplice made his work a lot easier.

What we would do, Ron having planned the raid in careful detail,
was this: we would walk or maybe take a bus, it doesn't matter, to a
Woolworths some distance from where we lived and there I would act
as decoy while Ron did the robbing. I would stand at the boring end of
the toy counter, the bit where they had dolls and skipping ropes and
other things of interest only to small girls, and from there would attract
the attention of the assistant, giving her some spiel about trying to
decide on a birthday present for my then non-existent little sister.
Meanwhile at the other end, Ron was filling his pockets with such

desirable objects as penknives and toy soldiers. Then he would give me
the nod that he had grabbed about as much as he could reasonably
steal and I would break off negotiations with the assistant, saying that I
would have to check my piggy bank to see how much I could afford,
and we would make our separate ways to the exit.

Outside and some distance from the shop, Ron and I would split the
proceeds and go home modestly congratulating ourselves on a job well
done.

We did this quite often and never got caught because Ron was a very
accomplished thief. But there was something else about him which,
now I come to think of it, struck me even then as distinctly odd. There
were just the two of us; I don't remember anything like a gang or even
the odd hanger-on. And, as kids do, we played fantasy games. My fantasies revolved around cowboys and Indians, cops and robbers, knights
and dragons – in short, any situation which ended satisfactorily with the
good guy (me) slaughtering somebody who deserved no better. Ron's
fantasies, however, were far more sophisticated: they included girls, not
real girls – we didn't know any of those – but girls he had conjured up
in the more febrile recesses of his mind. And these games, otherwise
packed with chases, murders, robberies, massacres and similar atrocities
beloved of healthy young males, always ended up with Ron rescuing an
imaginary damsel in distress and falling into a passionate clinch with
her. He would wrap his arms around himself, close his eyes and plant
fervent kisses on the air. I went along with this because I didn't want to
upset him and pretended to snog a girl of my own but my heart wasn't
in it. In those days I hadn't the slightest interest in girls and couldn't see
any reason for them, but that final embrace was of vital importance to
Ron, the whole point of the game, and I was just smart enough to
know that I would mock it at my peril.

I wish now that I knew more about him, his background and what
became of him in later life. When after a year or so I left Taunton I lost
all track of him for ever but every now and again I still think of him. His
precocious interest in sex might not be all that unusual today but it was
exceptional in the 1940s, when people tended to remain childlike and
innocent until comfortably into their teens. And his expertise as a thief

was also remarkable in one so young. Maybe he grew up to be a master criminal or a serial sex offender or both. When I knew him, either of these possibilities certainly seemed more likely than that he would settle down to an uneventful life in a neat little house with a devoted wife and 2.4 children.

But – and this is a thought that has just occurred to me as I write – I wonder why nobody in my grandparents' house ever asked me how I came to have such an endless supply of new penknives and toy soldiers. Because nobody, including my mother, ever did, despite the fact that at my age and with Mum and Dad paying two lots of rent and house-keeping, I rarely had more than a couple of pennies in my possession at any given time.

On the other hand, maybe their indifference was not really so sur-prising. Deep down they probably knew I'd nicked these things and thought it better to say nothing because thievery was in the maternal genes.

Woolworths again, in Edgware this time when I must have been six, pushing seven. I was with Mum and Rick, who is four and a half years younger than me. He was still being shoved around in a pram but he was big enough to sit up and wriggle about and as we paused by the toy counter, soon in another location to be the familiar scene of my crim-inal activities, he grabbed a couple of lead soldiers and dropped them nonchalantly into his pram. Then, as my mother stood there, frowning slightly as if trying to remember why she'd come into the shop in the first place, he grabbed a couple more. And a couple more . . .

Not at that time being a larcenist myself, I was horrified. 'Mum,' I said, in my clear, piping voice, 'Mum, look what Ricky's doing.'

She clipped me sharply round the ear. 'Shut up,' she said. 'Just shut up.' Then she swiftly tucked the soldiers under the pram cover and we took them out of the shop unpurchased.

So perhaps I do Ron an injustice. He may have turned me into an active criminal but it was Mum who made me mentally prepared for it. And years later, when I was in my teens, I became her – unwilling – accomplice, too . . .

But before then, and back in Taunton, life went on as it usually did under my grandparents' roof, which is to say that periods of calm were followed by frequent and vitriolic rows, invariably stirred up by my grandmother. Granddad never took any part in them, having learned long ago that if he did everyone would unite and turn on him.

Gran's policy was to divide and rule. She was never particularly happy on those rare occasions when all the siblings were getting along well together, possibly because this suggested that she wasn't needed and she positively demanded to be needed. So one of her children always had to be the bad guy and most often it was my mother who was elected.

Perhaps I'd better explain the familial setup. My grandfather, Harry Crafford, came from money, or anyway recently from money. His own family had at some time in the nineteenth century owned several hotels in London, though his father had gambled them away by the time Granddad met Lizzie, his future wife. She came from poverty, an Anglo-Irish background of ill-paid menial work. How they met I was never told but he was immediately smitten by this beautiful girl with raven hair so long that she could tuck it under her when she sat. If on his part, though, it was love at first sight, it was not on hers. He had, apparently, caught her on the rebound, soon after she had been dumped by a man she had confidently expected to marry and she seems to have accepted my grandfather's proposal largely to spite the previous feckless lover. Hardly a happy basis for a relationship, even without the fact that, from what I gleaned over the years, Granddad's mother was by no means best pleased when he announced his intention of marrying this Lizzie.

'She's a lovely girl,' his mother said, 'but you will have to bring her up to your standards.' That, however, was not the way it turned out. Gran, though ignorant and with no interest in furthering her own education, or indeed providing much of it for her children, was a woman of formidable determination and made it perfectly clear that she had no intention of tearing up her roots and changing class. I'm not making any judgements here; I'm not saying that middle class is better than working class. I'm merely saying that, had she played her cards right with her mother-in-law, she could have had the opportunity of a better, or anyway more affluent, life than she had ever known and she rejected it. She was content in the social basement and Granddad, if he wanted her, was obliged to join her there.

So he did. With what money he had, after his father's squandering of the family fortune, he bought a shoe shop in a street of narrow, terraced houses near the Elephant and Castle and there he and Gran brought up their family. They had eleven children of whom those who survived to adulthood were Alf, Arthur, Fred, Charlie and Denis, along with Louise (known as Louie), Mary (known as Polly) and my mother, Elizabeth (known variously as Lizzie, Betty, Hetty or, among her siblings to whom aspirates were an unnecessary luxury, 'Ettie). She, the youngest of the daughters, was the second Elizabeth in her family, the first having died in infancy. Presumably determined to have a daughter to bear her own Christian name Gran simply passed it on to the next one who came along.

You might have thought that this would have made my mother the favourite. On the contrary, she was figuratively – though not literally – the runt of the litter, the least considered of them all. Like her brothers and sisters – like my father indeed – she was educated at a London County Council school, which reckoned its remit fulfilled if it could turn its pupils out into the world, aged fourteen, just about able to read, write and add up. Mum deserved more than that. When she was eleven she had the chance to go to a much better school but on the day she was to take the entrance exam Gran made her stay at home and clean the windows instead. I don't know why. Didn't want one of her children getting above herself perhaps. But it upset Mum a great deal because – and I'm damned if I can see why – she loved her mother and craved her approval. Not that she ever received much of it. Her usual role, in Gran's master plan of family domination, was to be the scapegoat.

I can remember many occasions after the war when Mum and I would trot innocently round to Gran's house, there to be greeted by everyone present (my easy-going Granddad always excepted) with verbal abuse for some offence of which she was presumed guilty. Occasionally one of her brothers or sisters was victimized instead but, whoever the chosen miscreant was, the pattern was always the same: a blazing row, in which the passions and language were fierce, followed by several days of implacable, brooding resentment on Gran's part until the appointed victim came round with a humble apology for misdeeds never knowingly, or even actually, committed and was regally pardoned.

I remember an early example of my grandmother's petty malice, because, to my shame, I was a part of it. It was in Taunton, April Fools' Day, and Gran called me in to deliver a message to my mother. Mum was in a house across the road, one of those frequent rows having caused us briefly to move out of the grandparental home, and what Gran said was: 'Go and tell your Mum your Dad's on the phone and it's urgent.' I didn't want to deliver the message because I knew that Dad wasn't on the phone but Gran said, 'Go on, do as I say. It's all right, it's just an April Fools' joke', and because I was more scared of her than I was of my mother I did as she said.

I still feel guilty when I remember how Mum's face lit up when I delivered the message, how she hurried across the road only to be greeted with cries of 'April fool!' and cackling laughter and how she came back in tears. In wartime it was a miserable joke to play on a woman whose husband was away in London where the bombs were still falling.

It was also about that time that I realized how much my grandmother disliked me. I was playing in the front garden with Rick when Gran came out of the house, went up to my brother and handed him sixpence, saying, 'Here you are, son. Go and buy yourself an ice cream.' And then she turned and walked away. There was no sixpence for me and, young as I was, I knew that a deeply pointed message had just been delivered. Years later when I recounted this episode to my mother she wouldn't believe me while Rick, the happy beneficiary of the sixpence, still reckons the explanation was perfectly simple – he was clearly much more lovable than I was. That may well be true but I took it hard, as I'm sure I was meant to.

On the other hand, I cannot recall Gran ever hitting me, though she was a powerful woman who, even in her seventies, could break great lumps of kindling wood across her knee. Besides, her antipathy towards me was offset by my grandfather's amiability. So I kept out of Gran's way as much as I could and enlivened my days with a good deal of scrumping in the local apple orchards and a bit of light thievery with Ron, which was really the sum total of my criminal career.

Well, no, that's not quite true, actually. There was, as I said, a time when I became my mother's accomplice . . .

It was several years later, after the war, and the fact that I was a most reluctant accomplice is no excuse. We were back in Edgware by then, I was a teenager, enrolled at a public school, and I knew perfectly well that what I was doing on her behalf could only be construed as theft.

Dad was in Australia producing a film called *Eureka Stockade* when the scam began and I don't think he ever knew anything about it, even though it continued long after he came home. And what was going on was as follows: Mum had a friend named Doris, who worked as an assistant in a local greengrocer's shop and regarded her job as a licence to steal. But to steal she needed a little help, which was where Mum – and sometimes I – came in. Every now and then Mum would give me a ten shilling note (50p) and a long list and send me off to buy the fruit and veg – whatever was in season in those austere days before everything was available all the time. The admonition was always the same: 'Don't let anyone but Doris serve you.'

So I would lurk among the other customers, letting numerous people go ahead of me, until Doris, a large, very stout woman, was free, whereupon I would thrust my list and the money into her hand and wait. Sometime later she would present me with a bulging shopping bag and say, 'This is for your Mum.' Most times she would give me change as well, though I was clearly holding a lot more than ten bob's worth of goods. Then she would give me a second, equally bulging bag, and I would carry them both home. The second bag was Doris's and she would collect it from my mother after work.

I used to hate doing this because I was terrified of being caught and marched off to the police station by the shop's manager. Every time I was sent on this nefarious errand I would say, 'Do I have to?' and my mother would reply, 'Yes, you do. You'll be all right.'

I could, no doubt, have struck a pose of moral rectitude and refused to do it but it was never easy to say no to my mother. She was a woman of immense charm, which she could turn on or off depending on her whim, but like her own mother she could be extremely stubborn and determined. If she wanted you to do something you'd better do it – or else. In the end it was easier to slink furtively to and from the greengrocer's than not to go and, besides, it was useless trying to point out the criminal nature of her deal with Doris because she genuinely didn't appear to see the wrong in it. The greengrocer was flourishing and well able to withstand the loss, so what was a bit of fruit and veg here or there? Arguing that she had no need to steal these things, that while not rich we certainly weren't poor, would also have been a waste of time. What appealed to her quite as much as the saving of money was the thought that she was getting something for nothing. In a way, it was just a game to which the element of risk gave an added thrill.

But this criminal activity was only a part of her and a very small part at that. She also had a sharp eye for business. In the late 1940s she bought a modest wool shop and made it prosper. Whenever we moved home, which we did several times, it was she, not Dad, who chose the new house, haggled with the estate agent until the price suited her and then, in due course, always sold at a profit. What she would have liked to do was to invest in the property market, buying flats and houses to rent. But Dad was financially too cautious to back her in this, which was a great pity because, given her head, I'm sure she would have made the family fortune.

Above all, though, she was a wonderfully devoted and fiercely protective mother. Everything she did was for us, for me, for Rick and later for Valerie, our sister, who was born in 1946. We were brought up in an atmosphere of love and loyalty to one another and whatever Mum stole, or managed to wangle on the black market during the war – an egg here, a slice of meat there, a pat of butter somewhere else – was for our benefit, never hers. And talking of eggs . . . One day she found a rotten egg in her meagre wartime ration. So she took it back to Sainsburys – not then a supermarket, of course, but still a very large grocery shop – and showed the stinking thing to the girl who had sold it to her.

'What am I supposed to do about this?' the girl asked.

'Give me a fresh one instead,' my mother said.

'Well, I'm not going to. It's part of your ration and if it's bad, hard luck.'

'Oh, yeah? Well, you have it then,' said Mum and threw it in her face. The girl screamed, the manager turned up at a run, my mother yelled and in the end she walked out of the shop with a fresh egg. And that sort of belligerence, the insistence on fighting her corner and never backing down, was as much part of her character as the streak of larceny which, as I said, ran in the family.

In that slum street in south London where she was born and brought up pilfering was not only an accepted way of life but pretty well a necessity if you were to make ends meet. My grandfather owned a shoe shop, yes, and was therefore a man of comparative substance in this underprivileged neighbourhood but there was never much money around when the children were young and living at home.

When someone in the street died, everybody chipped in to help pay the funeral expenses. If somebody was in debt and the bumbailiffs were on the way, the neighbours held a whip-round to stave them off. Nitty Norah, she who searched for head lice, was a frequent visitor to the local school. The Horseradish Lady, prematurely aged, her eyes permanently bloodshot, her fingertips red and raw from handling the pungent roots she chopped, was an established figure in the neighbourhood, turning up every week to set up her little stall and sell her wares, her sore eyes weeping copiously the whole time.

At best, the residents of the street scraped a living and a shoe shop owner was no great exception. It was not until their children were grown up and gainfully employed that my grandparents could afford to move to the middle-class respectability of Edgware and the early deprivation was never truly forgotten by any of them. So the family's unspoken motto, amoral though it may have been, was: If you can nick something and get away with it, why not? Thus they were inclined to nick away here and there and since the people from whom they nicked were never aware of it nobody really suffered. Well, not to the family's way of thinking.

Nearly all the siblings were on the fiddle, one way or another. After the war Uncle Alf, a printer with the London *Evening News*, regularly came home with desirable and extremely cheap goods which seemed to have fallen mysteriously off the back of somebody's lorry. And Uncle Charlie, a sound editor at Elstree film studios, was always in possession of a thick roll of bank notes, the result of dealing in virgin film stock which I doubt was ever, strictly speaking – or perhaps in any manner of speaking – legally his to dispose of in the first place.

In the Elephant and Castle days, before she was married, my mother had a friend named Jimmy Dinnegan, another denizen of the street where she lived, who was a fairly serious thief and, on occasion, did time for it.

Mum, who must have been in her late teens, had just started working in the film industry as an assistant in the cutting rooms and for a while, indeed, was the girlfriend of Ray Milland before he went to Hollywood to become an international movie star and win an Oscar for *The Lost Weekend*. Moving in such exalted circles – hugely exalted by the standards of the Elephant and Castle – she obviously needed lots of new clothes and Jimmy was the man who provided them for her. He had, it seems, an equally criminal contact in a large dress shop in the West End of London and on a Saturday morning Mum and a couple of friends would meet Jimmy, Up West, and take their pick of what the shop had to offer. How they concealed their pillaging from the owner was not revealed to me but they must have been good at it because they were never caught.

Well, Jimmy was caught but not, I think, when stealing from the dress shop. It must have been something rather graver than that because the last time he was convicted he was sentenced not only to prison but to several strokes of the cat-o'-nine-tails. After that, by all accounts, he was a reformed character. According to my mother, he found the experience of being whipped so humiliating that, when he had served his time, he made a vow to go straight and kept it. I remember him vaguely because, much later on, he came to our house in Edgware a couple of times when I was very young – tall and slim, he was, elegantly dressed and with a small, neat moustache and a splendid

head of hair, greying at the sides. Distinguished looking is the phrase
that comes to mind; certainly you would never believe, to look at him,
that here was a man who had tasted the cat.

It was my mother who told me, after Jimmy was dead, about the
flogging and the reformation and both she and my father would cite
the unhappy man's experience as clinching evidence that use of the
cat-o'-nine-tails, or indeed any form of corporal punishment, should be
immediately reintroduced into the judicial system. Come to that, they
wanted hanging back as well. As convinced Tories they – especially
Mum, now a reformed character herself except when urging her tiny
grandson Howard to pinch apples from market stalls – were very hot on
crime, though unconvinced about the causes of crime. Poverty?
Deprivation? They – Mum, in particular – would have none of it. We
were poor, we were deprived and we turned out all right. Well, yes,
Mum, but . . . Oh, never mind. She never could see that what she did
so often in her youth was itself criminal and neither, I suppose, could
her siblings.

They were – the uncles far more than the aunts – a wonderfully
high-spirited bunch and when I was young they scared the shit out of
me partly because, taking a lead from their mother, they all seemed to
dislike me. But maybe in part I was to blame, too: I was a shy, reserved
kid who, unless sternly ordered to do so by my mother, would never kiss
or hug anybody, while the uncles believed in physical, though entirely
platonic, demonstrations of affection towards their nieces and nephews.

But when I grew up and felt I could hold my own in their company
I came to know and become fond of them, Alf, Charlie and Denis in
particular. They were all sharp, quick-witted and possessed of a sly, dry
Cockney humour and, in a group, would seize upon one of their
number to be the butt. When they were young men, apparently, the
affable Fred was the victim of choice.

He would turn up in, say, a smart new shirt. One of the brothers
would say solemnly, "Ere, that's a nice shirt, Fred', and promptly tear
one of the sleeves off, whereupon another would agree, saying 'It is, an'
all' and rip off the other sleeve, after which the rest would take turns in
removing the buttons and reducing the rest of the shirt to polishing

rags. Fred, according to my mother, never seemed to mind and tended to join in the general mirth, though after a bit he did take care not to wear a new shirt when he was going to meet his brothers.

My mother outlived them all and missed them to the end of her days. When she was in her late eighties she and Denis, her junior by about a dozen years and then in remission from lung cancer, would talk often on the phone, reliving the old days and bemoaning the fact that they were the only ones left.

Denis told me of one of these conversations once. 'Bit bloody gloomy these days, isn't she, your Mum?' he said. 'She kept saying, "Which of us'll be next, Den, which of us'll be next?" and I thought: well, I hope it's you but I didn't like to say so.'

In fact, it was Den and after that, with my father gone, too, Mum kind of gave up on life. Towards the end – she died, nearly ninety-one, a week before Christmas 1998 and about a year after she had given up smoking for the good of her health – she became increasingly frail and querulous. Her mind was still sharp and active but her body had tired of the struggle. She could walk only a few yards at a time and then with difficulty. Dad had died in February 1993, a week before his eighty-second birthday, and since then she had lived alone in their house in Hertfordshire. This was her own choice. She was ferociously independent and would not have wanted to live either with Rick and his wife, Christine, or with my wife, Diana, and me, even if we had offered. And no, we didn't offer – not because we were callous and didn't care but because all of us, Mum included, would have found sharing a house insufferable, unless it was my mother's house and that she wouldn't have minded. Ideally, she would have liked Valerie to give up her own life and family and live with her. But that was never an option because in the early 1980s Val, her then husband Bernard Williams, a film producer who had worked extensively with Stanley Kubrick, and their three children had moved to Los Angeles. Mum never really forgave her although it seemed to me that Val and Bernie had done the wisest thing. The film industry in Britain was in a dire state and if Bernie were to exploit the international reputation he was beginning to acquire, Hollywood was the place to do it.

Val, therefore, wasn't around and her absence was a constant source of disgruntlement to our mother, who believed a daughter's place was in the maternal home. When, alas, my sister's marriage broke up, Mum was given to muttering grimly, 'See? I told her she should never have gone to bloody America. I said it would never work. She should have stayed here, where she belongs.'

So in Val's absence Rick and I and Chris and Diana did what we could: between us we called in to see her each day; while she was still able and willing to go out we would take her to restaurants and every Sunday she would come to my house or Rick's for lunch; we provided her with meals that she could heat in her microwave for the rest of the week; Rick looked after her financial affairs, the paying of bills and suchlike, and we also made sure that she always had enough money and plenty of food in the house.

You think I protest too much? Well, maybe I do. At the very end, a month or so before she died, when she could no longer fend for herself we found a pleasant nursing home for her, a few minutes drive from both Rick's house and mine. There we, or her daughters-in-law, or one or other of her grandchildren popped in to see her every day. But there, too, she died alone, never having liked the place and always clinging to the forlorn hope that one day she would be strong enough to go back to her own house.

If you wonder whether I feel guilt, well, of course, I do. She was never neglected in her old age but neither was she cosseted as her own mother had been and as she would have liked to have been. But Gran had two bachelor sons, Alf and Denis, to live with and attend her until she died; Mum did not. And besides in those last two or three years her temper was such that had she moved in with Rick or me verbal violence at the very least would have been the constant and inevitable result.

During the time she was still looking after herself at home and on those days when I was working too late to visit her, I would telephone and this was an ordeal for which I had to steel myself. Because the conversation invariably began like this: 'Hi, Mum, how are you?' – 'Bloody awful, son . . .' and there would follow a litany of her ailments, her aches, her pains and how – in her mind, though not in fact – she had somehow been done down by whoever had called in to see her that day. I used to dread those phone calls and always felt depressed after them.

It's a hard thing, a somehow shameful thing, to admit that your mother's death came as a relief but hers did. She had never prepared herself for old age or maybe she had thought that for some indefinable reason she would be given a kind of dispensation – that she might grow old but the ravages of age would never afflict her. And when they did, in the form of a mild stroke and a heart that needed a pacemaker, she reacted with frustrated rage. 'Why am I still here?' she would ask frequently. 'Why am I still alive? That Bloke Upstairs must really hate me or he'd have taken me years ago.' And to this she would add bitterly, 'Don't grow old, son.'

So when she died we all consoled ourselves with the thought that it was for the best, that it was what she would have wanted, because in her physically inactive state she hadn't been happy for a long time. But who knows how true that might be? If there is an afterlife – and I hope there is – I rather fear she might be waiting to tell me I was wrong.

I don't mean I would be afraid to meet her again; far from it. I loved her and she loved me. If we are honest we know that the number of people who truly, unquestioningly, unshakeably love us can easily be numbered on the fingers of two hands, or maybe just one. My mother loved her children with a fiercely protective passion. But she was never slow to tell us if we had screwed up or somehow fallen short of the standards she had set for us.

I would call in to see her and straight off, even before the filial and maternal greetings had been exchanged . . . 'You looked bloody awful on TV last night, son,' she would say. 'Big bags under your eyes, hair all over the place. Tell 'em to light you better.' She hardly ever commented on the content of the programmes, the things I'd actually said, the things I thought I was best at. It was the appearance that counted: she wanted everyone else to think me as good-looking as she believed me to be, because she was proud of me. She gloried, more than I did, in the nice pieces that were sometimes written about me in the newspapers and railed, far more than I did, about the crap that was also written, as it always is, about people in the public eye.

In her declining years she would come back from the various hospitals she had to attend, or the old people's lunch club she frequented occasionally in her village, and say, 'I don't know how it is, son, but somehow everyone seems to know I'm your mother.' Since I had not had occasion to tell anybody this might have been a touch baffling if I hadn't suspected that maybe she had let the odd word slip herself . . .

During the war we had a Morrison shelter in our flat in Edgware, a neat device made of steel that fitted into a bedroom and was long and wide enough for two or three people to lie in but hardly high enough for anyone but a child to sit up in. If a bomb had landed nearby and the building had collapsed I suppose this contraption might have saved the lives of those in it, though I wouldn't bet the mortgage on it. Still, that was the theory and, thank God, in our case it was never put to the test. But – maybe before the flight to Taunton or perhaps after our return from Hassocks – Mum used to put Rick and me to bed in the Morrison shelter and, when the air raid warning sounded and we could hear the guns and the bombs, she would give us the most delicious sweets I have ever tasted. They were chewy, lemon-flavoured toffees and I can still, vaguely, conjure up their flavour at the back of my mouth and with the taste comes the memory of Rick and me chewing away in our shelter, while Mum sat outside, feeding us sweets, and the bombs fell ten miles away in London. I cannot remember her joining us in the shelter; that was our place, the place where she prayed that we would be safe. Her place was outside the shelter, ministering to us and pretending, even though she was terrified, that all was well, that what was going on was exciting and an adventure but nothing to be afraid of.

As a result I don't remember being afraid. My strongest memory of the war in Edgware, which was where we were closest to danger, was of going out the morning after the air raids and collecting shrapnel in the streets. Sometimes, mysteriously, we would come across pieces of parachute silk but we never knew how they got there or whether the person who had worn the parachute was one of our lads, a German pilot or, wow, a spy, who might even as we examined and wondered about the silk be hiding in a garage or a garden shed nearby, ready to shoot us if there was any danger that we might discover his whereabouts.

Once in the 1960s when I was interviewing Noel Coward the name of Anna Neagle cropped up in the conversation. When you were interviewing Coward almost any name you had ever heard of was likely to crop up. Anyway, Neagle, who was married to her producer and director, Herbert Wilcox, was one of the great British stars of stage and screen during the 1930s and 1940s. And Coward said, 'Dear Anna. Herbert looked after her so well that the Second World War passed her by unnoticed.'

I mention this because you could almost say the same about Mum and me. Almost but not quite. If it had been remotely possible Mum would have ushered Rick and me through the war without either of us being aware of it. But when a bomb drops in your back garden you can't help but notice, especially when as a result Mum became deaf in one ear and I became an asthmatic. I'd always been a sickly, chesty sort of kid – I nearly died of pneumonia when I was three – but the asthma I attribute firmly to Hitler and so, as a matter of fact, did all the doctors Mum dragged me to see.

My paternal grandfather, so I'm told, had a favourite saying: 'One father can support ten children but ten children can't support one father.' He had a good number of children himself and because he was usually hard up they were raised for the most part in even greater poverty than my mother's family, so I suppose he meant financial support. Well, I would plead innocent of that charge, not that I was ever really put to the test. If you're doing all right financially and your parents are occasionally in need of this or that it's no big deal to help out.

But at the end of my mother's life I was guilty of a much more culpable lack of support. One day in December 1998 Diana and I called in to see her in the nursing home. It was the day of Rick's pre-Christmas party and among other things I'd gone to discuss her travel arrangements. The first thing that became clear, however, was that she was too ill to go to a party. She wasn't in any pain but, as she pointed out in what had become her usual forthright way, she certainly wasn't well.

Now flash back a few years and if the positions had been reversed she would have been fluttering solicitously around, full of tender care and sympathy. I didn't do that. I was in a bad mood that day, God knows why, and short of patience. I wasn't unkind but I wasn't kind either, maybe because she had been crying wolf an awful lot lately. Frankly, I was too busy suppressing irritation to be very sympathetic.

'I want a doctor,' she said. So, while I stayed and talked to her as encouragingly as I could, Diana went to consult the matron on duty who, reasonably it seemed to us, said she didn't think there was any point. The most a doctor would be likely to do was transfer my mother to the local hospital, a place she had been in a lot and disliked even more than she disliked the nursing home. She was better off, the matron thought, where she was: she had a comfortable room, there were nurses on duty and there was a panic button beside the bed in case of emergency.

Mum wasn't convinced. She still wanted a doctor but since none was coming she settled for the next best thing and allowed Diana to put her to bed. We stayed a while longer until she dozed off to sleep and then we left.

About one o'clock the next morning, some time after Diana and I had returned from Rick's party, there was a phone call from the nursing home. Mum had died in her sleep about forty minutes earlier.

I wish now that I had insisted on calling a doctor, even though I'm sure that would only have delayed things for a short while. I wish I had spent more time with her that last afternoon. Above all I wish I had been nicer to her. That was the very least she deserved.

Chapter Two

A MORNING IN THE SUMMER of 1940. A Sunday I think it was and if it wasn't it is now because my memory insists that it was a Sunday. I was at my maternal grandparents' house in Edgware. At that time Mum, Dad, Rick and I lived in a flat about a mile away but we spent a lot of time at Gran's house, largely because she insisted upon it.

Dad wasn't there that day but my mother was and so was a selection of my aunts and uncles and most of us were hanging around the kitchen when one of the uncles charged in.

'Outside, quick,' he said. 'Dogfight.'

Everyone rushed into the front garden and stared up at the sky and all along the road the neighbours were doing the same. You learn things quickly in wartime and even at seven or thereabouts I knew what a dogfight was; I knew I wasn't being dragged out to watch a couple of mongrels having a go at each other. What I saw instead was something I had never seen before and was never to see again and the memory of it has remained vivid all my life.

High above us on this cloudless day but not so high that we couldn't identify the red, white and blue roundels on the wings of one plane and the black swastikas on the wings of the other, a Spitfire and a Messerschmidt were trying to blow each other to pieces. We watched them manoeuvre, each seeking the advantage of height and the sun, whirling, swooping and climbing. Memory says we saw smoke from the guns in the wings of the aircraft and even the lines of tracer bullets but maybe this isn't so; maybe memory filled in such details later.

Mum, the uncles, everyone in the street was shouting encouragement to the Spitfire pilot. 'Go on, boy, get the bastard.'

And suddenly he did. Suddenly smoke, thick, black smoke billowed out of the Messerschmidt and the plane started falling, or rather gliding swiftly downwards, obviously out of control. Where it crashed I have no idea, nor do I know whether the pilot baled out, though if he did none of us saw him.

All along the road people were shouting, applauding, laughing and weeping. And then the Spitfire pilot, as if conscious of his admiring audience down below, did a cocky, triumphant victory roll before setting off in pursuit of the crippled Messerschmidt. It's hard to describe the onlooker's feelings at such a moment but amazement was among them and awe and a savage joy that someone, one of the bad guys, had probably died up there that day. Along with these there was satisfaction that the result had been one up to us and sod you, Adolf. But a few months later Hitler got his own back.

By then the Blitz was full on, air raids on London every night, and I suppose for reasons of comfort and companionship Mum, Rick and I had taken to sleeping at Gran's house. My father wasn't in the army then; he was called up a little later. But he had already been co-opted by the War Office to work on a curious concept called Sonic Warfare and he was getting home late at night. Understandably, my mother didn't fancy being in our flat, alone with two young children, while the air-raid sirens went off and the noise of the Luftwaffe bombing the hell out of London was clearly audible even as far away as we were in Edgware.

The day I'm thinking of was already a significant one at my grandparents' house. The Anderson air-raid shelter which had been installed in the back garden had just been finished and furnished with bunks and drinks and iron rations and for the first time my brother and I, along with the womenfolk, were to sleep in it. But Dad was working late again and it was decided that none of us should go into the shelter until he came home to say goodnight to Rick and me. So we children were put to bed, temporarily, in the front room, the parlour, and quickly fell asleep.

What woke me up was the most godawful noise and the sensation that the house was falling down. A huge, framed picture, some kind of gloomy Victorian print, fell off the wall on to my legs and it seemed as if a vast, malevolent creature had seized hold of the house and was trying to shake it to bits. My parents rushed into the room to grab Rick and me and we joined the others in the hall. I don't remember panic, simply a dazed disbelief that this could be happening to us. There was plaster everywhere and great, gaping cracks in the walls and the house still seemed to be shaking a bit.

Family legend has it that when the bomb dropped my grandfather was in the hall and the blast hurled him against the front door with such force that his nose went straight through the stained glass window at the top before he was hurled backwards again. When he had recovered and checked himself for injuries he discovered that his nose was a little sore but otherwise undamaged and there was a small, nose-shaped hole in the glass. Whether this is apocryphal or not I couldn't say but the family believed it and it's at least possible; blast does very strange things.

We gathered together coats and blankets and spent the rest of that night in the communal air-raid shelter at the end of the road. The next day the house was still standing but quite uninhabitable and when the adults went to look at it they discovered that the bomb had fallen directly on the brand new, unused garden shelter. Anyone inside would have been killed instantly.

That was when we all moved to Taunton. I say 'all' but I'm not sure how many of us there were. Gran and Granddad obviously, Mum, Rick and me but not Dad because he had to stay in London. All the uncles apart from Denis had been called up by then and besides, like the aunts, all but Denis and Alf were married and had their own homes, mostly within a few miles of Edgware, so I suppose only Denis actually lived with us, though the others visited from time to time. Denis was much the youngest of the siblings, a sort of afterthought or, perhaps more accurately, an accident because I don't recall any overt displays of affection between my grandparents and can't imagine them joyously deciding to have another child when the rest of the family were grown up or in their late teens.

Louie and Polly were occasional visitors, though as far as I was concerned they were never a welcome sight because both of them were founder members, along with their mother, of my anti-fan club. Gran didn't like Dad either, partly because he was brighter and more successful than his in-laws and partly because he was half-Jewish, on his own father's side, and an ill-disguised anti-Semitism was among my grandmother's many less endearing traits. 'That Yid,' she used to call him, though never to his face, when he had done something that his brothers-in-law hadn't, like gaining a commission in the army.

The house in Taunton was smaller than the one in Edgware though comfortable enough, but even there Hitler wouldn't leave me alone. A few days after we moved in a bomb fell barely a hundred yards down the road and though, apart from the noise, we were unaffected it was a nasty shock. Why even the most rabid Nazi should have wanted to bomb a modest suburb of Taunton nobody could imagine but it was a reminder that if you lived on a comparatively small island in wartime you could run but you couldn't hide.

Every night all those present would gather round the radio at nine o'clock to listen to the news on the BBC Home Service. The war wasn't going well for the Allies but there was never any defeatism in the household, rather a confidence that everything was sure to turn out all right in the end.

'You know what they ought to do when the war's over and we catch that bleedin' 'Itler?' my grandmother said once when the news had been particularly glum. 'They ought to 'and him over to a crowd of women, mothers. They'd tear the bastard to bits.' She nodded slowly, savouring the thought with grim relish, and since she clearly had in mind a bunch of women, mothers, exactly like herself what she had conjured up was a chilling prospect. Even Hitler didn't deserve that. Oh, I don't know though – yes, he did.

One night the newsreader, Alvar Liddell or whoever it was, announced that, as was often the case, enemy aircraft had dropped bombs at random and – I promise you this is true – my grandmother sighed and shook her head sorrowfully. 'I do feel sorry for them poor buggers,' she said.

'What poor buggers?' said my grandfather.

'Them poor buggers at Random,' said my grandmother. 'They're always getting it.'

That my father didn't seem to figure too much in my early years is probably because my recollection of anything that happened before the Second World War is at best vague. I have subliminal recall of a house in a close in Mill Hill, of a maid called Lydia and a huge, ferocious Alsatian dog which, so I was told, acted as my minder and of which all the local tradesmen lived in dread because of its tendency to leap, snarling, at them, to put its front paws on their shoulders, and shove them against a wall if they came anywhere near my pram.

There was, too, a holiday in the south of France which comes back to me in short, rapid flashes, like the fragmented memories of an amnesia victim in a Hollywood movie. 1938. Ste-Maxime on the Riviera. Cloudless skies, hot sun, warm sea, a long, golden, thinly populated beach and a hotel that seemed to be the height of luxury, though it probably wasn't. We met a young German couple there, who spent a lot of time with my parents during the ensuing fortnight. As people do in such circumstances, they all vowed to keep in touch afterwards and maybe they did – for a year or so anyway, after which the postal service between Britain and Germany was kind of interrupted.

My father was born in 1911 and always celebrated his birthday on 23 February until, when he was in his late seventies, he consulted his birth certificate and discovered that he had actually been born on 25 February. His background, generally speaking, was even more impecunious than my mother's, although there seem to have been brief interludes of affluence in his family. One of his sisters boasted that she had been born in a flat in Park Lane, Mayfair, but their more familiar habitat was another of those slum streets around the Elephant and Castle.

Dad was the second youngest of eleven children. I recall only a few of his siblings – George, Emile, Celestine, Marjorie, Colette, Gerald and Sadie – because we never had much to do with them except when I was a child. The incidence of French names – my father's full name being Leslie Armande Norman – was because of my paternal grandfather, a somewhat mysterious figure who was certainly born into an orthodox Jewish family but who also claimed, on what evidence I don't know, to be French. Like my paternal grandfather he came from money, from a family which manufactured and retailed boots and shoes in the Brighton area.

I never knew either of my paternal grandparents; my grandmother died before I was born and my grandfather soon afterwards. But I do know they were very poor. My grandfather had been trained to be a chiropodist, a prospect which he detested. He wanted to be in show business and, as soon as he could, he left home and the chiropodist's trade to join a circus. This was merely the first of a number of jobs, most of them pretty menial. But his own father, presumably a man of stern Victorian principles, was furious and refused to support him. Later, when Granddad was working as an assistant to a conjuror, he fell in love with and married one of the three girls – 'The Three Graces' – who were part of the act. This resulted in a permanent rift with his father who disinherited him because my grandmother was a Gentile who refused to convert to Judaism. As a result their eleven children were brought up in a loose sort of way as Anglicans and for the most part in poverty.

What other jobs my grandfather did are unknown to me but some of them were obviously more rewarding than others, hence the erratic shift between Park Lane and the slums. What does seem to be established, however, is that at one point he was associated with, or more probably employed by, some people who imported a pair of Siamese twins to exhibit them publicly in Britain. Family legend claimed that they were the first such twins ever to be so exploited in this country but that's obviously not true. Even so they were a rarity and, in the less politically correct days of my boyhood, my grandfather's part in this grisly enterprise was recounted as something to be proud of.

Dad was educated, to the age of fourteen, at Cork Street Elementary

School in South London, whereafter – sharing his own father's fasci-
nation with show business – he worked for various firms connected
with the then silent film industry in and around Wardour Street.
Despite his meagre schooling he was obviously very bright and before
he was seventeen he was promoted to Despatch Manager at one of
those companies. But as talking pictures were introduced his ambition
was to become actively involved in the production side of movie
making, so when an opportunity arose to train as an editor he took it,
even though it meant demotion and a cut in pay.

It was while he was thus employed, by an outfit called De Forest
Phonofilms, that he met my mother, who was also working as a trainee
editor in Wardour Street. He was immediately smitten; by his own
admission more smitten than she, although there was clearly a mutual
attraction because they started going out together. And when she joined
British International Pictures at Elstree in Hertfordshire in 1929, he
swiftly followed her.

'He was a poor-looking sod,' she said, remembering him affectionately, which she didn't always do. 'Boils on his face and neck. Shabby
suit, frayed shirt. He couldn't even afford underwear. He gave all his
pay to his mother. They were very hard up, that lot.'

Clearly she must have found something attractive about him, boils
and frayed shirt notwithstanding, because they started going out
together and pretty soon decided to get married. Up to this point Dad
had never met my mother's family, an oversight which, naturally, they
set about rectifying immediately, so she took him home to introduce
him to the assembled clan.

'Mum,' she said, proudly, 'this is Les. We're going to get married.'

Gran took one look at him, didn't like what she saw, grabbed a carving knife and yelling, 'You bleeder! You're never going to marry my
daughter. I'll swing for you first', chased him round the room and out
of the house. And that, give or take the carving knife, pretty well
summed up their relationship until the day she died.

Nevertheless, my parents did marry, at a registry office on 31 January
1931, and it wasn't until the wedding day that Mum (birth date: 11
March 1908) found out that dad was only nineteen and three years

younger than herself. By this time there must have been a grudging acceptance on Gran's part that there was nothing she could do to stop the marriage because they went back to her house for the wedding night. Gran, however, exacted her own kind of sadistic revenge by refusing to allow the newlyweds to share the same bed, or even the same room; Mum slept with her sisters and Dad with a couple of her brothers.

My parents remained married until Dad's death, more than sixty years later. I was born on 21 August 1933, whereafter Mum gave up work, Rick (more correctly Richard) on 3 February 1938 and then, a world war intervening, Valerie on 1 August 1946. We would have had twin brothers if, around 1944, my mother had not miscarried, fairly late into her pregnancy, when we were living near the army camp where Dad was stationed at Ballantrae in Scotland.

How happy my parents were it's hard now to say. While I was growing up and well into my adult life they seemed very happy together although some time in 1948, soon after Dad had returned from several months in Australia where he had been producing *Eureka Stockade* for Ealing Studios, they called me into their bedroom and asked how I would feel if they divorced.

I said I would hate it because I loved them both and they smiled and nodded and never mentioned the subject again.

Much, much later when Mum and Dad were rowing bitterly my mother told me the reason for this question. While he was in Australia Dad had had an affair, far more than an affair in fact: he and a woman whose name I never knew had lived together for most of the time he was there. How my mother found out she never told me and it wasn't something that Dad and I ever discussed. He didn't mention the matter and I didn't feel it was my place to ask. Yet he must have been aware that Rick and Val and I knew about this Other Woman because there was in Mum a streak of vindictiveness, inherited from her own mother, which meant that when she was hurt or angered she would strike back with every weapon she could muster. And in those years towards the end of their life together when she and Dad argued often and quite fiercely she would surely have let him know that she had told their children of his one – and, as far as I'm aware, only – act of infidelity.

But . . . Did he tell her about his love affair because he wanted to end the marriage and begin a new life with another woman in Australia? Did he, on the other hand, confess all out of feelings of guilt and contrition? Or did Mum, a remarkably intuitive woman, simply guess that something had been going on? The first explanation is unlikely: because of his work Dad was often an absent father but he was always a devoted one, who would not lightly have given up his children. So I would imagine it was a combination of the last two – her intuition forcing a confession – that brought everything into the open. She herself once told Rick that she knew about the affair because, when Dad returned from Australia, she found lipstick-stained handkerchiefs in his laundry. I find that hard to credit. Dad was no fool; he wouldn't have brought incriminating evidence like that home with him.

But however she found out, the fact is that Dad had had an affair and Mum never really forgave him. And though I would not say this ruined their marriage thereafter, it certainly cast an occasional cloud over their last forty-odd years together, a cloud that tended to grow blacker and presage an unpleasant storm whenever some otherwise unrelated hiccup occurred in their relationship.

All this, however, was way in the future, unimagined and unimagineable, as the war dragged on and we moved from Edgware to Taunton and then, life with Gran becoming intolerable even for my mother, to the rustic peace of Hassocks, in Sussex. While we were there I was enrolled at the first of my two public schools, Hurstpierpoint College, and Dad became ever more involved in Sonic Warfare.

Chapter Three

B Y THE END of the 1930s my father was reckoned to be just about the best film editor in Britain. First with British International Pictures (BIP) at Elstree and then with Warner Brothers–First National at Teddington he cut a variety of films ranging from an early Laurence Olivier outing, *Potiphar's Wife*, in 1931 to musicals with Richard Tauber (*Blossom Time* and *Hearts Desire*), to *Mimi*, a musicless version of *La Bohème* starring Douglas Fairbanks Jr and Gertrude Lawrence, and such Max Miller comedies as *Everything Happens to Me*. That few of the films were much good and none has outlasted its time was hardly Dad's fault.

Put simply, editing is a matter of assembling the film shot by the director – and there could be several hours of it – into a coherent, and much shorter, whole. If the director is himself an editor (David Lean, who was Dad's peer, comes to mind) he will oversee this process closely, in which case the cutting and splicing of the film frequently becomes merely a technical craft. But since few directors have served their apprenticeships in the cutting rooms the editor is often not only vital to the film but an artist himself, since it is he who can heighten the drama, comedy or romance by judicious selection of the footage to be used. First a rough cut, usually a sprawling assembly of the story in chronological order, is made, then the fine-tuning begins. Footage is added, subtracted, or just shortened and sharpened, then the music, background sound and/or special effects are included and more fine-tuning goes on until the movie is the desired length and as good as it can be, given the material.

Dad was both an excellent technician and a creative artist. Indeed, he was so well-regarded that early in the war he was offered the staggering sum of £100 a week to take over production at the BIP studios in Welwyn Garden City. A few years later I was bragging about this to one of my prep school friends, who refused to believe me. 'Never,' he said. 'Not £100 a week – £100 a month, maybe.' I could see his point. In 1939 at Teddington Dad was earning £1,000 a year, quite enough to afford the rent of a four-bedroom house, a car, a live-in maid and regular holidays. Five times that amount would have been almost unimaginable wealth.

Mind you, it was all academic anyway because before he could accept the job the army had claimed him or, more accurately, he had come to the attention of a certain Colonel Disney 'Boy' Barlow. This Barlow was a career officer with rather more imagination than most of his kind, for he had conceived the idea of deceiving the enemy with sound. He was sure it was possible but, having no technical knowledge at all, had no idea how it could be done.

And that, in 1941, was where my father came in. Barlow made enquiries within the film industry and these led him to Dad, who was not only a brilliant film editor but an accomplished sound editor as well. What Barlow wanted and what Dad provided was a film soundtrack of a staff car approaching from the distance, followed by a dispatch rider on a motorbike, the sound of the motorbike's engine ticking over, then roaring up again and disappearing back whence it came, followed by a convoy of heavy vehicles, including tanks, drawing up, stopping and being refuelled. For good measure the old man threw in the sound of cooks preparing to feed the troops.

It worked – certainly for Barlow, who went off to report to his superiors in a state of much excitement, not, however, to be heard from again for some time. Meanwhile, Dad carried on working at Teddington Studios, although there was little enough to be done there, feature film production not having a particularly high priority in time of war. And while he was doing that he and all his close relatives were, as he learned later, being vetted by Military Intelligence to discover how trustworthy they were.

His next contact with Barlow came in the form of a request, well, a summons really, to report to the Hyde Park Hotel in London where he was asked to explain his soundtrack and how he had gone about putting it together to half a dozen or so other colonels and the like. And after that, giggling quietly to himself in the belief that he must have stumbled into the plot of some melodramatic B movie, he was asked to sign the Official Secrets Act.

Matters became even more melodramatic a little later when he was called in to see the head of Warner Brothers at Teddington and was told that while he would continue working at the studio his salary was now being paid by the British government to which he had been seconded. This came as something of a surprise to Dad since hitherto nobody had bothered to tell him, much less ask whether he minded being seconded or not.

More time passed, then Barlow popped up again asking Dad to write and direct a documentary film, for the eyes of top military brass only, to explain his hush-hush project. With Warner Brothers' co-operation the film was duly made on a closed set and, according to the account my father wrote of it in an unpublished memoir, was truly awful, all the performers being – in the interests of secrecy – army officers, none of whom showed quite the acting ability or animation of the Talking Clock. But apparently Barlow was pleased with it, especially as it led to him being given the go-ahead by the War Office to demonstrate his idea to a bunch of high-ranking army and navy officers.

This event took place at Chipping Camden in the Cotswolds. In order to prepare for it my father asked permission to recruit some people of his own, to go with the odd-job collection of volunteers that Colonel Barlow had rounded up. One of those Dad picked was my uncle, Charlie, himself a sound editor in peacetime but then Gunner Crafford of the Royal Artillery, although to enable this lowly private to mix on equal terms with senior officers the pretence was made that he, like Dad, was actually a civilian.

Just before midnight on the chosen day, the officers were rounded up and transported to a stretch of farmland where they were asked to take note of the terrain they had crossed and to imagine themselves on a battlefield, or whatever part of a battlefield people of such exalted rank might occupy, with a strong enemy force directly in front of them. It was further suggested that they might listen carefully to everything they heard and make notes about how they would counter the opposing army.

And then the makeshift lights were turned out and the assembled brass hats were left in total darkness and, for a while, silence. Some of them were beginning to complain that all this was a frightful waste of time, bearing in mind that cigars and brandy were awaiting them at the plush hotel they had just left, when, in the distance, they heard the cough of an engine, then a vehicle backfiring. From the left flank came the roar of an even more powerful engine, soon to be joined by the noise of others and the clatter of tank tracks. It was impossible to tell how powerful the advancing force was but the onlookers turned towards the sounds, straining to catch sight of the attackers, whereupon another, larger, force of heavy tanks advanced towards them from the right, slewing on hard ground, splashing through water, their engines protesting as they crested steep hills.

The assembled officers could see nothing but those who had duly taken note of the terrain could tell roughly where the vehicles were – just there, over to the left – no, over to the right – no, no, directly in front of them.

Suddenly the sounds stopped. Again the night was silent. And then the lights were turned on and the officers discovered that the only military vehicle to be seen was a single Churchill tank that had crept up, unnoticed in the general uproar, behind them.

The whole auditory illusion had been created by my father and his team, using 35 millimetre film recordings which were transmitted through speakers on 15 cwt army trucks some distance away. Everyone, especially the very senior brass, was hugely impressed and Colonel Barlow was instructed to put his Sonic Warfare notion into action a.s.a.p.

For Dad the immediate effect of this was that, in 1942, he was called up. He wasn't exactly pleased; given his choice he would have remained a civilian, working in the film industry but still doing his bit for the war effort by helping Colonel Barlow. The army, however, doesn't operate like that, being distrustful of civilians or anyone else whose life it can't dominate for twenty-four hours a day. And in truth the call-up could have come at a worse time for my father. Like everyone else, he had finally been laid off by Warner Brothers at Teddington and though he had then edited an Edgar Wallace film called *The Case of the Frightened Lady*, starring Emlyn Williams and Gordon Harker, at Beaconsfield Studios that job, too, had come to an end and he was unemployed and spending a week with the family when the call-up papers arrived.

He was, by his own admission, a hopeless soldier. Never at the best of times remotely interested in male fashion he carried his sartorial carelessness into the army, even to the extent of wearing his gaiters back to front. Once this trifling error had been pointed out to him, however, he rose to the astonishing height of acting unpaid lance corporal and might well have remained there had not Colonel Barlow intervened once more.

Dad was in the Royal Army Ordnance Corps at the time and one day he was marched into the presence of his commanding officer to be told that he had applied for a commission. Dad staunchly denied it, knowing he had done nothing of the kind. But the CO was adamant: *somebody* – Colonel Barlow, as it turned out – had applied for a commission on his behalf and therefore he must try for one whether he liked it or not. Before that could happen, however, he was instructed by an orderly sergeant to report to the Camouflage Training and Development Centre in Daker Street, London, W1.

Dad said: 'I'm a Londoner and I've never heard of Daker Street.'

'What does it say on your orders?' said the sergeant.

'Daker Street, sarge.'

'Then report to bleedin' Daker Street!'

'Even if it doesn't exist?'

'Yes, even if it doesn't fuckin' exist report to bleedin' Daker Street!'

Dad, showing more initiative than the army could expect, or even possibly want, reported instead to Baker Street where indeed he found the Camouflage Training and Development Centre which turned out, not at all to his surprise, to be connected with Colonel Barlow's outfit. Barlow himself was ensconced at Laggan House, an old Scottish mansion near Ballantrae in Ayrshire, and there Dad was dispatched to help set up the Sonic Warfare unit. Since he would be working on equal terms with officers he was disguised – as Uncle Charlie had been at Chipping Camden – as a civilian.

Returned from there a fortnight later to his own unit in Leicester and his true rank as acting unpaid lance corporal he was ordered to report to an Officers' Selection Board. At first this did not go well, mainly because the board was under the impression that my father was in the Royal Artillery, rather than the Ordnance Corps, and kept plying him with questions about gunnery, a subject on which Dad's knowledge was not so much non-existent as positively dangerous to his own side.

Although he was able to point out the error he was none too sanguine about his prospects, especially as the bombardier waiting outside to send him on his way said, 'I wouldn't count my chickens if I were you. You're not officer material, are you?'

Generally speaking, he probably wasn't. True, the film industry, which he loved, and the army, which he didn't, were both renowned for bullshit but military bullshit was far too earnest and much less fun for his taste. Besides, the film industry is largely populated by the kind of free-thinking mavericks who have no wish to conform that the army tends to despise and Dad was one of those.

Nevertheless, he became an officer and was sent to Laggan House to join Colonel Barlow full time. And here they trained units which eventually put Sonic Warfare into effect.

But what exactly was Sonic Warfare?

As Dad explained it the aim, quite simply, was to make the enemy move his reserves. If, for example, battle had been joined and neither side appeared to have an advantage, the Sonic Warfare unit would create the illusion of an auxiliary force advancing on perhaps the enemy's left flank in the hope that the opposing commander would deploy his reserves to deal with it, whereupon the British would launch a counter-attack on the now weaker right flank.

As the war dragged on it was used with, apparently, some success in Europe. I say 'apparently' because even today very little is known about it in this country. It's different in America where people are allowed to know about things that were done in their name and where Philip Gerard has published a book on the subject called *Secret Soldiers*. Here, my daughter Samantha decided a year or so before Dad died to write his biography, with particular reference to Sonic Warfare, but the Public Records Office at Kew told her that information on the subject was not available to the public. Just like wartime really, when it was so hush-hush that Barlow's unit disguised itself under the innocuous and misleading title of the Light Scout Car Training Centre.

Whatever happened in Europe Dad learned of it second-hand because, except on two occasions, he stayed in Britain training the crews, eventually rising to the rank of major. His first visit overseas, thanks to Douglas Fairbanks Jnr, was to America in 1943. Fairbanks, an Anglophile later to be given an honorary knighthood for his contribution to Anglo-American relations, had visited Laggan House in his capacity as an American naval captain and had been impressed by what he saw. Someone, he suggested, should be sent to the USA to interest American forces in the idea.

The someone chosen was Dad, who spent seven splendid weeks in New York and Washington, enjoying the kind of unlimited food and drink that, in wartime Britain, he had almost forgotten had ever existed. Socially he had a glorious time, being treated everywhere as a gallant defender of freedom, though there was one occasion when, resplendent in British army officer's uniform and standing outside the Plaza Hotel in New York waiting for a car to collect him, he was mistaken for a doorman by an American matron, who tipped him a nickel for holding the door for her.

Militarily, however, his trip was a failure for all manner of reasons. For a start he didn't seem to have been equipped with any of the tapes he had successfully made in Britain when he flew out. Instead, the Americans – already sceptical, I suspect, because Sonic Warfare hadn't

been their idea in the first place and therefore eager to disparage it –
asked him to make a new tape at the Astoria Studios in New York. He
was happy enough to do that but the equipment, conditions and technicians provided were woefully inadequate, far below the standards he
was used to even in Britain in wartime, and the result, despite his best
efforts, was disappointing. The outcome was that Washington showed
no interest in Sonic Warfare and after seven weeks Dad came home.

What he brought home included a large box of assorted American
chewing gum, of a variety that Rick and I could only marvel at. We
knew about basic American chewing gum, of course, because it was
common practice among the British young to accost GIs in the street
with the plaintive request, 'Got any gum, chum?' And the Yanks were
very generous. They might heave a resigned sigh as they did so but they
would invariably hand over a strip of Wrigley's gum, the plain straightforward grey stuff which, nevertheless, tasted like ambrosia to us. But
what Dad brought home was a different class – there was bubblegum,
liquorice-flavoured gum, green gum, strawberry gum, every kind of
gum you could imagine. I'd like to say that we shared it with our friends
but I'm pretty damn sure we didn't. This was treasure trove and you
kept that to yourself.

He also brought back silk underwear and nylon stockings for my
mother and this was probably the only time in their married life that he
gave her a present she actually wanted and deeply appreciated. Until he
died he always gave a lot of thought to what he would buy her on her
birthday and at Christmas and somehow he always got it wrong.
Jewellery, clothing, watches, scent – he would give them to her,
giftwrapped, and wait expectantly for her response which, as I recall,
was invariably the same. She would look at the gift, whatever it was, and
say, 'Oh, son, you shouldn't have got this for me' and then put it away,
never to bring it out again. The 'son' – a nickname she had bestowed
upon him after their wedding day when she discovered the difference
in their ages – was an indication of gratitude and affection but it didn't
mask the fact that the present was never quite what she had wanted or
expected. It wasn't a matter of cost – cheap or expensive, she didn't
mind – it was simply that the gift never seemed quite to hit the spot.

Dad was still based at Laggan House at the time of the American trip and to have his family close to him had installed Mum, Rick and me in a house in Ballantrae, about a mile or so away. What I remember of our time at Ballantrae, where we stayed for several months, was that I nearly drowned there. I was about ten and had just learned to swim and one day, a cool, overcast day, I went to the beach alone to practise this new skill. Nobody was with me and the beach was otherwise deserted. Confident of my new-found prowess I swam directly out to sea, a truly stupid thing to do, until my arms grew heavy, at which point I decided I'd better go back. Good idea, only I should have thought of it earlier. I was a hundred yards or so from the shore and the tide if not actually going out was certainly on the turn and I barely had the strength to stay afloat, let alone swim. And to make things worse there was the increasing sense of panic, the knowledge that I could very easily die out there. I tried to push this thought out of my mind while I doggy paddled, rested and doggy paddled some more, always hoping that a strong swimmer might miraculously appear to rescue me. I don't know how long it took me to reach a point where I could let my legs down and stand with my head above water. Fifteen minutes maybe? It could have been less but it seemed like an awful lot more. I was exhausted by the time I crawled up the beach to my towel and clothes.

Ever since then I've been nervous about getting out of my depth even in a swimming pool but obviously I'm a slow learner because, many years later, the same thing happened again. I was on holiday in Catalonia with my wife Diana and our two young daughters, Samantha and Emma, when the girls' beachball drifted away and out to sea. The first I knew of this as I lay dozing on my towel was when the girls started yelling, 'Dad! Dad! Get the ball, quick.'

Devoted father that I was I plunged in after it, not bothering to stop and consider what I was doing. I damn nearly got the thing, too, but somehow it was always fractionally out of reach and this was so frustrating that, still not thinking or even taking note of where I was heading, I became obsessed with grabbing it and bearing it triumphantly back to my daughters. But after a bit I was aware of something ominous. The ball was no longer just out of reach; it was now quite a long way out of reach and the reason for this was not that it was moving any faster but that I was moving more and more slowly. My arms ached, my legs ached, my chest ached. So I stopped and belatedly took stock of my position and it wasn't good. I was way out in the bay, so far that I could only recognize the girls because they were the ones leaping up and down at the water's edge and shouting. What they were shouting – and I could only hear it dimly – was, 'Go on, Dad, you can do it!'

But I couldn't. I could hardly move. I waved to them feebly in the hope that they would understand that I needed help and, shades of Stevie Smith, they waved back, not realizing that I was pretty close to drowning. I waved some more, rather more urgently now, the girls waved, too, and a couple of strangers lolling about on the beach joined in as well. I tried shouting 'Help!' but my head went underwater and I almost choked.

Panic set in, just as it had in Scotland, and for a moment I thought I was going to die for the sake of a bloody three quid beachball. There were no boats, no swimmers anywhere near me and every moment I seemed to be getting further from the shore. Thankfully the panic, though not the fear, passed and I began to do what I had done as a ten-year-old in Ballantrae – I doggy paddled and rested, doggy paddled and rested, gasping for breath and bitterly watching my unconcerned, unaware family reading books and sunning itself on the beach. When, finally, I could stand I dragged myself towards a rock and leaned on it to pull myself out of the water but as I put my hands down my arms collapsed, all the strength drained from them, and I fell on my face.

I staggered back to the family and the girls said, 'You didn't get the ball then' and carried on sunning themselves.

We found the beachball that afternoon. It had drifted round the headland and come ashore in a small cove a couple of hundred yards away. The next time it floated out to sea I watched it go and the girls said, 'Aren't you going to get it, Dad?'

'No,' I said. 'It'll come back.' Maybe it would and maybe it wouldn't but one thing was for sure: I was buggered if I was going after it again.

*

Dad's second trip overseas on behalf of Sonic Warfare was to Burma. This was some time after the D-Day landings when things were going well for the Allies in Europe and more and more thought was being given to the war against the Japanese in the Far East.

To this end the Light Scout Car Training Centre modified its equipment to deal with jungle warfare. The sonic equipment was redesigned to be operated from Jeeps or even mules instead of Scout Cars; small, portable speakers, each pushing out fifteen watts and each carefully camouflaged, were strung together about thirty yards apart on thin wire and so tuned as to give the impression of troop movement along a given front. Extensive trials were held and deemed successful. But the trials took place in Scotland, whose terrain isn't noticeably similar to that of Burma, and so it was decided that someone should go to Burma and see how it all worked there.

It was Dad who came up with this idea, arguing that it was essential to know what effect humidity would have on the soundtracks, how the density of the jungle might distort the sound waves and what kind of indigenous noises should be added to the tracks to convince the Japanese troops that the apparent army advancing on it was indeed in Burma and not poncing around on the shores of Loch Lomond.

Bad move on Dad's part. Putting forward an idea in the army is tantamount to volunteering and so he found himself 'volunteered' to go to Burma, a country he had positively no desire to visit, especially at a time like that.

Together with another major from his unit, one Tommy Watkins, he was flown to the Far East via Malta, where they arrived in time to witness an air raid on both the harbour and the airfield on which they had been billeted overnight. Bearing in mind that hitherto Dad's experience of foreign travel had consisted entirely of our holiday in Ste-Maxime and his visit to the USA, this must have been a traumatic experience. Matters became no less traumatic when, on their arrival in what was then Ceylon, Major Watkins promptly became ill and was taken to hospital, leaving Dad to travel on alone to No. 2 Light Scout Car Field Park on the Indian mainland, which he remembered as being insufferably hot, and from there, via Calcutta, to Ramree Island, just off Burma.

Hitching lifts on whatever form of military transport was available, he eventually found his way to his intended destination where he joined up with the Second Light Scout Car Company and prepared to put Sonic Warfare into effect.

The first task was to spend time in the jungle at night to note and record the noises that would have to be added to the soundtracks. To this end the local commanding officer detailed a platoon of Pathans to escort the old man to a suitable spot. Dad and the Pathans were obliged to communicate by sign language, grins and nods, neither being able to speak the other's language. Pausing only to stop for tea every hour – the Pathans' idea, not Dad's, though he found these ten-minute breaks exceedingly welcome – and with the troops hacking their way through undergrowth with machetes, they eventually arrived at what was deemed to be the ideal place. There a slit trench was dug and, after more tea, the Pathans collected their bits and pieces, saluted the English officer smartly and shoved off on a mission of their own.

Dad was left with his recording equipment, his field rations, his slit trench – and what the hell do I need a slit trench for? he wondered, uneasily – alone in the middle of the Burmese jungle. To him, every noise – and there was plenty of noise – was either a marauding beast of prey or, even worse, a marauding Japanese soldier. Like the man of war he had, theoretically, been trained to be he took out his army issue. 38 Smith and Wesson only to discover that it was still covered by the protective grease in which it had been issued. He cleaned it, loaded it, sat on a fallen tree and spent fearful hours just listening, partly in the interests of Sonic Warfare and partly, as he frankly admitted, out of sheer terror. At some stage during the night he finally realized what the slit trench was for – to hide in. He duly hid in it. He daren't make tea because that would have meant lighting a fire and alerting any Japanese soldiers who might be marauding in the vicinity to his presence. He daren't use his torch either for much the same reason. So he spent the night in darkness while an army of gigantic ants and the occasional snake passed by. At one point, discovering that leeches had infested his trousers, he did light a cigarette – and to hell with the Japanese – in order to burn them away.

Dawn came but not the Pathans and, as the day wore on, Dad began to wonder whether he was expected to find his own way back to base, a difficult feat since he had neither a compass to guide him nor a machete to clear his way and had not the remotest idea where he was. So he stayed put and another awful night passed, along with the best part of another day until, in mid-afternoon, he heard the sounds of people approaching him. The Japanese, without a doubt. He checked his Smith and Wesson and wondered whether, even in mortal danger, he could actually shoot to kill another human being.

The question remained unanswered for ever because the approaching bodies turned out, at last, to be the returning Pathans. They seemed pleased to see him but not nearly as pleased as he was to see them. When, eventually, they all returned to base it transpired that they shouldn't have left him alone in the first place but somehow this instruction had not been conveyed to them, possibly because even intelligent unilingual Pathans can't always understand orders no matter how loudly they are barked at them in English.

While he was in Burma Dad was, finally, able to find out whether or not Sonic Warfare really did work. According to family legend (our family is full of legends) it happened like this: once again Dad was left alone in a jungle clearing, only this time with full Sonic Warfare equipment to replicate the sound of vast troop movement. We, his children, knowing nothing of the technology involved, used to imagine him sitting up all night winding a gramophone to entice the Japanese army towards him while the real British forces, undetected in all the cacophony, crept up on the enemy's rear. And it worked – in a way. Come the dawn (legend has it) Dad's little clearing was suddenly invaded by soldiers – only these were British soldiers, furiously accusing the old man of having done his job so well that the Japanese, instead of moving to engage the supposed advancing force, had taken the infinitely wiser course of scarpering.

Reality, as ever, was more prosaic. The British 14th Army was planning to trap a large Japanese force between the sea on the enemy's left flank and a river in front of it. To confuse the enemy Dad and his unit were to pump out the sounds of motorized forces approaching the river from the other bank and also, under the cover of a smoke screen, the sounds of bridge building. The hope was that the Japanese would be sufficiently impressed by all the racket to attempt a river crossing further down, thus leaving a vulnerable force behind to protect their rear, or would advance to attack the troops who were apparently coming towards them from the opposite bank, in which case they would have to call up their reserves and the 14th Army could fall on them from behind.

Dad and his unit were, in fact, in considerable danger, imminently expecting to be shelled to eternity by the Japanese guns. But it didn't happen.

As in the legend, so in reality – the idea was sort of successful. The only soldiers Dad and his companions saw were members of the 14th Army. For whatever reason, and he never did find out, the Japanese had decided they were outnumbered and had simply slunk away. Perhaps they had retreated towards the north or perhaps there weren't as many of them as intelligence had led the 14th Army to suppose. In any event there was no battle. But at least Sonic Warfare could be perceived to have worked, if only in a negative way.

Chapter Four

I N 1945 EALING STUDIOS sent the director Harry Watt to Australia to
film *The Overlanders*, the story of a drover who, two years earlier, had
taken a thousand head of cattle on a 2,000 mile drive across the country to save them from the threat of Japanese invasion. It was a kind of
western without the gunplay and raised its star, Chips Rafferty, to the
status of national icon.

Harry was a distinguished documentary maker with credits such as
Night Mail and *Target for Tonight* to his name. But hitherto he had
only made two feature films, *Nine Men*, a semi-documentary war story,
and *Fiddlers Three*, a farce starring Tommy Trinder. *The Overlanders*
was a much bigger enterprise than anything he had been used to before
both logistically and – since it cost about £150,000, a respectable sum
in those days – financially. Perhaps because of the scale he fell back on
the techniques with which he was most comfortable and shot it like a
documentary. There was excellent action material, good performances
and plenty of atmosphere but the story simply didn't hang together in
the way a feature film should.

The shooting finished, Harry took his film back to Ealing where a
succession of editors attempted to give it the necessary cohesion and,
one by one, came to the conclusion that it couldn't be done. Michael
Balcon was on the point of scrapping the whole thing when Charles
Frend who, like my father, had been an editor before the war and was

now a director said, 'I know one man who could make this work for you – Les Norman.'

'Then get him,' said Balcon.

There was, however, a slight snag: Dad was still in the army. The war was over but he wasn't due for demobilization for a few months yet. Balcon, though, was not a studio head for nothing; he knew people, the right people, he knew which strings to pull. He contacted the right people and pulled the right strings and Dad's demob was miraculously brought forward. Even so he played hard to get, insisting that he wasn't interested in joining Ealing unless he got as much money as he had been earning before he was called up. How much was that, they asked. Twenty quid a week, he said defiantly. Done, they said, and he'd been at the studio for some months before he realized that, even in 1945, he had sold himself cheap. But in a way he was always inclined to do that. He had a load of talent but very little self-confidence. When he died I wished fervently that he was still around, not only for the obvious reasons that I loved him and missed him but so that he could read the glowing obituaries which turned up in practically every newspaper and could learn at last just how good he had been.

With *The Overlanders* he lived up to everything Charlie Frend had said about him. What the film lacked was linking shots, moments that would ease the transition from one scene to another without a lurching jolt. There was no chance of going back to Australia to shoot them so Dad took a camera unit to Kew Gardens and there filmed footage of water, plants, grass waving in the wind. This stuff he used as the scene breakers that Harry had forgotten to shoot. There was one sequence in particular when the thirsty cattle smelled water ahead and grew restless. The cattle were filmed in Australia; the water they could smell at Kew.

The film was a great success and established Harry Watt's reputation, the vital work my father had done being unknown to the critics. But that was the editor's lot and, for the most part, still is. Time after time he/she will pull the director's chestnuts out of the fire and hang around, unsung in the background, while the so-called auteur modestly accepts the praise.

Not that Dad felt any resentment towards Harry Watt. Indeed, they became good friends and as, respectively, producer (Dad) and director (Harry) went on to collaborate on such films as *Eureka Stockade* (an historical drama about Australian goldminers rebelling against the Establishment in 1854), *Where No Vultures Fly* (an early warning about animal poaching in Kenya) and *West of Zanzibar*, a sequel to *No Vultures*.

For Dad the success of *The Overlanders* brought rapid promotion. He edited two more films for Ealing – *Frieda*, in which the Swedish actress Mai Zetterling plays the German war bride of a British soldier (David Farrar), still a ticklish subject in 1947, and *Nicholas Nickleby*, directed by Alberto Cavalcanti and starring Derek Bond and Cedric Hardwicke. After that he became a producer, or rather an associate producer since, officially, every film turned out by Ealing was produced by Michael Balcon. This was a little hard on people like my father because Balcon was less a producer than a gifted promoter of films. Nothing was made at Ealing without his say-so and while the actual hands-on work was done by others, the so-called associate producers, it was always Balcon who took the credit.

This, remember, was in the days before directors were accorded the godlike status they have been granted since. In Britain in the post-war era the studio system, copied from the Hollywood model, still prevailed and directors were regarded as technicians who did their masters' bidding, the masters being men like Michael Balcon. To do him justice Balcon was never an ogre like Jack Warner, or Louis B. Mayer at MGM or Harry Cohn of Columbia. He once said, 'I always look for people whose ideas coincide with mine and then I'm ready to give them a chance to make a name for themselves.' And because he did that he attracted the loyalty of contract directors and producers such as Alexander Mackendrick, Basil Dearden, Charles Frend, Michael Relph, Robert Hamer and my father. Dad, in fact, was too loyal and to the detriment of his own career stayed with Balcon until after the studio had been sold and the Ealing name faded into history.

The first film Dad produced was *Eureka Stockade*, in 1948. He followed that with *Where No Vultures Fly* and then, in 1952, he was asked to direct *Mandy*, the story of a little girl who was born deaf. Mandy

Miller played the title role, with Jack Hawkins and Phyllis Calvert as her parents. At the same time Charles Frend was ready to start directing *The Cruel Sea*, based on Nicholas Monsarrat's novel, but said he would only do it if my father would produce it for him.

Dad turned down the chance to direct *Mandy*, not because he thought he was incapable of doing it but because several visits to the school for deaf children in Manchester, where the film was to be shot, had so moved him that he was sure his approach would be too senti-mental. So he stood aside to let Alexander Mackendrick direct while he acted as producer. And when that film was finished he went on to join Charles Frend in the making of *The Cruel Sea*.

Mandy, however, had a bizarre effect on Dad. He felt that to be born deaf was the most appalling affliction and for ever afterwards was terrified that it would be visited upon his own grandchildren. So when, in their turn, my daughters, Samantha and Emma, Rick's sons, Mark and Matthew, and Val's children, Dana, Vanessa and Howard, were born and were still very young he would creep up behind them in their cots and clap his hands as loudly as he could just above their heads.

If they woke up with a howl of protest – as, understandably, most of them did – his fears were assuaged. But Howard, who was not remotely deaf but a very sound sleeper, was oblivious to all the handclapping and simply slept on. Dad was distraught and nothing anybody said could comfort him. His worst nightmare, he persuaded himself, had come to pass and his youngest grandson was stone deaf. We found him slumped miserably in an armchair, muttering on about, 'Poor Howard, poor little devil, lost in his lonely world of silence.' It was only several days later, by which time it had become perfectly clear that Howard, when awake, could hear everything that went on around him, that he was finally comforted.

Meanwhile, as Dad climbed the ladder at Ealing and went off to Australia to make *Eureka Stockade* and have the love affair that was to scar his marriage, I was already enrolled at Highgate School. It stands impressively on the top of Highgate Hill and is a respectable minor public school, one of the oldest in the country having been founded by

Sir Roger Cholmeley – pronounced Chumley – an Elizabethan lawyer and politician, in 1565, which event is celebrated in a perfectly excruciating school song. It begins like this:

> Fifteen hundred and sixty-five,
> Glorious Bess was then alive.
> Up Highgate Hill, sedate and slow,
> As a great chief justice ought to go,
> Rode Sir Roger Cholmeley-oh,
> Cholmeley-oh,
> Cholmeley-oh,
> Rode Sir Roger Cholmeley-oh.

Mercifully, I've forgotten the rest of this doggerel except for one couplet – 'Here is the place for a school, I trow/Quoth Sir Roger Cholmeley-oh, Cholmeley-oh, etc.' – but I do remember that even at the age of thirteen I found it a cringe-making number to sing and we had to sing it at school assemblies about twice a term.

Generally, though, I have warm enough memories of Highgate. I turned out to be rather bright and, more importantly, pretty good at games, being a fair cricketer and a useful goalkeeper and such a combination leads to a pleasantly smooth passage through a public school career. Only in one serious respect were Highgate and I at odds: the school's aim was to turn out leaders of men and I didn't want to be one. I didn't want to be a follower of men either; I just wanted to be left alone, to do my own thing and go my own way and in that respect I was a severe disappointment. The school did its best to rectify this deficiency in me. When I went into the sixth form I was appointed house monitor, which meant I could lord it over the other boys in my house. What my housemaster, the Revd Charlie Benson, a gentle, amiable man with a huge Adam's apple, and the headmaster, Geoffrey 'Ding-Dong' Bell, who was white-haired and not at all amiable (at least to me), were saying was: okay, like it or not we've made you a leader of men so get on with it.

It didn't work. Usually such a promotion was followed, within a year at most, by a further promotion to school monitor and even to school prefect at which lofty rank you were permitted in those days actually to cane other boys. By the time I got into the sixth form I regarded this practice with deep suspicion. Caning other boys has never been one of my ambitions; I've never wanted to cane girls either. So I suppose my mildly bolshie attitude was fairly apparent and the school gave up on me as a leader of men. A house monitor I became and a house monitor I remained for two whole years.

I said I turned out to be rather bright and I did but it wasn't always so. For the first couple of years I was an idle little swine, never actually bottom of any class but always within easy touching distance of it. One day, however, my third form teacher, Tommy Twidell by name, changed my life. It was near the end of term and he had told us to get on with reading our set books while he looked at our reports from other teachers and added his own comments. So I was sitting there, dozing happily over *David Copperfield* or whatever, when all hell broke loose.

Tommy leaped up from his desk on the dais at the front of the room and, his face dark with barely suppressed rage, charged down the aisle to where I sat, grabbed me by the shoulder, shook me like a rat and – to the inexpressible delight of my classmates – proceeded to tell me what a lazy, good-for-nothing, headed-for-the-gutter, layabout sluggard I was. I was wasting my time, he said. Far worse, I was wasting his and, not incidentally, I was also wasting my parents' money. There was no room in a school like Highgate, he said, for anyone as contemptible as me and unless I did something about it he would make it his business to see that I was kicked out.

I think that is still the most humiliating experience of my life. Other teachers had certainly reprimanded me in the past but I had never before been subjected to anything like this. Even now I can see the glee on the faces of my friends – all of them deeply relieved, of course, that he had picked on me and not them – and I can feel the overwhelming shame. When we broke up for the holidays I spent days of deep anxiety waiting for my report to arrive. I knew it would be bad and it was. On the day it came I saw the envelope with the Highgate crest lying on the mat and thought about running away from home. Too late. Dad picked up the post, opened the envelope and . . . This was probably the worst bit of all. He read the report, frowning, and said, 'This is not very good, son. It's not very good at all. I know you're doing your best but do you think you could try a little harder?'

That was awful. Doing my best? I wasn't doing anything like my best and I knew it perfectly well. If Dad had railed and ranted and walloped me I could have slunk away persuading myself that I was hard done by. As it was I just stood there, reliving the shame and humiliation that Tommy Twidell had heaped upon me.

Never again, I thought, never again.

When I went back to school I worked as I had never worked before and had my reward – and glorious it was, too – when at the end of term as we read our set books and Tommy marked our reports, he glanced up with a faint smile and said, 'You appear to have made considerable progress this term, Norman.' Considerable progress? I'll say I had – I'd hoicked myself up from eighteenth or nineteenth to the top three or four in every subject and it was fear that had done it, the fear of Tommy's biting scorn and disapproval. And I'm forever grateful to him. He had instilled the work ethic in me and I found that I liked it. For the rest of my time at school I was regarded as one of the brainy ones. I worked hard, I passed my exams well and when I moved on into the wider world outside Highgate I knew that I was intelligent, that I could cope.

I owe all that to Tommy. If he had let it ride that day, had simply written me off as a loser and a no-hoper, as a lesser teacher might easily have done, I truly believe that that was what I might have become. But he had seen something more in me and if his method of bringing it out was startling and painful it succeeded. It's one of my lasting regrets that I never told him how grateful I was. After I left school I kept meaning to write to him and thank him but I never got round to it, a lingering residue I expect of the laziness he had detected in me. And then he died and it was too late.

So, yes, Highgate did well by me and I have only warm feelings towards it but I was not a natural public schoolboy. I've never been a gregarious person, much more of a loner, really, and public schools don't approve of loners. I had one very good friend at Highgate but in the holidays I would often spend my time playing football in the park at Edgware with kids from state schools and once they'd discovered that I was good in goal and had forgiven me for the fact that my accent wasn't quite like theirs, they accepted me as one of their own. The one thing I was quite unable to do, though, was get along with girls and I blame Highgate for that.

I was a day boy and therefore at home in the evenings and at weekends, so you might think that I would have had every opportunity to meet girls. Not so. By the time I began to realize that there was something about the opposite sex that could cause strange and delicious stirrings in me I was in the fifth form – a late developer sexually as well as intellectually, you see – and studying hard for School Certificate. I do mean hard as well. I'd do three hours of homework every week night and about the same on Sundays. That left little time for meeting girls because my Saturdays were written off, too – school in the morning, compulsory games in the afternoon. So all I had was Sunday afternoons and where, in the late 1940s and early 1950s, could you pick up girls on Sunday afternoons?

The local cinema seemed the only option and I tried that often but never with success. The trouble was that I simply did not know how to talk to girls and since boys' public schools took great pains to keep their charges away from the wicked temptations of such creatures I never actually met any. Near my home at Edgware was the all-female North London Collegiate School, a place bursting with nubile teenagers, and I would often watch them with wistful lust as they passed by. But I never approached them. I was not a bad-looking kid and now, with hindsight, I suspect that some of them might not have been averse to a chat-up line. But I didn't know what to say to them. What interests did this exotic species have? What could I say to attract their attention? I had not the slightest idea, although I was just smart enough to realize that something on the lines of 'I see the Spurs lost again on Saturday' probably wouldn't do it.

So girls were in every sense a mystery to me and when I went to the cinema on Sunday afternoons I had nothing better to do than watch the films while other luckier, smoother blokes were snogging happily in the back row. The knowledge I thus acquired of the movies came in handy later on but I wasn't to know it then.

I cannot remember a time when the cinema was not part of my life. When I was about five Lydia, my parents' maid, used to take me to children's Saturday matinées. What I remember about the films I saw then was a lot of men on horseback charging around firing six-shooters, the ones in white hats being the good guys in pursuit of the ones in black hats. The black hats often wore big moustaches, another sure sign of villainy in these movies, and the episodes usually ended with the words: To Be Continued, thus ensuring that we all came back for another dollop next week. It was those Saturday matinées, along with my parents' enthusiasm, that gave me my abiding love of films and westerns in particular.

Later, towards the end of the war when we were back in Edgware, I would often go to our local cinema, the Ritz, by myself. In those days there were only two categories of censorship in Britain – U, meaning the film was suitable for anyone, and A, children admitted only with an adult. The H for horror certificate had been suspended in 1942 and X – strictly for grown-ups – was only introduced some years later. So if the double bill – and it was always a double bill then – consisted of two U certificates there was no problem; unaccompanied children were welcome. But if one of the films was an A I was not allowed in on my own. What to do? Well, what I did, what loads of kids did with their parents' knowledge and approval was – and it seems unbelievable now – approach an adult, proffer my money and say, 'Please, mister, can you take me in?' It wasn't always a single man; sometimes it was a woman or a couple but often it was a man on his own. And then together we would approach the box office where he, or she or they, would buy the tickets and once inside the auditorium we would separate.

Nobody in his right mind would allow a child to do that today. But in the war years and after it went on all the time. There must have been paedophiles around in those days, of course there were, but I was never molested and neither was anybody else I knew. Maybe we were just lucky, our parents being more trusting, or simply ignorant, than parents are now. But then it was altogether a more trusting age. When I was about thirteen my parents would, quite happily, let me travel from Edgware to White Hart Lane to watch my favourite football team, Tottenham Hotspur, play at home. There were crowds then of around 50,000, all standing on the terraces and no attempt was made to segregate the supporters; there was no need because there was never any trouble. Wearing my Tottenham rosette I would wander into a crowd of, say, Arsenal supporters, who would look down at me and say, 'You can't see anything from here, son', and then they'd lift me up and hand me down until I was as close as I could get to the pitch.

Nor did the result of the game alter the good-natured mood. There would be a lot of banter between the home and away supporters but no punch-ups, no knives, no enraged groups knocking someone to the ground and giving him a kicking. Perhaps such things did happen at football matches in the 1940s but I never witnessed even the suggestion of violence. Indeed, it wasn't until I was long grown up that I first felt the slightest twinge of anxiety or unease at a football game.

This is not to suggest that the 1940s were a less violent age. We'd just fought a world war and things don't get much more violent than that. And maybe therein lies the answer: the men who lifted me down to the front of the terraces had fought in that war; for six years their lives had been dominated by violence and perhaps they'd had enough. Compared with what they had known, maybe the result of a football match, however disappointing, simply wasn't worth getting worked up about.

Against that, however, I have to say that the only time I have been homosexually molested was when I was on my way to White Hart Lane. I was standing in a crowded Tube compartment when I felt someone stroking my buttocks and looked up to see a man, a youngish, mid-twentyish sort of fellow as I recall, smiling down at me. I was so startled, so petrified that I simply grinned weakly back at him and tried to move away but in the crush of bodies that was impossible. I may have been only thirteen but I knew what was going on here. I did not, however, know what to do about it. So I moved as far away as I could, a matter of a couple of feet at most, and he moved after me, still touching me. By now I was really frightened but, thank God, the train pulled into the station, my station – Manor House – and I got out and ran as fast as I could to the exit. What I also remember is that I did not mention the episode to my parents because I knew that if I did they would never again let me go to watch the Spurs on my own and in those days I loved the Spurs with a burning passion. I had done since I was ten and first started playing football myself. It was the name that grabbed me. Not Tottenham – nobody could be stirred by a name like Tottenham – but Hotspur, which seemed to me to be wildly romantic and passionate and so much more fascinating than all the Citys and Rovers, Wanderers and Uniteds.

I've supported them through thick and thin – mostly thin – ever since and nowadays when I hear of trendy media people who suddenly reveal themselves to be lifelong supporters of Manchester United or Arsenal, or any other team that might conceivably win the Premiership, I curl my lip with the scorn that is the right of one who has given his allegiance to a bunch of, generally speaking, under-achievers and no-hopers for nearly sixty years.

Chapter Five

I WAS SUPPOSED TO go to Cambridge University. Public schoolboys did in those days – Cambridge, Oxford, London, maybe Durham. Redbrick universities hadn't really been invented then and if they had no public school would recognize them except with disdain. I suppose it was easier to get into Oxbridge at that time, so long as you had the right background and enough intellectual ability to pass the entrance exams. My form master was confident that I could manage that. It was simply a matter, he thought, of my deciding which college I fancied and what I would read there.

I wanted to go. Sort of. Three years of swanning around with my contemporaries, maybe even getting to know a few girls, sounded very attractive. On the other hand, I'd never lived away from home and was nervous of doing so. I would miss my parents, my brother and my little sister and besides nobody I really liked at school was trying for Cambridge that year.

Why Cambridge rather than any of the others? I'm not entirely sure even now. It was more convenient to my home in Edgware than, say, Oxford but I don't think that really entered into it. Mostly I suppose I chose the Light Blues because they were the ones I always supported in Varsity matches. At school you were obliged to support one or the other and somebody I didn't like much said he was Oxford so I chose Cambridge. Not that it mattered because I didn't go.

I was still dickering – shall I, shan't I? – when I learned, from where

I cannot recall and how accurately I do not know, that because my father earned more than £5,000 a year (a princely sum in 1950) he would have to fork out fairly heftily on my behalf whichever university I went to and whether I won a scholarship or not and that sort of clinched it. Suddenly I was overcome with the kind of absurd nobility that can afflict you at seventeen and give you the truly potty idea that it would be a far, far better, and certainly more romantic, thing if you were to sacrifice yourself for the greater good. My parents, I decided, had already spent too much on my education and, since Rick still had a few years to go at Highgate and Val would soon enough enrol at whichever primary school my mother happened to approve of that term, I would no longer be a burden upon them.

So I told my father I didn't want to go to university. Later and for several years I was to regret this decision, especially when I got to Fleet Street and watched Oxbridge graduates, no more gifted than I, climbing the ladder ahead of me simply because they were helping each other up the rungs.

I broke the news one afternoon as Dad and I sat in the garden, discussing my future. He was very disappointed because he and Mum had always vowed that their children would have the kind of education that class and poverty had denied them. And here was their first-born turning the opportunity down.

I could have been persuaded to change my mind but on this occasion Dad, who had always paid me the compliment of treating me as an intelligent, thinking being, now made the mistake of treating me as an intelligent, thinking being and after a little argument accepted my decision. If he had simply said, 'Shut up. You're going to university and that's that' I would have gone. But he didn't and so I didn't.

The question now was: what job did I want? When I took School Certificate and matriculated with some ease the headmaster, Geoffrey Bell, had his own ideas about what I should do. I didn't much like old Ding-Dong and he didn't like me. When, after matric, we were called into his study, one by one, to discuss our futures, his greeting – and I can still hear the grudging note in his voice – was, 'You did much better than I expected, Norman.' Oh, thanks, Ding-Dong. I'd actually got the best matric in the school that year. A little praise, the odd word of congratulation, wouldn't have come amiss, would it?

Anyway, his suggestion was that I might become a lawyer or maybe, since my main subjects were French and German, an international salesman for some big company like ICI and as soon as he said this I knew he had no knowledge or understanding of me whatsoever. Me – a lawyer, or a salesman? I may have been arrogant (actually I was arrogant) but I was also painfully shy. The very idea of standing up in court, or trying to flog chemicals or the like to some uninterested Belgian made me cringe.

So the law was out, likewise selling. What else might I do? The film industry appealed. For some time I had had vague notions of following in Dad's footsteps, of getting a job in the cutting rooms and, like him, working my way up to editor, producer and, as he ultimately did, director. I believed then and still do that the best directors are those who understand the editing process. To watch my father go onto a movie set was to watch a man who knew precisely what he was doing. He had the whole picture mapped out in his mind, knew the mastershots and close-ups that he wanted, knew where the cuts and dissolves, the fade-outs and fade-ins would come. Not a shot or a moment was wasted. In the years to come I was to see other directors dithering about, doing take after take, not because they were striving for perfection or because there was anything wrong with what they had shot previously but because they had no clear idea how the picture would cut together and therefore felt obliged to cover every possible option.

Dad became a director in 1954 when he made an excellent suspense thriller called *The Night My Number Came Up*, starring Michael Redgrave. But long before then he would often take me to the studios during the school holidays and I would spend the morning and afternoon watching him on the set as he conferred with the director, the actors, the cameraman and ensured, as a good producer should, that all problems, large or niggling, were swiftly resolved and unlikely to get in the way of the business of making the movie. In between, at lunchtime, he would take me into the executive dining room where Michael Balcon held court, surrounded by directors and producers like Charlie

Frend, Sandy Mackendrick and Robert Hamer, and writers such as T. E. B. Clarke, who won an Oscar for his screenplay of one of the great Ealing comedies, *The Lavender Hill Mob*. It was during those lunches, when I listened to all these creative people discussing their work, seeking advice from each other and generously offering it, that I began to acquire both a background knowledge of the film industry and an abiding respect for its most able practitioners.

So on that sunny afternoon I told Dad that I fancied the movies and he said, well, okay but . . . On the face of it the British film industry was doing well: Ealing Studios was the jewel in its crown but Rank was also churning out pictures from Pinewood, as was ABC at Elstree, and Shepperton, too, was in full production. And television – only the BBC in those days – was not yet making significant inroads into the audiences. Beneath the surface, though, things were not so good. Even then Hollywood films were more popular than the indigenous product, money was tight and the studios were cutting back. The British industry, in short, was going through one of its regular crises, so what chance had I?

Dad reckoned he could wangle me a trainee job at Ealing, no problem, and by pulling a few strings could even arrange a union ticket – absolutely vital in those days. But with around 2,000 experienced technicians already out of work there was a fair chance that I could find myself laid off before I'd got my feet under the table. 'This is not a good time to go into the film industry, son,' he said. 'You might be all right for a few years but long term . . .'

Thus in a few minutes and with a few words any aspiration I might have nurtured to become the next Alfred Hitchcock was dashed.

And I really don't regret it. I might have done at the time but even then at the back of my mind was the thought that if I went into the film business I would always be Leslie Norman's son, only here because of his dad/not as good as his dad/must be a disappointment to his dad. I can't say I was relieved when Dad spelled it out for me but I wasn't shattered either. A little sad, perhaps, a little disappointed, about sums it up.

What else then? Well, ever since I can remember I had been writing – short stories, essays that I scribbled down in the privacy of my bedroom and never showed to anybody. French and German may have been my specialist subjects in the sixth form but I was better at English and liked it more. I've always loved the richness of the English language and I think this passion for words has much to do with the fact that I have a tin ear; music is a mystery to me. I can't hold a tune, I can't even remember a tune unless it's accompanied by lyrics by the likes of W. S. Gilbert or George Gershwin, Cole Porter, Irving Berlin, Jerome Kern or the Beatles. The Beatles were the last pop group, probably the only pop group, that I truly appreciated, not because of their music – I'm not remotely qualified to judge that – but because of their lyrics.

I know that in lacking music I'm missing something desperately important but I only know that because other people, my wife Diana in particular, tell me how vital it is to them. There was a time when I thought that I could acquire music, learn it, grasp it, possess it by trying harder and I went through a period when I would spend hours listening to Diana's records of Mozart and Beethoven. But then, just as I thought I'd cracked it, she would turn on the radio and listen raptly as music poured out and I would say, 'That's nice. What is it?'

'Beethoven's fifth,' she would say, a little surprised that even I didn't know that, and I would realize that I had been listening to it, all the way through, only the previous day and I still couldn't recognize it.

But at seventeen, because of my love of writing stuff down in exercise books, journalism appealed to me almost as much as the movies. Indeed, at that time I had an ambition to become a foreign correspondent for the *Daily Express*. Now I can't think of anything I would hate more but in the 1940s and 1950s the *Express* was a great newspaper. It led the way in circulation and the quality of its writers with the rest of the popular broadsheets – the *Daily Mail*, the *News Chronicle*, the *Daily Herald* – trailing way behind. The *Daily Mirror* was the leading tabloid, up there with the *Express* in sales figures, with the nasty little *Daily Sketch* a long way back. In fact, compared with *The Sun*, the *Mirror* and the *Daily Star* today the *Sketch* wasn't really all that nasty. But it was nasty enough as I was to discover a few years later when I went to work for it.

In any event, that day in the garden my future was determined: I was to become a journalist. And I've never regretted that either. Indeed, the newspaper experience I acquired proved invaluable when I moved into television and radio and wrote my own scripts. Journalism develops a news sense, an instinct for what will seize the readers' (or viewers', or listeners') attention; it gives you an appreciation of the fact that the most important elements of any story are who, what, where, when and why; and it teaches you to grab the audience's interest with your first few sentences.

I took my A-levels and then left school, a month or so short of my eighteenth birthday. Highgate had been an enjoyable experience and had served me well but now that part of my life was over and unlike some of my contemporaries I had no desire to cling on. For a couple of seasons after I left I played football for the old boys – the Old Cholmeleians – but that was simply because I wanted to play football not because I wanted vicariously to extend my schooldays. Since then I've visited the school no more than half a dozen times, always by invitation and often to talk to the sixth form.

After leaving Highgate I enrolled at Pitman's College in Southampton Row in London to learn shorthand and typing. While I was there I kept an eye on the situations vacant columns in *The World's Press News* and in November 1951 applied for a job as a reporter on a weekly newspaper called the *Kensington News*.

It occupied a narrow building in Kensington Church Street – a small reception area, the printing works and the managing director's office downstairs, the editorial room on the first floor. The editor, unusually then even for a local paper, was a woman, Barbara Denny, and she had a regular staff of three, plus the occasional freelance contributor. I went to see her on a Friday afternoon, got the job and on the Saturday I had my first journalistic assignment, covering a fête that was opened by Douglas Fairbanks Jnr. I didn't actually speak to Douglas Fairbanks Jnr; I merely jotted down his opening address and took as many names as possible of those present, especially mayors, borough councillors and other local bigwigs. It seemed to be enough because when I wrote my report on Monday morning – in longhand, nobody having yet thought to provide me with a typewriter – it was greeted with approval.

On that Monday, my first full day of work, I started at 9 a.m. and got home to Edgware about midnight. In between, apart from writing up the fête, I had covered the local Darby and Joan club in the afternoon and a meeting of the British Legion at night. Such things were important then. Darby and Joan clubs, run by volunteers to give the elderly and otherwise housebound a weekly outing, were always well attended by senior citizens scoffing sandwiches and buns and, that soon after the war, the British Legion had a healthy and vociferous membership, though I haven't the faintest recollection of what they talked about that night.

This sort of day was to be the norm for the next year and more. I covered the Darby and Joan clubs, the British Legion, baby shows – there were a lot of them in those days – fêtes and local amateur dramatic productions, of which there were tiresomely many. I also kept in touch with crime by phoning the police stations every day and interviewed minor local celebrities, usually up-and-coming actors and actresses. Our freelance film and theatre correspondent, Denis Duperley, a West Indian who also wrote for the *Jamaica Gleaner*, tended to keep the better-known interviewees for himself. Denis was my closest mate at the *Kensington News*. The other two staff members were friendly enough but we had little in common and anyway, at eighteen, I was very much the office junior. I don't think I ever called Barbara Denny by her first name; she was always Mrs Denny to me but then this was a time when people still had surnames and insisted on other people observing them. Nowadays I have the feeling that if you phoned and got through to, I dunno, the head of the biggest company in the land, a voice would come on saying, 'Hello, I'm Sharon, I'm the boss. Who am I talking to – Barry, is it? How can I help you?' All very well if you already know Sharon personally but the chances are you don't, yet you're plunged at once into a redundant intimacy that is as phoney as it is unsought. I have scores of acquaintances whom I know reasonably well but I haven't the faintest idea what their surnames are because they have never volunteered them.

However, Denis must have been about thirty but he always treated me as an equal, not as a kid, and besides he was the only one among my colleagues who was happy to pop out for a drink and a chat in one of the neighbourhood pubs. Sometimes when he was away I would stand in for him as film critic and after a few months I also wrote columns of my own. The joy of reading my byline for the first time has never quite faded; even today I still get a kick out of seeing my name at the top of a piece in a newspaper or a magazine.

One of the regular columns I wrote was on the lines of 'On This Day Fifty Years Ago'. The *Kensington News* was an old-established paper and I would look through the back numbers and write what was intended to be a humorous column about the quaint things people did in the past. For the most part what I wrote was merely facetious rather than funny and I was dimly aware of that even at the time. But writing this stuff taught me a lot about how hard it was to be funny or witty in print and the lessons came in handy later on.

They were long days on the *News*. I rarely got home less than twelve hours after I set out; often it was more like fourteen or fifteen hours. And for all this work I received a weekly wage of £3 5s or – after deductions for income tax – £2 19s 6d. From that I paid my Tube fares to and from Notting Hill Gate and bought my lunch five days a week. I still lived at home and by way of rent, and after the necessary expenses there wasn't a lot left over, I bought my mother a packet of Du Maurier cigarettes every Friday evening. I did not, however, ask my parents for extra money; that they fed and housed me was enough.

The *Kensington News*, which covered the south-west London area, isn't there any more but it was a profitable little paper in the early 1950s, though it faced strong competition from the *Kensington Post* and the *West London Observer*. I knew quite a few of my rivals from the other papers, was once comprehensively scooped by one of them, and what we had in common was a desire, eventually, to work in Fleet Street. In this aim I was alone at the *News*. Barbara Denny was perfectly content where she was. Indeed, she had only ever worked for two publications. She had started on the *News*, had left briefly for *The Nursing Mirror*, decided she didn't like it and returned to the *News*. How my two fellow staff members saw their futures was unknown to me but working for national newspapers didn't appear to be on their agendas.

The rival papers, however, were full of people eager for Fleet Street and many of them made it. The editor of the *Kensington Post*, Geoff Pinnington, went on to become the editor of the *Daily Herald*, where he was joined by Doug Verity, Ken Drury and John Mossman. Thomas Wiseman, then a wunderkind film critic on the *West London Observer*, was snapped up by the London *Evening Standard* where his scathing film reviews made him the scourge of the movie industry before he went on to become a respected novelist. Gerard Garrett, of the *Kensington Post*, also became a show business columnist for the *Standard* and, incidentally, one of my closest friends in Fleet Street. And though I was younger than any of these they seemed to take me seriously because I, too, wanted to work for a national paper.

Perhaps the oddest person around the west London newspapers at that time was Michael Winner, who was then sixteen or seventeen, still at school and headed for Cambridge University. Later on, of course, he was to become a noted – some, thinking of his *Death Wish* films, might say notorious – film director and producer but in those days he would crop up from time to time contributing film reviews and show business articles to the *Post*. None of his colleagues seemed overly fond of him but on those occasions when we met on an assignment he struck me as all right, a bit bumptious and cocky, a bit full of himself. So what else is new? He's pretty much like that now. But he could then and can still, when the mood is upon him, be a most engaging and amusing companion. He can, too, present himself as somebody quite objectionable but that is a side of him that seems to have developed later, later even than the time towards the end of the 1950s when I was obliged to fire him from the *Daily Sketch*.

But that time I was scooped. It was John Mossman, whose brother James became a well-known TV presenter, who did it to me. It happened at the House of Commons where our local MP, a Tory – in Kensington, what else? Are you kidding? – was hosting a reception. I'd never been to Parliament before and regarded this as an opportunity to look around and enjoy myself. Which is precisely what I did. The booze flowed freely – free being the operative word – and to a boy who couldn't afford more than a couple of pints of bitter a week this was not to be missed. Not to put too fine a point on it I got thoroughly pissed. Didn't do a stroke of work. Never occurred to me even to say hello to the MP.

Mossman, on the other hand, talked to him at length and while there wasn't a word about the reception in the *News* that week, the front page of the *Post* was devoted to Mossman's interview in which the MP expounded on all manner of important local issues. Why I wasn't fired I do not know; I should have been; I deserved it. I do remember that Mrs Denny was not pleased but maybe she took my youth and inexperience into account. She didn't even tick me off too much and very decently never referred to the matter again. I, on the other hand, never forgot it. For the rest of my career on newspapers I lived in dread of being scooped and from time to time, inevitably, I was but not too often.

During the summer I left school I played cricket for Ealing Studios where my partner as opening batsman was Ron Elliott, a good friend of my father's, Ron having been the unit accountant on *Where No Vultures Fly*. Ron was in his mid-thirties and he and his wife, Sylvia, became friends of mine, too. When they emigrated to South Africa, where he was to work at the Killarney film studios in Johannesburg, we began writing regularly to each other and this correspondence and friendship became particularly important towards the end of 1952.

After I had been on the *News* for twelve months I began to realize that every day I was doing precisely what I had been doing on the same day the previous year. It was all becoming routine; I was learning nothing new, so I began to cast around for a job elsewhere. I wrote to various provincial dailies all of whom turned me down on the grounds of youth and inexperience, so I seemed to be stuck where I was, at least for the foreseeable future.

That being so I thought I should at least get a rise in salary. So one day I accosted the managing director and told him I wanted more money. He said he would think about it and let me know.

A week later he called me into his office. 'About your application for an increase,' he said. 'I've been thinking it over very carefully. You've done well here and you obviously have a considerable flair for

journalism.' My hopes rose. I'd been expecting a rise to £3 10s a week
but with this encomium it could be £4 or even £5. Then he said, 'I'm
sure it's only a matter of time before you get a job in Fleet Street and
that being so there isn't any point in my giving you more money.'

As brush-offs go I thought it was pretty neat but it was still a brush-
off. So in my letter to Ron that week I told him about it and he wrote
back saying: why don't you come here? A group called Argus South
African Newspapers owned among other publications *The Star*, an
evening paper in Johannesburg. They also had a London office in
Fleet Street where they recruited quite a lot of journalists from Britain.

So I wrote to them, went to Fleet Street for an interview and was
offered a job on *The Star* at the staggering wage of £9 a week. They also
offered to pay my passage out on condition that I stayed in South Africa
for at least three years. Since I wasn't sure I wanted to do that I accepted
the job but not the fare and when my letter of appointment was duly
received and acknowledged resigned from the *Kensington News* with
considerable satisfaction.

Although, now I come to think about it, the managing director probably felt just as satisfied as I did, arguing that my rapid departure only
showed how right he had been not to waste any more money on me.

Chapter Six

I LEFT FOR SOUTH AFRICA on 6 March 1953, the day after Josef Stalin died. It was the day after Sergei Prokofiev died, too, but there wasn't much mention of that in the newspapers of 6 March; it was Stalin who occupied all the space.

I wept copiously that morning. So did my parents and Rick and Val. Not for Prokofiev, still less for Stalin, but for me and the fact that I was about to embark on the biggest adventure of my life and nobody knew when we would see each other again. The whole family had come to see me off on a cold, foggy day and as I stepped aboard the train second thoughts hit us all, especially my mother. Neither she nor Dad had really wanted me to go, although he believed that it had to be my decision. After all, I was nineteen and at that age he was already married, compared with which taking a job in another country was no big deal. But it took a lot of courage and pain for Mum to agree, finally, that if this was what I wanted to do then I'd better do it.

I'd been to Johannesburg before. At the end of 1950 the family had joined Dad in Kenya, where he was making *Where No Vultures Fly* and had stayed for several weeks. Ron Elliott was there, too, and it was during this time, when I made a number of trips with him from Nairobi to the film location in the Amboseli National Park, that he and I became friends.

When we left Kenya Mum, Rick, Val and I flew to Johannesburg for a week before going on to Durban and catching the Union Castle liner home. We were lodged in a first-class hotel and, because Ealing was making the film in conjunction with John Schlesinger who owned, among other things, the Killarney studios, there were plenty of people to entertain us and show us the sights. So it wasn't the prospect of returning to Johannesburg that caused the tears, trepidation and second thoughts that day in March – it was the wrenching knowledge that I was leaving the family and going off to fend for myself.

I hung out of the window of the railway carriage, waving and weeping, until the fog and a curve in the track took the station out of sight.

And then I perked up. Whatever else youth is, it's resilient. By the time I'd boarded the Union Castle liner at Southampton, found my cabin and explored the ship homesickness was already being replaced by excitement. To be on my own, away from parental supervision, answerable only to myself and with no work to do for two whole weeks was bliss. All I needed now was a shipboard romance and I promptly found one, for I fell deeply and mutually in love with a very pretty girl from Harrogate, Jean Kemp, who was my age and who, with her parents and little brother, was emigrating to Bulawayo.

It began a couple of days out when the ship stopped for a few hours at Madeira and I went ashore to look around with Jean, another English lad and a South African girl with whom I had been tentatively dallying. Neither the South African nor I were really keen but we were both unattached, we had freedom and opportunity and a little light flirting seemed a pleasant way to pass the time.

I hadn't spoken to Jean much before we went ashore but at some stage as we wandered around, that mysterious man-woman thing happened and the hormones kicked in, hers as well as mine. By the time we returned to the ship we were holding hands and planning to spend the evening together. Matters just progressed from there and for the rest of the journey we were pretty well inseparable.

This was not, you must understand, a question of mere sex; this was the real thing, this was love, passionate and undying. The depth of my affection was such that I even found myself being nice to her little brother, undoubted pest though he was with his insistence on attempting to tag along wherever we went. Trying to avoid or shake him off during the day was difficult in a confined space like the second-class accommodation on an ocean liner but fortunately the little blighter went to bed early.

Meanwhile, after a slow start, other passengers were having a riotous time. The ship was passing full of young women on their way to southern Africa to join their husbands or fiancés who had gone on ahead to find jobs and homes. For the first couple of days they were extremely proper and exceedingly well behaved. But, then, suddenly and for some reason – 'excitation by locomotion' a friend of mine called it – they all went wild. At night the corridors were packed with flushed, dishevelled women charging in and out of men's cabins and this went on until a couple of days before we reached Cape Town when they brought the orgy to an end and reverted to being the prim, composed creatures they had been the day they embarked at Southampton.

A long journey on an ocean liner is like time out of life; it divorces you completely from the person you had been before you stepped on board and the person you would be when you disembarked. It doesn't exactly destroy your inhibitions but it certainly packs them away in a trunk labelled 'not wanted on voyage'. Or it did for those young women. Jean and I observed their antics with amusement and even a mild sense of superiority. They were simply sowing what was left of their wild oats; we were not. We were committed to each other and as a pledge of my devotion I gave her a treasured possession – a giraffe hair bracelet, which I had acquired when I was in Kenya. She said she would wear it for ever.

The day we stepped ashore at Cape Town was the last time I ever saw Jean. She and her family, like most of the passengers, were travelling onwards by regular trains; I, however, had long ago booked myself on the Blue Train, the southern African equivalent of the *Orient Express*. It cost me, I remember, £20 and everyone said what a waste of money it was. To the extent that I spent most of the journey mooning over my lost love I suppose it was but at least I was mooning in the greatest luxury the railway had to offer.

For several months Jean and I did write to each other, missives full of love and yearning. But after a while the gap between her letters grew longer until finally I received a short, polite note informing me of the weather in Bulawayo (excellent) and the state of health of herself and family (nothing to complain of). It ended with no particular expression of affection and the subscription: PTO. When I turned over I found, attached to the back, a clipping from the *Bulawayo Chronicle* announcing her engagement to some other bugger, whose existence had hitherto been unknown to me.

I'd had girfriends before Jean. Sort of. But she was my first love and it took me a while to get over the jealousy and heartbreak. But I did get over it, once I'd stopped feeling sorry for myself and remembered that Johannesburg was full of pretty girls.

Besides, the work kept me busy enough. I was accepted quickly at *The Star* because I was young, inexperienced and had never worked in Fleet Street. South African journalists were suspicious of old Fleet Street hands, arguing reasonably that however much they might swagger and bluster, as indeed they did, such people would never have emigrated to South Africa if they'd been able to cut the mustard in London. But for a biddable young person like me, eager to learn, *The Star* was the perfect training ground. It didn't go in much, if at all, for fine writing but it did insist on total accuracy. This, of course, is a laughable concept in modern British journalism, which never allows the facts to get in the way of a good story, but at that time and in that place carelessness with the facts was guaranteed to get you fired.

There was a reason for this, quite apart from the old-fashioned idea that a newspaper ought to tell the truth as far as it possibly can. Politically, the country was split between the ruling Nationalist Party, which consisted almost exclusively of Afrikaners, and the opposition United Party, dominated by English-speaking South Africans. The two parties, and indeed the two races, regarded each other with suspicion and hostility and since *The Star* supported the United Party it was very closely scrutinized by the government for signs of bias or subversive propaganda. It was the law of the land that every report, however brief, on a political meeting had to carry the name of the journalist who wrote it so that the government could keep an eye on him if anything he had written aroused its disapproval. It made us all very careful not to impart any personal spin to our reports, though what exactly would have happened had we done so is not clear. I never heard of anybody being hauled up before the authorities for real or alleged dishonesty or inaccuracy in reporting a political meeting but the fact that one was identifiable and therefore accountable acted both as a threat and a deterrent. It certainly ensured that our political reports were accurate and if we could be accurate in those we were expected to be accurate in everything else as well.

On the most appalling aspect of the country's political system – apartheid – the two major parties were pretty well agreed; they both thought it was a good thing. Blacks (or coloureds, or Indians) were not allowed to vote or buy land or cohabit in any way with white people. We were 'blankes' (Europeans), they were 'nie-blankes' (non-Europeans) and socially, domestically and, in particular, sexually we were completely segregated. Even the benches at bus stops were segregated and God help any African who dared to sit on a bench designated for blankes.

White people of even modest means employed black maids and house (or garden) 'boys' – all black males were referred to as 'boys'; often their employers didn't bother to learn their servants' names but simply called them John, just as the 'girls' were universally known as Mary. House girls were lodged in concrete huts in the garden. If married they were not allowed to have their husbands or children with them. They had to live in one of the African townships, as did John, the garden boy. And all black people had to carry passes detailing who they were and where they worked. To be found without a pass or to be found with a pass but in the wrong district was to be sent to prison. Simple as that.

The townships – Alexandra being probably the most notorious of them – were frightful, consisting of a few small, cheap houses and countless shanties made up of odd pieces of wood, corrugated iron and anything else that might provide some kind of primitive shelter. There were no roads, just mud paths down which water and sewage constantly flowed. Services such as electricity and drainage were either basic or, more likely, non-existent. I went to Alexandra a couple of times when I was covering the crime beat for *The Star* and returned again forty years later for the BBC Radio 4 programme *Sentimental Journey*. The place hardly seemed to have changed except that it had recently been provided with quite a decent cricket field. Why, for God's sake? Did it not occur to anybody that for people living, through no fault of their own, in filth and squalor a cricket pitch might come rather low on their list of priorities?

For a young, single white man, particularly one with initially at least only a minimal understanding of the country's politics, South Africa was an ideal place to live. For the whole time I was there, nearly two years, I stayed with Ron and Sylvia Elliott in the comfortable, whites-only suburbs just outside the city. I gave Sylvia £3 a week for my board and lodging and lived pretty well on the other six quid. They didn't run to a tennis court and swimming pool but a lot of their friends did and the weekends were taken up with tennis and swimming parties, barbecues and the like. And when the party was over we all just walked away; the servants would clear up the mess.

Professionally, too, the living was easy. *The Star* was Johannesburg's only English-language evening paper, its competition being *Die Vaderland*, which was printed in Afrikaans, but we didn't bother too much about that. *Die Vaderland* had its own, stridently Nationalist, agenda and very few people read both papers. So the work was quite relaxed and also varied. Young reporters like me were switched around every three months from one beat to another. I started off covering the hotels, interviewing anybody of any celebrity whatsoever who happened to be in town. From there, I was switched to the crime beat, to covering the magistrates' courts, to subediting and to reporting on the High Court. Every now and then they let me cover a football match and after a while, probably because they knew of my family connections, they asked me to stand in for Oliver Walker, the paper's film and theatre critic, whose son Peter went on to play cricket for Glamorgan and England.

My big break, though, came when I was sent to run the paper's branch office at Germiston, which was about fifteen miles from

Johannesburg and, though a pretty small place, was reckoned to be the sixth largest city in South Africa. This was not quite such a grand appointment as it might seem because the office consisted of me and a secretary and besides there wasn't, in truth, a great deal going on in Germiston.

But I scurried around picking up news items wherever I could and augmented these with a number of feature articles or, as *The Star* called them, 'specials'. My chief inspiration for the latter came not from my own initiative but from the London *Evening Standard* which, in those days, sent thick, weekly compendiums of its daily editions to South Africa. I would scan the features in these and steal any ideas which might be adapted to Germiston, interview the appropriate towns-people to give my story a local flavour and send the result to *The Star*. When, eventually, I returned to Johannesburg I got a lot of praise from the news editor, Theo Cutten, for my initiative. Neither he nor anyone else knew where my ideas had come from because nobody else seemed to read the *Standard*'s weekly edition. I was pleased with the credit I was getting but rather ashamed of the reason for it. Stealing other people's ideas struck me as a pretty shabby thing to do. But I was naïve at the time and didn't realize that that was what journalism was all about.

So life proceeded on its easy course. When Ron and Sylvia moved to a bigger house in a better suburb I went with them. Some time during 1954 my father came down from Kenya, where he had been producing *West of Zanzibar*, and I spent a week with him in his suite at the Carlton Hotel in Eloff Street. One night, courtesy of John Schlesinger whose company was producing the show, we went to see *Les Folies Bergères*, a touring company from Paris, at one of the theatres and later joined the cast at supper. I was given the place of honour next to the leading lady, a gorgeous young woman who spoke reasonable English with that thrilling accent known only to Parisiennes, and made a total prat of myself. She was not much older than me but a whole generation senior in maturity and sophistication and I sat there throughout the meal overawed, overwhelmed and largely silent. The more she tried to persuade me to talk to her the more inarticulate I became. At one point, possibly desperate to find some kind of topic on which we might exchange more than a few words, she asked me what I did for a living and I told her I was a journalist. 'You don't seem like a journalist to me,' she said. She might have meant it as a compliment but I don't think so. The way I read it, accurately I fear, was that a journalist, *any* kind of journalist, should be able to conduct at least a coherent conversation with a beautiful woman. I remember her (though not her name) vividly to this day but I imagine she forgot me as soon as the meal was over.

Dad's parting gifts to me before he flew home were a tailor-made dinner jacket, a twenty-first birthday present which I wore for years, and a down payment on a Morris Minor, my first car. This was a bit optimistic of him since up to that time I had never even driven a car. But one day there it was in Ron's driveway so I embarked on a series of eight lessons, took the test and failed. A few lessons later I retook the test and failed again, the examiner placing undue emphasis, I thought, on the fact that I had scraped against another car while trying to overtake it in a traffic jam. On the third attempt I passed. But in between times, unlicensed, I had tried to impress a girlfriend by driving her home, which only goes to show what stupid things young men will do when urged on by the libido rather than the brain. We'd been out to dinner – a fair amount of wine having been consumed – and she was understandably worried about catching a late bus and then having to walk some distance along deserted paths.

'Don't worry,' I said, confidently. 'I have a car.'

So we caught a bus to Ron's house (I couldn't possibly afford a taxi) where, taking care not to wake the Elliotts, I retrieved my keys and took her home. I had just failed my second test, had never driven in the dark before and now set off along black, unlit tracks to drive her several miles into the boondocks. When we arrived – it seemed like hours later, though it couldn't have been – her parents were asleep and generous payment in kind was clearly on offer. But by then I was far too nervous to take advantage. So I simply kissed her goodnight and went home, driving very, very slowly and terrified in case I should hit somebody, well aware that if I knocked over a European I would probably go to jail and that even if I 'only' hit and killed a black person it could be mildly embarrassing. As it happened this was the end of that particular relationship; the girl in question was so offended by the way I had rejected her grateful overtures that she never went out with me again.

But, not to worry, there were always other fish in the sea . . .

The Star was understandably eager that its unilingual reporters should learn Afrikaans. As one of those unilingual people I could understand that. In the Johannesburg magistrates' courts and at political meetings in Germiston I had often found myself reporting on events that were being conducted in Afrikaans, a language with which I was unfamiliar, and to understand what was going on I had to find someone who would translate for me, something I never liked doing because, give or take a few notable exceptions, the Afrikaners were probably the most unpleasant race of people I have ever encountered.

Most of the police in Johannesburg were Afrikaners and they were brutal. One Saturday morning when I was covering the crime beat I was taken out by a couple of Afrikaner cops in a squad car. It was a quiet morning, nothing much going on, until we came to a kaffir beer hall. Kaffir beer was the only alcohol permitted to Africans; it was a rough, thin liquid which no white man would ever drink and the only place it was obtainable was in the designated beer halls. This particular hall was as quiet as anywhere else that morning, only the sounds of conversation and laughter, people having a nice time, coming from within.

The cops pulled up outside and got out of the car. I was about to follow but . . . 'You stay here, man,' they said to me and went into the hall. For a moment there was silence inside the place and then the conversation and laughter were replaced by yells and screams. This went on for quite a long time and then the two cops came out, putting away their truncheons. 'That's better,' they said as they got back into the car. As we drove away I looked back and saw a few men stagger out of the beer hall, their heads, faces and clothing covered in blood. Did I report this, either in the paper or to the cops' superior officers? No, I did not. The policemen would have denied it and I knew perfectly well that the senior officers would unquestionably have taken their word rather than mine. It was just an ordinary, everyday event in Johannesburg; there was nothing anyone could do about it, so best to forget it.

The only time I ever felt in danger while I was in South Africa was when I found myself among a crowd of Afrikaners. One evening after work and not long after my arrival in Johannesburg, I was having a beer in a pub with another young reporter when a bunch of about half a dozen hefty Afrikaners came in and began muttering among themselves and scowling in our direction.

'Oh, Christ,' said Terry, my companion, 'they're coming over here. Listen, if they ask what we do we're clerks, okay? We work for *The Star* but we're just clerks and we only earn £5 a week.'

'Why?' I said.

'Just trust me.'

The Afrikaners came over, beer glasses in hand, and formed a menacing ring around us. 'Hey, man,' said the ringleader, 'who are you?'

Terry gave them our names.

'Are you Englishmen?'

I said I was; it didn't go down well.

'What the bladdy 'ell are you doing in our country, man?'

The signals from Terry were clear: play it cool, play it down. I said there was no work in England and South Africa seemed a wonderful country to live in. They were not appeased. Where did we work? Terry told them.

'The fucking *Star*? You work for the fucking *Star*?'

Terry said, 'Yes, but we're only clerks.'

They muttered among themselves and then the ringleader asked: 'How much do you earn?'

'Five pounds a week,' said Terry and suddenly the tension eased. They earned more than that, therefore they were our superiors. I can't say they became friendly but the hostility diminished and after a few minutes they went back to the bar and lost interest in us.

We left quite soon. 'What on earth was that about?' I said.

'Listen,' Terry said, 'if we'd told them we were reporters and how much we earned they'd have followed us outside and beaten the hell out of us. It's happened before.'

Much the same sort of hostility was evident when I covered Nationalist Party meetings, where I swiftly learned to keep my head down and speak only when spoken to. For most of the time I was dependent on bilingual colleagues to tell me what was going on but sometimes I was the only reporter present and had to ask the officials for a precis of the proceedings. Grudgingly they would tell me; after all it was a splendid opportunity to put their story across in the best possible light, since I was in no position to contradict or argue with anything I was told. But always the help that was offered was accompanied by insults delivered, in tones pretty close to hatred, at my newspaper and reporters who couldn't even speak the language.

I was trying to speak it, ugly, bastard tongue that it is. Dutifully, I attended the private lessons which *The Star* had arranged for the handful of us, Australians and Englishmen, who were unilingual. Our teacher was an English-speaking South African, fluent in Afrikaans, called Chloe Spilhaus. Her parents were big-time wine growers in Cape Province and Chloe worked in the administration offices at the paper. She was about my age, tall, dark and much fancied by her pupils and for once I was in pole position because all the others were married and she wasn't about to get involved with married men.

So Chloe became my girlfriend and for the second time in my life I found myself burbling to a woman about marriage, although that came later and in another country.

For a while things couldn't have been better in Johannesburg. I'd been given a hike in pay to £12 a week, I was happy in my digs, I had my own car, the climate and the countryside were wonderful and there was Chloe. But, without realizing it, I was beginning to grow up. When I arrived in South Africa, nineteen years old, a very Conservative (with or without a capital c) ex-public schoolboy, I believed – as I had been taught at school to believe – that my elders were always right. So when Ron and Sylvia and their friends, all several years older than me, behaved instinctively as though anyone who wasn't white was inferior to themselves, I assumed that that was the way it was. They weren't really racist; they didn't hate the non-whites or treat them badly – they simply behaved, more or less, as if such people didn't exist or certainly

didn't need to be considered. Thus to them – and to me – it was perfectly natural that if we were walking along a crowded pavement and a
black man or woman was coming towards us he, or she, should step
into the road to allow us to pass. Blacks were servants, or menials or
labourers, not through any fault of their own but because they were naturally inferior and could not aspire to anything else. Admittedly, they
weren't educated but that was because education would be wasted on
them. And, God help me, I swallowed all this and went along with it for
a year or more.

But then, gradually, I began to think again. As a reporter I came into
contact with far more Africans, Indians and coloureds than did the
average white South African. I covered court cases in which the non-
European defendants were charged with political offences, trivial
things for the most part which would pass unnoticed in civilized countries but which there were punishable by terms of imprisonment. And
after a while I realized that these were often highly intelligent people
and, what's more, in their demand for basic civil and human rights they
had rather a good point.

Now it began to worry me that black people automatically stepped
off the pavement to let me pass. To an extent, actually a very large
extent, it was the Elliotts' house boy, Adam, who helped to change
my mind. He was a Zulu, the same age as me, and quite often when
I was babysitting for the Elliotts' two young children I would go into
the kitchen to talk to him. It had to be in the kitchen because people
like Adam weren't allowed in the other rooms unless they had a job
to do.

Like me he was keen on sport and quite knowledgeable about it,
especially boxing. At that time the Empire flyweight champion was a
Zulu named Jake N'Tuli. He had won the title in England because he
certainly wouldn't have been allowed to fight for it – against a white
opponent! – in South Africa. He was a very good little fighter and,
armed with the information I had brought from England and whatever
I picked up from reading the weekly editions of the *Evening Standard*,
I kept Adam abreast of his career. We got along very well and I enjoyed
those chats in the kitchen.

But then Adam left to take a better paid job in a factory and I didn't see him again for several months.

The next time we met came at a rather significant moment for me. I was covering the High Court, the Old Bailey as it were of Johannesburg, and various disturbing things had been going on. In the same week I had sat through two rape trials. In the first an Afrikaner had been accused of snatching a young African woman off the street, bundling her into his car and taking her to a deserted place where he had raped her. He was found guilty and given a suspended sentence.

In the second an African gardener was charged with raping his white employer's wife. As I listened to the case it seemed to me, as surely it should have done to any impartial onlooker, that the man had been set up. All the evidence, not only the alleged rapist's, pointed strongly to the woman having fancied 'a bit of dark meat' (in the elegant South African phrase) and seduced him, not once but several times. It was only when she feared she might be pregnant by him that she yelled rape. The defendant's case was certainly based on the woman having instigated everything that happened but, hey, she was white and it was her word against that of a black man. No contest. He was found guilty and condemned to death. A suspended sentence for a white man; the noose for a black.

One morning, in the aftermath of these two cases, the High Court was adjourned at about 11 a.m. and we of the press corps went across the road for a coffee. As we were coming back Adam came along on his bicycle, spotted me and greeted me and we stopped to catch up with each other's news. We only chatted for a couple of minutes because he was on his way to clock in at the factory and when he left I hurried to catch up with my colleagues on the High Court steps.

And there a journalist from *Die Vaderland* turned to me and said, 'Hey, man, you shouldn't be seen talking like that to a kaffir in the streets.'

That was the moment when I decided I couldn't live in South Africa any more. Had I been a brave man I might have stayed, joined one of the dissident political groups and protested against apartheid. But I didn't have that kind of courage and besides I was realistic enough to know that any such action on my part would have led, at best, to house arrest and, at worst, to imprisonment and God only knew what kind of violence at the hands of the police.

What to do then? The trouble was that having been in South Africa for a little under two years I wasn't yet ready to go home. Besides, this was a big continent of which I had seen very little. A transfer to one of the other Argus newspapers in South Africa wasn't the answer because the political situation would have been exactly the same there. But Argus also had papers in Southern and Northern Rhodesia (Zimbabwe and Zambia as they now are) and that rather appealed.

So I asked for a transfer to the *Rhodesia Herald* in Salisbury (Harare), explaining that I wanted to widen my knowledge of southern Africa. Because the Argus group had every reason to believe that I was going to settle in the country and because the kudos I had acquired in Germiston had marked me out as a man to watch, this was regarded as an enterprising notion on my part. The transfer was negotiated without difficulty, I was given a rise to £15 a week and in November 1954 I set off to drive myself to Salisbury, through the Transvaal to Beitbridge and then along a hair-raising narrow road, with a sheer drop often of hundreds of feet on one side, through the mountains of Southern Rhodesia. I was alone in gorgeous but deserted countryside among a people who had no cause to like me but at no time did it occur to me that what I was doing might be a little risky. Nor, even late at night, had I ever felt in danger in Johannesburg, certainly not from Africans. Forty years later, when I went back for *Sentimental Journey*, downtown Jo'burg had become a no-go area at night time, especially for white visitors, and I wouldn't have contemplated driving any great distance alone. Apartheid, thank God, had gone and the Africans were, belatedly, on the brink of taking charge of their own country but not everything had changed for the better.

The journey to Salisbury took three or four days because I was in no hurry and on the last night of the trip, 230 miles from my destination, I stayed at a hotel in Bulawayo. Out of curiosity I looked up the Kemps in the telephone book. They were there all right but I didn't call them. Jean was probably married by now and somehow I suspected that my turning up unexpectedly and asking if I could have my bracelet back wouldn't have been entirely welcome.

The *Herald* had found me digs in a boarding house not far from the office. But I wanted a place of my own and was lucky enough to find one. A subeditor, married but separated from his wife, was going on temporary transfer to the group's paper in Ndola, in Northern Rhodesia, and wanted to sublet his flat while he was away. I was his man and so, for the first, and only, time in my life I lived on my own. The rent I paid included the services of a black house girl, who cooked my breakfast, did my laundry and cleaned the flat, for the most part in silence. Her grasp of English was minimal and anyway we had little to talk about.

I was living now about twenty minutes drive from the office and a fascinating drive it was, especially at night. The journey, to and fro, took me through whites-only suburbs where African prostitutes would accost drivers at every traffic light, offering deliciously naughty pleasures. I was often tempted because some of them were very beautiful but I never availed myself of the delights they proferred. It was fear of disease that held me back not, as would have been the case in Johannesburg, the fear of prosecution for having illegal sex.

In a way the presence of these black hookers – and the fact that they were allowed to ply their trade unharassed, for the most part anyway, by the police – underlined my belief that I was right to go to Salisbury. Such women were unknown in the white suburbs of South Africa but here they were at least tolerated. Certainly miscegenation was disapproved of in Rhodesia but for social, not legal, reasons. There was no policy of sexual apartheid there; I could if I had wanted to have taken a black mistress or, I suppose, a black wife. Quite a few white men did so, although these were poor whites, the trailer trash of the town, who had no social standing to lose and it was not uncommon to see them walking along, hand in hand, with black women. Admittedly, I never saw a black man walking hand in hand with a white woman. That was not acceptable but the reasons were racist, not legal, and had much to do with the white man's fear of the black man's legendary potency. True, a white man of the middle class or above who openly consorted with a black woman would have been socially ostracized. But a lot of well-connected people – including a senior official of the city council – were known to have black girlfriends on the side and so long as they remained on the side and out of public view nobody (except perhaps the white wives) objected.

In short, things were better in Rhodesia. There was racism, certainly, but without the crackling tension that was so apparent in South Africa. What was more, in Salisbury if a black man stepped off the pavement to let me go by he did so out of politeness, not because it was demanded of him.

Work for the *Herald* was much as it had been for *The Star*, with a few bucolic differences. A hippopotamus suddenly cropped up in the outer suburbs, wandering into people's gardens and eating their vegetables, and I was detailed to chronicle its activities for a week or two until it was driven back to a wilder place where it belonged. And before then, when I had only been there for a day or two, a freelance correspondent sent in a paragraph about a housewife who had come across a green mamba in her kitchen and beaten it to death with a broomstick. I thought this was amazing: a green mamba was about as deadly a snake as you would wish to meet and I insisted on going out to interview the heroic housewife. The news editor wasn't keen but I put that down to occupational cynicism. So I talked to the housewife in the very kitchen where the events had taken place and even looked with awe upon the body of the snake. I wrote, I may say, a graphic and thrilling account of the events but next morning all the paper published was the correspondent's original paragraph.

I marched angrily into the news editor's office, brandishing the offending page. 'Why?' I asked.

He shrugged. 'Happens all the time,' he said. And, actually, it did.

On another occasion I was physically threatened, for the only time in my life, for doing my job. I was covering the magistrates' court where a middle-aged, trailer trash white woman, a sort of Hell's granny, was found guilty of some violent offence. In the courtroom, looking on, was her son, a brute of a bloke who was serving in the Rhodesian army.

As I walked out into the street he grabbed me by the shoulder. 'One word of this gets into your fucking paper,' he said, 'and I'm coming after you with my rifle.' I believed him; there was nothing in his demeanour to suggest I shouldn't.

I went back to the office and reported the encounter to the news editor, who was furiously indignant. 'To hell with that,' he said. 'We're printing the story. We're not scared of him.'

Well, no, there was no reason why the news editor should be. But I was scared and for a week after the story appeared – quite prominently displayed to prove the news editor's courage – I spent an awful lot of time looking over my shoulder for an irate man with a rifle.

At Christmas, the first I had ever spent away from family or close friends, I was thrilled to learn that Chloe was coming to Salisbury to spend the holiday with relatives. The fact that I was there also had something to do with her decision.

We spent the afternoon of a dull, overcast Christmas Day alone on a hillside just outside the city and, among other things, discussing the future. By then, my dreams of Fleet Street having been reawakened, I had already decided that I would go home within the next few months and Chloe said she wanted to come with me. The question was should we be married first, or should we wait until we got to London? We decided to wait. She stayed in Salisbury for a few more days before I saw her off back to Johannesburg, each of us vowing undying love.

And so I embarked on my last few months with the *Rhodesia Herald* before, at the end of May 1955, setting off on the long drive to Johannesburg to spend a week saying goodbye to the Elliotts and other old friends. I went to *The Star* office looking for Chloe but they said she had gone to Cape Town, which was odd because she hadn't told me she was going. And then, glancing idly through back numbers of the paper, I came across the announcement of her engagement, again to someone I'd never even heard of before.

So that was that – a perfect symmetry to my South African adventure: dumped at the start, dumped again at the end.

Actually, I was quite relieved this time. Chloe was a wonderful girl but the idea of marriage between us was always absurd, never more than a soppy dream. So I set off in good spirits to drive to Cape Town,

through the Karoo where I had to stop to let a family of baboons cross
the road, to take myself and my little car home. Again it was a memorable journey through wonderful countryside and the voyage back to
England, though sadly lacking in romance on this occasion, was again
a gloriously irresponsible time out of life. Even the fact that I had to
share a cabin with a young South African suffering unashamedly from
gonorrhoea was of no great concern.

Two weeks after leaving Cape Town I arrived back in Southampton
to find the entire family waiting for me on the dockside.

Chapter Seven

I HAD CHANGED A lot in the time I had been away, grown independent I suppose and possibly selfish, too, and some of this was immediately apparent as the family came forward to greet me joyously and I found, to my horror, that I felt awkward, almost estranged, in their company. These were the people I loved best in the world; I had been longing to see them for weeks but I couldn't show the unrestrained affection which they deserved and which indeed I felt. Val, who was nearly nine at the time and loved me dearly, drove back to Edgware with me in my car and was almost in tears by the time we arrived. I wasn't the brother she remembered; I didn't seem to know anything about her or her recent life; I was too polite – like a stranger. My parents, and Rick, too, were hurt by my apparent aloofness. I couldn't then and can't now explain this curious attitude of mine but I know it took several weeks before they, and I, felt I belonged again.

The family had moved while I was away, to a house on the Canon's Park estate, still in Edgware, and just down the road from Max Bygraves, though we saw little or nothing of him. A few years later he starred in *Spare the Rod*, a sort of British *Blackboard Jungle*, which my father directed but by that time Max had moved away.

Arrived home, I pottered around for a few weeks looking for a job. Jack Worrow, an old friend of my father's and the head of publicity at Ealing Studios, arranged an interview for me at the *Evening Standard* but it didn't go well. Theo Cutten, the news editor of *The Star*, had provided me with a most glowing reference, saying that any time I wanted to return to the paper there would be a job for me; if no vacancy existed one would be created. You'd think that might have impressed the bloke at the *Standard* and I expect it would have done if only I'd shown it to him but I didn't. I was too shy. So all he saw was a kid pushing twenty-two – young for Fleet Street in those days – with a less than overwhelming CV. Unable to think of anything else to offer me, even to please Jack Worrow, he suggested I might do the odd football report and sent me off to think about it.

I didn't think about that; what I did think about was that I'd been a bloody fool not to show him my reference and I didn't make that mistake again. As a result I was offered jobs on the *Derby Evening Telegraph* and the Scottish *Daily Mail*, neither of which appealed much. An offer from the Press Association was more interesting because it was in London but I didn't fancy the anonymity of agency work. The London connection was important because on a visit to Ealing Studios with my dad I'd fallen in love again, this time with a very pretty blonde secretary there. She was a little older than me and on the rebound from what appeared to have been a rather abusive relationship. I was deeply besotted with her, which was why Derby and Edinburgh were out of the question. I simply had to be in London and in the end, again thanks to Jack Worrow's contacts, got a job with the *Daily Sketch*.

In all sorts of ways this turned out to be both good news and bad. It was good news that I was working in London and, at last, on a national newspaper, bad that my girlfriend dumped me almost immediately and went back to her abusive boyfriend and probably worst of all that it was the *Daily Sketch*. This was an unpleasant little newspaper, a struggling tabloid bobbing along in the wake of the *Mirror* which in those days, under the aegis of Cecil King and Hugh Cudlipp, was infinitely better than it has ever been since.

The editor of the *Sketch* was Herbert Gunn, a tall, imposing man with a fine head of steely grey hair and a journalist of considerable, though now fading, reputation, fading because running the *Sketch* couldn't have been anybody's idea, least of all his I imagine, of an ideal job. He took me on at a salary of £17 a week – well below the union minimum – and got away with it by claiming that I was a trainee gossip writer. He was right in a way. I'd never done any gossip writing and was soon to discover that I didn't like it, though I was stuck with it for about four years. But this was a seedy way to take on cheap labour and typical of the *Sketch*, which should have had Cheap and Seedy printed on its masthead.

The editor of the paper's gossip column, published under the pseudonym of Simon Ward, was Alan Gardner, a plump baby-faced man who was a lot tougher than he looked and really loved gossip writing. He didn't have to do it; his family had a thriving toy business within which a much better-paid post was his for the taking. But he was a newspaper, and gossip, junky and very good at his job. I got on well with him, as I did with David English (later Sir David and the mastermind behind the remarkable success of the present tabloid *Daily Mail*), who was the features editor.

I was slightly in awe of English, who was only a few years older than me but light years ahead in political and journalistic skill. I didn't like his methods – the way he slanted the news to fit the paper's needs – but then and later they were amazingly effective. He knew exactly what the readers wanted and would cheerfully spin the facts to give it to them.

In 1956 when the EOKA uprising in Cyprus, led by Archbishop Makarios and General Georgios Grivas, was at its bitterest and most violent I was sent there to write a feature about it. I don't recall being given any particular brief; I was merely told to liaise with Simon Wardell, the paper's correspondent in Nicosia. Why the *Sketch* should have sent me remains a mystery. I was a gossip writer, for God's sake, and a very inexperienced one at that. Maybe they thought I might be killed, in which case it would be no great loss to the paper but would make a hell of a story.

What I do recall is armed British troops everywhere, barricades, the sound of gunfire, not all of it very distant, an air of great tension and a hotel full of hardened Fleet Street hacks getting stuck into the booze every night. In their company I was a stranger. They didn't know me, had never heard of me and weren't about to help me in any way, though they were quite happy for me to buy them the odd beer.

Simon Wardell, in truth, wasn't much more help. He was a tall, slim, fair-haired man who had been the first editor of the *Sketch* diary and had indeed lent it his name though without the final 'ell'. Now he was living in semi-retirement in Cyprus and seemed to welcome my company. He had a dry wit and slightly effete manner and I don't think the Fleet Street hacks liked him much more than they liked me. He was very useful in that he drove me around in his car and introduced me to British officials but he seemed to have no more idea than I about what I should write, except that one afternoon he came up with the notion that we should try to get an interview with General Grivas.

Like nobody had thought of this before? Every correspondent on the island had been trying to get to the general and been turned away with contempt. Simon, however, came up with a new approach. We wouldn't attempt to contact Grivas through official sources but instead we would get into Simon's car and go and look for him.

'Where?' I said.

'Oh, up in the hills. EOKA stronghold up there,' said Simon. 'We're bound to find him.'

And so we set off. Now, admittedly, this harebrained scheme was the result of a well-lubricated lunch but it was a ludicrously dangerous thing to do. EOKA was so well established in the hills that even British troops didn't go there. In every village the walls were covered with slogans supporting EOKA and *enosis*, the movement for union of Cyprus with Greece. Mostly the streets were deserted but such passers-by as there were regarded our car with a mixture of hostility and disbelief. Blithely ignoring all this, Simon and I stopped off at various tavernas for a beer and to enquire of the locals, 'Can you tell us where we might find General Grivas?' Needless to say nobody could – or if they could they wouldn't. When I thought about it later it seemed miraculous to me that we hadn't been beaten up or even killed. Maybe the fact that we were obviously some way from sober and therefore not to be taken seriously stood in our favour. For the most part people just ignored us, although they clearly weren't happy to have us in their midst. Simon and I spent the whole afternoon racketing around the villages and popping into tavernas and finally returned to Nicosia no wiser as to the whereabouts of General Grivas than we had been when we set out.

What nonsense I sent back to the *Sketch* by way of copy I have mercifully forgotten and in any case it never appeared in print. My story was handed to David English, who promptly threw it away and concocted one of his own. It was all about the anxious wives of British soldiers in war-torn Cyprus waiting in the barracks, never knowing whether their husbands would survive to come home in the evening. To that extent what he wrote may well have been the truth but the embroidery around the rest of it was pure invention.

Fortunately the English version went down well and in a quite unjustified way some of the credit for that attached itself to me. I hardly returned a hero but I wasn't accused of having failed either, although in fact I had.

With hindsight I now realize that English must have seen some merit, or anyway promise, in me because after the Cyprus trip he rather took me under his wing, asking me to do a number of features, all of which he rewrote pretty well from top to bottom. But comparing his versions with my own and allowing for his additions and twists I began to see how feature articles should be written for popular newspapers and in the end some of my stuff was published much as I wrote it, so I was rather grateful to him.

Meanwhile, there was the gossip column. I had quite a talent for writing gossip, no talent at all for acquiring it. At that time the Fleet Street columns had a morbidly obsessive interest in the adventures and misadventures – especially marital – of the aristocracy. And one day I was sent to a house in Chelsea to interview a peer of the realm, whose wife had run away with the Master of Foxhounds in whatever county the peer had his country estate. His lordship himself answered the door, which threw me a bit because I'd been expecting a butler. 'Who are you?' he asked. I told him.

'What do you want?'

I told him that, too, in a faltering sort of way – 'Well, you know, your wife and the Master of Foxhounds . . . gone off together . . . I was just sort of wondering what you . . .'

'What the hell's it got to do with you?' he said and right away he had me. I was stuck for an answer, knowing perfectly well that his marital unhappiness had nothing at all to do with me or the prurient readers of the *Daily Sketch*. I was mumbling something about letting him tell his side of the story when he slammed the door in my face. I couldn't blame him; I'd have done the same.

I wandered unhappily away and phoned Alan Gardner to tell him what had happened. 'Go back,' Alan said. 'Bang on the door again. Keep at him.' Easy for him to say and probably, if he'd been there, that's what he would have done. But I didn't have the heart for it.

So I bought a newspaper, found a coffee shop nearby and sat there for a peaceful hour before phoning Alan again. 'He's still not saying anything,' I said, which after all was the truth; certainly he wasn't saying anything to me.

'Well, keep at it.'

'Oh, I will,' I said. 'I won't let him get away.' Then I went back to the coffee shop and did the crossword puzzle. An hour and another phone call later Alan congratulated me on my diligence, commiserated with me on the peer's non-co-operation and told me to come back to the office. That sort of thing happened several times. If people were happy to talk to me, then I was happy to question them. Otherwise, I was useless and later – on the *Daily Mail* – Alan realized this and used me mostly to cover non-contentious gossipy events and to rewrite other people's copy.

I was also hopeless at inventing stuff. One night I was sent to the Royal Opera House at Covent Garden where Princess Margaret was to attend a performance. She was big news in those days, this being soon after the crass decision by Buckingham Palace to oppose her projected marriage to the divorced Group-Captain Peter Townsend. The public wanted her to marry him and, had she done so, it would have given the royal family's popularity no end of a boost. But the royal advisers stood on protocol and precedence and made a huge mistake. Townsend was – oh, the horror of it – a divorced man and a commoner to boot; impossible that he should be allowed to taint the royal blood. True, the princess was later permitted to marry another commoner, Anthony Armstrong-Jones, and that was a popular decision but still the royal advisers learned nothing. If they had been paying attention to the public mood they would, much more recently, have allowed Prince Charles to marry a woman of his own choice rather than being intent on finding him a 'suitable' bride in Lady Diana Spencer (who turned out to be quite unsuitable) and by so doing would have avoided the ensuing neurotic fiasco and the seething unpopularity which subsequently attached itself to the entire royal family.

However, that night at the Royal Opera House I was in attendance along with a couple of women, tough old boilers, from rival gossip columns and Margaret turned up half an hour late. The boilers and I enquired the reason for this from her equerries, ladies-in-waiting and the Opera House staff but nobody could, or would, explain it. The boilers, both of whom ignored me the whole time, went off together, whispering in what I rightly assumed to be a sinister manner. For the next morning, while the *Sketch* carried my lame story about the unsolved mystery of the princess's lateness, the other two papers revealed without fear of contradiction that just as she was about to step into her car to go to the opera Margaret decided she simply must change her dress.

There was no evidence for this whatsoever. It was, in fact, a total fabrication but the old boilers, wiser than me, knew that the royal family would never deign to deny or comment upon such a story, however untrue it might be. Besides, it appeared in two papers so it must be true, mustn't it?

So there I was, deeply in the shit. Bert Gunn called me into his office, pointed to the rival stories which, trivial though they were, were certainly better than mine and asked why I hadn't written the same kind of thing.

'But it's all lies,' I said. 'They made it up.'

Gunn was not appeased. He ticked me off and sent me away with the strong impression that my true fault lay not in having missed the old boilers' fabricated story but in not having had the initiative to invent something even more outrageous.

Even so I hung on at the *Sketch* and was eventually given a pay rise that brought me up to the union minimum. When I'd been there about two years Alan Gardner left to take over the *Daily Mail*'s gossip column and give it a brand new image under the pseudonym of Paul Tanfield. (Actually, on his first day in charge they called it Peter Tanfield before deciding the following day that Paul sounded better.) To my surprise, Gunn asked me to succeed Alan as editor of the Simon Ward column. I accepted, asking only for increased pay in exchange, a request that struck me as no more than reasonable. Gunn said he would think about that and let me know in three months.

Three months went by. The column was okay – not brilliant but then very few gossip columns are – and I was happy enough sitting in the office, sending people out on assignments and rewriting their copy. One of the people I had to send out was Michael Winner, now down from Cambridge and working as a freelance journalist for the *Sketch* diary and also for the *Evening Standard*'s 'In London Last Night' column. He was willing enough but his heart wasn't in it because he was already planning his entry into the film business. David English was aware of this and didn't like him, so one day he took me aside and told me to fire Winner. This was not a task I fancied. Michael may not have been the best of gossip writers but he was no worse than anybody else and besides firing people struck me as a most unpleasant thing to do. But English insisted so, during a lull in the day's proceedings, I told Michael the bad news. 'English says I've got to fire you.' I must say he took it very well. Maybe it was no surprise to him; maybe he just didn't care. After all, it wasn't as if he were going to be destitute – his father was very rich and anyway it wasn't too long afterwards that he directed his first film.

Fairly soon after Winner's going, though in no way because of it, I left the *Sketch* as well. The three months having gone by I went to see Gunn and remind him about the promised rise. He said he would give the matter further consideration and let me know. Now, it was his policy every day to put up a bulletin on the newsroom notice board giving his forthright – sometimes downright vicious – opinion of that morning's paper. In the preceding three months the gossip column had come in for its fair share, no more, no less, of mild compliments and occasional insults. But now hardly a day passed without Gunn railing against the inadequacy of the Simon Ward column. 'What has gone wrong with our diary?' he would ask on a more or less regular basis. I used to dread going into the office, knowing that public calumny was bound to be heaped upon me yet again. After about a month of this Gunn summoned me to his office.

'Well,' he said, 'you've seen what I have to say about the diary. In those circumstances I can hardly give you a rise, can I?'

'No,' I said, realizing at last that what was wrong with the diary was that its editor wanted more money, 'and in those circumstances I can hardly stay here, can I? So I'll give you my resignation.' He clearly wasn't shattered but I think he was surprised. If he had wanted rid of me he would have fired me. The purpose of those daily attacks in the bulletin had not been to make me quit but to make me humble, make me scared, make me grateful that I still had a job and to keep the wage bill down.

I wrote my resignation and handed it in and, as a result, had a final showdown with the man I disliked most on the *Sketch*, Cyril Morton, the managing editor. He was a large, fat, and it seemed to me brutal, man who commanded the paper's newsroom like Charles Laughton bestriding the poop deck in *Mutiny on the Bounty*. He was a bully and everyone, including me, was afraid of him. Within minutes of my resignation landing on the editor's desk he came roaring over to me, surrounded by acolytes.

'How can you do this to Gunn?' he shouted so that everyone could hear. 'You owe him everything. He dragged you up from the gutter . . .'

That did it. Sheer fury gave me a courage I had no idea I possessed. I leaped up from the desk and yelled back at him. 'What did you say? He did what? He dragged me up from *where*? How dare you . . .'

And the bully deflated. He stepped back with an alarmed look on his face, possibly due to the fact that my fists were clenched, and he must have thought I was about to hit him. 'I didn't mean that literally,' he said. 'I mean he took you in when no other paper would and . . .'

'And now I'm going,' I said. 'I have my own career to think about.'

He recovered enough to sneer. 'Your *career*? What career?'

'The one I'm going to have somewhere else.' I took another step towards him and this time he turned and walked away mumbling to himself. It was only a little victory but it was a nice note on which to leave the *Sketch* and the *Sketch* was a good paper to leave. Because in those days the national newspapers had a greater fear of libel and lawyers and contempt of court than they do now, it was never as brutish or sadistic as the red top tabloids of today but it was brutish and sadistic enough. On the other hand I learned a lot there, not least that wherever I went in future there was not a dirty trick anyone could play on me that I hadn't seen done better at the *Sketch*.

One amazingly good thing did, however, happen to me while I was at the *Sketch*: I got married. Early in 1957 the Moscow State Circus came to London – no big event nowadays but huge at the time. On the Sunday evening they arrived I was sent to Earl's Court to report on how they were settling in. Every daily paper had somebody there, including the *Daily Herald*, who had sent a remarkably pretty, fair-haired girl called Diana Narracott. I had never met her before but I felt an immediate stir of interest and made it my business to introduce myself. She wasn't much impressed. I was a comparative newcomer, while she, though only twenty-three as I was, had been in Fleet Street for ages, had in fact at the age of twenty been the youngest reporter working there. She was very popular with all her colleagues – most of whom, as I discovered later, fancied her – and she really didn't have a lot of time for someone who worked for the *Sketch* (yuk!) and as a gossip writer at that. I mean, for heaven's sake, a girl had her standards.

I went away thinking wistfully how nice it would be to see her again and wondering whether I should phone her at her office. I was still summoning up the nerve to do that when it became unnecessary, for a couple of days later I met her again, at St Margaret's Church in Westminster, where we were both covering a society wedding. I don't

really know why she was there because this was very much a gossip
column event and Diana didn't do gossip. This time we got along a
great deal better possibly because, there not being many real reporters
around, I was one of the few people she recognized. So we covered the
wedding more or less together and discovered – a hugely important
point this in any relationship – that we laughed at the same things.
Even so, I still didn't have the nerve to ask her out and went back to
wondering what she would say if I phoned her. 'Get lost', perhaps. 'Go
out with someone from the *Sketch*? Are you mad?' These and many
other put-downs all seemed possible, so I didn't call.

But again it became unnecessary. On the Friday of that week I was
sent to Shepperton film studios where Charlie Chaplin was about to
make *A King in New York,* by no means one of his best films but at the
launch party before shooting had even begun we weren't to know that.
Chaplin was easily Britain's biggest movie star at the time and there was
much interest in his activities; indeed, earlier in the week I'd been
lurking around the Savoy Hotel, hoping to get a word with him. As it
happened I failed and this launch party at Shepperton was the only
occasion I ever met him, not that I can recall a single word he said
because meeting Chaplin for the first time was totally overwhelmed by
the fact that I was also meeting Diana for the third time. Fleet Street,
or the newspaper part of it, was a very small community, not unlike a
village in size, and it really was rather odd that in eighteen months I
had never before set eyes on Diana yet now I bumped into her three
times in a week. Fate. Had to be. Again we got along very well but again
I couldn't summon the courage to ask her for a date until, at the end of
the launch party, my greatest asset came to my aid. I'm talking about
my car here. In the mid-1950s not many people, even journalists, had
their own cars but I did. And as Diana was about to join our fellow
hacks on the coach that was to take them back to London I moved in
and tentatively offered her a lift. She accepted. I drove her to
Paddington Station where she was to catch the night train to Torquay
and spend the weekend with her mother, Aeron, and her younger
brothers, Tony and Roger. I don't think anything as racy as kissing took
place before we parted but I did at least ask her if she would like to

come out with me sometime and – ah, bliss – she said she would.

We arranged to meet for dinner at the Trocadero in Piccadilly on the following Tuesday and from then on matters took their course. Even the fact that whenever we went out together I had to drive her back to her flat at Wanstead, in Essex, many miles from my own home in Edgware, didn't dampen my ardour.

A few months later we were engaged and on 12 October 1957 we were married at St Margaret's Church in Edgware. The reception was held, at my mother's insistence, at my parents' home. Just before the engagement – yes, bended knee and everything – Mum had told me that if I ever married she hoped it would be to somebody like Dee. I took this as maternal approval but actually it wasn't. She didn't really want me to get married at all. Her ideal scenario, I think, would have had all her children living at home for ever but once she realized that I was not to be deterred she made the best of it and insisted on taking charge of the arrangements. This was made easier for her by the fact that Dee's parents were divorced. Her father, Arthur Narracott, Air – or as they called it in those days, Aeronautical – Correspondent of *The Times*, had married again and didn't see much of his daughter, while Aeron, her mother, simply lacked the resources to finance either the wedding or the reception, to which Diana, a much more gregarious soul than I, kept inviting more and more people.

My parents didn't mind but Aeron did. 'Stop doing that,' she told her and in a way was quite relieved when, a week or so before the event, Diana succumbed to 'flu and, confined to bed, couldn't go around inviting anyone else. But one day Diana awoke from a feverish sleep, saying she had had a curious dream in which she had seen 'little people', leprechauns, elves and the like. 'Oh, God,' said Aeron. 'I bet she's asked them to the wedding.'

The reception was not especially grand but it involved a marquee in my parents' garden and a lot of people turned up, among them Richard Attenborough and his wife Sheila Sim, Donald and Diana Sinden and other notable actors of the time, such as Bernard Lee. Fleet Street was well represented, too, and so was the Veuve Clicquot, which nearly turned the happy event into a major tragedy.

Dee and I were going to Majorca for our honeymoon. We'd booked with a package deal firm that offered special rates to civil servants and members of the National Union of Journalists and we had to check in at a terminal at the top of the Edgware Road, near Hyde Park, at about 11 p.m. Dad, who had knocked back his full share of champagne, volunteered to drive us there. In those days people didn't take drink-driving as seriously as they do now, or rather they did – they drank seriously and then drove seriously, or as seriously as was possible in the circumstances. We'd hardly been on the road ten minutes when we drifted into the wrong lane and . . . 'Dad, look out!' I yelled, as a thundering great lorry came roaring towards us. Dad swerved and we and the lorry missed each other by inches.

But it was close, by God it was, and that moment is one of my most abiding memories of my wedding day.

In the end we reached the terminal with time to spare and immediately became the centre of attention. For a start Diana was wearing what could only have been a bride's going-away outfit, complete with blue hat, while her maid of honour, Trixie Neuburger, was still in her wedding gear with a coronet of flowers tipped rakishly over one ear and one of the ushers, in full morning dress, was so drunk that three times he got himself a cup of coffee from a machine and, in the process of raising it to his lips, tipped it down his chest. To our fellow travellers waiting there we must have seemed like the cabaret turn.

Finally, to our relief, we got aboard the coach, said goodbye to Dad and the rest of the entourage and headed off for Blackbushe Airport where thick fog had descended and all flights were cancelled, with the result that Diana and I spent our wedding night leaning against each other, bolt upright, on a wooden bench. Not a great start but somehow, forty-odd years, two daughters and three grandsons later, we seem to have survived.

The cost of that honeymoon – yes, we both enjoyed it immensely, thank you – is worth recording in view of current prices. The flight plus full board at a modest but pleasant hotel in Porto Cristo was £37 10s each. In the evenings we and two other couples on the trip drank at a bodega near the hotel. Everything in the bodega, from wine to brandy, was tuppence (the equivalent now of less than 1p) a glass, except for champagne, which was half a crown (12½p) a bottle. One evening everyone on the trip went to a nightclub where I bought a round of eleven champagne cocktails and a glass of Madeira, which set me back twelve shillings (60p).

Admittedly, even at that time the prices were ridiculously low but, my word, things have changed.

Chapter Eight

MARRIED NOW, LIVING in a large, dark flat in Highgate filled with somebody else's horrible Victorian furniture and, within a month or two, out of work, having left the *Sketch*, I had to decide what to do next. This was not a happy time. For both Diana and me the first year of marriage was appalling, largely my fault, I think. Cutting the umbilical cord with my family was much harder and more painful than I had ever imagined it would be. Highgate being only a short drive from Edgware both my parents rather expected me to be at their beck and call. One night my father phoned, saying, 'Son, get over here. Olsen and Johnson have just dropped in.'

I wanted to go. Ole Olsen and Chic Johnson were the stars of an anarchic and in some ways seminal 1940s film comedy called *Hellzapoppin'* and I'd have loved to meet them. But . . . 'Dad,' I said, 'I can't just drop everything. Diana's cooking dinner.' This was pretty loyal of me, really. In those days Diana could cook only two dishes – shepherd's pie and cauliflower cheese. I rather liked shepherd's pie, though it's surprising how fast you can become bored with it, while cauliflower cheese was something I had always loathed. I think cauliflower cheese was on the menu – indeed, it was probably the entire menu – that night. I thought wistfully of Olsen and Johnson and the mouth-watering food my mother would provide and reckoned it was very grown-up of me to turn my father down. Not, however, all that grown-up. I sulked around the flat all night and I'm sure it was my sulks, along with my inability to remember that, as a married man, it was not a good idea to stay late in the pub with my mates, that helped make life so hard for Diana in that first difficult year of marriage.

It was the curtailment of freedom that hit us both hardest. Marriage meant that I could no longer spend carefree weekends at Edgware and Diana could not nip down to Torquay whenever she wanted. Instead we were often penned up in Victorian gloom in Highgate with, literally, no money to spend on anything but basic survival rations. Why we stayed together, squabbling constantly, during those first twelve months neither of us can now understand. Probably it had something to do with the shame we would have felt at throwing in the marital towel (not to mention having to give back the presents) within a few months of the wedding that made us determined to stick it out for at least a year.

We weren't helped much by the fact that at that time we both resented and disliked each other's families, Arthur Narracott always excepted. We saw little of him but when we did see him he was affable and charming and there was absolutely nothing to resent. Besides, I understood that he played cricket for Devon and for me anyone who has played even Minor Counties cricket is somebody to be admired. So I got on well with Arthur while I was learning slowly but, as it turned out, inevitably to love Aeron. She was the perfect mother-in-law. Never interfered, except on my side even when I was clearly in the wrong. There were, I realized later, several occasions when Diana would take a much-needed break in Torquay and complain that she simply couldn't put up with me any longer but Aeron always sent her back. Had I known about it at the time I would have wondered whether she was doing either of us a favour but I know now, without doubt, that she was.

My own mother, who had liked Diana very much before we were married, now took against her so obviously that even I was shrewd enough not to let slip how unhappy I was. Mum guessed that things weren't going well but I never told her so because I suspected that if I had she would have urged me to walk away from the marriage and cut my losses. Indeed, I thought of doing that myself, as did Diana, about once a week. Not that it was all bad. We had our good times but they were outnumbered by the bad and the bad were made worse by our lack of money. Diana was buying a house for her mother and brothers in Torquay and what with that, the rent for the Victorian mausoleum and running the car there never seemed to be a lot left. Once we had ten shillings (50p) to see us through an entire weekend, part of which we spent playing endless games of cribbage. Diana was good at crib but this wasn't her day and after I had beaten her sixteen times in a row she threw a hairbrush at me with the passionate and somewhat garbled cry of, 'You can take so much but this is a straw!'

If there is any moral to our early experience of married life I suppose it's this: the first year is the worst. If you can stick that out things are bound to get better. Anyway they did for us. Gradually, over the years, I formed a great affection not only for Aeron but also for Diana's brothers, Tony and Roger, and their families. And Dee, who had always been fond of my father, Rick and Val, developed a warm relationship with my mother, who came to realize that she had been right in the first place – Diana was exactly the sort of girl I should marry.

Oh, and by the way – Diana is an excellent cook nowadays and I'm not bad either.

Meanwhile, as we both struggled to adapt to somebody else's way of life and cauliflower cheese followed shepherd's pie relentlessly on to our dining table, I joined the *Daily Mail*. In fact, I did this within a week or so of leaving the *Sketch*. Alan Gardner swung it for me. As editor of the Tanfield column he put in a good word for me with the paper's news desk and I was offered a job as a reporter. I was grateful but also suspicious. What was in it for Alan? There had to be something and I was pretty sure what it was: he wanted me to join him on the gossip column. Of course, he denied it when I so accused him. 'No, no,' he said. 'I know you're fed up with gossip writing. I just thought I'd help you get work as a reporter.' His round blue eyes shone with an innocence that I had come to regard with alarm.

And I was right to do so. After six weeks as a reporter – and I didn't do badly – I learned, not at all to my surprise, that Alan was urgently in need of a deputy on the Tanfield column and, by sheer chance, I fitted the bill perfectly. So there I was – lumbered with gossip writing again. But before that happened I had one memorable assignment as a reporter, memorable not for the story but for the kindness of Nick Tomalin, a very fine journalist, who was later to be killed while on assignment in the Middle East.

The story itself concerned a group of Oxford undergraduates who had been guilty of some minor infraction of the Official Secrets Act and I and Nick, whom I had never met before and who was then working for the *Daily Express*, were sent to Oxford to interview them. Both of us, dispatched in haste, arrived with only a few quid in our pockets, which was awkward because it was late by the time we rounded the students up and we were obliged to stay overnight at the Randolph Hotel. Naturally, we phoned our respective papers with the reporter's traditional demand: send more money. They said they would but by the next afternoon it still hadn't arrived.

I was desperate. The *Mail* told me to stay another night but my father's film *Dunkirk* was having its West End premiere that evening and I wanted above anything else to be there. I begged and pleaded with the news desk and eventually, reluctantly, they agreed to send someone to replace me. Which was fine but how was I to get to the West End? It was late in the day and I was broke. All I had was my return rail ticket and small change, not nearly enough to get myself to the railway station, then home to Highgate to change into dinner jacket before getting a cab to Leicester Square.

Nick noted my distress and asked what was wrong. I told him. 'That's no problem,' he said, turned out his pockets and gave me all the money he had on him, which wasn't a lot but was enough, just about, to suit my needs. Given that we were at best acquaintances and that he had to stay another night in Oxford it was a remarkably generous act and one I have never forgotten. I paid him back, of course I did, and he accepted the money as casually as he had made the loan. I never really met him again after that, which I regret. He went on to much more serious journalism while I was stuck with Paul Tanfield and our paths hardly ever crossed, except occasionally in El Vino when we would nod amiably enough to each other.

As for gossip writing, well, it hadn't changed. Our most coveted stories still revolved around the marital misfortunes of the famous and/or

the aristocracy and since I was going through a pretty querulous marriage myself I now had even more sympathy for the victims. Knowing
that I was more likely to offer the betrayed and the cuckolded a shoulder to cry on than a tough line in questioning, Alan kept me away
from such stories, sending out harder-nosed reporters to do the dirty
work. Compared with the kind of stuff British newspapers print now –
all those orgasm by orgasm revelations by the discarded boyfriends or
girlfriends of minor celebrities – what we wrote was pretty innocuous.
Snide, oh it was certainly that. Prurient, too, and imbued with spiteful
triumph at the downfall of the great and good or at least the richer and
better known than us. But it was far less explicit and, because of that,
less crude than the fare regularly served up by the newspapers of today.

I think this is a more brutish and uncaring age – and, no, that's not
another way of saying, 'Ah, life was better in my young day' because in
all kinds of ways I'm damn sure it wasn't. On the other hand newspapers didn't inflict emotional pain and humiliation on people as
casually as they do now. We might have wanted to but if so we were
restrained, partly no doubt by the libel laws but also by what I can only
think of as an odd sense of decency. Yes, by all means expose the liars
and the cheats but leave it at that – don't then knock them down and
put the boot in with a blithe disregard for the misery you might be causing. There was a universal, if generally unspoken, belief in something
called 'society', which meant that we were all to some extent responsible for and should use a modicum of care in our dealings with each
other.

But then Margaret Thatcher came along to show us what a laughable self-delusion this was. 'There is no such thing as society,' she said
and suddenly no holds were barred. We all suffer to a greater or lesser
degree from greed, meanness and envy but until Thatcher's pronouncement these unsavoury qualities were largely kept in check.
Previous governments indeed had rather encouraged us to keep them
in check. No man, they implied sagely, was an island. But then along
came Thatcher to tell us that John Donne, the man who said it first,
was an idiot. Look after number one, she said, and so we did. Of course,
some of us weren't able to and became homeless and beggars and,

thanks to the glorious idea of 'care in the community', were joined on the streets by bemused mental patients who had been let out of hospitals to fend for themselves. And this brave new world was reflected and to an extent shaped by the press which, finding itself unshackled by the new morality, felt free to say what it liked about anyone regardless of the pain that might be caused.

Would we, given the opportunity, have behaved similarly in the fifties and sixties? Probably. Human nature hasn't changed; licence has. But because of the constraints of the time we were perforce more circumspect and used the stiletto rather than the cudgel, were spiteful rather than cruel. Even so, the collective efforts of the Fleet Street gossip columns brought forth a much-publicized attack on us by Penelope Gilliatt, the novelist and critic and wife of the playwright John Osborne. But, scathing though it was, her article had no lasting effect. Soon enough it was forgotten and we went back to business as usual, no doubt keeping a particular eye out for anything unsavoury concerning Ms Gilliatt or Mr Osborne, for that is the way of journalists: right or wrong they insist on having the last word.

The highlight of the two years or so I spent on the Tanfield column was a remarkable weekend in Monte Carlo. Some kind of festive event was going on and Monaco was therefore the place for Tanfield to be. The *Express*, then still the front runner among middlebrow broadsheets, went further than the *Mail* and sent Logan (Jack) Gourlay, one of its star writers, to cover the occasion. On arrival we teamed up and decided that since all the visiting big hitters were sure to be in the Sporting Club casino that night we'd better go there, too.

It was my first glimpse of real wealth and the way its owners squander it. At one point I wandered into the chemin de fer room and watched, aghast, as Gianni Agnelli, the owner among other things of the Fiat car company and the Juventus football team, lost £15,000 on the turn of one card. I reckon that's a lot of money to lose even now but in the early 1960s it was the equivalent, to me, of about five years salary. My horror must have been pretty evident because the casino attendants, shrewdly sussing that I wasn't exactly in Agnelli's league, suggested politely that I might find some of the other gaming rooms more interesting. So I went away and joined Jack at a roulette table. He was playing with the generous expenses provided by Lord Beaverbrook, I with the more modest sum grudgingly released to me by Lord Rothermere or his minions (the *Mail* was notoriously stingy with expenses) but we both did pretty well. He won about £100 and I won a tenner. Who knows? We might have gone on to break the bank if Jack hadn't knocked the croupier off his stool. It was an accident, of course, a mere stumble, which I certainly don't attribute to the wine we had drunk at dinner. But Jack stumbled, the croupier fell and somehow we didn't feel terribly welcome there any more.

The next day Jack and I parted company, he to collect material for his piece, I to join up with the *Daily Mail* photographer, David Steen. It was Saturday morning and the research I had done before leaving London suggested that on Saturday mornings Princess Grace (the movie star Grace Kelly as was), wife of Monaco's ruler, Prince Rainier, regularly took her two young daughters to the public swimming pool. So, on the off chance, that's where David and I went and there she was – Princess Grace, looking gorgeous in a modest one-piece bathing costume, splashing about in the children's paddling pool with the princesses Caroline and Stephanie. I was not exactly dressed for the occasion, having left my swimming trunks at the hotel, but undeterred I took off my shoes and socks, rolled up my trouser legs and strode into the pool to accost the royal personage. She looked a bit startled but, considering that these must have been among the more unusual circumstances in which she had ever conducted a press interview, she couldn't have been nicer. Why did she bring her children here when they presumably had an Olympic-sized pool of their own? It was good for them, she said. Kept them in touch with their parents' subjects, gave them an idea of how less privileged people lived, kept their feet on the ground (or anyway in shallow water). This was obviously American democracy at work, although when you consider the later lives of the two princesses, it's doubtful whether it had any lasting effect. Was she herself, I asked, happy? Oh, yes, she said. Would she ever make another film? She thought not. I said it was a shame and meant it and she, a touch wistfully it seemed to me, agreed it might be.

Inconsequential though it was this exchange would obviously make an excellent lead for the column and in theory David and I could now relax. But we felt we were on a roll. Who else could we go and bother? 'Who else is around?' David asked. 'Well,' I said, 'Somerset Maugham has a villa somewhere around Cap Ferrat.' 'Okay, let's go and see him,' David said. I had no real idea of Maugham's address, nor did I know anyone in Monte Carlo who might give it to me. So I looked him up in the phone book and, to my astonishment, he was in it. I phoned the number and got through to Maugham's secretary and longtime companion, Alan Searle, and asked if I might pop up and have a word with the great man. Even more to my astonishment Searle said yes. 'Come for drinks this afternoon,' he said.

Now this may not sound much of a result (to borrow a football phrase) but in those days Maugham, well into his eighties, was still a revered literary figure, slightly reclusive and rarely interviewed. David and I could hardly believe our luck. We grabbed a taxi and headed up towards Cap Ferrat and the Villa Mauresque before Searle could call back and cancel the arrangement. But when we arrived it was clear that he would never have done so; we were actually welcome because he and Maugham were quite obviously lonely. They lived in extreme luxury in a beautiful villa but hardly ever saw anybody. They either did not know or did not like their neighbours. 'Lord Rothermere,' Maugham volunteered at one point and with icy distaste, 'has a place nearby. The ugliest villa on the entire *cap*.'

We had drinks and canapés and then Maugham, walking with difficulty and lovingly tended by Searle, showed us his paintings – wall-to-wall Impressionists as I recall, plus in the hall near the front door a huge 1902 Picasso from the blue period. 'I've had it for years,' Maugham said. 'It's one of Picasso's favourites. He keeps trying to buy it back from me but I won't sell.' His smile was full of grim pleasure.

Then we went into his study where, mounted on one wall, was a large panel covered with paintings of Polynesian women, flowers and scenery. It was wonderful and I said so.

'Do you know what that is?' Maugham said. 'It's the door of Gauguin's hut in Tahiti.' And then he told me how he came by it.

When he was researching his novel, *The Moon and Sixpence*, which was based on the life of Paul Gauguin, he followed the painter's progress to Tahiti and found the house, no more than a hut really, in which he had lived. It was empty, almost derelict. Gauguin had been so poverty-stricken that he could not afford canvas or even paper on which to paint and had instead painted on the door and windows. The windows had long since been shattered by local kids hurling rocks at them but the door and the pictures upon it remained intact. Maugham immediately sought out the owner of the hut.

'I want to buy that door,' he said.

The owner, knowing a mug when he saw one, was too fly for that. 'I can't sell you that door,' he said.

'Why not?'

'Because I'd have to buy another one to replace it.'

'How much would that cost?'

The owner sucked his teeth, possibly wondering how much he could take this sucker for. 'Five shillings,' he said.

'All right,' said Maugham. 'Here's the money.' And the deal was done. How much was the door worth when I saw it there in Maugham's study? 'Oh, about £10,000,' he said, casually. And that was forty years ago, long before the price of paintings shot up into the millions. Even then I wondered at Maugham's obvious pride in the cheapness of his acquisition. He must have known, when he bought it, that it was worth infinitely more than he was paying. Couldn't he at least have given the poor Polynesian sod a few quid extra? But no. The rich don't stay rich by paying more than they're asked.

As the taxi took us back to Monte Carlo I remarked to David on how hospitable Maugham and Searle had been, how pleased they had seemed to see us. 'Yes, well,' said David. 'It must have been nice for the old dears to entertain a couple of good-looking young lads like us.' Oh, they're a cynical lot, journalists.

By now, what with a few other titbits, I had what I knew to be a splendid Tanfield column and on the Sunday morning, as David flew home to London, I sat down to write it. But in the course of racketing around Monte Carlo we had bumped into a French journalist, who told us that Joseph Kennedy, father of JFK, was staying at the Hotel du Cap. So when I had phoned my copy to Fleet Street I went up to the Cap, this time (wisely as it turned out) taking my swimming trunks with me. These days, having covered getting on for twenty Cannes film festivals, I know the Hotel du Cap pretty well. It's where all the movie people with delusions of grandeur stay while the festival is on – a luxurious place, so snooty that it won't accept credit cards. Given the astronomical nature of its prices I can only imagine that the guests have to turn up with pantechnicons full of cash, or at least bankers' drafts, to pay their bills. Nowadays any journalist breezing in with the intention of buttonholing someone as lofty as the father of the American president would be lucky to get beyond the gate. But way back then hatred and suspicion of journalists was not nearly as rife as it is now and I wandered into the hotel and asked where I might find Mr Kennedy and was told he was down at the restaurant, Eden Roc, on the seafront. There I learned that he had finished his lunch and was now bathing in the sea – just down there, along the path and beyond the swimming pool. I looked and spotted him – a long, lean elderly figure wallowing alone in the water and quite close to the shore.

I stripped down to my trunks and waded in after him. As with Princess Grace the element of surprise worked in my favour, that and the fact that no matter who you are it's hard to stand on your dignity when you're treading water in the Mediterranean. It wasn't, in truth, much of an interview. I didn't ask him about his days as a bootlegger in the 1920s, or his gangster connections or his affair with Gloria Swanson, though I did ask him to explain why, as US ambassador to London before the war, he had been so defeatist about Britain's chances and so apparently pro-German. His answers were as bland and evasive as you might expect. But he chatted amiably enough about JFK and his other sons and what with the circumstances in which the interview was conducted it made quite a nice piece. The *Mail* was very pleased with me when I got back and didn't even query my expenses too closely.

But such trips were rare. Generally speaking gossip writers operated in the West End of London, interviewing debutantes and the like, covering charity balls and keeping an eye out for illicit aristocratic rumpy-pumpy. Not a very noble occupation; indeed, a distinctly grotty occupation and one from which I finally escaped about the same time as Alan Gardner. He had written a novel, a thriller, and when Harry Weaver, a fellow member of the Tanfield staff, asked him what it was about, he said, 'It's about 120,000 words. Americans like thick books.' How much the Americans liked it I don't know, though it was quite successful in this country. But either because of the book or because it was now time to take his place in the family business, Alan left Fleet Street.

So, too, did a man named Edward Goring. He was the *Mail*'s show business correspondent but he'd had enough of national newspapers – been there, done that, got the byline – and had accepted an executive job on a provincial daily. A vacancy was thus created and I was asked to fill it, probably in the belief that, because of my father, I would have a better contact list within the film business than anyone else on the staff.

The immediate result of this appointment was that I moved out of the newsroom to share an office with Cecil Wilson, the film critic, Roy Nash, the education correspondent, Julian Holland, a senior feature writer, and Bernard Levin, then the theatre critic and later an astringent columnist, first for the *Mail*, then *The Times*. I was in particular awe of Bernard and Julian, who seemed to spend most of every day arguing fiercely and articulately about politics, books, the theatre, society and anything else worth arguing about and for a long time I sat at my desk and hardly said a word. Their conversations fascinated me and made me realize how basically ignorant and uneducated I was, so I merely listened in silence until one day one of them, possibly carried away by the heat of the discussion, made a remark that struck me as preposterous and, somewhat to my horror, I found myself saying so.

Both of them immediately turned towards me, this insignificant show biz writer, with cool courtesy. 'Yes?' said Julian. 'What makes you say that?' I told them and they thought about it. 'You may have a point,' said Bernard and from that day onwards they always included me in their conversations. Julian became my closest friend on the *Mail* and Bernard, though less inclined than us to waste his time in the Mucky Duck, had an equal place in my affections. Between them they completed my education, arousing and stimulating my hitherto dormant interest in literature, the theatre and politics, encouraging me to think for myself and making me realize that maybe I could become more than just a gossip writer or reporter. Their effect upon me and my development was more agreeable but no less profound than that of my form master Tommy Twidell on the day he leapt off his dais to berate me. I owe them both more than I could ever repay.

Show biz writing – about film and theatre in my case – suited me far better than the gossip column. For a start the people I was writing about were more interesting. I'm not starstruck and never have been. Even as a child I was accustomed to the company of famous actors, who would come to my parents' house and talk to my father about their career, financial and marital problems. Thus from the start I was aware that even movie stars are just people. They might be prettier and more celebrated than you and me but you can't see daylight between their feet and the ground as they move about. When you get right down to it they're just working stiffs like anybody else. Their work may seem particularly glamorous to the outsider but it doesn't imbue them with superhuman qualities. True, some of them appear to think it does but you find stupid people everywhere.

The downside of show biz writing, which was as competitive as everything else in Fleet Street, was the midnight phone call from the news desk and for a while this was a fairly regular event. I'd just be dozing off when the phone would ring and the night news editor would say something like, 'Look, old boy, there's a story on the front page of the *Express* that Elizabeth Taylor's been taken ill. Get us a piece for the second edition, will you?' I'd sit up with sinking heart, grab my contacts book, and start ringing people who were even less pleased to be woken up in the small hours of the morning than I had been. I don't mean to suggest that this only happened to me; my rivals on the other papers suffered the curse of the midnight call as well. Nobody's perfect; nobody can cover everything that happens every day. You miss things. Tough. It's part of life and you get over it.

But matters became truly serious when Jimmy Thomas was fired. Jimmy was a highly experienced show business reporter for the *Express* and we, his younger competitors, had much respect for him. But one night he got the dreaded call from his news desk. Dougie Marlborough, the *Mail*'s TV correspondent, had a two paragraph story on the front page that Jimmy had missed. Get it, he was told. He tried but failed. The next morning it hardly seemed to matter because Dougie's story had merely been a space filler, so inconsequential that it vanished after the first edition. But Jimmy hadn't got it and Jimmy was fired.

Now this was really alarming. Something had to be done. Fair enough that all the show biz reporters were trying to put one over on each other but if our own papers were going to stab us in the back nobody was safe. So we got together – Mike Walsh of the *Express*, Michael Wale of the *Sun* and I – and worked out a *modus vivendi*. Each night we would call each other and reveal what stories we had written that day. If one of us had an exclusive he would tell the others what it was and provide the source of the information. This would enable the competitors to get the story themselves at a civilized hour, rather than after midnight. There was one proviso: he whose exclusive it was must be given a one edition lead; the others must not submit their own copy until 10 p.m. at the earliest. This worked out splendidly. The next day the one who had found the story in the first place would casually point out to his news desk that he had beaten the rest of the Street by a full edition, while the others would, just as casually, apologize to their own news editors for having originally missed it, adding, 'But there wasn't too much harm done. I caught up for the second edition.' This would often lead to congratulations and questions like, 'How were you on the ball so fast?' asked in admiring tones. To these you just gave a modest shrug and murmured something like, 'Well, I keep my ear to the ground, you know.'

With this arrangement in place life was much more pleasant for us all. The midnight phone call became a thing of the past except on those rare occasions when somebody who wasn't in the inner circle happened to stumble upon a story that the specialists had missed.

To make life even more pleasant I came to an arrangement with Dougie Marlborough that he would have Fridays off and I would have Sundays, so every Friday I would cover his beat and every Sunday he would cover mine. Late one Friday afternoon, the film and theatre scene being quiet, I was in the BBC press office in Portland Place along with the rest of the telly correspondents when Martin Jackson of the *Express* turned up with a tasty little story. Dutifully he gave the details to the rest of us and I got on the phone to check it out. Meanwhile, Tom Merrin of the *Daily Sketch* said, 'Here, Martin, show us what you've got.' Martin handed over his copy. 'Not a bad story that,' said Tommy and proceeded to dictate what Martin had written, word for word, to his own paper.

Martin was understandably outraged. 'You might at least have changed it,' he said. 'I haven't got time,' Tommy said. 'You change it.' So Martin had to rewrite his own story before dictating it. Since he'd taken considerable pains over the first draft what finally appeared in the *Express* wasn't quite as good as Tommy's story in the *Sketch*. But they were good friends, Tommy and Martin, good friends of mine, too. We used to cover the cabaret scene together and the cabaret scene was lively in London in the 1960s – the likes of Betty Hutton at the Stork Club, Sophie Tucker and Lena Horne at the Talk of the Town. Tommy wasn't particularly welcome at the Stork, which was run by a man named Al Burnett. We who were invited to review the cabaret acts were provided with an excellent supper and plentiful wine but Tommy didn't think this was enough. He felt we should have champagne as well, plus bottles of whisky and gin on our table to welcome us, by way of aperitifs, when we arrived. And these things were duly provided. The fact that the *Sketch*, not being much interested in cabaret acts, hardly ever used his copy thus making his presence more or less redundant didn't bother Tommy at all. Eventually, however, it bothered Al Burnett who, coming across yet another invitation about to be sent to Tommy, rounded on his PR man. 'Why do we invite him, can you tell me that? He comes here, eats all my good food, drinks like a fucking camel what has just come out of the desert and never gets a fucking word in the paper.' Allowing for a certain hyperbole this was generally true but somehow Tommy always seemed to get his invitation and the rest of us were glad of it. Nights at the Stork Club would not have been the same, and not nearly so well lubricated, without him.

It was then a very agreeable life as a show business reporter. The hours were long but the company was good and I was happy enough to stay there, moving upwards – or at least sideways – until the Night of the Long Envelopes, apart from one occasion when I put in my resignation. This happened in 1964, the day after Peter Sellers married Britt Ekland. The wedding, which took place in Surrey, where Sellers had a house, was one of the big news events of the year. She was twenty-two, blonde, Swedish and gorgeous and he was thirty-eight and an internationally popular movie star. This was my big day, the big day for all of us show biz writers, and I was duly there outside the registry office, polishing up my aphorisms, when Vincent Mulchrone appeared on the scene. I couldn't believe it. Vince was the *Mail*'s star feature writer. Why was he here, muscling in on my story?

Well, he said, he didn't want to be there; indeed, he had argued against it, being a professional who had no wish to offend a fellow professional by invading his territory. But the editor, Michael Randall, had insisted: the Sellers wedding was the big story of the day, of the week, probably of the month, and only Vince Mulchrone should cover it for the *Mail*. If this in itself were not bad enough, my fellow show business writers were hanging around, eavesdropping, as Vince explained the situation. I accepted matters graciously. 'Fuck it,' I said. 'Fuck it, fuck it, fuck it.' And I went home. I was furious; Diana was furious; it was an insult, nothing less. Resignation from the paper seemed the only dignified course open to me, so the first thing next morning I demanded an interview with Mike Randall.

'Yesterday was a bloody humiliation,' I said. 'And I'm just here to tell you that I'm resigning forthwith.' I remember the 'forthwith' – it's the sort of word people only ever use on occasions like that.

Surprisingly, Mike apologized, even sympathized. 'But put yourself in my position,' he said. 'Yesterday morning Vince was named Descriptive Writer of the Year in the Hannen Swaffer Awards and I just had to get him in today's paper. The Sellers wedding was the obvious story, the only story for him to cover.' I can't say my heart bled for Mike but, angry though I was, I could see the logic of his argument. And then he came on with the soft soap, telling me how very much he did not want me to leave and how he regarded me as one of his star writers (though obviously not as starry as Vince) and so, in the end, I decided not to resign.

But it was odd that it should have been Peter Sellers who, innocently in this case, nearly brought my association with the *Mail* to an end. Later on he came close to doing it again, although on that occasion he tried to have me fired.

Chapter Nine

W HAT CAN I SAY about Peter Sellers? He was a brilliant mimic and a fine comic actor. He was also unscrupulous, duplicitous and a liar, only I didn't know that at first. Indeed, when I first got to know him around 1960 we appeared to be good friends. I didn't see a lot of him but he was very much a rising star and I used to phone him regularly for quick interviews and news stories. In those early days he was married, blissfully as far as the press knew, to the actress Anne Hayes and, when we'd got the business part of the phone calls out of the way, he and I would chat about holidays we had recently taken, the state of our respective families and whatever car had most recently taken his fancy. It was fine. I felt we had a real relationship going. I liked him and I got the impression that he liked me. He trusted me and I trusted him. That was my mistake.

One morning, soon after Sellers had made *The Millionairess* with Sophia Loren, his public relations man, Theo Cowan, issued a brief press statement to the effect that Sellers and Anne had agreed to separate. It was all very amicable, according to this statement, and neither party wished to say more. The news came as a shock and naturally I phoned Sellers at once to commiserate and find out the details.

He was grateful for my sympathy but begged me, as a friend, not to press him for further information. The situation was so delicate, so much not of his choosing that any comment could sway the balance irrevocably, make the break-up final and that was the last thing he wanted. He said. It was his fervent hope that he and Anne would, sometime soon, be back together again. He said. So, please, would I play it down, as a favour to him? I said I would and he thanked me, adding that if at any time he changed his mind and decided to talk about the situation I would be the first to know. He sounded sad, almost broken. Well, of course he did – he was a bloody actor. But I believed him.

I wrote a discreet, sympathetic piece and told the news desk that Sellers was not talking to anybody and why. And the news desk, revealing a quite unusual sensitivity, agreed that he was wise to adopt such a course. What I should have done was to go round to Sellers's house and accost him. But I didn't; he was a mate and had appealed to my friendship to leave him alone. So I went home instead.

The next morning the shit hit the fan and I was standing right underneath. A crime reporter – not a show business man but a *crime* reporter – from the *Express* had got an exclusive interview with Sellers the previous night. It being, presumably, a slow news day as far as crime was concerned this reporter had been dispatched to doorstep Sellers's home, had accosted him as he returned from a night out, had been invited in and given the full, graphic details of the marriage break-up. I have no recollection of what appeared in the *Express*, except that there was much emphasis on how heartbroken Sellers was and that, as I found out later, it was all lies anyway. It was Sellers who killed off the marriage, not Anne; it was Sellers who went home, during the filming of *The Millionairess*, to tell his wife that he was madly in love with Sophia Loren and was confidently expecting to make his life with her. He hadn't actually told Sophia Loren any of this but that all tied in with his general lunacy. In his own way he was touched with genius but also in his own way he was touched with madness. The stories of his behaviour towards Anne, his violence and cruelty, have been chronicled elsewhere and I have no wish to go into them now. The point is that at the time of which I write none of these things was known: as far as the world was concerned, Sellers was the good guy, the wronged guy, the guy most deserving of our sympathy.

Meanwhile, as far as the *Mail* was concerned, I was the heavy, the bad guy. Sellers was supposed to be my friend and yet he had talked not to me but to a mere crime reporter on our biggest rival. I had no explanation, no excuse except that I had trusted the man. As soon as I could escape the tongue-lashing from the news desk, I put in a call to Sellers. What about his promise that I would be the first to know? What about that? Oh God, he felt so guilty but none of it was his fault. The guy from the *Express* had just been there, taken him completely by surprise. He was so flustered he didn't know what he was doing. He had screwed up, yes, he was man enough to admit that and could I ever forgive him? I forgave him. For the first time but, fool that I am, not for the last.

Flash forward a couple of years. December 1962, Rome. Sellers was there to film *The Pink Panther*, something which, he told me, only came his way because Peter Ustinov had turned it down. That didn't seem very significant at the time. *The Pink Panther*? Just another comedy, wasn't it? Might turn out all right, might not. In the event, of course, the role of Inspector Clouseau, several times reprised, was the one for which Sellers became best known. Odd now to think that if Ustinov had liked it better all that international fame and popularity might never have come Sellers's way.

Anyway, we were mates again, Sellers and I, and I took him to dinner at a restaurant renowned for the quality of its baby lamb. We talked very little about his role in *The Pink Panther* – at this stage there was nothing much to say – and besides he was more interested in talking about himself and the state of his life. In the past month his father had died and he had begun divorce proceedings against Anne. Although she was in no way the guilty party it had been agreed that Sellers, not she, should bring the action, presumably because it would be better for his public image that way. Not that I knew that at the time; nobody did.

Suddenly, as we were going through the events of the previous month and everything that had led up to them, he broke down, voice and lips quivering, the odd tear dripping into his gravy. He'd had an awful year, he said, the like of which he would not want to live through again. In effect, he was having to start a new life and it was his intention to do so away from Britain. Of course, there were good financial reasons for somebody such as himself, the nation's highest paid film star, to want to escape from Britain where, under Harold Macmillan's government, income tax was punitive enough to make the rich squeak with pain. So, yes, naturally money had something to do with his decision, though he was not greedy for it. What he wanted to do, he said, was to earn enough to provide for his children. (Another lie. When he died he left the vast bulk of his fortune not to his children but to his third wife and widow, the actress Lynne Frederick.)

But, in fact, he said, financial considerations were a side issue. What really made him want to leave and start afresh elsewhere was his general unhappiness, the misery of the past year. True, his mother and the children were still in England but his father was gone, so was his marriage and the work that awaited him was in America, not Britain. So he would sell his flat in Hampstead and move . . . where? Switzerland, he said, seemed a good place. 'David Niven is there and so is old Coward. But I don't know that it would do for me. Perhaps I'll go to Jersey or Guernsey. Somewhere not too far away – because I shall miss Britain.'

Today when movie stars live wherever they like in the world and nobody cares, this doesn't seem like much of a story. But it was then. Peter Sellers turning his back on Britain would cause waves of indignation and, in some cases no doubt, grief. The question was: did I believe him? Oh, he was convincing enough, sitting there being all emotional over his baby lamb but I had learned enough from my previous experience to know that Sellers at his most convincing could also be Sellers at his most deceptive.

When I left him that night I went back to my hotel room and carefully transcribed my notes. Yep, he'd certainly said all those things but . . .

The next day I went to the film studios where they were making *The Pink Panther*. Sellers was in jovial mood for this was his element, the place where he was the centre of all attention, where the main concern of everybody from the director Blake Edwards down to the clapper boy was to keep him happy. At lunchtime and at Sellers's invitation I joined him, Edwards and a handful of others to watch the rushes, the footage they had shot the previous day. They all came out in excellent mood for we had seen some very funny stuff up there on the screen. It was then that I took Sellers to one side. 'What we were talking about last night, Peter,' I said and read out his quotes to him. 'Did you really mean all that?'

'Oh, yes,' he said. 'Every word.'

So I wrote my story, which appeared on the feature page under the headline: 'Sellers Talking: Why I'm Getting Out,' with a cross-reference on page one. It was a minor scoop on which I was much congratulated and, as I knew it would, it created quite a stir.

A few weeks passed and Sellers flew back from Rome to be greeted by reporters at Heathrow wanting to know more about his reasons for leaving Britain and where he had decided to live instead. He denied everything. My story, he said, had been a total fabrication, not a word of truth in it. Leave Britain? Perish the thought. I read all this with a disbelief that drifted into weary cynicism. Sellers had screwed me again and again he had done me harm. His denials did not pass unnoticed at the *Mail* and for a while my stories were zealously double-checked for accuracy.

The worst, however, was yet to come.

June 1964. Things were not going well for Sellers. The year had started promisingly with his marriage to Britt Ekland but his latest film, *The World of Henry Orient*, had opened to indifferent reviews and in April, newly wed and working on a Billy Wilder film called *Kiss Me, Stupid*, he had had a heart attack in Hollywood (causing Harry Secombe to send him a cable with the cheerfully unsympathetic message: 'That's what you get for all that Swede-bashing.') Not everybody was convinced about the severity of the heart attack. One of the producers of *Kiss Me, Stupid* had remarked that Sellers 'would do anything to get out of this movie' and Billy Wilder commented, 'What do you mean "heart attack"? You've got to have a heart before you can have an attack.' The making of the film had been fraught from the start, not least because Sellers, who was used to freewheeling and doing his own thing on set, could not adapt to Wilder's insistence that the script was sacrosanct and the cast should not mess about with it. In any event, however grave – or not – the heart attack was it enabled Sellers to drop out of the movie, to be replaced by Ray Walston (who collected pretty decent reviews) and to justify himself with a paranoid attack on Hollywood. It wasn't just Wilder and everyone else connected with *Kiss Me, Stupid* who hated him, he reckoned, it was Hollywood itself. It was, he told the London *Evening Standard*, a place where they 'give you every creature comfort except the satisfaction of being able to get the best work out of yourself . . . As far as film-land is concerned I've taken the round trip for good. The noise and, to coin a phrase, the people.' In short, 'I have had Hollywood, love.'

The result of this outburst was a telegram he received signed by, among others, Billy Wilder and Sellers's erstwhile co-stars on *Kiss Me, Stupid*, Dean Martin and Kim Novak. The message was brief and to the point: 'Talk about unprofessional ratfinks.' A ratfink was a word of deep opprobrium used in the film and the telegram was widely publicized by the senders, which was where I came in.

By now Sellers was back home at Elstead, in Surrey, and I called him to ask how he reacted to being called a ratfink. The way things turned out his comments on that subject were hardly more than a footnote to the story I wrote. Once again he was friendliness personified, as if the inconvenience (to put it mildly) that he had caused me in the past had never happened. I was 'love', I was 'mate' and he opened his heart to me. Yes, indeed, he had had it with Hollywood and not only Hollywood but with acting itself. 'I'm seriously thinking of giving it all up,' he said. 'At the moment I just don't feel like ever working again.' He wanted to use his recuperation from the heart attack as a period for contemplation. No, no, he wasn't disillusioned with the film industry: he loved it. 'But it may be that the time has come for me to do something entirely different. I don't know what. It could be anything.' Directing? Screen writing? Yes, these were possibilities but right now his inclination was to 'wander around the world and do nothing for the rest of my life'.

Again this was quite a story: Sellers, Britain's biggest movie star and still only thirty-eight, on the point of throwing it all in. But again I was dubious. I read my notes and checked the salient points with him once more. This, I said, was what I was going to write: was he happy with it? Yes, he was.

Mike Randall, the *Mail's* editor, was off that day leaving Derek Ingram, his deputy, in charge. I wrote my piece and showed it to Derek. 'What do you think of that?'

'Good story,' Derek said. 'But does he really mean it?'

'Who knows? It's what he said.'

'You've run it past him again?'

'Yes.'

'Okay then,' Derek said, 'we'll go with it.'

And we did. Front page stuff.

The next day Theo Cowan, still Sellers's personal publicity man, was on the phone to Derek. Sellers denied every word of my story. He had never said anything of the kind. It was a tissue of lies. I had made it all up and Sellers wanted an immediate and prominent retraction. Derek, God bless him, was having none of this. Barry Norman, he said, did not make stories up. The paper stood by every word I had written and there would certainly be no retraction. Any future action was entirely up to Sellers.

Predictably there was no future action and the story died away. But what, I thought at the time and have often thought since, if I had not been on the *Mail* for so long, what if I had been a young reporter, new to the job. Who then would the paper have believed – me or this famous movie star with his PR backup and veiled threats of litigation? In such circumstances I reckon there's a fair chance that I would have lost my job. Would Sellers have cared? The hell he would. The feeling I had then was that though we had known each other for so long it would not have bothered him in the least if his preposterous denials and demands had caused me to be fired. For him only himself, his image, his personal comfort and happiness mattered; everyone else was expendable.

As far as I was concerned that was the end of it. I made it clear that, whatever the story, I would never talk to Peter Sellers again and as a writing journalist I kept my word. The only other time I met him was in 1974 when he was making *The Return of the Pink Panther* in Gstaad and then, as the presenter of a film programme for the BBC, I had no option but to interview him. This time I met him as if we were strangers, snubbing his attempts to revive the old, and as it had transpired phoney, cameraderie that we had previously shared. The interview was brief and businesslike and though we were both in Gstaad, staying at the same hotel, for the whole weekend I didn't speak to him again.

Thinking back on it now I wouldn't go so far as to say of Sellers, as Robert Loggia did of the Jeff Bridges character at the end of *Jagged Edge*, 'Fuck him, he was trash.' He wasn't trash. I admired him a great deal as an actor, in the first *Pink Panther* movie, in *Dr Strangelove* and, at the end, as the idiot savant in *Being There*. But he was a very disturbed and egocentric man whose empathy with other people was virtually non-existent and whose vision of the truth was whatever suited his own purposes best. So, 'fuck him' – yes, I would certainly say that.

Chapter Ten

ONE EVENING IN 1964 Diana and I were going to the National Theatre, then housed at the Old Vic, to see Laurence Olivier in *Othello*. This was early in the run – maybe the second or third performance – of a production that was to be the hottest ticket in town that autumn. We arrived early and went into the pub next door, the familiar haunt of the National Theatre company, most of whom I knew pretty well. We were having a drink with one of them, Colin Blakely, when an unremarkable middle-aged, middle-sized man, grey hair, grey suit, came into the bar and greeted me amiably.

'Oh, hi,' I said. 'This is Diana, my wife.' They shook hands, I bought him a half pint of bitter and we chatted inconsequentially about this and that before he emptied his glass, said, 'Oh, well, better go and get ready, I suppose', and left us.

'Who was that?' Diana said.

'That?' I said. 'That was Laurence Olivier.'

I said earlier that I have never been starstruck and that is true. But Olivier I held in something pretty close to awe. In the theatre I saw him only in the 1960s in plays like *Othello*, *The Dance of Death*, *Love for Love* and *The Merchant of Venice* and by then, aged sixty or thereabouts, he was physically past his prime. Nevertheless his presence and impeccable technique were such that he is the greatest stage actor I have ever seen or ever expect to see. Here I must confess that I never saw John Gielgud except in films or on TV and I know there are many people who claim that in the theatre he was Olivier's equal or even superior. As to that I cannot argue. But if Gielgud was truly the better actor he must have been something pretty damn special.

Among many other attributes Olivier seemed to be a kind of human chameleon, taking on the shape of whatever character he happened to be playing. As Captain Edgar in Strindberg's *The Dance of Death*, for example, he was short, almost square, bull-necked and florid. As Tattle, the fop, in *Love for Love* he was effete and soft. And in private life he often adopted the guise in which Diana had seen him, that of the greying, ageing suburbanite, especially when he was travelling home at night on the train to Brighton. 'I sit there,' he told me once, 'with a script or something in front of me and nobody recognizes me. They think I'm a bank manager about to cancel somebody's overdraft.'

That night at the Old Vic he came on to the stage totally transformed from the man we had seen in the pub. He seemed to be about seven-feet tall, dark, lithe, almost boneless, gliding rather than walking across the boards, his voice a full octave lower than I had ever heard it. This was not a mere impersonation of a Moor, far less a caricature: if Moors were not really like this, we felt, then they should have been.

A couple of days later when I was congratulating him on his performance he said, 'Joanie [his wife, the actress Joan Plowright] was in the dressing room waiting for me when I came off stage. I said, "Hold on a moment – I must have a shower." I went into the shower as Othello and came out as myself and Joanie's jaw dropped six inches in sheer disappointment.' I told Diana that and she nodded understandingly; her jaw would have dropped, too.

I first met Olivier in 1963 when he gave a press conference to announce his plans for the new, long-awaited National Theatre, of which he was the first director. After the conference a few carefully selected journalists, of whom I was one, were invited to stay on and join Olivier in a lunch of apples, cheese and maybe a glass of wine. Although he was now married to Joan Plowright his divorce from Vivien Leigh was still fresh in the public, or anyway the media, mind. It had been a much-publicized event from which he emerged rather badly, largely because he refused to talk about it while Leigh suffered no such inhibitions. Her side of the story was widely circulated, his was not; therefore, unfairly as it turned out later, Olivier was regarded as the villain of the piece. It was only after Vivien Leigh's death that we learned she had been a manic-depressive and that her consequent erratic behaviour, more than any deficiencies on his part, had been the principal cause of the marital break-up. But that day in Olivier's office at the Old Vic none of us knew these things. Vivien Leigh was still perceived as the wronged woman and some of my colleagues among the chosen few of us chewing apples and cheese, being starry feature writers, went away and wrote long thoughtful pieces about Olivier's previous heartbreak and how he had bravely fought through it to find new happiness. Nor, of course, did they forget to reprise some of the spicier details about the sad ending to the marriage of Britain's most celebrated theatrical couple. I, on the other hand, was simply there to write a news story about the plans for the National Theatre and this is what I did. Mine was a straightforward piece that made no reference to Vivien Leigh and though I had no way of knowing it at the time I couldn't have done anything smarter.

The next morning Virginia Fairweather, the National's publicity woman, phoned me at the office. Larry, she said, was furious with the starry feature writers – 'absolutely *furious*, darling' – but he simply *loved* my story. Certain people would not be welcome any more at the Old Vic but any time I wanted to talk to Olivier I had merely to call her and she would arrange it. And that's pretty well the way things went. I don't suggest that Larry – yeah, I called him 'Larry'; he asked me to – would speak only to me but I think he spoke more happily to me than to most of my colleagues. It was a matter of trust. I didn't misquote him or make fanciful allusions to his broken heart (of which there was no sign anyway, now that he was happily remarried and had started a new young family) and therefore he spoke to me quite frankly. I'm sure, too, that he rather enjoyed my obvious admiration of his talent.

When it was announced that for a fee of £250,000, an enormous amount at the time, he had agreed to play the Mahdi to Charlton Heston's General Gordon in *Khartoum*, I said to him in my naivety, 'It must be an awfully good part if you're going to do it.' He looked at me a shade suspiciously, as if I were maybe taking the mickey but when he realized I wasn't he grinned and said, 'Barry, dear, we don't always do everything for the artistic values.' In other words he was doing it for the money but he trusted me enough to know that I wouldn't write that. And if I had it would have come as an awful blow to dear old Chuck Heston, whom I also spoke to about the film and who was positively overwhelmed at the idea of sharing a screen with Olivier.

I've met Heston several times and rather like him. I don't like his ultra-conservative right-wing views and his support of the American gun lobby but you can't help feeling a certain affection for a movie star who blithely wears a wig as bad as his. He must be able to afford something much better but he appears happy with the one he's got and I kind of admire him for that. I first met him when he was filming *El Cid* in a Spanish town called Peniscola – inevitably pronounced 'peniscolour' by the attending journalists – and I was slightly wary of him. After all, he was a big star, surrounded as big stars always are by people who kept telling him what a big star he was, and he exuded a rather striking gravitas. I was somewhat impressed by that until one day on location I joined his table at lunchtime and heard him talking about 'the historical *jean-ray*'. I had no idea who this Jean Ray was – a Frenchman presumably, given Chuck's pronunciation of Jean. Maybe he was a little-known friend of El Cid. But then Heston went on to mention other *jean-rays* – the western, the horror, the science-fiction *jean-rays* and the penny dropped. Oh, right, that *jean-ray*, Chuck. Got you. All of a sudden he seemed pleasantly human and fallible. I mean, simply because he was a movie star why should anyone expect him to be fluent in French and to know that *genre* wasn't exactly pronounced the way he thought? So what with that and the wig I had a bit of a soft spot for him anyway and his undisguised admiration for Olivier clinched it. He once told me that he had been asked to play Henry V, a part he coveted, at Stratford, Ontario, but had turned it down because he had seen Olivier's film version sixteen times and had been so overwhelmed that he felt he would be on a good hiding to nothing. For a journalist to be starstruck is dangerous and you only have to look at the nonsense served up by some of the bouncing bimbos, of both sexes, who interview movie stars on television to see why. But for an actor to be starstruck is rather admirable: it means that he has an ideal, a level of excellence to emulate, and that he will work to improve his own craft in the hope of reaching the desired standard. I think Heston did that. He is not a great actor but he did get better because he knows what great acting is and strove to produce it.

However, all this is a long way from Olivier. I remember him most and with the greatest affection for the time he took the National Theatre, on its first overseas visit, to Moscow in 1965. I travelled with them, rather grandly, as a first-class Intourist passenger, which meant that on arrival I was entitled to a chauffeur-driven car and a guide. Both of which things I got but not initially. Initially, we were all taken by coach from the airport to the Ukraine Hotel, which was the biggest and undoubtedly the worst in Europe. At that time Russia was a bloody awful place to visit; I don't know what it is like now because I have never wanted to go back. But then it was a place of shortages and bread queues and innate suspicion of foreigners.

Arrived at the hotel we all had to queue up to check in – and I mean all of us. There in the middle of the queue, looking decidedly pissed off, was Laurence Olivier. Nowhere else in the world would he have been treated like that; nowhere else in the world would he, having waited his turn to sign the register, have been obliged to carry his own cases up to his room. Virginia Fairweather told me that having got there he sat on the side of the bed, drummed his feet on the floor and said, 'I want to go home!'

But his troubles were nothing compared to mine. There I was, lining up with the rest, confident that when I presented my impressive Intourist documents (Intourist being the official Russian tourist agency) I would be ushered through without let or hindrance. Fat chance. When finally I arrived at the desk the receptionist, a bespectacled blob of a man, looked slowly and carefully through my papers and said, 'You are not on the list.'

'What? Of course I am! Check again.'

He checked again. 'You are not on the list.'

Famous actors, Billie Whitelaw, Frank Finlay, Lynn Redgrave

among them, shuffled impatiently behind me. 'What am I supposed to do then?' I asked.

'Wait some time,' he said.

Naturally, I interpreted this as imperfect English. Clearly what he meant to say was 'Wait a moment'. But I was new to Russia and was soon to learn that what he meant was what he said. I waited some time. I waited until everyone else had been checked in and then I took my papers back to the desk. The receptionist read them carefully once more. 'You are not on the list,' he said.

'I bloody know that,' I said. I have a very short fuse and patience is not one of my virtues. 'You've already told me twice. What do I do now?'

'Go over there,' he said and pointed to a desk on the far side of the vast, gloomy foyer. I picked up my papers and trudged across to confront another receptionist, who spoke no English, only a guttural French. He read my papers, shook his head, muttered things. 'Comment?' I said.

'Là,' he said and gestured towards the first receptionist before pointedly returning to business of his own. Wearily, I went back across the foyer and slapped my papers on the desk yet again. The bespectacled blob barely glanced at them. 'No, too late,' he said. 'I close now.' And he went away.

By then I was pretty desperate. It was getting very late, I had a story to write and phone through to the *Mail* and I was homeless, stuck in this dreary foyer with only a sofa to serve as a bed, always assuming – which was unlikely – that the hotel staff would let me sleep there. Rescue, however, was at hand in the shape of my friend Felix Barker of the London *Evening News*. Though only a third-class Intourist traveller himself he had been given a room without question and now he came down to the foyer in search of a bar, as any self-respecting journalist would.

'Felix,' I cried. 'Help!' and told him of my plight.

'That's all right, old boy,' he said. 'I've got two beds in my room. You can use one of those. You can use the phone as well.' He handed me the key. 'Now, have you any idea where the bar is?'

I stayed, illegally, in Felix's room for about three nights before Intourist grudgingly admitted that I was in Moscow as of right. But even then they didn't give me a room of my own: I had to continue sharing with Felix until he went back to London a few days later. God knows what the house-mother made of us. 'House-mother' was the name we gave to the elderly woman who sat opposite the lift on our floor – every floor had one like her – and made note of the comings and goings of all the guests. This, we believed – the entire National Theatre company believed – was merely the obvious face of surveillance. We were all convinced that our rooms were bugged and when any of us made even a vaguely anti-Russian remark we would look under the bed and, for the benefit of the suspected hidden microphones, say, 'Sorry, only joking.'

This was not necessarily as paranoid as it might seem. Among the Intourist guides attached to the theatre company was a young, red-headed lad called Vladimir. He was a nice kid and, a couple of days after our arrival, he joined a bunch of us, journalists mostly, for a drink. We were all drinking vodka, which seemed to be the only hard liquor available in the hotel and after a while he asked, 'Do you like vodka?'

'Yeah, it's okay,' we said. 'How about you?'

'I like whisky,' he said.

As it happened I had a bottle of duty-free Scotch in my room and suggested we all go up there and drink that. Vladimir joined us enthusiastically and there, possibly no less influenced than the rest of us by the booze we had consumed, he started telling us how much he admired England and America and how much he would like to visit those countries. He was not confident that he would ever be able to do so because in those days Russia, like most dictatorships, seemed less concerned with keeping foreigners out than keeping its own citizens in. It turned out to be a very jolly drinking session and we all parted on the best of terms.

The next day there was no sign of Vladimir. Nor was there the following day. So I approached the head Intourist guide, a young but darkly scowling woman, and asked her where he was.

'Who?' she said.

'Vladimir,' I said. 'Young bloke, early twenties, red hair.'

'No,' she said firmly. 'There has not been anyone like that here.' And we never saw him again, nor did we ever learn what had become of him. He was a non-person.

It was a very odd place, Moscow, at that time. On day one several of us went to the famous department store, GUM, which was actually not so much one store as a collection of many stores. Somehow – terrible oversight for a journalist – I had come away with only one pen and it was fast running out of ink. So I went all over GUM trying to buy a ball-point pen. I might as well have asked for the keys to the Kremlin. Oh yes, they knew about ballpoint pens, all right; they'd had some only a few days ago and were almost certain they'd have some more next week. But right now, well no, they couldn't oblige, although they did have these pencils . . .

I bought a pencil and bumped into Anthony Nicholls, tall, grey haired, splendidly elegant and one of the older members of the National Theatre Company. He was looking shocked and indignant in equal measure. 'You'll never believe what's just happened,' he said. 'A young man came up to me and said, "I Roshan playboy. I geeve you good time tonight for one English pound." Bloody cheek! Fancy picking on me.'

Once I'd got my official status sorted out I used the Intourist car, driver and guide to do some sightseeing. Felix, an ardent Chekhovian, was anxious to see the great man's grave, so we went to the cemetery and found it. Rather elaborate it was, too – a comfortable-sized plot with railings around it, a bit of statuary and a tree growing over the grave itself.

'Is that a cherry tree?' Felix said, excitedly. 'I'm sure it is. It must be. What else would they plant but a cherry tree? I must have a souvenir.' Reverently, he plucked a leaf and took it back to our guide. 'Look,' he said, holding it out carefully on both hands. 'Is this the leaf of a cherry tree?'

The guide took it from him, held it up, scrutinized it. 'Yaas,' he said. 'Is cherry tree.' Then he screwed it up and threw it on the ground. The distraught Felix hurried back to pluck another leaf. This time he kept it well away from the guide.

Dad (centre), me and Laurence Harvey on set during the filming of *The Long and the Short and the Tall* in 1960.

Dad in his late thirties . . .

. . . and again a year or so before he died.

Our wedding day. From left, Diana Sinden, me, Diana, Richard Attenborough kissing Diana, Donald Sinden kissing Dickie and Dickie's wife, Sheila Sim.

Mum (with Dad on her left) shaking hands with the Queen at the Royal Premiere of *Dunkirk* in 1958.

Flash forward thirty years or so and I, too, meet the Queen at a Royal Film Premiere. (That's Maureen Lipman, partly obscured by H. M.)

I don't remember what the question was but Sophia Loren doesn't seem to have liked it much.

I thought young Albert Finney should do more theatre work; he thought he shouldn't. Here he's probably telling me why.

Photographer David Steen, Somerset Maugham and me at Cap d'Antibes.

With Georges Simenon, creator of Maigret, at his Swiss home.

John Mills at his home in Buckinghamshire in the 1970s. He doesn't look much different now. I do.

Richard Burton in Milan, the day after he fell asleep while I was interviewing him.

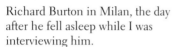

Dirk Bogarde at his farmhouse in Grasse. He didn't go to Cannes because it was full of all the people he'd hoped were dead.

Peter Finch, who worked with Dad on *The Shiralee*. Finchie said it was his favourite film.

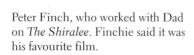

On location in Beverly Hills for *The Hollywood Greats*. Producer Barry Brown is third from the left.

Beverly Hills again, this time with Barry Brown and Gene Wilder.

Bruce Thompson and me. Which of us believes the bottle is half empty?

Back to Beverly Hills, with Liz Ekberg (left) and Helen Cook.

Francis Ford Coppola, who made us go to him.

Director John Schlesinger who learned his trade at the BBC and went on to higher things.

Steven Spielberg apparently insisting on a close-up at his Amblin' Studio in California.

The young Martin Sheen, later in *The West Wing* to be the finest president America never had.

1978 and Superman, Christopher Reeve, comes to town. Barry Brown is on his right.

Charlton Heston, whose hankie turned out to be cardboard and cotton.

Me in Dallas. Oh, and the bloke with his back to camera is Clint Eastwood.

Al Pacino, not that tall but a hell of a good actor.

Eric and Ernie with the chorus singing 'There is Nothing Like a Dame'. Half the nation watched us that night.

With my award for being Pipesmoker of the Year in 1987. Another year I was voted Best Dressed Man on TV.

Later I went to Chekhov's house, which wasn't very impressive, and in the company of Joan Plowright to Tolstoy's, which was a large, wooden building whose contents didn't seem to have changed since he wandered off to die at the local railway station in 1910. Tolstoy had a lot of children but, so we were told, only one who, he felt, might have inherited his genius. Alas, this boy died of a fever at the age of eleven or thereabouts and his room was still exactly as it had been on the night of his death. His exercise books were open on his desk, his little nightshirt was folded neatly over the back of a chair. Joan and I, who both had young children, left the house sobbing brokenly.

On a more brutal note there was the time when Felix and I, having spent a morning looking at paintings and the English silver – 'the biggest collection of English silver in the world', they told us – in the Kremlin treasury, were returning to the hotel for lunch. We were nearly there when a drunk staggered into the road in front of our car. At the speed we were going it would have been easy to avoid him but instead of slowing down the driver hit the accelerator, hit the drunk and sent him sprawling into the gutter. The man was not badly hurt because he lurched to his feet, shaking his fist and cursing, but I couldn't believe what I had seen. Neither could Felix. We discussed it over lunch and decided that what our driver had done could only have been deliberate. We knew that the authorities were clamping down on public drunkenness in Moscow but this did seem to be taking matters a little far. In the afternoon, Felix having a piece to write, I went out in the car on my own.

'Tell me,' I said to the guide of the day, a young man memorable only for almost lethal halitosis, 'why did the driver deliberately knock that drunk down?'

'Oh no, Mr Norman,' he said. 'You are very much mistaken. That is not what happened. The man threw himself in front of the car. The driver could not avoid him.' And in this way in Soviet Russia history was rewritten while you waited.

Meanwhile, the National Theatre Company was taking Moscow by storm. They were performing, and were the first western company to do so, in the Kremlevsky Theatre within the Kremlin itself. On the opening night we all travelled by coach from the hotel to the theatre. I sat beside Billie Whitelaw, who was playing Desdemona, and we ate caviar out of a tin with a shared spoon. Give or take the tin and the spoon this might sound a little grand but, in fact, caviar and smoked sturgeon were just about the only things worth eating at the Ukraine Hotel. For the week or so that I was there I lived on them, hard-boiled eggs, yogurt and vodka; the rest of the food was disgusting.

The opening production was *Othello* and when it was over the entire packed audience stood up and started walking determinedly towards the footlights. For a moment they looked like a lynch mob but then the applause started and went on for ages, only stopping when Olivier stepped forward and delivered a speech of thanks in, so I was told, perfect Russian, a language of which he had no knowledge whatsoever. *Othello* was a triumph, so was *Hobson's Choice* but the audience reaction to *Love for Love* must have been disconcerting for the cast. Whether it was because of bad instantaneous translation – very probable – it rapidly transpired that Russians couldn't seem to get a handle on Restoration comedy. Congreve's wittiest lines went by in silence and only Olivier, hamming it up as Tattle, raised the occasional laugh. But again the audience rose and walked to the footlights and although the applause wasn't as ecstatic as it had been for *Othello* it was generous enough. The National was a tremendous hit and I said so in the *Mail*.

Those first few days in Moscow were exciting and busy but after all three plays had been premièred the rest of the press went home, while I stayed on to write a couple of feature articles and now began a period of intense loneliness. Any big city can be lonely if you're a stranger in it with nobody to talk to but Moscow was the worst. Hardly any Russians, except the stern and formal Intourist guides, spoke English and those who did were clearly afraid to fraternize with foreigners. Taxi drivers couldn't understand where I wanted to go, there was nothing to buy or even look at in the shops unless you went to the Dollar Shop, which was exclusively for the use of visitors and accepted only foreign currency, and I didn't like to walk too far from the hotel because I couldn't read the street signs and was scared of getting lost.

All very well, you might think, but not that bad. I wasn't really alone surely because the National Theatre Company was there. True enough but I hardly saw them. They worked late at night, then had supper together and slept for most of the day. Sometimes I would drop in on them at supper just to talk to somebody but one night it became clear that I was no longer welcome. No explanation was given, not at first, but people with whom I had hitherto been getting along very well turned pointedly away as I approached and if I persisted in talking to them they were polite but cold.

What had happened? Well, as I later learned, a few other members of the company had flown in for a day or two from London and one of them, for reasons best known to himself, had circulated the rumour that I had been systematically rubbishing the company in my reports and reviews. Informed of this I denied it strenuously but nobody believed me, treating me instead like a viper they had innocently been nurturing at their bosoms.

As I think about it now it all seems very strange. Surely somebody in the company must have been in touch by phone with London and would have asked what the papers were saying. But apparently not and maybe that isn't quite as odd as it might appear because the telephone link between Moscow and London was erratic at best. At eleven o'clock one morning, a day or two before I came home, I booked a call to the *Daily Mail* to dictate a feature article I had written. There was, I was told, a delay of one hour. At noon I tried to call again. Still there was a delay of one hour, just as there was at one o'clock and two o'clock and three o'clock. At four, with my deadline getting perilously close, I had another go, with exactly the same result. And now, in a state of desperation, I lost it. 'What is it with this fucking country?' I yelled at the operator. 'You can get a man into space but in five hours you can't even get me a phone call to London? You're rubbish, that's what you are.' Then I slammed the phone down, cooled off and started wondering what would happen to me now. The KGB was sure to have been listening in and wouldn't like what I'd said about their country. I sat and waited for a knock on the door but instead of that the phone rang and the operator said, 'Here is your call to London.' Being Mr Nice Guy for five hours had got me nowhere; foully abusing his country had brought the right result in two minutes. But that was Russia in 1965.

However, that came later. Before then there was my period of ostracism when my sense of loneliness and isolation became complete. For a couple of days when I wasn't using the Intourist car I didn't talk to anybody at all. Word of all this finally got back to Olivier, who had no more idea of what I had been writing about the company than anybody else and was therefore faced with a choice: was he to believe the rumours or my denials? To my eternal gratitude he chose the latter. One night at the company supper he stood up to make a speech, something he had not done before. He began by thanking them all for their hard work and dedication in making the visit such a success and then he asked them to drink a toast to 'Barry Norman who, even as we sit here, is locked away in his room writing yet another article to tell people back home how well you have all done'.

This was an act of trust; without even asking for my side of the story he had put himself on the line for me, which was a brave and generous thing to do. If the rumours had turned out to be true he would have looked gullible to say the least but he took that chance. From my point of view the result was immediate: the next day people were talking to me again and when, a day or so later, more people came in from London bringing press cuttings with them I was completely restored to favour. What I had written about the National's trip to Moscow was the truth: they had been greeted with acclaim and had shown themselves to be splendid ambassadors for the British theatre and, by extension, for Britain itself. To have said anything to the contrary would have been a distortion of the facts. And when the gist of my stories had been conveyed to the rest of the company I was more popular than I had ever been. I was pleased for myself but even more for Olivier. He had, as it seemed to me, followed his instinctive belief that I was trustworthy and he had not been let down.

I had one other odd experience in Moscow. I was sitting in my room, writing, when the phone rang and a seductive female voice started gabbling at me in Russian. We had all been warned at a Foreign Office briefing prior to our departure that prostitutes targeted foreign visitors in this way, so I listened until she came to the end of her spiel and then I said, 'I'm awfully sorry but I don't understand Russian.'

'Niet?'

'Niet.'

A pause then she started again, even more seductively this time. She had a very nice voice which, whatever she was saying, was pleasant to listen to. When again she stopped I said, 'Well, it's been terribly nice talking to you but since I don't understand a word you're saying perhaps we'd better hang up now.'

She ignored me and carried on until she ended on what was clearly a question which, from the intonation, seemed to demand a Yes or No answer. Da or Niet – which was it to be. I flipped a mental coin and decided on Da.

'Da,' I said.

There was a sharp intake of breath at the other end of the line. 'Da?' she said.

'Da,' I said firmly.

Now there was another pause, longer than before, until speaking for the first time in English and with a note of sorrowful apology in her voice she said, 'I am terribly sorry.' And then she hung up.

What on earth had I said? That my wife was with me? That I already had a prostitute? That I was homosexual? I never found out because she didn't call again.

Chapter Eleven

I WAS OFFERED A prostitute once. It was in Madrid where I had gone to report on the making of some epic movie, of which an American producer named Samuel Bronston made several in Spain in the 1960s. There were about six journalists on the trip and the publicity man was hospitality itself. Drinks in our hotel, dinner in one of the city's best restaurants and then on to a night club, by which time none of us was remotely sober. We watched the floor show – flamenco dancing probably; it usually was in those days – and at one point I went off to the loo. When I returned there was what I took to be an elderly woman sitting in the chair next to mine. In fact, she can hardly have been more than forty and was not at all bad-looking but since I was at least ten years younger she seemed elderly to me. She smiled affectionately as I sat down and moved her chair nearer to mine. It soon became clear that she spoke no English.

'Who's she and what's she doing here?' I said to the publicity man, a tall, bespectacled and rather shabby-looking Englishman.

'Her name's Maria,' he said, 'and she's for you.'

'No, she's not,' I said. 'I don't want her.'

'What? You must be joking.'

'No, I'm not. I don't want her.'

'But you must! I got her specially.'

'Look,' I said. 'I don't want her.'

He heaved a deep sigh. 'Oh Christ,' he said. 'That means I'll have to have her again. That'll be the third time this month.'

For several years I thought this was a one-off occurrence, an unusual example of excessive hospitality on the part of a lone PR man. But then I went to Rome, once more on a film location, in the company of another English journalist and almost the first thing he said to the PR man – a different PR man – was, 'Look, old boy, just to let you know – I won't need a woman on this trip. I've got the girlfriend with me.'

'Okay,' the PR man said.

I was astonished. I had no idea that pimping for journalists was part of a publicity man's job; certainly, with the exception of the time in Madrid, nobody had ever offered to pimp for me. Maybe if I'd asked . . . Oh, well, come to think of it, perhaps better not. I mention this only to point out that the perks in show business reporting were nothing like as extravagant as people might think, or at least they weren't in my experience. When I took on the job at the *Daily Mail* I heard mouthwatering tales of how, at Christmas time, the major film companies would send round cases of wine, champagne and hard liquor. I was even told of one journalist who, having been sent a case of Scotch, phoned the donor in a state of outrage. 'Look here,' he said, 'you know I don't drink whisky. I'm a gin man.'

'Oh, sorry,' said the repentant PR bloke, 'I'll send some gin round at once.' And he did. Or so the story went. Well, it was probably apocryphal but I remember looking on with envy as Cecil Wilson struggled home with some tasty-looking Christmas loot. Unfortunately by the time I'd been in the job long enough to qualify for all these good things, austerity had crept in. The great and wonderful Lew Grade (later, of course, Lord Lew) always sent me and several others a bottle of champagne but apart from that I was lucky if some inferior sherry came my way. On the other hand I was often taken out to lunch by a publicity person trying to interest me in interviewing somebody or other and on these occasions, though I ate and drank well, I was always careful to keep my demands reasonable, not wanting to be under an obligation. But there, too, I discovered that I was missing out.

Rome again. Another film location and again I was there with one other English journalist. The publicity man, highly apologetic, said that he wasn't able to take us out to dinner that night; he had a meeting so would we mind eating at the hotel and charging the bill to his room? We said that was fine and repaired to the dining-room where I looked through the excellent menu and decided upon the dishes I knew I liked. My colleague, by contrast, was running his finger slowly down the price list and choosing only the most expensive items. He did the same with the wine list. Whether he had ever in his life tasted the things he was ordering I seriously doubt but they were there, they cost a great deal, he wasn't paying and he was going to have them.

But this was a time when film companies offered journalists first-class return flights to locations, splendid hotels and lavish meals in return for which they hoped for, rather than expected, sympathetic write-ups. Neither they nor we construed these things as bribes; they merely oiled the wheels. As for downright bribery, well, I've never encountered it, though many times I have wished that someone would attempt to bribe me. It's not that I'm particularly, or indeed at all, venal – it's just that I would love to know what my price is. When you get right down to it I rather doubt that anyone, including myself, is totally incorruptible; in the end it's a matter of price. Would I give a rotten film an enthusiastic review if somebody offered me £1 million? I like to think not, although the question is academic anyway. No review could possibly be worth that kind of money and anything less would be too contemptible to contemplate. So I am able to sit back smugly and assert that, although probably not incorruptible, I have never been corrupted.

In any event, during my time covering show business for the *Mail* I was grateful for much smaller favours than bribes. The theatre was part of my beat and one day I went to the Royal Shakespeare Theatre at Stratford-upon-Avon to interview Diana (now Dame Diana) Rigg, who was to appear there in *Twelfth Night*. It was out of season, hardly anyone was around, and as she and I sat down to talk over a cup of coffee I became painfully aware that unless I found a loo, like immediately, I could not be answerable for the consequences. This is not normally the kind of thing you confide to a beautiful woman but I had no alternative.

'I have to pee,' I said, 'and I can't remember where the loos are.'

'Come with me,' she said briskly, as practical and down to earth as all the best women are. So I followed her around the corridors in a state of increasing desperation, my knees clamped firmly together, as we found first one, then another men's lavatory that was locked. From my expression she clearly saw that matters were urgent.

'Okay,' she said. 'There's a ladies down here that I know is open because I used it myself this morning. You can go in there.'

'But . . .'

'Oh, don't worry.' She opened the door, went in, checked out the cubicles. 'All clear,' she said. 'Go on. I'll stand guard. I won't let any-body in till you've finished.' And that she did. Now this was something greater than any bribe and would in itself have justified the glowing piece I wrote about her. Not that I would have written anything else anyway because, like most men in the 1960s, I rather fancied Diana Rigg and for a while I deluded myself into thinking that she fancied me, too. This came about as a result of our first meeting in Chelsea when she had just been cast to play Emma Peel in *The Avengers*, prob-ably the most popular television series of the decade, and the publicity people had arranged for us to have dinner together. It all went – to my mildly besotted mind – remarkably well and I went home thinking, well, you know, if I'd made a pass there . . . But men are fools, able to con themselves into thinking anything that suits them, and the cool awakening came a year or two after the incident at Stratford when I interviewed her again, this time at the National Theatre where she was playing Lady Macbeth, and she said, 'Do you still live at home with your mother?'

Never in the time I had known her had I lived at home with my mother. I had always been married with children. But with an awful clarity I saw myself through her eyes: a thirty-something wimp, asexual at best, a mummy's boy. No wonder she had been so relaxed and at ease that night in Chelsea; she must have thought she was perfectly safe with someone like me. Other journalists might try to jump on her but not this sad bloke who lived at home with his mum.

Even so I had, I think, a friendly relationship with her as I did with

Maggie Smith. She (now, like Diana Rigg, a Dame) was someone I liked and admired a lot. She was – still is – a wonderful actress but during the early 1960s she was continually overlooked. Each time she appeared in a new production in the theatre the critics greeted her ecstatically as if she were somebody who had never been discovered before. This narked her considerably, as well it might, and perhaps because I sympathized we got along well. One afternoon, towards the end of 1966, when, finally recognized and established, she was one of the biggest stars at the National Theatre, she phoned me at the office. Would I come to her flat after work for a drink and a chat? There was something important she wanted to tell me.

Intrigued, I went. Robert Stephens (later Sir Robert; I'm talking about really distinguished actors here) was also present. He, too, was a big star at the National having recently enjoyed enormous success in Peter Shaffer's play *The Royal Hunt of the Sun*. The position, Maggie said, was this: she and Bob were planning to marry but unfortunately his divorce had not yet come through and – this was the crux of the matter – Maggie was pregnant. The question was, how could they keep this from the press? The first problem, as I saw it, was that I *was* the press and this was a terrific story, front page stuff even in those less prurient days. But I knew and liked them both and they were appealing to me as a friend. How could I help them? We sat down and worked out a plan of campaign. Maggie had already decided that, quite soon, she would take a sabbatical, claiming that she had been working very hard (which was true) and needed a rest. Then she would quietly disappear until either the baby was born or they could get married. Fine. But what if, in the meantime, another paper should get a hint of what was going on? In that case, we decided, they would fob off all enquiries and come immediately to me so that I could break the story in as sympathetic and least hurtful a way as possible.

I went home that night knowing that, if the *Mail* found out, I could get fired for what I had just done. Not only had I turned my back on a first-class exclusive story I had actually conspired to cover it up. And I didn't care. It seemed to me that here were two very nice people who found themselves in the kind of quandary that could happen to anybody and that, when you came right down to it, it was nobody's business but their own. The next few months were a little fraught. Every day I scanned the papers, fearful that somebody else might have stumbled upon and broken the story but fortunately that didn't happen. Unfortunately, I derived nothing at all from my inside information, although that was nobody's fault. The first intimation I had that the story was dead and any danger of scandal was past came in a paragraph in the stop press column of the London *Evening News*, which merely said that Maggie Smith, who, a week or so earlier, had married Robert Stephens at a private ceremony had given birth to a baby. And that, to my relief, was the end of it. I had, and have, no regret at all about my behaviour.

I realize, of course, that such an attitude would make me a hopeless failure in popular journalism today but then I've never seen it as part of a newspaperman's job to inflict misery and sniggering publicity on people who don't deserve it. Corrupt or mendacious politicians, yes, hit 'em with everything you've got because what politicians do – running, or as often as not, screwing up the country – affects the rest of us. If they turn out to be crooked or – a depressing characteristic of all our recent governments – arrogant they deserve everything in the way of opprobrium that you can hurl at them. I don't know what happens to people when they get into Parliament but whatever it is it does seem to happen fast. One day they're creeping around constituencies ingratiating themselves with the party of their choice in the hope of selection and the next they have the letters MP after their names and they're chucking their weight about. Have they overnight become better and wiser people? Of course not. For the most part they are still the same self-seeking chancers that they always were.

The best politicians (and I've been lucky enough to know a few of them) are those who retain a sense of humility and their own fallibility. There are never many of them about but I'll give you an example of one, probably the most honest politician I have ever met – Shirley Williams, Baroness Williams as is (and if it's beginning to sound as if I don't know anybody who hasn't got a title I assure you this is simply coincidence). When she was plain Mrs Williams in the 1970s she was both my MP at Stevenage in Hertfordshire and the Minister for Education in the Labour Government.

When Diana and I, staunch Labour supporters at the time, moved into the village where we still live you could have held a mass rally of the local Labour Party in the telephone box. But along with a handful of equally or even more devoted supporters we got the number up to around 100 at which point we invited Shirley to a cheese and wine party. To our surprise, since as a Cabinet minister she must have been rather busy, she accepted. She talked to everyone and when it came to my turn I asked her a question. I can't now remember what it was and anyway it doesn't matter. The interesting part of our exchange was her response. 'I don't know the answer to that,' she said. For a politician to express ignorance of any subject was unusual enough but then she said, 'I'll find out for you.' Yeah. Right. Like she'd got nothing better to do.

Six months later we invited her to another party, again she came and the first thing she did was to approach me and say, 'You remember that question you asked me?' Actually, I didn't; I'd forgotten it a long time ago but I nodded confidently and said of course I did. 'Well,' she said, 'this is the answer . . .' and gave it. A small incident, no doubt, but that she should have remembered when I had not and had taken the trouble to seek out the facts impressed me greatly. I was a huge fan of Shirley from then on and so was Diana. It was largely because of her that when the Labour Party self-destructed after the 1979 General Election and Shirley went off with the rest of the Gang of Four (Roy Jenkins, David Owen and Bill Rodgers) to form the Social Democrats Diana and I followed.

That was in every way an appalling election, not least because the misguided voters of Stevenage replaced Shirley with a Conservative named Tim Wood, whom I met only once and then briefly, though I'm sure that if you like the Conservative sort of thing he was a perfectly good MP. But in our house he was always known as Doom Wit because Aeron, my mother-in-law, caught a glimpse of one of his election posters, which happened to be upside down though she didn't know that, and asked in a spirit of genuine enquiry, 'Who is this fellow Doom Wit anyway?'

Following Shirley was not, however, an easy thing to do. A new political party requires all sorts of things – money, obviously, but also people, willing helpers to do the hard groundwork. Shirley immediately spotted one of these in Diana, although Diana herself was initially unaware that she came anywhere near that category. A Social Democrat convenor for the whole of Hertfordshire was needed. 'Oh, Diana will do that,' Shirley said confidently, not bothering to consult Diana. And when Diana protested, saying, 'I haven't the faintest idea how to be a convenor', she airily brushed this petty objection to one side. 'You'll soon work it out,' she said, which is how it proved.

Diana became and remained the convenor for Hertfordshire until the pact between the Social Democrats and the Liberal Party came to an ignominious end after the 1987 election. That, you may recall, was when milords – as they now are – David Owen (SD) and David Steele (Lib) took a pace backwards, aimed carefully and shot each other in the foot. For Diana and me this was the end of the Social Democrats. Sod them and sod David Owen was what we thought. Sod David Steele, too, come to that. Diana had worked like a galley slave on behalf of this bright new hope of British politics only to discover that with a few notable exceptions (Shirley among them) it consisted of people no less dumb than those who ran the other parties.

I had done my bit, too. At various times and in various election campaigns I had stumped round Stevenage, along with Robert Powell (best known for playing Jesus on television but also a grossly underrated comic actor), on behalf of Ben Stoneham, our 1983 candidate, had gone walkabout alongside Roy Jenkins when he contested Warrington in 1981 and, again in 1981, had spoken on Shirley's behalf at a rally in Crosby, when she won the by-election there. Actually, Shirley should never have contested Crosby; she should have waited until 1983 and stood again for Stevenage, which I'm convinced she would have won back and which, if she had so wanted, she could be holding still. I was not alone in thinking that but Shirley is a hard woman to convince and she believed that winning Crosby would be a significant achievement for the infant Social Democratic Party. So, to be fair, it was. But she lost the seat at the next General Election and thus brought her career in the

House of Commons, which could ill afford to lose her, to a premature end.

Since then I have spoken at rallies and the like on behalf of Paddy Ashdown and Charles Kennedy because these, too, are politicians I like and trust. But on the whole I believe that people who actively want to become MPs should automatically be disqualified from standing for any seat anywhere and when I look back over the sleaze, arrogance and all round nastiness of the 1990s I see no reason to change my mind. So, to return to a point I was making earlier, bad, crooked, venal and lying politicians should be exposed mercilessly and, to their credit, British newspapers do that pretty effectively. But when it comes to lascivious revelations about the marital problems and sexual misadventures of actors and other entertainers the contemporary press loses my sympathy and clichés about crushing butterflies on wheels come to mind.

Chapter Twelve

IN THE SUMMER of 1959 Diana and I moved to a house in a village in Hertfordshire. Actually, what we acquired on a 999-year lease at a ground rent of £30 per annum was a terrace of four tiny labourers' cottages in a pear-shaped piece of land. They had gas and running water but no electricity or indoor sanitation and unless somebody like us agreed to convert them into a habitable dwelling they would be torn down.

My father found them for us or rather his agent, Leslie Linder, did. Dad had been looking for a place in the country where he could read and write screenplays in peace and quiet and Leslie, who had a hankering for something similar, found two lots of these condemned cottages in Hertfordshire. In the event neither of them moved there, Leslie because the block he had chosen was structurally unsound and had to be demolished and Dad because the village was only about twenty miles from Edgware and he rather wanted something a little more remote and distant.

At the time, Diana and I were living in a furnished flat on a second floor in Victoria and not liking it much. If we left the bedroom window open only a fraction we would come back at night to find the pillows coated with grit thrown up by the passing traffic and the kitchen was so terminally filthy that we never used it for anything more than boiling a kettle.

So, in the belief that it was time we had a house of our own, Dad passed his block of cottages on to us. We first went to see them on a damp, grey day in autumn and what I remember most from that visit was the sight of a huge rat running along the side of the road. Was this really the place for us – a pair of sophisticated Londoners? As it turned out it was, initially because it was all we could afford. With considerable help from an excellent architect, Martin Priestman, who lived in the village, we took the place and converted it into a four-bedroom house at a total cost of £3,600 of which £400 was a council grant. (Mind you, it has cost us far more since, what with adding rooms, acquiring extra land and buying the freehold, thus disposing of any nagging worries we might have had about where we would go when the lease ran out.)

Our intention originally was to stay there for a few years, sell the house and move to something more expensive, then do the same thing all over again and economically no doubt that would have been the clever way to go. But unexpectedly we found ourselves sucked into local life. In London we had lived in three flats in three different areas and had never known our neighbours, except in Victoria where there was a young bloke who obviously fancied Diana and made a pest of himself, certainly to my way of thinking.

But in the village, where our next-door neighbours were an elderly hedger and ditcher, who had served in the First World War, and his wife, who had never been to London and had no desire to go, we were received with instant and genuine friendliness and offers of help as we set about decorating our new home. Life there revolved around the church, the pub and the cricket club and soon we became involved in all these things, especially the pub which was the centre of social activity. It was there that I was signed up for the cricket club. I hadn't really played since I left school but I wanted to and the club was eager for me to join if only because I was one of the few people who had a car and would therefore be invaluable in transporting other players to away matches.

So we settled in and stayed. If we had followed our initial plan and moved and kept moving we might well be living in a small mansion by now in some fashionable part of the Home Counties populated by media and show business people. But we would both have hated that. What we acquired by staying put was much more to our taste – roots, a sense of belonging and a little haven in which what you do for a living is unimportant and nobody is impressed by it anyway.

Both our daughters were born in our house, Samantha in December 1962, and Emma on 29 February 1964, which means she only has a proper birthday every four years. As a child she manipulated this very well in non-Leap Years, insisting on celebrating both on 28 February and 1 March.

Samantha (known from babyhood as Mamfie because that was the closest the 2-year-old daughter of a friend of ours could come to pronouncing her name) arrived three days after Christmas in a snowstorm and at the start of what was to develop into a bitterly harsh winter. We had expected her a little earlier but she was in no hurry and was still unborn on Christmas Eve, a deeply cold but clear and starry night, when Diana and I walked to church for midnight Mass, Diana toddling along beside me in black stretch pants and a bright red top looking not so much like a ship in full sail as a large robin redbreast.

I was beginning to wonder whether she was going to stay like that, not bothering to give birth at all, until early in the morning of 28 December she nudged me awake. 'Something's happening,' she said. 'Better get Mum.'

Mum, Aeron, a trained nurse, was sleeping in the room next door. I went in, woke her and explained the situation. She got up and joined Diana and I crawled into the bed just vacated by my mother-in-law and promptly fell into a peaceful sleep. What was happening next door, I felt, was women's work, nothing to do with me. But a few hours later I was awakened again, by Aeron this time. 'I think you should call the midwife,' she said.

I got up and went downstairs to the phone. By now it was snowing hard. 'I know the village,' the midwife said, 'but how do I find your house?'

'There's a little green just outside,' I said, 'with a telephone booth on it. You can't miss it – it's the only light in the neighbourhood.'

Some while later I heard a car chugging up the lane around the corner and went out to meet it. Just as well I did, because as I stepped on to the green the light in the phone box went out. If I hadn't been there, waving madly, the midwife would have sailed on past, blinded by the swirling snow, probably never to find us at all.

I sat beside Diana, holding her hand, as she went through the ago-nies of labour, gripping me with a passion that had more to do with resentment than affection and cursing me roundly. 'It's all your bloody fault,' she said, which I thought was a bit hard since it takes two to make a baby. 'I hate men.'

I wanted to be there for the birth but the midwife foiled me. As the contractions became more and more frequent she said, 'Go down and boil some water, lots and lots of it.'

Obediently I did so. I filled as many kettles and saucepans as I could find and watched them boil and then I went back upstairs to ask what I should do next, there to find my beautiful daughter, still attached by the umbilical cord, lying in her mother's arms. My first reaction was wonder at the fact that there in the room was somebody who hadn't come in through the door; my second was anger at the midwife, who had cheated me by sending me away to boil all that bloody water, because it now became clear that she had simply not wanted me around at the moment of delivery. She was a middle-aged traditionalist who believed that childbirth was an exclusively female mystery in which men should take no part.

Later in the day our doctor, who lived in the next village, came in to check that all was well but then the snow really set in, the local roads became impassable and we didn't see either him or the midwife for another week. Thank God for Aeron and her nursing skills.

A couple of hours after the birth a friend of mine, unaware of recent events and merely looking for a playmate, called in to invite me down to the pub. 'I can't,' I said. 'But come in and have a drink. I've got champagne. Diana's just had a daughter.'

'Oh, shit,' he said and scuttled away, a somewhat startling reaction but perhaps understandable in his case. Though childless himself he used to dress as Santa Claus for the Christmas jumble sale in the village hall and entertain the local children in his grotto. But because he didn't really like children he could only face this ordeal after downing several large brandies, so his breath as he 'Ho, ho ho-ed' at the poor little mites was about 100 per cent proof and they would stagger out of the grotto half-sozzled.

Samantha Jane, so-named because Diana liked the song in *High Society* and we were both on a big Jane Austen kick at the time, was crying lustily as she was born and didn't stop for about three months. Diana bore the brunt of this. A year or so after we married she left the *Daily Herald* to take a job with more regular hours on a magazine. She didn't really want to do so because she was very happy at the *Herald* but she felt that one of us should be around most of the time to make a home. Then when Mamfie came along she gave up full-time work because, although on two salaries we might just have afforded a nanny, she didn't want anybody else bringing up her baby. Neither did I. And when I was at home I did what I could to help, doing my share of nappy-changing, getting up in the middle of the night and, at breakfast time, stuffing baby compound into my daughter's mouth or, depending on which way she turned her head, her ear.

Fourteen months after Mamfie's arrival Emma was born, the same midwife in attendance. At first events proceeded much as before – curses and imprecations from Diana, her fingernails drawing blood. But then came the crucial moment and from the midwife the expected demand for boiling water. But this time I was ready for her and I stood firm. 'No,' I said. 'You didn't need the water last time and you don't need it now. I'm staying here.' And I did until Emma miraculously appeared, as beautiful as her sister, and I realized, to my astonishment, that tears were streaming down my face.

The names we had actually chosen for her were Alexandra Emma, the first being Diana's choice, the second mine after my favourite Jane Austen novel. But on the day she was born Princess Alexandra also gave birth and an awful thought occurred – people might assume that I had been so naff as to name my child after a member of the royal family.

I am, I have to say, a royalist and can see no good reason why Britain should become a republic. Indeed, I can muster a very strong argument against it: if this country were a republic we would almost certainly have had to suffer President Thatcher throughout the 1990s and even beyond. I rest my case.

But supporting the royal family is one thing; being perceived as the sort of person who fawningly borrows their names is something else again. So although our younger daughter was christened Alexandra Emma the Alexandra was redundant from the start and she is known by that name only to the Inland Revenue.

Thus Diana and I entered into the realm of parenthood, a blissful state marred only by the fact that you are doomed to worry about your children until the day you die. But you don't realize that until much later, which is just as well because otherwise nobody would ever have a family.

Chapter Thirteen

IN DECEMBER 1963, A few months before Emma was born, I went to Madrid to interview John Wayne. I met him only twice; brief encounters both of them but memorable, at least for me. The reason for this first encounter was that he was making a film called *Circus World* with Claudia Cardinale. It turned out to be a pretty duff movie but that's beside the point. The fact that he was making it at all was a big event because Wayne was big. He remained big throughout his lengthy career and was still big at the end of 1999 when, twenty years after his death, he came second to Harrison Ford in a poll to discover America's all-time favourite film star. In 1963 he would have come first by a street.

It was a warm, sunny day and the interview started out in much the same way. Movie stars were different then, much more approachable and relaxed than they have since become, certainly as far as the British press is concerned. They no longer trust British journalists, believing that though what they say may be quoted accurately the comments between the quotes are likely to be snide and derogatory. The journalists might argue that it is not their job to provide advertising hype but to be honest and forthright. To which the stars would reply that honest and forthright doesn't come into it and that the British press represents or has even helped formulate a society that envies and resents anyone else's success and wants to see it belittled. Go figure. But at that time things were different and the unit publicist took me to Wayne's trailer on the film location, introduced us and left me there. Just the two of us. No steely-eyed personal PR person to tell me what I might or might not ask of the great man or to butt in if the conversation strayed from the prescribed tracks.

Wayne and I got on well. At first. He was big and bluff and friendly, rather good company actually, and if his answers to my questions were on the bland side, well, that was hardly surprising. Movie stars always give bland answers. I blame all that money and celebrity. They're so rich and so famous that they rapidly lose touch with real life. Wherever they go they're surrounded by hired hands whose jobs depend on them listening earnestly to their employers' opinions, however banal, and laughing uproariously at their jokes, however feeble. And even when they meet other people, not employed by themselves, these are usually producers, directors and studio executives who are anxious to sign them to film deals and who, therefore, also listen earnestly to their opinions and laugh uproariously at their jokes.

After a few years of all this sycophancy, to say nothing of fan worship, the movie star forgets that essentially he is an ordinary Joe, whose good fortune is that he happens to be more photogenic than the rest of us. He begins to believe that his opinions and jokes are actually worth listening to, that he is not just fortunate to be where he is but that he deserves to be where he is because he is more gifted, more special than other people. There was an element of that in Wayne, a suggestion that by talking to me at all he was doing me a considerable favour. That he was amiable, at least until things went a bit pear-shaped, was not because he wanted me to like him – why should he care? – but because he wanted me to convey a warm image of him to my readers.

His modern counterparts have adapted this attitude to television interviews. While the interview is being conducted they're bright, amusing and friendly but this is not for the benefit of you, the interviewer. They don't care what you think of them; they care what the camera thinks of them and what the TV audience, which will finally watch all this stuff, thinks of them. And when the camera is switched off you get the brief handshake and perhaps a patronizing touch on the shoulder and then they move off to the next interview location and you are history, instantly forgotten.

Is this offensive? Not in the least. Amusing is what it is; you can expect nothing else because such a lordly attitude towards all who are far less rich and famous than themselves is in the nature of the beast, although in my experience this applies largely to American movie stars who, because Hollywood dominates the world's cinema, are bigger and better known than those of other countries.

But there's more to it than that. In their own land American stars enjoy a celebrity and adulation that is unmatched anywhere else. And that, I believe, is because secretly America yearns for a royal family and having carelessly rid itself of any claim to one as far back as 1776 has spent the intervening centuries looking for surrogates. In the early 1960s John and Jackie Kennedy fitted the bill perfectly despite being, as we were to discover later, quite as dysfunctional as any other royal family. Since then the person I suspect America would most have liked to claim as its unofficial queen was the late Princess Diana who, being blonde, beautiful and a skilled self-publicist, met all the criteria for New World royalty except, of course, that she wasn't American.

So in the absence of a Princess Diana of its own or, since the Kennedys, a presidential family with the remotest claim to glamour, the nation makes do with movie stars. These are its royalty; they are treated as such and behave as such. When they appear in public their court travels with them – managers, agents, secretaries, hairdressers, make-up artists, personal trainers, manicurists, gofers and even, representing a kind of Household Cavalry, bodyguards.

You may wonder – I often do – what they have done to deserve their status and I suppose the simple answer is that they represent the American Dream come true. They are rich, they are famous and though they inhabit a make-believe world within it they exercise real power, at least until another monarch comes along to usurp them. To emulate them, to have what they have, is a dream that millions of people seem to share. To become a real king or queen is impossible for all but a handful of people but to become an ersatz one is at least on the cards no matter what your background, as John Wayne proved.

He came from comparatively humble stock, the son of a drug store owner in Iowa, but nevertheless rose to an eminence even other movie stars have never quite shared. Just before he died the American Congress struck a gold medal in his honour and, at the tearful behest of his friend and frequent co-star, Maureen O'Hara, it bore the simple inscription: 'John Wayne – American'.

Later they named schools and airports after him as if somehow he personified all that was best in America. But, for God's sake, he was only an actor – and, if the truth be told, not a particularly good actor at that. He never *did* anything; he just played at doing things – winning battles, shooting people, slaying Red Indians. He was certainly a great movie star but an extraordinarily hollow figure to elect as a kind of national symbol. Only in America . . .

However, on that day in 1963 he was a benevolent enough monarch until, I forget how, the conversation turned to politics. A presidential election year was coming up in America – Lyndon Johnson for the Democrats versus the ferociously right-wing Senator Barry Goldwater for the Republicans – and, in a moment of aberration I found myself saying: 'I do hope Goldwater doesn't get in.'

I can't imagine why I said it. I knew perfectly well that politically Wayne was so far to the right as to regard Attila the Hun as a prototype communist. But having said it I knew at once that I had made a grave tactical error, for Wayne drew himself up to his full considerable height and said, in the tones of one putting a commoner in his place: 'Senator Goldwater happens to be a very close personal friend of mine.'

Since this was clearly a pronouncement and in no way an invitation to engage in a discussion of the senator's merits, or lack of same, you would think, would you not, that I'd have had the sense to shut up. But, no. On I went, trying both to justify my criticism of his close mate and to appease Wayne, who was showing signs of wishing to bring the audience to a premature close, and in so doing managed the neat trick of putting both feet into my own mouth. 'Well,' I said, desperately, 'he's not as bad as that dreadful Joe McCarthy.'

Senator McCarthy was the man who spearheaded America's appalling communist witch hunts of the 1950s and in the more liberal climate of 1963 it seemed a safe bet that nobody would approve of him any more. Unfortunately, Wayne did.

'I happen to believe,' he said, 'that Senator McCarthy was one of the finest Americans who ever lived.'

Very soon after that I was removed from his presence and he showed no perceptible sign of being sorry to see me go. Well, it was my own fault. I should have remembered Wayne's reaction to *High Noon*, the western in which marshal Gary Cooper, abandoned by his fellow townsmen, has to take on the killers by himself and in the end throws his badge to the ground. Wayne regarded this as the most un-American action he had ever seen, akin to 'belittling the Medal of Honor'. If that seems a touch extreme you have to know that Carl Foreman, who wrote the screenplay, maintained that the film was, in fact, an allegory, that Cooper represented the man standing up for his beliefs, the killers were the witch-hunting House Un-American Activities Committee and the townspeople were the mass of American citizens who stood by doing nothing and allowed the persecution to go on. Wayne was not about to have any truck with communist propaganda like that.

I should also have remembered that when the attentions of HUAC threatened to end Foreman's career by blacklisting him and causing him to move to England, Wayne said: 'I'm glad we drove that sono-fabitch out of America.'

Anyway, after Madrid nearly six years went by before my second encounter with Wayne. Two events, regarded equally as of vast national importance, were taking place at the time: the centenary of the completion of America's coast-to-coast railway system was being celebrated and Wayne's latest film *True Grit* – for which he later won his only Oscar – was to have its world première. Paramount, the studio which made the film, decided to hijack the centenary celebrations to publicize their movie.

The railway had been built by a horde of Irish labourers starting out from the east coast, and a similar horde of Chinese starting from the west and somehow they actually contrived to meet at a town called Promontory in Utah. So it was at Promontory that both the centenary festivities and the world première were to be held, though what on earth *True Grit*, a droll western, had to do with railways has always baffled me.

Still, Paramount had invited me to cover this doubly auspicious occasion for the *Mail* and I was thrilled to accept. I had never been to America before but had long been fascinated by the country and, like a lot of people, I imagine, had the feeling that going there would in some indefinable but agreeable way change my life. In my case this turned out to be totally erroneous but I don't suppose I'm alone in that.

However, along with two other European journalists – a jolly free-lance from Munich and a rather cynical young man from *Paris Match* – I was flown to New York, put up at a hotel near the airport, taken to dinner in Manhattan and, the next day, flown to Denver.

There, after a night at the Denver Hilton, we boarded a train that would take us to Promontory. By this time about fifty journalists had been assembled, the others representing newspapers from all over America. There might have been the odd radio reporter among them but there was nobody from television. Video tape hadn't been invented yet and the making of TV reports was still a cumbersome business involving lots of lights and ten-minute rolls of film. TV crews were a pain; nobody wanted them around.

The reason we were on this train was that Wayne was also aboard. Whenever the train stopped, which it did several times, he would stand in the doorway waving and chatting to the quite respectable crowds of people who had turned up to gaze upon him. Most of the time, how-ever, he was installed in the club car at the back and the journalists were split into groups of half a dozen or so, each of which in its turn was ushered into the presence. The interviews began at about 8 a.m., but the German, the Frenchman and I, being non-Americans and therefore pretty low on the totem pole, were not summoned until half-past eleven. As we and a few people from unimportant American papers waited near the club car for the previous group to come out, the waitress approached me and said, 'Do you know how many bourbons he's had this morning?'

Not having been around to count them I did not and said so.

'Fifteen,' she said. 'Do you believe that? Fifteen!'

Now to my way of thinking fifteen miniatures of bourbon, each a double, represented a pretty solid day's and, come to that, night's drinking. For anyone to have consumed them all before noon was awe-inspiring. A bit alarming, too. What kind of shambling, bellicose wreck, I wondered, would we find when we got into the club car?

In fact, Wayne was okay – a little flushed as to the cheeks perhaps but what could one expect? He greeted us all amicably, waving what I assumed to be his sixteenth bourbon, and fortunately showed no sign of recognizing me. Introductions were made and the German, the Frenchman and I sat back politely and allowed our American colleagues to start the interview. Pretty boring stuff it was, too. 'How did you enjoy making the film, Duke?' they asked and he said, 'Fine.'

'So how was it with the director, Henry Hathaway, Duke?' That apparently was equally fine as was working with his young co-star, Kim Darby. The American journalists scribbled this tedium earnestly into their notebooks while the Frenchman, the German and I began to shift restlessly in our seats. And then somebody mentioned Vietnam. The war there still raged and Wayne had recently returned from a goodwill visit whose purpose presumably was to urge the US troops to do better.

During his visit the bicycle he was using had been struck by a Vietcong bullet. Wayne wasn't riding it at the time; it had been deposited in some bicycle parking lot while he, no doubt, was in the officers' mess enjoying a well-deserved bourbon. But the fact of the bicycle having been wounded was regarded as a narrow brush with death and there was much discussion of the incident within our little group culminating as I recall (and I may be imagining this but what the hell) with a suggestion that the bike might be awarded a Purple Heart.

Wayne brushed aside discussion of any possible danger he might have faced with the modesty becoming to an all-American hero but the turn the conversation had taken seemed to me to open the way for a more interesting interview. I do not as a rule ask actors for their political views on the grounds that their opinions carry no more weight than, let us say, those of my milkman, the guy who runs the corner shop or indeed mine. But Wayne was different. He was always throwing in his political twopenn'orth on behalf of the hawks and the rest of the far right, so I asked him what he thought about Vietnam.

'Well,' he said, 'I'll tell ya. It's easy to stop that war. All you have to do is call up Kosygin on the hot line and say, "You send one more bullet, one more gun to Vietnam and we'll bomb Moscow."'

And here I made my first mistake. I laughed because I thought he was joking. But unfortunately he wasn't and from this point onwards as he downed yet more bourbon he turned his disgruntled, liverish gaze upon me. I had laughed at him. People did not laugh at John Wayne; they might laugh with him but never at him. I was, therefore, the enemy.

This was a time when students were demonstrating, even rioting, not just in Europe but also in America. I sympathized with them; Wayne did not. Indeed he dismissed them all as 'just a buncha jerks'. What's more, they were obviously left-wing jerks and he had strong views about both left-wingers and jerkdom. 'In my day at college,' he said, 'you got a D for being a jerk. Now you get an A. That's the difference. Look, if you're a socialist in your first year at college, okay. But if you're still a socialist when you leave you're the dumbest sonofabitch that ever drew breath.'

I forbore from mentioning that, as I recalled, he hadn't even graduated from college, having been there only on a football scholarship, which he lost anyway when he damaged a shoulder. Did football scholars get As? Or were they D-level jerks? It hardly seemed the time to raise the question.

By now he was ignoring everyone else in the compartment and addressing himself only to me, his antagonist, waving a meaty forefinger and prefacing his remarks with, 'Lemme explain sumpun to ya.' Every now and then he would temper some particularly forceful statement by saying, 'Look, I'm not speakin' from up there on the mount,' which I took to be a biblical rather than an equine reference.

I suppose the sensible move on my part would have been to let him rant but I couldn't bring myself to do that. He was talking nonsense and I felt the least I could do was disagree with him. But this only made him angrier and soon I was a 'goddamn pinko liberal'. I'm not sure I didn't become a 'goddamn pinko liberal faggot' than which Wayne had no greater insult to offer. My colleagues listened to and made notes of our exchanges in rapt silence until eventually he said something so outrageous – and what it was I have never been able to remember – that I said, 'Oh, come on. You can't be serious.'

His face, already a glowing red, turned even darker. 'What do you mean, I *cahn't* be serious?' he said, mimicking my English vowel sounds, and turned to the Americans in the compartment, inviting them to join him in mocking this foreigner in their midst. But what he had forgotten is that Americans are very courteous people and they had been rather embarrassed both by his mimicry and the ferocity of his attitude towards me. Instead of sharing in his mirth at my expense they were looking out of the window or examining their fingernails or whistling soundlessly to themselves and that made him even crosser and his expression showed it.

The time had come, I felt, to defuse the situation. 'That's very good,' I said. 'I didn't know you could do an English accent.'

And that finished it. His face turned puce and he lumbered up out of his chair, growling angrily, with the obvious intention of having a go at me. For a moment I didn't know what to do. I certainly wasn't going to fight him. After all, he was a very big man and if he just fell on me he would probably kill me. The thought occurred that we were on a long train and I was pretty sure I could outrun him and I was about to put this to the test when a handful of Paramount publicists interposed themselves between him and me. 'It's okay, Duke,' they said, nudging him back to his chair, 'it's cool, it's cool', and handed him another bourbon.

To me they said, 'I think the interview is over now, don't you?' and ushered me out of the club car. And that was the last time I talked to him. We were all in Salt Lake City for a couple of days and Wayne was much in evidence most of the time but whenever I set off to engage him in light-hearted conversation there always seemed to be a publicist at hand to insist on showing me something of enormous interest in the opposite direction.

When *True Grit* had been duly premièred and the centenary of the railway celebrated Paramount flew me back to New York to do some

interviews which they would arrange. In the event they arranged nothing until the night I left, when they fixed up for me to interview Nicol
Williamson, who was playing *Hamlet* on Broadway, in a Sixth Avenue
bar on my way to the airport, thus making me realize that the much-
vaunted American quality of 'get up and go' was simply another myth,
probably put about by Hollywood. But they treated me very nicely,
lodged me at the Plaza Hotel, provided theatre tickets, gave me lunch
in Chinatown and one evening one of the publicists took me to a
friend's apartment where Norman Mailer, who was running for mayor
of New York that year, was addressing a group of supporters.

I contributed a couple of dollars to Mailer's fighting fund and afterwards, with the publicist and a handful of others, went on to another
apartment where the host provided drinks and then said, 'Okay, who's
got the grass?'

This was my first encounter with marijuana or indeed any drug
other than nicotine and alcohol and when the joint came my way I
passed on it. I had a cigarette in one hand and a gin and tonic in the
other and I reckoned that was just about as much in the way of recre-
ational substances as I could handle at the moment. The joint,
followed by others, went on its way, always passing me by until the host,
who had been inhaling deeply, looked across at me and said, 'I think it's
time I had a drink. What are you drinking?'

'Gin and tonic,' I said.

'Hey, that sounds good only, see, we're outa tonic.'

'Well, bitter lemon's okay,' I said.

'Yeah, right, only we don't have any bitter lemon.'

'Then I don't know what to suggest,' I said.

He took another drag on the joint. 'We got chutney, though,' he said.
'How do you think gin and chutney would taste?'

At that point I decided I had been wise to forgo the marijuana if it
could make a person even contemplate drinking gin and chutney and
indeed apart from one drag at a party in Los Angeles several years later
I have never tried it.

One way and another, though, it had been an interesting introduction to America but the most interesting part of it was the least

expected. It had been my assumption that because Americans and I spoke more or less the same language there would be a bonding between us but in fact during the two or three days in Salt Lake City I found I had far more in common with the German and the Frenchman. We laughed at the same things – yes, Germans do have a sense of humour – liked and disliked the same things and preferred each other's company. This is not to say that the Americans were in any way unpleasant – well, Wayne was, I suppose; they were, on the contrary, perfectly friendly and welcoming. But as my plane took off from Kennedy Airport I realized that perhaps the most important thing I had learned over the past week or so was that I was a European first, an English-speaking person second. And though I have now been to America literally more times than I can remember, have enjoyed every visit and made a lot of American friends I still feel exactly the same way.

Chapter Fourteen

IN HIS BIOGRAPHY *Richard Burton: A Life* Melvyn Bragg includes an extract from the diary of said Burton for 29 May 1969 in which I am mentioned. I am described therein as being 'bright as a button' and I have no quarrel with that but the reason I am mentioned is that during the course of the previous day I had asked what Burton describes as 'the unavoidable question', namely, 'Why don't you come back to the theatre?' He then proceeds to give his reasons why he wouldn't go back to the theatre and implies that the discussion took place in the presence of Elizabeth Taylor, his then and indeed future wife, who was 'quite savage' with me in his defence, so savage indeed that I had tears in my eyes, whereupon she gave me a kiss.

A nice little story. Unfortunately it's not quite true.

What really happened . . . Well, to understand what really happened we have to go back to Gstaad in December 1968, where the Burtons had arrived to spend Christmas in their Swiss home. They had come early because two of her – and by adoption his – daughters, Liza, aged eleven, and Maria, aged eight, were appearing in the end of term play at the exclusive and expensive Tournesol School where they were both pupils. The *Daily Mail* photographer Roger Bamber and I were on hand to cover this momentous event at which, as I wrote, the senior Burtons turned up – he in a mink coat, she in sable – looking 'like a pair of glamorous teddy bears'.

At the time I knew them both rather well so after the play Roger and

I were invited to the Burtons' villa for drinks and then, various other junior members of the clan also being present, accompanied them to dinner in a restaurant in town. While we were at the villa I looked through Burton's bookshelves – you can tell a lot about people from their books, just as you can from the contents of their bathroom cabinets – and found a copy of my first novel, *The Matter of Mandrake*. This was very gratifying and I said as much. 'Oh, yes,' said Burton gravely, 'we love it.' This would have been even more gratifying if the condition of the book had not suggested that nobody had even opened it, let alone read it. But then Burton was always inclined to be economical with the truth, particularly if a little white lie would please somebody he liked and at that time, when I saw him quite often, he did like me.

Anyway, I wrote my piece, light-hearted and affectionate, about the play, the performers and the two distinguished members of the audience and forgot about it. Until 28 May 1969.

That was the day of the press call for the forthcoming film *Anne of the Thousand Days* in which Burton was to play Henry VIII to Genevieve Bujold's Anne Boleyn. The Fleet Street contingent, reporters and photographers, were taken on coaches by the movie company to Shepperton Studios where the two main principals, in full costume, granted us audience. When the talking and the picture taking were done the journalists, myself among them, headed back towards our coaches but Burton took me to one side.

'You don't have to go yet, do you?' he said. 'Come upstairs, luv. Have a drink.' So I did. And in his dressing room he and I, along with various members of his entourage, got stuck into the vodka. Now in those days boozing with Burton was a perilous business because no heeltapping was allowed; you had to match him drink for drink. He would drain his own glass, hand it to an acolyte to be refilled and frowningly instruct his drinking companion to 'finish that up. It's time for another one.'

Since his capacity for alcohol was far greater than mine I rapidly found myself, tongue loosened by a couple of massive vodkas, bringing up the 'unavoidable question' mentioned in his diary. I had and retain a great affection for Richard Burton because he was always very nice to me. But I believed then, and still believe now, that in many ways his was a wasted life. In his early days, playing classical roles at the Old Vic, he was not only a bobby-sox idol – girls would hang around the stage door for hours waiting to see him – but widely regarded as a potentially great actor. That most perceptive of critics Kenneth Tynan saw him as the natural successor to Laurence Olivier, than which there is no greater praise in the British theatre. But a potentially great actor is what he remained, his promise never truly fulfilled. He was, I think, both lazy and too readily seduced by the easy pickings of Hollywood. The work he was offered there was undemanding to an actor of his skill, the financial rewards were attractive and the fame, especially after his marriage to Elizabeth Taylor, was too glittering to be resisted. The film offers came to him too soon and too abundantly with the result that though the cinema might have gained another star the theatre lost something much rarer, an actor who should have been great.

So that evening at Shepperton Studios I brought up all these thoughts of mine – well, not the laziness; that might have seemed a bit insulting – and asked why he had more or less ignored the theatre for so long. As he gave his answers – the sheer tedium of long stage runs, the boredom of repeating the same speeches night after night, the intellectual snobbishness that made people think the cinema was trivial and only the theatre was important – the discussion became warm but never heated. And at the end of it, still friendly, he gazed upon the latest vodka on which I was embarked and said, 'How are you getting back to town? Christ, you're not driving, I hope.'

I said I wasn't; I said I was hoping someone might get me a cab. 'Don't worry,' he said. 'I'll give you a lift.' So we got into his chauffeur-driven Rolls-Royce and headed back to London and on the way I said, 'Richard, I've been drinking your booze all night. Let me buy you one.'

He thought that was a good idea so we stopped at a pub and went in. The place was not too full but if the drinkers who turned idly in our direction as we entered recognized him they gave no sign of it. We stood at the bar where I ordered us pints of bitter and in the course of conversation, apropos of nothing at all, he suddenly said, 'Do you know, I've never been unfaithful to Elizabeth. Not once.'

Why he told me that I have no idea. Certainly it wasn't in response to any question I had asked. And whether what he said was true I also have no idea. As I had already learned – not only in Gstaad but even earlier – he was capable of saying almost anything he thought you might want to hear. But at that moment, as he spoke, I would have sworn he was telling the truth.

We finished our drinks and carried on towards the Dorchester Hotel where he and Taylor were staying and as the car turned into the forecourt he said, 'Come in and say hello to Elizabeth.'

I said, 'Richard, I can't. I've got to get back to the office. I've already missed one deadline.'

'Oh, don't worry about that. Come on in. I insist. She'd love to see you.'

I was on the point of feeling flattered by this when realization hit me: he was late home for dinner and he was scared to go in by himself. I thought of the old joke about the British working man staggering home from the pub and throwing his cap through the door. If his wife didn't throw it out again he was okay; if she did he had better make himself scarce. That night I was to be Burton's cap. Well, it seemed the least I could do . . .

We went up to the Oliver Messel suite which he and Taylor occupied and he opened the door, peered in and said, 'Darling, I'm home. Look who I've brought to see you.'

Taylor appeared in the hallway. She didn't seem too happy to start with, even less so when she spotted me. 'Oh, it's you,' she said and swept back into the sitting room, where we joined her, and Burton occupied himself with pouring drinks and providing social chitchat. I joined in the chat; Taylor didn't. She sat a few feet away staring fixedly at me in silent disapproval. The atmosphere was heavy to say the least.

After a while when both Burton and I had run out of nervous nonsense to exchange she leaned forward, turned the full power of those violet eyes on me and said, 'I don't like you.'

From her earlier demeanour I had kind of gathered that but I was genuinely puzzled. 'Why not?' I said.

'Because of that time in Gstaad,' she said. 'You made fun of my children.'

And that upset me. It was a monstrous accusation. 'I did not,' I said. 'I would never do such a thing. I took the piss out of you and I took the piss out of him but I did not make fun of your children.' If, as Burton said, there were tears in my eyes, that's when they appeared and they were tears of indignation.

Taylor looked at me thoughtfully for a few moments. 'You know something?' she said. 'You're right.' And that's when she got up and kissed me.

We parted amicably and I went back to the office to write my report of the photo call, which included a quote from Burton saying that he intended to give up acting in two years time when he would be forty-six. It was utter rubbish and I knew it even then. But what can you do? If that's what they say, that's what you have to write.

My relationship with Burton went back to the mid-1950s when he and his first wife, Sybil, went into tax exile in Switzerland. By then he was becoming big in Hollywood – two Oscar nominations under his belt already – and was earning a lot of money. This was very pleasing to him but even more so to the British Inland Revenue, which promptly demanded 90 per cent of it – and that under a Conservative government, the Conservatives being, you understand, the party which doesn't believe in high taxation.

As with Noel Coward before him and Peter Sellers later, the prospect of one of our biggest stars leaving the country to fill his boots and his bank balance did not go down too well with the populace. All very well for him, people grumbled, he's an actor, he can live anywhere but what about the rest of us who are stuck here with this bloody government and these bloody taxes?

The departure of the Burtons was, therefore, a muted occasion, he giving polite but guarded answers to questions about his motive for leaving. I was merely one of several asking these questions and there was no noticeable rapport between us.

The next time we met was in Rome in 1962. He was there to play Mark Antony to Elizabeth Taylor's Cleopatra in Joseph L.

Mankiewicz's film of that name. This was a production that had already caught the attention of the world's press, largely because it was so fraught with problems. It had started out, under the direction of Rouben Mamoulian, at Pinewood Studios in 1958 and that was a pretty daft decision in the first place given the British climate. Indeed, it was the climate that had the last laugh because partly as a result of its rigours Taylor was taken seriously ill and the production had to be postponed.

When it restarted two years later in Rome the director had been changed and so had the leading men – Peter Finch (Caesar) giving place to Rex Harrison and Stephen Boyd to Burton. What with all the alterations in locale and personnel and the scrapping of an expensive set at Pinewood the cost was already astronomical before a foot of film had been shot. The very existence of Twentieth Century Fox, the studio producing *Cleopatra*, seemed to depend on its success.

But suddenly all these considerations were as nothing in the light of the rumours emanating from Rome. Burton, husband of Sybil and father of two, was said to be having a tempestuous affair with the biggest movie star in the entire world, Elizabeth Taylor, wife of Eddie Fisher and mother of four. Could this possibly be true? Surely not. The *Daily Mail* sent me to Italy to find out.

When I got there I discovered that Taylor wasn't talking to anybody but Burton was. Sort of. I met him at Cinecitta Studios and took him to the commissary for coffee. Was he, I asked over a double espresso, having an affair with his co-star? Come on, Richard, you can confide in me.

He looked me frankly in the eye. 'No, luv,' he said. 'It's all a lot of talk. There's absolutely nothing to it.'

He was lying and I knew it. What's more he knew I knew it. And on top of that I knew he knew I knew it. It was a perfect stand-off and all of a sudden both of us started grinning. We couldn't help it; the whole situation seemed so ludicrous. We chatted together for quite a long time but he wouldn't change his story and I caught the next plane home, journalistically frustrated but aware that in a curious way he and I had become friends.

Thereafter I bumped into him quite often, always in a professional capacity. And in Rome again in 1966 he gave me a quite remarkable story, possibly to make up for the fact that he had given me nothing at all four years earlier. He and Taylor, by then absolute megastars by virtue of being the most famous film couple in the world, were there to make *The Taming of the Shrew* and it was really Taylor I had gone to interview. Of late she had taken to calling her husband 'Walter' when she wanted to annoy him, Walter being his middle name, which he didn't like at all but with which he was stuck and mention of it certainly irritated him. She urged me to call him Walter as well but since I couldn't see any percentage in annoying or irritating the man I was too fly for that.

Anyway, after I had interviewed her I thought I might as well interview him, too, but though he was always fun to talk to he didn't seem to have anything newsworthy to impart on this occasion and after a while we were both aware of that. But then he said, 'I'll tell you something I've never told anybody before', and embarked upon a curious tale of how, when he married Taylor, he gave away all his money.

He hadn't consulted anybody, he said; he had just decided to do it, ridding himself of £500,000, a considerable fortune in the 1960s. Why he had embarked upon this course, he said, even he didn't really know. It just seemed the right thing to do, a matter of starting afresh with a clean sheet, so he had distributed his largesse to charities and members of his family in Wales. This was really good stuff and my report dominated the main feature page of the *Mail*.

A couple of weeks later, however, I bumped into Burton's brother, Graham Jenkins, who worked for the BBC, in the foyer of Broadcasting House. 'That was a load of rubbish you wrote about Richard the other day,' he said. 'Gave away all his money? Nonsense. He never gave anybody a penny.'

He was very convincing. But why should Burton have said that if it wasn't true? To make himself look good? Yes, that possibly entered into it. But maybe, too, he didn't want me to go away empty-handed, with nothing to write, so he simply let his imagination take flight and perhaps what he told me he had done was actually what, out of guilt over his betrayal of Sybil and his children, he felt he should have done and perhaps he had also half-persuaded himself that that is what he had done. In the light of what Graham Jenkins said this, in any event, was what I came to believe: it was just a fairy tale.

But when I met Burton for the last time, in July 1977, I was persuaded that he had been speaking the truth. He was in London to prepare for a film called *The Wild Geese* and for almost the first time in my experience he was completely sober. He had given up drink, he said, because 'my metabolism must have changed. Until I was forty-five I never had a hangover. Now I get horrendous hangovers. I'm so ill I can't even get out of bed.' The current anecdotal evidence suggested that his doctors had told him that unless he gave up the booze he would die but that's not the point – the point is that he was sober. And in this state, unprompted, he reminded me of what he had said in Rome about giving away all his money and added that he had done exactly the same thing again when he and Taylor were divorced for the second and final time.

'A brave thing to do at fifty, wasn't it?' he said, a note of self-mockery in his voice. But to me there seemed no need for the self-mockery because this time I believed him. When he first told me the story in Rome it was for an interview; now, in London, the TV camera had been packed away and we were just chatting, reminiscing about old times. What he said would not be broadcast on television or printed in a newspaper. It was simply between us and he had no need to try to impress me. In those circumstances there would be no point in repeating something that was just a fabrication. Whether all his family had benefited the first, or second, time around I do not know. But now I did not doubt that he had done what he said and if that were so it was indeed a brave thing to do, at any age.

A year after that Roman encounter the Burtons were in the news again. They had become directors of Harlech Television, which had taken over the TV franchise in Wales. So off I flew once more to talk to them about this new turn in their careers.

Along with a bunch of wealthy friends they were floating about in the Mediterranean in a newly-acquired yacht, the *Odysseia*, just outside

Portofino in Italy. To Portofino, therefore, I repaired and sent a message to the yacht by speedboat informing Burton that I wished to speak to him. By return speedboat he said he would meet me in a bar on the quayside in an hour's time.

In those days, and for all I know still, Portofino was a trendy, upmarket resort, its quayside lined with smart restaurants, bars and boutiques. The Burtons joined me in the bar where I was awaiting them and their friends dispersed into the boutiques and started buying each other presents as if money was imminently about to lose all value and might as well be spent now while it still meant something.

Taylor had her leg in plaster and was walking with the aid of a stick as a result of a fall on the yacht a few days earlier but she was as eager to join in the buying spree as anyone. Nevertheless, she stayed with her husband and me long enough to share her views on being an incipient TV tycoon before the urge to hurl money about in the boutiques became too strong to resist. She and Burton were a couple who, notoriously, rowed a lot in public and at the tops of their voices but on this occasion they were getting along well. As if to prove it he would, every now and then, lean affectionately towards her, grasp one of her admirable breasts, squeeze it and say, 'Barp! Barp!' To which her response was a girlish, 'Oh, Richard!' No Walter this time, you notice.

After a while, however, she drifted away to join her friends in swapping gifts – watches, shoes, blouses and, when it began to rain, oilskin coats. I say rain but what fell from the skies was nothing more than a damp mist, hardly noticeable. Even so it was enough for Taylor and company to buy each other these designer raincoats in yellow oilskin. At one point when, resting her injured leg after the ordeal of so much shopping, she had rejoined us in the bar one of the friends came in with just such a coat and tossed it to Burton. 'Here, Richard,' he said, 'this is for you.'

Burton held it up with visible distaste. 'I don't want it,' he said and threw it over to me. 'You have it.'

Before I could refuse – and I wanted the thing even less than he did – Taylor snatched it away and gave it back to her husband. To me she said, 'I'm sorry but we can't let you have this', and to Burton,

'Richard, how can you be so rude? This man has given you a present. You can't just give it away.'

'Oh, all right,' Burton said and muttering token thanks screwed it up on the bench beside him, whereupon the shoppers, Taylor included, went away again to resume the arduous business of buying things.

As we left the bar Burton invited me to join him and the rest of the company at lunch in a restaurant just across the quay. I accepted and then he said, 'Everyone around here has had a present except you. Let me buy you something.'

I protested strenuously that I wanted nothing from him, that I was perfectly happy to go away giftless. I meant it, too, because I've always had a horror of being under any obligation to the people I have to write about or, later, to review. But he ignored me. Taking me firmly by the arm he led me into a boutique next to the bar. As we approached the door the place seemed to be empty but as soon as he entered shop assistants came pouring out of the woodwork with many an obsequious murmur of 'Ah, Signor Burton'.

He was wearing I had noticed, and quietly admired, a canary yellow pullover in the most delicate cashmere. Now, pointing to it, he said, 'I bought this in here the other day. I want another one for him. Charge it to me', and then he walked out, leaving me alone with the shop assistants. To them I insisted feebly that it was all a mistake, that I wanted nothing but they took no notice. Fastidiously, using only their finger-tips, they divested me of my Marks & Spencer woolly, which they dropped into a plastic bag, and then clad me in a cashmere pullover, the pale blue twin of Burton's yellow one. It was a perfect fit. Beaming, they put the plastic bag in my hand and shoved me out of the door.

I felt awful, knowing that I owed Burton something. Even worse, I had forgotten the name of the restaurant where I was supposed to meet the others. What to do?

At this moment of desperation relief was at hand. Towards me, quite alone, leaning on her cane and wearing a yellow oilskin raincoat came the limping figure of Elizabeth Taylor. 'You're joining us for lunch, I hope,' she said. 'Do you mind if I take your arm? This leg is a little painful.'

'Oh, please,' I said, proferring the arm. I'm like that; I don't mind who takes my arm, and together, slowly, we headed towards the restaurant, my mind still awhirl with doubts about the gift I had accepted from her husband.

And then she said, 'That's a nice sweater.' This was my cue. 'Yes, it is,' I said, 'Richard gave it to me . . .' whereupon I launched into a pathetic babble about how I hadn't really wanted it and shouldn't have accepted it, only there was nothing I could do because he had insisted and how bad I felt and . . .

Mercifully, she cut me short. 'Would you like to buy me a present?' she asked.

'Yes,' I said, 'please', and only then did I wonder what kind of present this woman, whose collection of jewellery was probably second only to that of the Queen, would expect. The Koh-i-noor diamond maybe? I was pretty sure I didn't have enough in my current account to cover it but what the hell. 'Anything,' I said.

'Well, a shop down here sells umbrellas that would go very nicely with this raincoat. Would you buy one for me?'

Would I? I almost dragged her into the shop where, crassly overriding her preference for a black umbrella on the grounds that a yellow one would perfectly match her coat, I parted with a fiver and presented her with her gift.

Outside she thanked me prettily, put the umbrella up to keep the mist out of her hair and, arm-in-arm, we proceeded slowly to lunch.

I have only met Elizabeth Taylor a couple of times since then and I imagine she has long forgotten that brief period when we were if not friends then at least on terms of social intimacy. But I have not forgotten her. What she did that day showed a remarkable degree of sensitivity. It was obvious that I was uncomfortable and embarrassed at being, in my mind if not in his, in Burton's debt and so she solved the problem simply and with the utmost grace.

The cashmere sweater must have cost Burton a great deal more than the umbrella cost me but that wasn't important. What mattered was that as Elizabeth Taylor and I left the umbrella shop what she was saying, without actually saying anything, was, 'We bought you a present. Now you've bought me one, so we're quits. Shut up.'

I've loved her for that ever since.

And so to my penultimate meeting with Burton. Once more it happened in Italy, this time in Milan where he was making a film called *The Voyage* with Sophia Loren, the last film by the great Italian director Vittorio De Sica.

I had not seen Burton for a few years, my life having rather dramatically changed course. I was no longer a show business writer but a columnist for *The Guardian* and, most significantly for me, a film critic, the presenter of a programme on BBC1 then called *Film 73*. It was in this latter capacity that I went with my producer, Pat Ingram, and a camera crew to Milan to talk to Burton about his career and his current film.

Elizabeth Taylor was not with him. She was in Rome, making a movie of her own. The couple had recently been reconciled after one of their many vituperative separations but, though I didn't know it then, the reconciliation didn't take and they had more or less decided to divorce. For the first time, that is. (Having married and then divorced they seemed to get the taste for it and did both things all over again but that was to come later.)

Burton, therefore, had gone to Milan on his own and, probably because whatever the state of their marriage he loved and missed Taylor, he was drinking heavily. By the time I arrived he had been there for some while and – I pieced this together from members of the unit – a pattern had emerged. At a certain stage of his daily drinking his libido kicked in and when it did his eye fell upon an extremely pretty Italian starlet, who had a small role in the film, and he would take her to bed. The next morning, full of alcoholic and postcoital remorse, he would ask her to leave. The remorse was such, however, that he started drinking again and at a certain stage of his drinking his libido kicked in once more and his eye would fall again upon the Italian starlet and he would take her to bed. The next morning . . . well, you can fill in the rest for yourselves. But the result was that when I got there Burton was in a terrible state while the poor girl hardly knew whether she was coming or going.

He and I met up on the evening of my arrival by which time he was already pretty sozzled and I suggested we do the interview the following morning but he said, 'No, let's do it now.' I was not happy about this, rightly fearing the worst, but he would not be gainsaid.

We set up our equipment in the middle of the hotel's huge and otherwise deserted ballroom, Burton insisting on holding a ratty little Pekinese dog called E'en So on his knee. The cameraman and soundman fiddled around getting the light and voice levels right, signalled that they were happy and Pat gave me the nod to start the interview. I began, as I always do in recorded as opposed to live conversations, with a couple of innocuous queries just to get everybody happy and relaxed and then I embarked on the biggie, a reprise really of the 'unavoidable question' I had asked him at Shepperton.

I was looking upwards rather than at him, snatching the right words from the atmosphere, when I heard a loud snore and glancing across at my interviewee discovered that he was fast asleep, chin resting on his chest. Nothing like this had ever happened to me before – somebody nodding off when I was in the middle of asking him a vital question. Bloody rude. I gave him a quick kick on the shin. 'Richard, wake up!' But he just shook himself slightly and snored again.

The cameraman looked at Pat, she shrugged and looked at me and I said, 'Let's go and have dinner.' Quietly we packed up our stuff and stole away, leaving him there still asleep, all by himself – give or take E'en So – in the ballroom.

Just before we went to the restaurant I sought out the leader of Burton's personal entourage and told him what had happened. He laughed. I said I would like to do the interview again the next morning, whereupon he laughed some more and said, 'No, that's it. You only get one shot. Tough luck.'

'Okay,' I said, 'then I'll tell you what's going to happen. Listen carefully. In my programme next week I will use the stuff we have just recorded and I will explain to the viewers how it came about. You think Richard will like that, do you – five minutes of him, pissed out of his head, on national television?'

'You wouldn't!'

'I bloody would and I will.'

All of a sudden he stopped laughing. In fact, now he couldn't do enough for me. Another interview? Of course, why hadn't I mentioned it before? Lunchtime the following day all right for me? Well, yes it was. Burton was only working during the morning and had the rest of the day off; the only problem was to keep him away from the booze until after I had spoken to him.

I did my best. I was on the set even before he was, fervently hoping that whatever scene he was shooting did not involve drink. For I remembered that when he was making *The Spy Who Came in from the Cold* he told me of one sequence in which he and another actor had to down a couple of whiskies. The props department gave them each a glass of flat ginger ale, the cinema's usual substitute for scotch, but Burton had waved it away. 'No, it's only a short scene,' he said. 'Won't need more than a couple of takes. Bring us some real whisky.' So they did and twelve takes later the scene was over. Well, in those days he could handle it. In those days he could drink all day and you would never know he had taken a drop. But I wasn't so sure he could do that any more.

Luckily, that morning in Milan no alcohol was involved. Between takes we stood on the sidelines drinking coffee and at one point after the beautiful Italian starlet, his bedmate, had been chatting to us and then gone away, he said, 'That girl fancies you.'

'Rubbish,' I said.

'No, she does. She told me. She thinks you're very handsome, very English.'

As usual I couldn't tell whether he was lying or not but anyway I wasn't to be distracted. Beautiful starlet or no beautiful starlet my job was to keep an eye on Burton. And when the final shot of the morning had been done and for the last time De Sica had ordered his cameraman to 'Checka da gate' I started propelling my interviewee towards the little room where my crew had set up, congratulating myself on the thought that this time both of us would be stone cold sober.

Unfortunately, the film Burton was making was a period piece and because he was dressed in Victorian costume he said he would like to change before we got started. I told him this was unnecessary; that I would explain on the programme why he was so dressed but he was adamant. 'Won't take five minutes,' he said. 'I'll be more comfortable. Come on.'

I went with him to his dressing room and there, as I feared, one of his acolytes was waiting with a large Bloody Mary so pale that it hardly seemed to contain any tomato juice at all. It was this, not the opportunity to change his clothes, that Burton had wanted and as he drank it I realized that my earlier fears had been justified. In the old days one Bloody Mary would have made no difference to his speech or thought processes; now it was enough to make him drunk and when, finally, we got down to the interview he was hardly more coherent than he had been the previous night. True, he didn't actually fall asleep but that was small consolation.

On reflection, it would have been kinder not to broadcast the interview and perhaps we shouldn't have done. But neither he nor his entourage asked us to withhold it and in any event we had no real choice. I had been in Italy for a week, had not seen the new films on release and had neither the time nor the material to write an alternative script. In editing the Burton conversation Pat was as kind to him as she could be but even so it was obvious to any viewer paying reasonable attention that the man was drunk. It was a sad, rambling, sometimes incomprehensible interview which, when transmitted, was greatly admired and greatly censured and horrified a lot of people.

We did not meet again until that time in London in 1977, when he had stopped drinking. He seemed physically to have shrunk but he was as amusing and friendly as ever. Drunk or sober he was always excellent company, except maybe that evening in Milan.

I didn't think he had seen the interview we had done there but he must have been in London when it was shown because he said, 'I think I was sloshed at the time. Was I?' I said I was afraid he was. He nodded ruefully and revealed that, after the programme went out, Ava Gardner, who was then also in London, phoned him and said, 'Come on round and I'll comfort you.' As I told him, that was a much better offer than I ever had but even so I was sorry that my programme had evoked such a response in one of his fellow stars.

In his biography Melvyn Bragg says that those who knew him best always called Burton 'Rich'. Obviously I didn't know him that well because I called him Richard, as indeed Elizabeth Taylor did when I was in their company. But I knew him well enough to like him a great deal, to be deeply saddened when he died at the early age of fifty-nine and to wonder frequently just how good an actor he might have been if he hadn't become so rich and celebrated when he was still in his early thirties. At an age when the great actors are still honing their skills he was world-famous and no doubt surrounded by people eager to tell him that he was great already, had given several splendid film performances to prove it and had no need to suffer the arduous and financially less rewarding business of testing himself against the classical roles on stage. If so, they were wrong.

There is a difference between stage and screen acting. In the theatre it's live and you only have one chance. Every time you tread the boards as Hamlet, or Macbeth or Lear you know you've got to get it right – all of it – here and now. On a film set you can make a mistake and stop and do it again, do it indeed as many times as you like. And that applies to every scene. Great acting in the theatre is a performance you can see taking shape before your very eyes. Great acting in the cinema is not one performance but the best bits of many performances artfully sewn together by the director and the editor. Neither is easy to accomplish but theatre acting demands quite as much skill and a greater degree of concentration, dedication and sheer physical stamina. In other words, it's harder to do well.

As a young man, particularly, Burton proved that he could do it well. But the great ones, the Oliviers and Gielguds, do it well and then do it again and do it better. Burton did not. He chose the cinema instead and though he gave many fine screen performances he never achieved the greatness that might have been his.

Chapter Fifteen

ONE EVENING IN January 1970 I was having a drink with Barry Humphries in the Mucky Duck. This was the time when he did drink, although as far as I know he hasn't touched a drop for many years now. He was already quite well known at the time for his creation of Les Patterson, the alcoholic, vomit-stained Australian Cultural Attaché, and Dame Edna Everage, Housewife Superstar, but he was not nearly as famous as he was to become.

A few months earlier, he told me, he had been asked by the *Daily Mail* to write an article about Ned Kelly, the nineteenth-century Australian outlaw, and had duly turned up in the features room one evening in merry mood and clutching a bottle of whisky. He spent many congenial moments chatting with Gordon McKenzie, the assistant editor in charge of features, and such other department executives as Alwyn Robinson and Peter Dobereiner before, the evening by now well advanced, they left him alone in Gordon's room to get on with it while they went home.

Around midnight Arthur Brittenden, the editor, was prowling the corridors and heard odd, muffled noises coming from Gordon's darkened office. He went in, switched on the light and found Humphries asleep on the floor, snoring gently. 'G'day,' said Humphries waking up and greeting the intruder courteously.

'Hello,' said Arthur. 'Who are you?'

'I'm Barry Humphries. Who are you?'

'Well,' said Arthur, 'I'm the editor of the *Daily Mail*.'

'Oh, shit, what a bastard of a job,' said Humphries. 'You poor sod, you shouldn't be here at this time of night, man in your position.'

Arthur thanked him for his sympathy and asked what he was doing there.

'I'm writing an article for you,' Humphries said.

'Oh, well, in that case I shan't disturb you.'

'Okay, sport,' Humphries said. 'Switch the light off on your way out, will you?'

By morning he had gone. The article never did get written.

Whether editing the *Mail* was indeed a bastard of a job I really couldn't say never having been asked to do it. But I worked under several editors all of whom for one reason or another were replaced in the end. So perhaps they could be regarded as poor sods. The first was Arthur Wareham, a serious man in late middle age and a graduate of the less racy pre-war school of journalism. He didn't encourage intimacy with junior underlings such as myself and indeed gave me a tongue-lashing one day when a peer of the realm complained that I had not so much misquoted him as invented a quote. Since he was quite right I had no defence. But the bollocking I got from Wareham shook me up to such an extent that I was careful never to invent anything again.

William Hardcastle, a bluff, burly man with prominent eyebrows, wasn't exactly a friend of mine either. As an editor he was inclined to mistake ruthlessness for strength and he was the only one to refuse me a rise in salary when I asked for it. A good few years later when we were both well known, I on television, he as the presenter of *The World At One* on BBC Radio 4, and we could meet on terms of equality I asked him why he had turned me down.

'Well, you weren't worth it at the time,' he said. 'If you came to me now I'd probably give you a rise.' He still didn't sound too sure, though, possibly not wishing to give the impression that radio had turned him soft.

Mike Randall was the first of the editors with whom I could claim to be on friendly terms and he was perhaps the hardest done by. In the late

1960s under his guidance the *Mail* was named Newspaper of the Year and deservedly so. Mike had realized that he had a bunch of good writers either on the staff or under contract and he just let them write pretty much what they wanted to. The result was a bright, confident readable paper, politically to the left of its proprietor, Esmond, Lord Rothermere, and none the worse for that. The accolade of Newspaper of the Year seemed to guarantee Mike's tenure of office for several years to come, especially as the circulation was very healthy. But when we had finished celebrating the paper's success the cover price, which had been artificially deflated for the past year, was raised to match that of our rival the *Daily Express* and the circulation promptly fell. I've never understood why the addition of an extra penny or two should have made so much difference. The paper was still as good as it had been the previous year, better than the *Express* anyway, but people simply stopped buying it and when they did Mike was booted out.

The last of my editors was Arthur Brittenden, a tall, slim, affable man with a ready smile and a core of steel. People coming out of his office after an unexpectedly tough confrontation were wont to remark bitterly, 'I've been smiled in the back again'. Here I have to emphasize that I never had cause to say that. I liked Arthur and he was always straight with me, except perhaps for that curious occasion when I was excluded from his inner circle. But I blame Julian Holland for that, though for nothing else. Julian, along with Bernard Levin, was a kind of guru of mine and a much-valued friend, a forthright, outspoken man who took no crap from anyone and who, when those he cared about fell from what he regarded as their highest standards, was quick to tell them so.

There were several occasions when I would arrive in the office preening myself on the fact that a number of people had already congratulated me on the piece I had written the previous day to find Julian reading it at his desk. His eyesight was very poor and he wore glasses like the bottoms of milk bottles. So he would hold the paper close to his nose and from behind it there would issue from time to time snorts of disapproval. Finally, he would cast the *Mail* aside and glare at me as I sat opposite him. 'That was a load of rubbish, wasn't it?' he would say.

'Not a decent quote in it. You just wrote yourself out of trouble.' And the galling thing is that he was always right.

I was not entirely surprised when he fell out of favour with the editor and took me with him, for it was not just his friends he was given to castigate. Many times he would read something in the paper, or a memo, perhaps, from on high, give a grunt of rage, leap from his desk and charge out, one shoulder hunched belligerently in what I always thought of as his Richard III stance. The rest of us would watch him go, shake our heads and murmur, 'He's off to give Arthur a hard time again.' And so it usually proved to be.

Bernard Levin who, in his day, was probably the most feared theatre critic in the land, gave up that job and became a daily columnist instead, delivering outspoken views on any subject from the appalling state of the government (it didn't matter which) to the magnificence of Wagner. In either capacity, critic or commentator, he was quite the most celebrated writer on the paper. He was also for a time possibly the most misunderstood man in the country.

In the early 1960s he was one of the star turns on *That Was The Week That Was*, BBC television's controversial satirical show, created by Ned Sherrin and fronted by David Frost. On it Bernard would interview someone in the news in a manner which, depending on your point of view, could be regarded as uncompromising or downright rude. The television audience, always suspicious of anyone as obviously clever as Bernard, decided he was rude and as a result he became the man people loved to hate. But this perception of him as an intellectual bully could hardly have been wider of the mark: he is, in fact, one of the kindest men I have ever met.

One day, when Samantha and Emma were about six and five, Diana and I were taking them to Trafalgar Square to feed the pigeons, said pigeons being a tourist attraction which had not yet, of course, aroused the ire of Mayor Ken Livingstone. En route, the family coming with me, I called into the *Mail* to collect some documents and make a couple of phone calls. Diana meanwhile chatted to Julian. When I had finished what I had to do the girls had vanished.

We found them a couple of minutes later in Bernard's office, sitting on his knees as he tried to teach them to type, a task which he regarded as more important than writing his column.

A couple of days later he came into my own office as I was preparing to leave for a lunch date. 'Have your girls read the Dr Seuss books?' he asked. I said they hadn't, largely because neither Diana nor I had then heard of them. 'Oh, but they must,' said Bernard, godfather to many a child. 'Go out and buy them at once.'

I protested that I couldn't, not that day, because I had to interview someone and I was already late. He muttered something uncomplimentary and went away.

When I came back from lunch there on my desk was a copy of every Dr Seuss book in print. Bernard had spent his own lunch hour going across London to Hatchards to buy them as a present for the girls.

On another occasion Diana and I were invited to Stratford-upon-Avon, to the Royal Shakespeare Theatre to see Peter Brooks's production of A *Midsummer Night's Dream* (still, incidentally, the most memorable show I have ever seen anywhere, either on stage or on screen). Bernard had a couple of tickets, too, and was taking his girlfriend of the time. But he couldn't drive and she had only a small and rather uncomfortable car.

So it was arranged that the pair of them should come to our house, which was roughly on the way, and transfer to our bigger, family car. Bernard and girlfriend would be in our house only long enough to drink a cup of coffee but even so he brought, as a gift for Mamfie and Em, an enormous box of paints. And though he rather spoilt the effect by encouraging the girls to decorate the white walls of our sitting room with murals of their own devising, it was a remarkably generous thing to do.

Diana drove us to Stratford and back. She always drives on the grounds that she is a nervous passenger and doesn't like speed. (The first part of this statement is true, the second is nonsense: she is, in fact, the fastest driver I know.) It was a long day, made longer by the fact that we came home by way of Oxford where we stopped for supper. By then it was late and all of us, Diana included, were very tired.

'Talk to me,' Diana said, 'or I'll fall asleep at the wheel.'

So Bernard, who was never averse to talking but that night was no less sleepy than the rest of us, kept her awake all the way home by telling her the entire story of Wagner's Ring cycle.

His inability to drive stemmed, it seemed to me, from an aversion to and total lack of understanding of machinery of any kind except a typewriter. Anyway, he said, he had no need to drive since he lived in the West End of London, regarded Regent's Park as the deepest countryside, and was inclined to yell 'Taxi!' automatically whenever he stepped into the street. But sometimes his inability to handle a car embarrassed him.

Once, when he and a different girlfriend were on the way to Glyndebourne, both in evening dress, she driving of course, he developed the paranoid idea that other drivers were looking at them and sneering – either at him, the non-driving wimp, or at her, the unemancipated chauffeuse. This troubled him but he couldn't think what to do about it until, as they passed through some small town, he spotted an old-fashioned draper's shop and asked his girlfriend to pull over. She did so, wondering what he could possibly want in a shop like that. When he emerged, the answer was clear for now he had one arm in a white sling, which he pointedly showed off to drivers of other cars whenever they had to stop for a traffic light.

Bernard left the *Mail* after the General Election of 1970. In his contract he had a clause that nothing in his column could be changed without his permission. At first as the election approached this didn't seem to present a problem. What Bernard proposed to do in the week before polling day, he told Vere Harmsworth (the future Lord Rothermere) and Arthur Brittenden, was to examine each day one of the important issues facing the electorate. Then at the end of the week he would tell his readers which way he thought they should vote.

Fine. Great idea, said Vere and Arthur. Go ahead. So he did. It was a finely balanced election between Harold Wilson's Labour Government and the Tory Opposition, led by Edward Heath. The *Mail*, naturally, favoured Heath and was not slow to say so in its editorials. Meanwhile, Bernard was casting an impartial eye over those matters which he believed should most occupy the thoughts of the electorate. Which way would he jump? The *Mail* was confident that he would follow the paper's own line. But then he wrote his final column and showed it to the editor and to Arthur's horror he was strongly urging the *Mail's* true blue readers to vote Labour. Brittenden immediately called Vere and they summoned Bernard and tried to persuade him to change his mind. He refused, so they sent him away while they discussed tactics together. Then they summoned him back and tried again and when he still refused to back down sent him away once more.

I became aware of this about 8 p.m. when, having finished the piece I was writing, I was on my way home. I thought I was the only one left on that floor and was surprised to find Bernard still in his office. I asked what he was doing there at this hour and he told me.

'Do you want me to stay with you?' I asked. 'Moral support and all that?'

'Please,' he said.

The first moral support I could think of was a few cans of beer from the Mucky Duck, so I nipped down to get them while he went back for the third or fourth time to argue with Arthur and Vere. I can't remember how many times he made the trip up and down the stairs to the second floor but eventually, about ten-thirty, stalemate was reached. Bernard refused to change his column and, contractually, Arthur and Vere knew they could not make him do so.

He took a taxi home and dropped me off at King's Cross Station. On the way he said, 'I'm going to resign.' I urged him to do nothing that night or even the next day, to think hard about it. He said, 'I really can't see that I have any alternative.' What surprised me particularly was that he seemed genuinely worried that this would be the end of his career.

I told him this was nonsense, that as soon as he left the *Mail* he would be snapped up, but that night he was not to be persuaded. In the event, of course, I was right. He duly resigned and was inundated with offers from other papers. Eventually it came down to a choice between the *Guardian*, for which he had written before, and *The Times* and he chose *The Times* because, he said, on the *Guardian* he would be writing for people who shared his left-of-centre views whereas on the traditionally right-of-centre *Times* he would be preaching to the so far unconverted.

Ironically, it turned out that the one who was converted was Bernard because over the years he moved increasingly to the right, even to the extent of praising Margaret Thatcher, one of the few things for which I found it hard to forgive him. Even so, and whether or not I agreed with his political views – which I did less and less often – he proved himself on *The Times* to be the outstanding commentator of his day and his column was always a joy to read. He was also as staunch a friend as anyone could want.

The thirteen years I spent on the *Mail* were happy ones for the most part. There is something invigorating about working in a newspaper office, not least because there is always an undercurrent of fear. Nobody ever actually tells you so but you know that you are only as good as your last story, or maybe your last two or three stories, and if they were not up to much you could find yourself out on the street looking for a job. Such knowledge concentrates the mind wonderfully.

But to this uncertainty as to one's future, which we all accepted as going with the territory, the *Mail* added a subtle twist of its own. I only became aware of it in my last few years when I was regularly writing feature articles and it worked like this: for several weeks, maybe three months, whatever I wrote went into the paper and was greeted with compliments all round (except maybe from Julian). My confidence rose and I knew I was writing well. Then, one day, my piece wasn't used. Nor was the next one, or the one after that, or anything I wrote for the next several weeks, until my confidence was shattered and depression set in, at which point I would find myself returned to favour as suddenly as I had fallen out of it. Until, that is, the pattern repeated itself.

I wasn't alone in this experience: it seemed to happen to everybody at one time or another, except perhaps Bernard and Vincent Mulchrone, the paper's most-valued contributors. What was the explanation? Well, there was none. I would ask for one, obviously, only to receive some such vague reply as, 'Well, space is tight at the moment'

or 'Not quite up to your usual standard', both of which were perfectly
valid except that if my work had not been up to its usual standard for
weeks on end I would have been fired. No question. The *Mail* then, as
no doubt now, was hardly a philanthropic organization or a rest home
for hacks who couldn't quite hack it any more.

In my more paranoid moments I did wonder whether this business
of keeping people on the wrong foot was some kind of official policy
but I came to the conclusion that it wasn't. I'm sure it wasn't written
anywhere or even discussed among the executives. Indeed, if I had
mentioned it to any of them I would have been met with incompre-
hension. Maybe it was just something in the air, part of the ethos of
the *Daily Mail*, an instinctive belief that an uncertain staff, a worried
and slightly frightened staff, was by definition a good staff that would
try harder. Even the executives themselves were not immune.
Periodically, Gordon McKenzie, an unexpectedly sensitive man,
would decide – possibly on account of pressure from above – that it
was time he had a mild nervous breakdown and retire to his bed for a
week, before returning refreshed and either rescue me from limbo or
cast me into it again.

Nevertheless, these were good days to be in Fleet Street. True, the
hours could be long and erratic but no day was ever exactly like the one
that preceded it or the one that followed. We would drift into the office
at about 10.30 a.m., hoping that we might get away by seven or seven-
thirty but also knowing that it could be two or three days before we saw
home again. Not to have your passport with you at all times was a sack-
able offence. Once I turned up at my usual time looking forward to a
quiet day only to be told that I was booked on the next plane out of
Heathrow bound for somewhere in Italy, precisely where I cannot now
recall. A well known British actress was reported to be wherever it was
for a romantic tryst with an Italian actor with whom she was allegedly
in love.

Yes, but where exactly? 'How should we know?' said the news desk.
'Find out when you get there. Go – now!'

I arrived in Italy with only a few pounds in my pocket, just enough
to pay for a cab from the airport to the hotel in which the office had

booked me a room. Well, no worries – the *Mail* was wiring money for me to a bank in the town.

Unfortunately, it turned out to be a bank holiday in Italy so there I was, penniless, with no access to the funds awaiting me and, in those pre-credit card days, no chance of persuading the hotel to advance me a few thousand lire. Even if my quarry had been in the vicinity – and I swiftly established that she wasn't – I'd have had no more chance of confronting her than if I'd still been in the office. I was stuck with nothing to do in a pleasant but dull hotel on a glorious day in an area, wherever it was, that looked interesting and I was too broke even to go out for a cup of coffee.

Other days, in London, were better – a lengthy lunchtime interview with a star or a director, a cocktail party and later a new production to watch at the National Theatre or, perhaps, Eartha Kitt to review in cabaret and then to talk to afterwards in her dressing room. The hours were long, yes, but they were flexible. Nobody cared how you filled your day so long as you provided the necessary copy at the end of it.

Quiet days, and they did happen sometimes, would involve a few phone calls in the morning, a thirst-quenching trip to the Mucky Duck, followed by a three-hour lunch with friends, a few more phone calls, a bit of obligatory writing and then an hour or so downstairs in the Mucky Duck again just to unwind.

It's very different now. For a start there is no Fleet Street any more, not as I knew it. In my day it was the heart of journalism, the most exciting street in the world. Now the newspapers are scattered all over London and the life of the journalist is altogether more sober. Alcohol and tobacco, the two essential crutches on which my contemporaries leaned, are frowned upon, if not totally forbidden, in newspaper offices today. The modern journalist, it seems to me, doesn't smoke (which is probably wise), drinks little (ditto) and spends his lunch hour at his desk with a sandwich and a bottle of Perrier or, if he is totally abandoned to high living, a diet Coke. He may be, and probably is, good at his job but I don't think he has as much fun as we did.

A few years ago at the Cannes Film Festival I bumped into my friend Victor Davis, once an excellent show business writer for both the

Express and the *Mail* and now a successful novelist. He looked shaken and I told him so.

'Well, I am shaken,' he said. 'I've just come from the publicity office in the Majestic Hotel and on the way out I passed a couple of young English journalists and, you won't believe this, one of them said, "Have you had a workout yet?" and the other one said, "No, but I've got the address of a very good gym just up the road." I mean, can you believe that? "Have you had a workout yet?" Christ, in our day it would have been, "Have you got laid yet?"'

Well, *ultra tempes, ultra mores* and in this more sober, more health-conscious and more politically correct era the behaviour of the people with whom I worked and whose company I enjoyed so much would no longer be tolerated. Not that I'm suggesting that ours was a Golden Age in Fleet Street, because it wasn't. It was so male dominated that women executives were almost non-existent. Now there are women editors, of daily papers as well as magazines. In my time, too, I can remember only one Asian on a national paper and no black journalists at all. Now there are if not many at least several, so some things have improved, though not everything.

In the 1960s the popular press, even the tabloids, believed that what its readers wanted to know was what was actually going on in the world. Political, economic and industrial news was the stuff of front page stories. If people wanted show biz trivia they would buy some such magazine as *Weekend* or *Titbits*. Today, when the banner headlines in the popular dailies are as likely as not to concern the activities of some third-rate actor in a TV soap, *Weekend* and *Titbits* would probably be regarded as serious newspapers.

So life was good at the *Mail* except that . . . Well, except that I knew I had gone as far as I could, or indeed wanted to, go there. By the beginning of 1971 I was merely treading water. Because this was a time when individuals in any industry were always in danger of the sack but large-scale redundancies were rare, I believed that I could probably stay at the paper pretty much as long as I wanted to. The question was: did I want to stay? I had in mind a dictum by the late Lord Beaverbrook (a dictum I now know to be nonsense) that if a man had not made his mark by the age of thirty he never would and it bothered me.

I was thirty-seven, a well-known (to *Daily Mail* readers) journalist and the author of two novels. But I couldn't claim to have made my mark in the world. What I should do, I realized, was escape the rut I was in and start again before it was too late. But I had responsibilities, a family to support. And while I was mulling over these things and wondering whether maybe, just maybe, I should take the chance and launch myself into the precarious and unknown world of freelance writing there came the Night of the Long Envelopes when all options were taken from me and my life was changed for ever.

Chapter Sixteen

EVEN THOUGH I had been prepared to volunteer for it, redundancy was a blow. The letters in our Long Envelopes explained that we were being ejected purely for economic reasons and there was no reflection on our undoubted abilities. Yeah, right. So why had we been singled out and not some other bugger? Redundancy is insulting. If you resign and your resignation is accepted your employers are saying, 'We think we can get along without you'. But if you're made redundant what they are saying is, 'We think we can get along *better* without you'. It hurts.

The effect, in my case, was to plunge me into a state of apathy. The *Mail* had, in fact, been very considerate, giving us one month's notice in addition to our redundancy pay and making it clear that during that month we would be expected to do the minimum of work for the paper and to use our time and the office facilities to find other jobs for ourselves. So did I do that? Not really. What I did was to hurl myself into bouts of pointless gardening, which is to say that I would dig a hole here and put the earth there and then do exactly the same thing somewhere else. Even I was astonished at this activity because gardening is something I have always hated. Nobody has ever thought of more ingenious excuses not to do it than I have. But now I gardened as if it were my profession and when I wasn't doing that I played endless games of Pelmanism with the girls, both of whom beat me soundly.

This intellectual lethargy, a refusal even to contemplate the future, was brought on by fear and desperation. I simply had no idea what I was going to do, how I was going to find the money to sustain a wife, a mortgage, two daughters, two dogs, two cats and two guinea pigs. Diana was wonderfully supportive. I knew she was deeply worried but never did she urge me to snap out of it, pull myself together and get out there and find work. Wisely, she left me to sort myself out in my own time, although since we'd never faced a crisis like this before she cannot have been at all sure that I was even capable of sorting myself out. In the meantime she decided that household economies must be made so she took the girls, then aged eight and seven, to one side, explained that I had lost my job and money would be a bit scarce, and told them they must use less lavatory paper in future. Now it was true that our daughters, hygienic little girls, were prodigal in their use of bog paper but it wasn't necessarily the first economy that would have sprung to my mind. Still, it was a start.

During this last dead month at the *Mail* I had one piece of luck. On the Monday after the Night of the Long Envelopes John Higgins, the Arts Editor of *The Times*, whom I knew from many evenings of reviewing plays together, took me to lunch and asked me to write one television review a week for his paper. For this he would pay me £15. We both knew it wasn't much but it was the best he could do and, at that stage, more than anyone else offered. If at that time any other paper had suggested taking me on, in whatever capacity, I would have accepted but no paper did and though I am now glad of that the general lack of interest in me only added to my sense of worthlessness and failure.

The one positive move I made was to arrange an appointment with John Anstey, the editor of the *Weekend Telegraph*, in the hope that he might let me write features for him. I turned up a few minutes early and waited in his secretary's office where, through the partition wall, I could hear Anstey chatting congenially with a woman, presumably one of his contributors. The time of my appointment came and passed and another fifteen minutes went by. The secretary apologized for the fact that I was being kept waiting and I nodded and sat there for a further fifteen minutes while the sounds of conversation and laughter continued on the other side of the partition wall. And at that point I stood up and said I really couldn't wait any longer. The secretary looked startled and said it would be difficult to make another appointment with Mr Anstey. I said I didn't want another appointment and went away in a sulk. I don't now blame John for keeping me waiting; there was no snub, slight or malice involved. As I discovered a few years later when I did write for his magazine he was not a man to do things by the clock. But at the time it seemed like another pointed rejection, another reason to believe that I was redundant not just at the *Mail* but everywhere.

And what added to my despair was the fear that family history might repeat itself. Soon after I came back from South Africa Dad drove me to London to buy me my first meal in a Chinese restaurant. On the way he had to stop in Piccadilly to see his then agent, John Redway, who had an office near the Athenaeum. What I remember first about this outing was that having arrived in Piccadilly Dad simply pulled over to the side of the road and parked there. All perfectly legal, no meters, no wardens, no parking restrictions, nothing. Just try doing that at lunchtime in Piccadilly nowadays. But the second thing I remember is that after Dad and Redway had finished discussing their business – the availability of an actress whom the agent represented and whom Dad wanted for a forthcoming film – Redway asked whether Dad was happy at Ealing Studios. He said he was. Redway said, 'What are you earning there now, Les? About £5,000 a year?' Dad said, yes, give or take and it was good money in the mid-1950s.

'The reason I ask,' Redway said, 'is that I could get you films to direct in Hollywood at £10,000 a time, no problem. Think about it.'

Dad said he would and when we left I said, excitedly, 'You're going to take him up on that, aren't you, Dad?' He said again that he was happy at Ealing but yes, he would think carefully about Redway's suggestion. He didn't though. Ealing and Sir Michael Balcon had given him the opportunity to become a producer and soon a director and he felt both affection and loyalty towards them. And that loyalty continued when, a few years later, Balcon sold the studios and made a deal with MGM, which in future would produce and distribute films made

under the Ealing banner. As part of the deal Balcon moved his operation to the MGM studios at Borehamwood – and Dad went with him.
During that period he made *Dunkirk* and *The Shiralee* (which its star,
Peter Finch, always said was his favourite film). Dad was justifiably
proud of both of them but he, like everyone else, must have known that
the glory days at Ealing were over, that this was when he should have
gone back to John Redway and asked him to deliver what he had promised. It was an opportunity missed. By the end of the 1950s Ealing
Studios had folded, Balcon had become an independent producer and
Dad was unemployed.

He did go on to make more films, notably *The Summer of the
Seventeenth Doll*, for Burt Lancaster's company, and in conjunction
with Balcon *The Long and the Short and the Tall*. But this was a bad
time for the British film industry and in particular its established figures. New, younger – and cheaper – directors were coming along and
there were not so many opportunities for the Ealing survivors. Dad
could have made commercials and worked in television while he
looked for a film to direct but he refused to do that, seeing both options
as retrograde steps. Nor would his pride allow him to go around looking for work. We, his family, urged him to go up to town and frequent
the clubs and restaurants where the movers and shakers of the film
industry hung out. Out of sight is out of mind; the way to remind
people you are still around, we said, is to be in their faces. But he
wouldn't do that. His self-confidence, always a delicate plant, had gone
and with it went his film career. He was only fifty when he made his last
movie, *Mix Me a Person*, and should have had many creative years
ahead of him. He knew that and as time went by I think he also knew
that he had blown it, that he should have swallowed his pride and
done the commercials and the television work while he fought his way
back into films, the only medium that really interested him.

All this became relevant to my own situation as I neared the end of
my month of gloom, gardening and Pelmanism because now an offer,
the more humble journalistic equivalent perhaps of the television offers
that Dad had scorned, came my way. Someone I had worked with on
the *Mail* a few years earlier asked if I would write short articles and

interviews for the Central Office of Information, a government publicity outfit that would syndicate my pieces around the country. The
money was poor, the kind of stuff they requested held no interest for me
and at first I felt insulted and, like Dad, was inclined to refuse. But what
was I to do? Nobody else wanted me. So I accepted and as, for the last
time, I left the *Mail* office one Friday night I could look forward to a
future in which I would earn £15 a week from *The Times* and, if I was
lucky, £7.50 from the Central Office of Information. And that was it. In
my last year at the *Mail* my annual income had for the first time
reached £5,000; now I would be doing well to make one-fifth of that.
Matters, however, were not totally desperate; the redundancy money, if
carefully handled, meant that I could struggle along for about a year.
But after that unless things took a distinct turn for the better I would
have to think about selling my house and moving the family into something much smaller.

On the Monday morning after the umbilical cord with the *Mail* had
been finally cut I wrote a short gossip item, which a friend on the
Daily Mirror had commissioned, and then realized that apart from
one television review I had nothing whatsoever to do for the rest of the
week. And what's more, the way things were shaping up every week
would be pretty much like that. It was a scary prospect but somehow it
jerked me, at last, out of my apathy. I had two options: I could either
wait, as Dad had done, for the world to beat a path to my door or I
could go out and beat on other people's doors. They say that nobody
learns from someone else's mistakes; that you have to make your own,
even if they are the same mistakes, before you can learn anything. I
decided that this was not true, that I would learn from Dad's experience, that I would not wait for an uncaring world to seek me out. So I
went and banged on executive doors all round Fleet Street, plying
people with ideas, and slowly this approach began to work. The odd
commission trickled in and as a result of one of these I made a decision
that turned out to be rather momentous.

A fellow redundee (if there is such a word) who had landed rather a
good job on the *Evening Standard* had asked me to write a long feature
about Surbiton, because . . . well, frankly I can't remember. I've just

reread the piece and although I think it's rather good I cannot at this distance in time imagine why anyone should have wanted it in the first place. However, I wrote it and handed it in and as I was leaving the office I bumped into a reporter who had also been made redundant by the *Mail* and who had been doing a bit of menial work for the *Standard*. He suggested we go and have a drink and though I didn't know him very well I agreed on the principle that redundees should stick together.

In the pub downstairs he asked how I was doing. Oh, wonderfully, I lied, how about you? 'It's awful,' he said, 'I can hardly get any work at all.'

I took a long look at him. Reading from head to toe, his hair needed a cut, his shirt collar was frayed, his tie was grubby, his jacket was crumpled, his trousers were baggy and devoid of creases and his shoes were dirty and I thought, though I didn't say: no wonder nobody wants to employ you; I wouldn't employ you – you look like a loser. And at that moment I conceived a cunning plan.

I invested some of my redundancy money in a couple of good suits, shirts and ties, gave my shoes a polish and, attired in all this finery, I did what we had advised Dad to do – I hung out where the Fleet Street movers and shakers went, in other words El Vino. I would go there once or twice a week, arrive early, grab a table in a prominent position, order a glass of wine and, looking affluent and at ease, have a stab at *The Times* crossword puzzle. When the hirers and firers, most of whom I knew if only slightly, came in I would greet them casually and, if they paused to chat, offer them a drink. Mostly they refused, suspecting a trap, fearful that if they sat down I would buttonhole them and plead tearfully for work. But for me this was a game of chess and I had planned several moves ahead. I would accept their refusals as casually as I had greeted them and carry on with the crossword puzzle.

After a while they would get used to seeing me there and relax. 'So, er, what are you up to these days?' they would ask cautiously and I would shrug and say, 'Oh, you know – reviewing for *The Times*, of course, writing another novel.' Actually I wasn't writing a novel at all but since I'd already published two it was a plausible lie. So because I was apparently doing well and looked affluent they lost any fear of my importuning them and began to invite me to join them at their tables.

What I was trying to pull off here, you understand, was a confidence trick. Doing well? Of course, I wasn't – a few bits here and other bits there maybe but essentially I was a loser masquerading as a winner. Whenever I joined a group at another table I was always careful to stand my round but I felt a sharp pain in the wallet every time I had to fork out for another bottle of wine because unlike the people I was drinking with I couldn't claim the money back on expenses. Indeed, one of the two things I had missed most sharply since leaving the *Mail* were the exes; the other was Fleet Street shoptalk. There was nothing I could do about the former but the latter was to be found at its most fascinating in El Vino. As I was to discover later, radio and television shoptalk are all about radio and television but Fleet Street shoptalk was something else again, for much of it involved scurrilous stories (many of them true but, alas, unprintable) about the sexual and even criminal activities of some of the best-known people in the world. Fleet Street shoptalk was the best and for lack of it I was suffering withdrawal symptoms. So I would sit and listen, relish the gossip and enjoy the feeling of belonging again – but never would I ask a favour of anybody. And because of that the hirers and firers began to proposition me, saying things like, 'Look, I know you're awfully busy but could you manage to do something for us?'

'Well,' I would say doubtfully, 'I suppose so. You don't want anything too soon, do you?'

'No, no. Could you perhaps do us a thousand words on so-and-so by, let's say, noon next Thursday?'

And I would appear to think about it and say, 'Yes, I expect so.'

When, soon afterwards, we went our separate ways I would immediately start work on the thousand words on so-and-so because I had hardly anything else to do between then and noon next Thursday.

One important lesson I swiftly learned in those first precarious months of freelancing and it's as true now as it was then, thirty years ago: at any given time, in any given medium, there is precious little real talent to be found anywhere. I had always been nervous of freelancing

because I didn't think I could compete with the successful practitioners. But now I discovered that I could and that it was actually quite easy.
I would deliver my thousand words well before noon on Thursday and
immediately there were two strikes in my favour – first, I had easily met
the deadline (and freelances were notorious for not doing that) and,
secondly, I had written exactly to length and freelances were notorious
for not doing that either. When, in addition, the commissioning editor
discovered that what he had been given was really quite well written his
joy knew no bounds. There were, of course, other freelances who could
match and in some cases better that but not, I soon discovered, very
many. A lot of people in newspapers, as in radio and television, can talk
the talk but precious few can walk the walk as well.

These things being so, more work came my way. John Higgins asked
me to do occasional show business interviews as well as my weekly TV
review for *The Times*; women's magazines such as *Cosmopolitan* invited
me to contribute think pieces. Gradually some kind of career structure,
or anyway work pattern, began to evolve.

One way and another then, thanks to my El Vino con trick, things
were already looking up when I received a phone call from Bernard
Levin, by that time well-established at *The Times*. 'If I were you,' he
said, 'I'd give Alastair Hetherington a ring.'

'Yeah?' I said doubtfully, Hetherington being the editor of the
Guardian and a man I had never met. 'Why?'

'He says he wants to see you because, well, I never told you this but
when you were made redundant I wrote to him and said that if he was
thinking of recruiting anybody from the *Mail* you were probably the
best bet because you were least likely to be drunk all the time, throw up
over the carpet or try to rape the managing director's wife.'

'Gee, thanks, Bernard,' I said, touched by this glowing encomium,
on the strength of which I contacted Alastair Hetherington. At his suggestion I went to his office at half-past ten one night, quite the latest
time in the day that I have ever been interviewed for a job. We did not
get off to a good start. For one thing he had clearly never heard of me
before Bernard's letter and that was a blow to the ego, considering all
those big bylines and pictures in the paper that I had enjoyed at the

Mail. And for another thing he thought I was a leader writer and I thought I wasn't. But a holiday relief leader writer was what he was looking for. Alastair had maybe half a dozen leader writers on his staff but it was summer time and, one by one, they were taking their holidays and he needed someone to fill in. So he was interviewing me for the job. I cannot think of any other reputable newspaper in the world that would, in effect, happily drag a total stranger in off the street to write its opinions for it. But that's what Alastair was doing. Only at the *Guardian* – and maybe only in those days, not now, at the *Guardian* . . .

As it happened I had written two or three light-hearted leaders during my final months at the *Mail* but these were think pieces uninformed by political or socio-economic knowledge and I had no particular desire to write any more. Actually, I kept telling him, I'm a show business specialist and what I'd really like to do, really, really like to do, is write film and theatre interviews for you. He wouldn't listen. Could you, he asked, write leaders about the political situation in the USA? No, I couldn't. Well, what about China? No, not that either. Er, the Soviet Union then? Nope. Right, well, ah, the economy here in Britain? No way, forget it.

We had reached an impasse, each of us no doubt wondering why we had wasted our time on this meeting, when apparently out of desperation he said, 'How about people? Do you think you could write leaders about people?' And I thought, well, some of my best friends are people, so I said, yes, I probably could. He seemed relieved. 'Go away and think about it,' he said, 'and come back next Thursday afternoon and tell me what you've decided.'

For the next week I read *Guardian* leaders until the information and opinions in them were coming out of my ears and the more I read the more I realized that I couldn't possibly write this erudite stuff. But on the Thursday afternoon I dutifully presented myself in the editor's office intent on confessing that I was unequal to the task he wanted of me and on making one more plea for consideration as a show business writer. As I walked into the anteroom Alastair's secretary said, 'Mr Hetherington is expecting you. Please go in.'

I went in and, to my horror, found myself in the middle of the

Guardian leader writers' conference. Alastair greeted me amiably. 'Do sit down,' he said. 'We'll come to you in a minute.' He didn't introduce me. The others present, senior executives as well as leader writers, simply stared at me in bafflement. They hadn't been warned that I was coming and they had no idea who I was or what I was doing there. Come to that, neither had I. Well, I knew who I was but that was about the limit of my knowledge.

One by one the leader writers, the real leader writers, went through their suggestions. A ticklish military situation on the Sino-Russian border? Grave nodding of heads and yes, yes, we ought to say something about that. The serious economic plight of Bulgaria (or somewhere similar)? Oh, yes, certainly. The implications of the impending American presidential election? Absolutely vital, no question. Israel, the Palestinians, the Middle East generally? Quite so, mustn't pass without comment. And so it went on until Alastair turned to me with an encouraging smile and said, 'Well, what do you think?'

At that moment I thought nothing; my mind was empty. What I wanted most urgently to say was, 'Please, may I go home now?' because I was out of my depth and knew it. But even in such a moment of panic that seemed altogether too wimpish and I started racking my brain trying to remember a story, any story, I had read somewhere that might be worthy of editorial comment and under Alastair's friendly smile and the puzzled frowns of the others I heard myself saying, 'Well, there's this woman in Sicily, who, like, put her husband in a chastity belt on account of he was always playing away from home and I thought, well, like, you know we could say something about well, you know, Women's Lib and like that and, you know, sort of . . .' I was horrified; I couldn't believe I was burbling on about such trivia and neither, clearly, could the real leader writers. But Alastair, to my eternal gratitude, smiled even more broadly and said, 'That sounds rather fun. Go away and write it.'

So I did and it was rather fun and he liked it and said, 'Can you come back tomorrow and do the same sort of thing all over again?' Well, of course, I could and I did and continued to do so, three times a week, for several months.

In the meantime I had a call from Wally Fawkes (the cartoonist Trog) suggesting that we meet for lunch. In our time together on the *Mail* he and Julian and I had often enjoyed three hour lunches together and I had missed these festive occasions. 'Great,' I said. 'High time we went out to play again.'

'No, no,' said Wally gravely. 'We must meet as grown-up business-men. I have a proposal for you.'

As grown-up businessmen, a role to which neither of us was remotely suited, we naturally agreed to meet at El Vino where, in com-pany with Keith McKenzie, who oversaw the artwork in the *Mail* – cartoons, comic strips and the like – we delayed serious discussion while we drank some wine. After that we went across the road for an Italian lunch and more wine and at some point during this bibulous meal Wally mentioned his proposal. He was the originator of Flook which, along with Andy Capp in the *Mirror*, was probably the best-known strip cartoon in British newspapers. Flook was a small, furry, mythical creature from whose point of view the strip cast a satirical eye over the social scene every day in the *Mail*. A long time ago Sir Compton McKenzie had written the story lines and the bubbles but for nearly a quarter of a century Wally's collaborator had been the jazz singer George Melly. Now, however, George had decided it was time to stop and Wally's idea was that I should replace him. I knew that (a) Flook was very dear to Wally's heart and that (b) George would be an extremely hard act to follow, so it was a huge compliment to be asked, especially as I was not at all sure that I could do it.

Therefore, despite the euphoria induced by the wine, I did not immediately agree. I said I would think about it and over the next week I concocted the outline for Flook's next adventure. Each story ran for about three or four weeks and needed a beginning, a middle and an end, preferably an end that would lead logically into the next story. This was not as easy as it might seem but, fortunately, I came up with a scenario that met with Wally's approval and so we two unlikely busi-nessmen went into business. Quite apart from the fact that Wally was one of my favourite people, what made this particularly gratifying was that having been kicked out of the front door by the *Mail* I was now sneaking in to Northcliffe House again through the back and I felt vaguely triumphant, or at least vindicated. Now I thank the *Mail* every day for making me redundant but at that time I was obsessed with a need to prove to the people who had so casually discarded me that they had been wrong.

(Incidentally, I learned later, when I had been writing Flook for some time David English, now the editor of the *Mail*, tried to persuade Wally to drop me in favour of the ultra-Conservative Auberon Waugh. Since one of Flook's strengths was that it gave an alternative view to that offered by the rest of the paper Wally's sardonic response had been, 'What – a right-wing satire in a right-wing newspaper? That'll be fun, won't it?' and the idea was dropped. But at least it shows that English had been a little economical with the truth when he told Peter Black how hard he had tried to keep me on.)

During George's tenure Flook had taken a wickedly sharp look at the nation's social pretensions but I was not nearly as knowledgeable about such things. Politics was my interest and, happily, Wally's too, so now Flook became more of a political satire viewed from as far to the left as we thought we could get away with on a paper like the *Mail*. For example, this was the time when Richard Milhous Nixon was president of the USA and the Watergate scandal was looming up and one of the Flook stories was set in the old Wild West and featured Millstone Dixon, who as marshal of Dodgy City was even shabbier than Nixon himself.

The way Wally and I collaborated was like this: a storyline having been agreed I would go away and write six episodes for the following week. These I would submit on Friday afternoon when we met in Keith McKenzie's office. Wally would read my script carefully, then suggest alterations, which I would fiercely reject before falling into a sulk. There would then be a lengthy silence while I glowered and Wally looked faintly concerned before Keith, the referee, said, 'Now, come on, chaps, we can sort this out.' Wally and I would ignore him. More silence. Then Wally would proffer other alternatives to my ideas. These, too, I would reject whereupon Wally would fall into a sulk. Now we were both glowering, not at each other but at our shoes. Keith would then offer tea all round, saying desperately, 'Surely we can find a compromise. Can't we? Time's getting on.'

Thus reminded that El Vino would soon be open for business Wally and I would swallow our pride, begin talking to each other again and finally reach the desired compromise. The sulks were childish, no doubt, but we forgave each other because what they proved was that we both cared deeply about the end product. When eventually all was resolved, this week's script and the outline for next week's having been settled, Wally would say, 'Let's take the pretty way home.'

This meant making our way to El Vino, which wasn't really very far from New Carmelite Street where Northcliffe House was, but taking the pretty way home made it quite a long journey, because it entailed calling en route into several pubs where congenial company might be found.

Looking back over my years in Fleet Street, I realize that drink seems to have played a significant, maybe too significant, part in the lives of myself and most of my contemporaries. And yet I can only think of one person I knew who was fired for drunkenness. He had been to a highly convivial lunch, lurched into the screening of the film he was to review and promptly fell asleep under the observant eye of the movie's PR man. No doubt sleep is also a form of criticism, though drunken sleep is probably less so. The way to cope with drunken sleep, particularly if you haven't seen a single frame of the film in question, is to read the production notes and then write a careful review on the favourable side of neutral. On this occasion, however, the sleeper, possibly waking in an irascible mood, slagged the movie off. Big mistake. Huge. Because the PR man and his assistant, who had noted every snore, complained to the critic's editor. It was a fair cop, everyone could see that and there could only be one result.

Certainly we did drink a lot. Alcohol and nicotine were our drugs of choice, though marijuana was not unknown in Fleet Street. We were heavy drinkers, yes, but mostly we were social drinkers rather than alcoholics and anyway drinking too much was a noble Fleet Street tradition.

Towards the end of his life, and thanks to Diana, his colleague on the *Herald*, I met Hannen Swaffer, who as a writer, critic and executive had been such a legendary figure in Fleet Street that for many years the annual newspaper awards were named after him. One night he invited us both to supper in his flat overlooking Trafalgar Square, a vantage point from which he confidently expected to watch rivers of blood flow down the gutters when the revolution came. On the matter of this forthcoming revolution Swaff was firmly on the side of those causing the rivers of blood so long as the blood was shed by the aristocracy and the Establishment. A sign of the times that anyone lucky enough to find a flat overlooking Trafalgar Square these days would have to be so rich as to be an early target for the revolutionaries.

However, during the evening Swaff told us about a night when, as a senior executive on the *Daily Mail* around 1920, he had been out for a few drinks and had rather overdone it. Returning to the office he realized after a couple of stumbling attempts that he couldn't possibly walk up the stairs so, ever resourceful, he tackled them on his hands and knees instead. He had crawled about halfway up when he met his employer, Lord Northcliffe, walking down. Northcliffe paused and frowned upon him. 'Swaffer,' he said, 'there's too much drinking in this office.'

Swaff gazed earnestly up at him. 'I know,' he said, 'I'm just going up to tell the bastards.'

Fifty years later things hadn't changed a lot. Though only one or two newspapers were actually in Fleet Street, many others were within a short walking distance and during my time it was in the local pubs that, after work, we would meet colleagues from rival publications. Consequently, there was an easy camaraderie among national journalists that can hardly exist today with newspaper offices scattered all over London. Modern practitioners of the journalist's murky trade may well lead healthier lives than we did but I can't help feeling that they are missing something important, because the comradeship and sense of solidarity that we enjoyed far outweighed the occasional hangover.

Chapter Seventeen

M Y STINT AS holiday relief leader writer at the *Guardian* lasted for the best part of four months during which time I even wrote a few serious editorials. For the most part, however, mine was the fourth leader, the light-hearted funny one, and I enjoyed those most. Writing funny is a lot harder than writing serious but it's also much more rewarding.

One day in October, however, I turned up at the office to do my bit and discovered that all the leader writers were back from holiday. Now the place had leader writers like other buildings had mice and when, after the conference, I came out to write my piece there was nowhere for me to sit. Even those leader writers who were not that day called upon to write leaders were not about to give up their chairs to me and in the end Alastair's secretary lent me her desk and typewriter and wandered round the office for an hour or so while I did my stuff.

I was not, therefore, surprised when, having read and approved my contribution to the next day's paper, Alastair began to explain that since all his leader writers were back he could no longer afford to keep me on. He said nice things about the work I had done over the last few months and hoped that in future he could call on me again but in the meantime . . .

I was ready for this. 'Tell you what,' I said, 'instead of doing three leaders why don't I write you a weekly column?' It was a cheeky suggestion but, hey, what did I have to lose? Alastair considered the proposition. 'That's a very good idea,' he said.

Now on any other newspaper I have ever written for if the editor said it was a good idea that I should have a column then I would have had a column and you better believe it. But on the *Guardian* it was different; each head of department was granted autonomy and even the editor could not override that. So . . . 'You'll have to go and talk to Peter Preston,' Alastair said.

Peter Preston, later the editor of the paper himself, was then the features editor and as such the arbiter of who should have a column and who should not. I went in search of him and by sheer luck found him, alone, in the men's room, having a pee and staring thoughtfully, as chaps do, at the porcelain on the wall. I installed myself alongside him, joined him in examining the porcelain and engaged him in conversation.

'I've just been talking to Alastair,' I said and told him about my idea for a column. Well, the opportunity was too good to be missed. I hadn't exactly caught Peter with his pants down but accosting him with his fly unzipped was certainly the next best thing. In such circumstances and at such a disadvantage what could the poor devil do except listen to what I had to say? So he listened and at the end he said, 'Well, that sounds all right. When could you produce your first column?'

'Monday?' I said.

'Okay,' he said and we, as it were, shook on it.

So now I became, as far as I know, the first person ever to write regularly each week under his own byline for both *The Times* and the *Guardian*. All right, I could be wrong; maybe somebody did it before me but if so I don't want to know. I like to cherish the idea that for however brief a time I was unique. And even if I wasn't unique at least I was unusual.

One way and another as 1971, which had begun so badly with redundancy, drew to a close things were really looking up. I was writing for the *Guardian*, I was writing for *The Times*, I was writing for various magazines, I was writing the script for Flook and, against all expectations, the indications were that in the tax year 1971–2 I would earn more money than I had ever earned before.

And at this point I had another encounter in a men's lavatory. Well, some years are like that; some years you can go to the loo as often as necessary and never meet anyone worth talking to. But other years every time you take a leak it's like attending a soirée and 1971 turned out to be one of those years.

As a regular television reviewer for *The Times* I had been invited, along with other TV critics, to a lunch at the Dorchester Hotel where we were addressed by the Postmaster General, Christopher Chataway. At that time the Postmaster General, a political office that doesn't exist any more, kept a stern governmental eye on the doings of television and in an off-the-record speech Chataway was giving us the benefit of his views, whatever they were. Nobody cared much anyway because to most of us Chataway was memorable largely for acting as pacemaker, along with Chris Brasher, when Roger Bannister broke the four-minute mile in 1954.

It was a good lunch and afterwards I made my way to the gents where I found myself alongside my old friend Martin Jackson, then chairman of the TV section of the Critics' Circle. And as we stood there, doing our business, Martin said, 'How do you fancy going on television?'

'What for?'

'Oh, I dunno – twenty-five quid, a few gin and tonics, a couple of sarnies and a car home, I suppose.'

'Sounds all right,' I said. 'What's it about?'

'Well, *Late Night Line-Up* want a dozen critics to talk about television over the last twelve months – you know, the best this and the best that and I thought you might like to talk about the best play of the year.'

'Okay,' I said. 'Count me in.'

We moved away from the stalls and went across to wash our hands. 'By the way, Martin,' I said, 'what *was* the best play of the year?'

He dried his hands carefully. 'No idea,' he said. 'What plays have you seen?'

I mentioned one. 'That'll do,' he said and so it was decided.

Now I had been on television before. Several years earlier, when I was show business reporter for the *Mail*, I had been one of the judges on an amateur talent contest run by Anglia TV in Norwich. It was a one-off appearance during the course of which I unfortunately allowed my attention to wander with the result that suddenly and for no reason at all I came to the conclusion that my opinion had been sought, so I gave it at considerable length, thereby interrupting the *commère* in the middle of her carefully scripted spiel. She was not pleased with me. Nobody was pleased with me and I was not invited back.

But time passes, wounds heal and in the summer of 1971 I had been asked, as a critic for *The Times*, to appear on a programme called *Open Night*, produced by Granada TV in Manchester. On this three different pundits each week, under the chairmanship of Michael Scott, discussed what was going on in television. What made the programme different was that the studio audience, which had been selected by Gallup Poll, was the same every week and they were encouraged to join in the arguments. As a result they were far more accustomed to being on TV, and therefore more relaxed and confident, than any of the pundits.

I had been asked to take part in a discussion of television sports coverage, so for a week I watched every sports programme on the box and duly arrived in Manchester confident that I knew my subject thoroughly. I was, therefore, a touch surprised when the first question the producer put to me on my arrival was, 'Well? What did you think of the film last night?'

'What film?' I asked.

'The BBC film about the presence of British troops in Ireland.'

'Oh, I didn't see that,' I said. 'I was watching *Sportsnight*.'

There was a horrified silence. 'Oh, Christ,' he said, 'didn't anyone tell you? We're not doing sport tonight, we're doing the Irish situation instead, with particular reference to last night's film.'

Well, no, nobody had told me but it was early yet and surely all was not lost. 'Get me a copy of the film,' I said, 'and I'll watch it now.'

'We don't have a copy,' he said, for this was a time before video tape was readily available, 'and what's more we can't get one.'

So what should I do? 'Read the reviews in the newspapers,' he said, 'and busk it.'

This did not turn out too well. My fellow panellists, who had watched the film and made copious notes, came across like experts while every time Michael Scott asked me to contribute the best I could manage was a hopeful shot in the dark. What's more the audience swiftly realized that I had very little idea what I was talking about. 'Rubbish!' someone in the audience would shout after I'd managed a few halting words. From across the studio someone else would say, 'What do you mean, rubbish? He hasn't said anything yet.'

'No, but he always talks rubbish.' And so it went on. It was a nightmare. But at the end of it the apologetic producer promised to make amends by inviting me back, presumably on the grounds that I couldn't possibly be worse than I was that night. Indeed, he did invite me back and though I cannot now remember what the television topic was on that occasion I was in fact worse than I had been the first time.

So I came to the conclusion, without any regret, that television was not a career for me. I had much respect for the people who did it well but I had no desire to join them. On the other hand, I also resolved to accept any offer to appear on both TV and radio, simply for the experience. At that time people were either newspaper, magazine, radio or television journalists – very few worked regularly in all, or even more than one, of those media. But redundancy had offered me an excellent opportunity to find out what I could and could not do. I was no longer pigeon-holed as I had been on the *Mail*; I could write about anything I wanted for anyone who wanted me. For a while in 1971 I wrote and broadcast a weekly newsletter from London for the BBC World Service, not because I particularly wanted to be on radio but to make myself comfortable with the medium. For the same reason I was happy enough to appear on *Late Night Line-Up*, arguing that the more often I was on TV the less likely I was to screw it up as I had on *Open Night*. If I became known as a reliable broadcaster, able to hold his own in general discussion, well, that would be another string to my journalistic bow.

Besides, the *Late Night Line-Up* appearance was less intimidating than anything before because I knew all the other participants and therefore had no inhibitions about interrupting them or rubbishing their opinions. And since they did the same to me we all had a pretty good time, especially as Martin had been quite right about the fee, the gin, the sarnies and the car home.

I left the Television Centre quite pleased with my performance and a couple of days later, this being early in 1972, received a phone call. 'My name,' said the caller, 'is Iain Johnstone.' (I had never heard of him.) 'I produce a film review programme called *Film 72*.' (I had never heard of that either.) 'It's shown on the opt-out slot on BBC1.' (Oh God, I thought, he's going to ask me to review it in *The Times*. But I couldn't because the opt-out slot was the one half-hour of the week when the different BBC regions put out their own programmes in their own areas; therefore this *Film 72* was only seen in London and the south-east and would be unknown to viewers and newspaper readers who lived elsewhere.)

'Yes?' I said cautiously.

'Well,' said the mysterious Johnstone, 'one of the reasons for the programme is to find new faces for TV. Now, I saw you on *Line-Up* and reckoned your appearance wouldn't frighten people too much and I like your column in the *Guardian* and what I was wondering is this: do you think you could take the same approach to films as you do to politics and the like in your column?'

'Are you asking me to present the programme?' I said.

'Well, yes.'

'But I've never done anything like that.'

'Oh, don't worry,' he said. 'It's easy. Look, come and have lunch at Television Centre next Tuesday and we'll talk about it.'

So I did. We had an excellent lunch and a bottle of what the BBC called Good Ordinary Claret and Iain kept telling me how easy television was. As we finished our meal and while I was still thinking doubtfully about his offer he looked at his watch and said, 'They'll have just finished recording tonight's programme and we still have the studio for an hour or so. Tell you what, why don't we go over there and I'll sit you in front of the camera and see how you look.'

Emboldened by half a bottle of claret I agreed but when we got into the studio I said, 'What am I supposed to do while I'm sitting in front of the camera?'

'Ah,' said Iain, 'it just so happens that I've got your *Guardian* column with me. You could read that.'

My *Guardian* column was a humorous, even satirical, look at current affairs and because it was supposed to be funny it was, for the nine years I wrote it, the hardest thing I had to do in any given week. There is nothing so subjective as humour. If somebody tells you a piece you have written is inaccurate or wrong-headed you can argue. But if they say it's not funny, you're lost. If people don't see the joke you can't explain it to them. Sometimes the pressure of trying to be funny was almost intolerable. There were many days when I would sit for hours at my typewriter and end up in the evening surrounded by pieces of crumpled paper with nothing written. That was when Diana would take me gently by the hand, sit me down, give me a glass of sherry and tell me to forget about it till tomorrow. Fortunately, the next day I was always able to come up with something because my subconscious mind, the most wonderful tool a writer has, had been working away on my behalf. And the odd thing is that those next day pieces, usually written in a state of despair, were often the ones that received the most gratifying response. Some weeks, not too often, an idea would spring fully formed into my mind and I would dash it off swiftly and easily and know that it was the funniest thing I had ever written. But nobody ever raved enthusiastically about pieces like that. I would compare them with the stuff I had turned out in desperation and try to spot the vital difference that made the desperate pieces more popular but I never could, which only goes to show, I suppose, that comedy is a funny business in every possible way. The only reliable yardstick I had was Diana; if I showed her the column and she laughed then I knew it was okay. If she didn't I would tear it up and find something else to write about.

I mention this because, having sweated blood over the *Guardian* pieces, I had them imprinted indelibly in my mind for days after I had written them, so when Iain asked me to read that week's effort to the camera I only had to glance at it occasionally as an aide-mémoire. Mostly, I had it off by heart and could simply recite it as I stared into the lens.

'Fantastic,' Iain said, when I had finished. 'Can you come in and review the films in two weeks time?'

'Well, yes, but hang on – what about the Autocue? I've never used one. I might be hopeless at it.'

'Oh, that's no problem,' he said airily. 'If necessary I'd be quite happy for you to sit there and read from a script.' In those days I was so naïve and inexperienced that I believed him; now I know that he would never have let me do any such thing but Iain was not only a brilliant producer, he was also a great conman, so when he added, 'But if it makes you feel happier come in next week and I'll have your *Guardian* column on Autocue for you', I stopped worrying.

The following Tuesday, I returned to the studio to try my hand at reading Autocue and found it a remarkably simple business. Effectively, Autocue reflected the script from a screen mounted directly below the camera back on to the lens, the operator rolling the words through to match the speed of the speaker. At any given time there were only about a dozen words on screen, so if you looked directly into the middle of them you could see them all. Therefore, especially if you had written the words yourself, there was no need for your eyeballs to swivel from side to side.

'Brilliant,' Iain said, 'you're a natural.' He probably said that to everybody but I was in a mood to believe him. So it was decided: I was told which films to see, when to submit the copy and when to turn up to rehearse and record. On my way out of Television Centre I bumped into the magazine writer Irma Kurtz, then coming to the end of her stint on *Film 72*. She was the second presenter and the first of the new faces. The original presenter when the programme was launched the previous autumn under the title *Film 71* was Jackie Gillott. The idea, as Iain had said, was to discover new people but wisely he had chosen to get the show established by a talented and experienced broadcaster and Jackie was both of those things. She was also beautiful and a gifted novelist but, alas, a manic-depressive and a year or so later she committed suicide.

But that day as we met on the forecourt Irma said, 'I hear you're taking over on *Film 72*. You'll hate it. I hate it. Television is awful.'

These were not exactly comforting words and they came back to me a few days later when my contract arrived. I had been taken on for a three-week trial period with an option for another three weeks, exercisable only by the BBC, so however much of a natural Iain thought I might be he wasn't exactly taking a big risk. But neither, I decided, was I. If Irma was right and TV was awful it was as well to find out now. Either way, I had nothing to lose.

I'd reviewed films before in Kensington, South Africa and Southern Rhodesia. Furthermore, as show business editor of the *Mail* I had appointed myself deputy theatre and film critic on the grounds that these were dirty jobs but somebody had to do them. More recently I had stood in once or twice for *The Times* movie critic, so I knew what I had to do. The only question was: how was I going to do it for this new medium? Since any decent journalist can write in whatever style he chooses, I could have adopted a blokeish tabloid approach or, just as easily, have been quite as po-faced and tight-arsed as *Cahiers du Cinema*. I decided on neither of these on the reasonable grounds that presenting a TV programme would be hard enough without pretending to be somebody I wasn't. So I wrote my reviews in much the same way as I wrote everything else and hoped that would be good enough.

On a Tuesday in February 1972 I went into the studio to make my debut as a television presenter. I felt excited, yes, but in no way nervous. This wasn't my work, this was just an interesting gig, a chance to get some useful experience. Television, after all, was merely a sideline. If, after my run on *Film 72*, my name was added to whatever list they kept at Television Centre of reliable guest pundits that was as much as I could, or did, hope for.

As it happened, and as I realized later, that was the best attitude to adopt. Had I gone in thinking, this is my big chance, probably my only chance, whatever I do I mustn't blow it, I would certainly have blown it. But such thoughts never crossed my mind. I'm not saying I was great that day but I wasn't bad and after my second appearance my contract was promptly extended to nine weeks, at the end of which time Iain said, 'If it were left to me I'd sign you up now to do the programme regularly but the Controller wants to carry on trying new people. I'd like you to come back later on, though, and do another six weeks.'

In that first run on *Film 72* I had learned a lot about television. First of all I had learned that Iain was right: it was easy – or, at least, it was easy to do it moderately well. But then it's fairly easy to do anything moderately well. The difficulties arise when you want to make the jump from moderate to good. That's when the hard work comes in, the time when you must sit back and analyse what exactly you're doing. Am I fidgeting in the chair? Am I moving my hands too much? Do I look as if I'm transfixed by the Autocue? Is the tone of the script right?

One thing I cottoned on to quickly was that television is a conversational medium. No matter how large your audience you must never believe that you are addressing the nation – you are, rather, talking, or better still chatting, to just one person. But which person? I invented one – an imaginary friend, gender unknown, who was rather more intelligent than me and a bit short on patience. And what, I decided, this person was saying was, 'Okay, tell me about the movie. What's it about, who's in it, what's it like? And don't bore me or I'll switch off.'

So, rule one: relax and when writing the script remember that it has to be spoken not read. Spontaneous is better than polished. But at the same time also remember that you're supposed to be a communicator, so use complete sentences and accurate English. And try, without forcing it, to entertain as well as inform.

Something else swiftly became apparent – television is a merciless exposer of the phoney. Just think Party Political Broadcast – no matter how sincere the speaker may seem you know the bastard's lying and that's because he knows he's lying. So, rule two: always tell the truth. If you think the film is crap you must say so, no matter how much you may hurt and offend the people who made it. Your obligation is not to them but to the viewers who might, on your recommendation, spend a small fortune taking their families to a cinema. If you're going to tell these people that a film is worth the financial outlay you'd better be sure you mean it. These things I decided for myself. Other people, studio directors and the like, offered their own helpful suggestions. Don't speak so fast, they said.

Why? Am I gabbling?

No, no, your diction's fine. It's just that you speak a bit fast.

Well, that's the way I speak. I'm comfortable with it.

All right, but don't write such complicated sentences for yourself.

Why not? Don't they make sense?

Yes, but most people on television use simple sentences.

Good for them. I like simple sentences, too, but sometimes I prefer complicated ones. Sometimes you need a complicated sentence and I believe the viewers are intelligent enough to understand that.

Okay, but you should smile more.

What for?

Well, sometimes you say quite funny things.

I know that. I work at it.

Then when you're saying something funny you should smile.

What, to let the viewers know a joke's coming up? Listen, if they think it's funny, they'll laugh. If they don't, they won't. End of story. Besides, I hate people who laugh at their own jokes.

So all these suggestions, well meant as they were, I rejected and continued to reject for the best part of thirty years. Be yourself. Never talk down to the audience. And for God's sake don't laugh at your own jokes.

Chapter Eighteen

ARLY IN MY initial run on *Film 72* I had two interviewees in the studio on the same day – James Stewart and Charlton Heston, both of whom came to the hospitality suite afterwards, those being the carefree days at the BBC when the licence payers' money was liberally spent and even opt-out programmes had hospitality suites with a generous supply of spirits, wine and various nibbles.

After a while Mrs Stewart discovered a mote, or anyway a speck of dust, in her eye and appealed for help.

'Does anybody,' said her husband, 'have a tissue or a clean handkerchief?'

There were no volunteers. Mrs Stewart continued rubbing gently at her eye while her husband looked around the assembled company and his gaze lit upon Heston. 'Chuck,' he said, 'you've got a handkerchief right there in your top pocket. Do you mind if . . . ?'

'No, no,' said Heston, taking a step backwards and clutching at his chest. 'It's . . .'

'Aw, come on, Chuck,' said Stewart and plucked the handkerchief from the pocket only to discover that it wasn't a handkerchief at all but merely a scrap of cotton attached to a strip of cardboard.

Heston snatched it back shamefacedly while a programme assistant went off in search of tissues. With movies and movie people, you see, all is illusion.

At this point, encouraged though I was by the comparative success of my first stint on *Film 72*, television played no particular part in my plans. Now that I had a pretty good idea how to cope with it I enjoyed it very much but this, remember, was a time before everyone's sole ambition was merely to be famous, never mind how. It didn't even occur to me that if I carried on appearing on TV some kind of fame would accrue and if it had it wouldn't have mattered much. As a writing journalist I was in greater demand than I could have imagined possible and it was in that line of work that I felt my future lay.

Thanks to John Higgins, I was regularly contributing articles to *The Times* and this led to another encounter with Michael Winner. By now he was a well-established and financially, if not always critically, successful film maker and he was directing a picture called *The Mechanic* in Italy. Along with Peter Noble, the editor of the trade magazine *Screen International*, I was flown to Naples and then driven along the coast to the hotel where the film unit was housed. But this was a leisurely trip and en route Peter and I decided to visit Pompeii, a place neither of us had seen before. I was naturally fascinated by such sights as the brothel with its faded but still erotic wall paintings and its proximity to the pox doctor's shop that advertised itself with a majestic penis above the door. Peter, however, being a total movie nut, equated everything we saw with the 1935 picture *The Last Days of Pompeii*. 'Look here,' he would say excitedly as I was trying to work out what exactly the people were doing to each other in a particularly faded painting, 'this must be the place where Preston Foster . . .'

Pompeii impressed him deeply. 'How did they manage to do that?' he asked when finally I dragged him away. 'It looks exactly like the film except there isn't a roof anywhere.'

The next morning, although it was early in the year, the weather in the coastal resort where we were put up was warm and balmy so I left my overcoat behind when we set off for that day's film location. This proved to be a mistake because the film unit was in the hills where the temperature was distinctly lower, a fact that immediately became apparent when I got out of the car to be greeted by Michael Winner wearing a large cigar and, below it, a luxurious sheepskin coat.

'Hello, my dear,' he said. 'You look cold.'

'I'm all right, Michael,' I said bravely.

'No, you're not. You look cold.' He turned to his first assistant director, who was also wearing a sheepskin coat, though an older and far
more battered one than Michael's. 'Give Mr Norman your coat,' he
said.

I was horrified. 'I don't want the man's coat!'

Michael took no notice. 'Give Mr Norman your coat,' he said again.

'Look, Michael, I don't want his coat. I'll be okay.'

Michael glared at the first assistant, who plucked at my sleeve and
took me to one side.

'Look, its fine,' I said, 'I really don't want your . . .'

'Take it,' he said. 'Please. If I don't give it to you my life won't be
worth living.' He took his coat off and, shivering, thrust it at me.
'Please,' he said again.

'Michael,' I said, 'what's this poor man going to wear?'

'Oh, wardrobe will find something for him,' he said airily and in this
he was right. Wardrobe did find something for him. The trouble was
that the scene they were shooting that morning was of a car exploding
and killing the people in it, so the only props wardrobe had brought
with them were rags, in a copious collection of which I next saw the
first assistant, looking like a tramp who had fallen on particularly hard
times.

It took a long while to set up the scene of the car exploding and at
first, despite meticulous preparation, it didn't work. All bystanders were
told to get well back and take such cover as they could as Winner
crouched down and said, 'Action!'

Somewhere nearby someone pressed a plunger – and nothing happened. 'Action!' said Winner again, rather more angrily this time.

Again the plunger was depressed and again nothing happened.

A hundred yards or so from the car about to be destroyed, Winner
rose up in his wrath. 'What the fuck's going on?' he roared and at that
moment the car exploded. It was a well-controlled explosion and nothing outside the immediate vicinity of the vehicle was in the remotest
danger but Winner, closer than most of us, looked shocked.

Soon after that the unit broke for lunch, the technicians and minor actors making their way to the location catering wagon while Winner and a dozen or so select companions, myself among them, were to partake of a proper lunch in a nearby restaurant. Because I stopped off to talk to a few people I was a little late getting to the restaurant and arrived just in time to hear Michael regaling his guests with his version of the dramatic events of the morning.

'When it didn't explode the second time,' he was saying, 'I stood up and then, at that very second, it went off.' Around the table there was the sharply drawn breath of horror. Michael nodded gravely. 'It was touch and go,' he said, 'whether I lived or died.'

I sat down in the one vacant chair. 'Unfortunately,' I said, 'he chose to live.' I don't think Michael was very amused.

Once, in an interview, Des O'Connor told me repeatedly that the key to his personality was that he loved people. I couldn't go along with that. I love people, too – some people. Others I dislike intensely and certainly when I see what people have done to the planet and each other I find it impossible to offer them my all-embracing love. Michael Winner, I feel, is more like me than Des O'Connor except that he probably loves even fewer people than I do and it shows in his films. He is a skilled technician but his movies lack warmth or empathy with his protagonists, especially the women. What he should have concentrated on was not directing but producing, for which he has exceptional gifts. He completes his pictures on, or under, budget and schedule and nearly all of them return handsome profits to their backers. Beyond that he is a very shrewd businessman. Long before anyone else he realized that after *The Magnificent Seven* Charles Bronson, though still virtually unknown in the USA, was a huge box office draw in places like Germany and South America. Therefore, by striking the right deal with Bronson he could recoup and maybe more than recoup a movie's cost elsewhere in the world before it had even opened in the United States. Hence films like *Chato's Land*, *The Mechanic* and the *Death Wish* series which, whatever you may think of them, made Bronson an international star.

Winner's record as a producer makes him worthy of far more

admiration than he has so far been accorded in his own land, although his flamboyant and sometimes downright boorish behaviour accounts for a certain withholding of admiration. As I said in the piece I wrote for *The Times*, 'To say that Michael Winner is his own worst enemy is to evoke a ragged chorus from odd corners of the film industry of "Not while I'm alive", but in a sense it's true.' So it is still. He can be a generous host and a most entertaining companion but he can also be rude and a bully, as if it amuses him to confront the world in the guise of a self-made shit. It's hard to understand why this should be so. It can't be financial disappointment because God knows he has made enough money. Perhaps what gripes him is that he wanted to be a great director and never became one. Not enough for him, I suspect, that as a producer he has few peers among his contemporaries in the British film industry.

Early one evening I was lolling about at home when I had a phone call from Ian Chapman, chairman of Collins, the publishers. He and his wife Marjorie, he said, were at the Dorchester Hotel to have dinner with the novelist, Alistair MacLean, and Alistair would like Diana and me to join them.

This seemed a good idea. At the time MacLean, author of *HMS Ulysses*, *The Guns of Navarone* and the like, was an international bestseller and, thanks to Ian, I was about to write a profile of him for the *Observer* and, later, worldwide distribution. So we dressed up and went to the Dorchester, there to find MacLean already well into his cups.

Diana took against him at once – and a day later was to take against him even more violently – because she thought he was rude to me. He may well have been but, if so, I took no notice because I had met him before, when he and I and Ian had gone to Amsterdam for the filming of his book, *Puppet on a Chain*. There it became apparent that MacLean was an alcoholic and, like many alcoholics, affable enough at a certain stage in his drinking but inclined to become spiky and unpleasant later on. Since for most of the time he was an amiable, kind and oddly vulnerable man I ignored the spikiness, attributing it to alcohol beyond his control.

At dinner Diana, still bridling at his supposed rudeness, sat next to him and ticked him off for his behaviour. He apologized. Not for a moment, he said, had he intended to be rude. Mollified, she began to warm to him and then melted completely as he confided that his son, Lachlan, had leukaemia. As he told her about it, she said on the way home, he was on the verge of tears and so was she. Come to that, so was I. Indeed, I was so moved that the next day I asked around to find out how bad Lachlan's condition was, only to discover that he didn't have leukaemia at all. He certainly had a skin and blood complaint that necessitated much hospital treatment but it was nothing as serious as leukaemia. When I told Diana this she was furious; MacLean, she said, had enlisted her sympathy and caused her a good deal of distress in the cheapest and most unforgivable way. That was it, she said – she would have no more to do with the man. And she kept her word.

I, on the other hand, was obliged to go to Geneva, where he lived, and spend two days with him in his villa overlooking the lake while I interviewed him.

When I arrived I discovered that he and I were the only residents. His wife, Gisela, and the family, he explained, had gone away for a few days. I didn't know it at the time, nor did he mention it, but the marriage was on the verge of break-up. Fortunately, he didn't mention Lachlan's 'leukaemia' either, which was a relief.

MacLean was a very rich man but he lived in comfort rather than affluence, his only luxuries being a Rolls-Royce and a huge Mercedes, both of which I had to drive when we went out for meals. He no longer drove himself, he said, because his sight was so bad; indeed, he was almost blind. This, I discovered later, was another wild exaggeration or sympathy-jerker. On the other hand I didn't mind acting as chauffeur, unfamiliar though I was with both cars, because he drank so much throughout the day and evening that he would have been a menace behind the steering wheel.

The drinking, it seemed to me, was the result of self-contempt. His novels had earned him fame and a great deal of money, neither of which he believed he deserved. He was a puritan, a son of the Manse, whose first book, *HMS Ulysses*, an instant bestseller, had been written in about a week and his success then and after appalled him. He was not a writer, he said, not a natural writer and not even the fact that his sixteenth and latest novel, *Bear Island*, the reason for the interview, had an initial print run of 100,000 copies in hardback and would automatically become a bestseller, could convince him otherwise.

'Basically, I'm a person who tells stories,' he said, dismissively, 'and what does that mean? How much is it worth?' He wasn't talking about money but the value of his work in the greater scheme of things and in his opinion it didn't amount to very much. At one point, sitting beside me in the Rolls-Royce, he said, 'I don't belong in this class. It's ridiculous.'

Like his fellow drunk and Swiss neighbour, Richard Burton, whom he disliked intensely, he said many things that weren't true but his sneering assessment of his own work clearly came from the heart, from an intense feeling of guilt that he had earned so much so easily. None of his books took much more than a week to write and none of them pleased him because they were never as good as he wanted them to be. Raymond Chandler, he said, now there was writer. MacLean's own ambition was to write one book, just one book, that could stand comparison with Chandler but he knew that it would never happen. And so he drank.

It was drink that caused his fallout with Burton, who had starred in the film of his book *Where Eagles Dare*. At a post-production party at the Dorchester the two men, both pretty well plastered, had had a drunken altercation that led to fisticuffs and, in MacLean's version anyway, a punch that felled the great movie star. They never spoke to each other again.

On the evening of the first day I drove us both to a restaurant on the shores of Lake Geneva where MacLean ate little but drank plenty and then we returned to the villa. It had been a good, interesting day and he had been charming company, so when he suggested a nightcap it seemed churlish to refuse, though I was tired and longing to go to bed.

He brought out the brandy and got stuck in and little by little his conversation became more and more slurred and incomprehensible until, in mid-sentence, he fell asleep in his chair. What to do? I could, of course, have left him there and retired but I was a little concerned. He was so drunk that I was afraid he might wake up, reel about, fall over and hurt himself. So I stayed there, reading a magazine, until eventually he did wake up.

It was about two o'clock in the morning. He snorted, shook himself, turned a bleary eye on me and suddenly I found myself in the middle of an Alistair MacLean thriller with him as the hero and myself cast as the heavy.

'What do you want from me, Barry?' he said in a distinctly unfriendly tone.

'Well,' I said, taken aback, 'you know. This interview . . .'

He shook his head, his gaze growing ever more baleful. 'No. You want more than that. What is it – money? You want money from me?'

'Of course not!' I said.

'I know you want something. Oh, yes. I know all about people like you. You inveigle your way into my home and you think you can fool me but you can't. I'm too clever for you. Get out.'

'What?'

'Get out of my house. Whatever it is you want I'm giving you nothing. Do you understand that? It hasn't worked, whatever your plan was, and I'm telling you to leave my house. Now!'

What was I to do? The villa was miles away from the nearest hotel and though I knew where the keys were I could hardly help myself to his Merc or his Roller. The only thing, I decided, was to enter into the drunken game he was playing.

I stood up. 'Very well, Alistair,' I said. 'You win. I'm leaving.'

'Good,' he said, nodding. 'You realize I have no alternative, don't you?'

'I do,' I said. 'Goodnight, Alistair.'

And I left him there and went upstairs to bed, wondering uneasily what he would do the next morning when he discovered I was still on the premises.

In fact what he did the next morning was to creep solicitously into my room at about seven o'clock, bearing coffee and toast, apologizing for waking me so early and making it clear that I was under no obligation to get up until I wanted to. Whatever wild scenario he had been playing out the previous night had gone completely from his mind and he made no mention of it during the rest of my stay.

We parted on the best of terms and though we never met again I – unlike Diana, who snorts derisively whenever his name is mentioned – retain a fondness for him. Taken drunk he could be a monster, taken sober – or not very drunk – he was likeable and somehow rather sad. He was right about his books: they really aren't very good. But he knew that and was prepared to admit it, to himself most of all. I've met a lot of hugely successful people but I think Alistair MacLean had the most self-awareness of any of them.

In the spring of 1973 Paul Fox, then Controller of BBC1, decided that he was fed up with all those rotating presenters on the film programme. Why not, he said, offer the job full time to that bloke from the *Guardian*? By now a good number of people had taken their turn at presenting the show but none of them wrote regularly for the *Guardian*. I, however, did, so the job was mine – if I wanted it. And by then, having done a couple more six-week stints I did want it. Mind you, through a misunderstanding I very nearly fell out of favour with Paul Fox. One morning when all the top BBC brass were gathered for the daily programme review meeting – otherwise known at the Beeb as the Chimps' Tea Party – he had complained bitterly that last night's film show had been presented by 'a bloke wearing a wig. I won't have wigs on my channel.' He was only appeased when Iain pointed out that I wasn't wearing a wig but merely suffering a bad hair day. However . . .

Among the things I had realized during my brief experience of the telly was that to enjoy watching yourself on the box you need to be a much closer descendant of Narcissus than I am. I have never derived pleasure from the process, partly because I've never been enamoured of my own appearance. Why couldn't I have looked like the young Paul Newman or Robert Redford or Tom Cruise or Brad Pitt? Not much to ask, is it? But mostly I disliked watching my programme because all I could see was what I was doing wrong, which really is why I watched in the first place – to keep an eye out for irritating tics and mannerisms and resolve to do something about them next time.

All these things I had learned quite soon and I had also learned that making television, sitting in the studio recording the programme, was the least enjoyable part of the job. Not that I was bad at it; indeed, I was rather good. From the start I imposed on every production team with which I worked one stern rule: anyone could change the script, so long as it was me. There was a good reason for this. Because every word that appeared on Autocue was mine I knew precisely how to read the lines and where to place the emphasis. As a result I hardly ever fluffed, which made me popular with the people in the control gallery, who disliked going back over the same passage time and again quite as much as I did. So I had no problem with recording or even, on various occasions over the years, going live. It was simply that while the business of actually making a programme was always interesting I never found it much fun.

What was fun was seeing the films – even the bad ones – and, most of all, writing the script. If I had been asked to appear on TV reading words written by somebody else I would have refused. I've never seen any point in that. No matter how successful a show, if all the presenter has done is read out another person's hand-me-down opinions then any fame and popularity he acquires are at least tainted. Television is, of course, full of such people and probably always has been and if they can live with it, fine. But it wouldn't have done for me. Ever since I left school I have taken a probably immodest pride in the fact that I have earned my living from writing – journalism, books, television, radio, whatever the medium the words, for better or worse, were always mine. But knowing that is a secret pleasure because somehow television audiences never seem to believe that you're capable of writing the stuff yourself. Over the years I was often approached by people saying things like, 'Love your programme. And what you said about so-and-so last night was very good. Who writes the script for you?' It used to drive me nuts. If I didn't write it myself, why did they think I was there? For my sex appeal and stunning good looks? Hardly, although for a while, before the ravages of time took their toll, I was known as 'the thinking woman's crumpet', a title I shared with Melvyn Bragg. Diana and the girls found this hilariously funny and so did I, actually, but at least, I thought, if I am the thinking woman's crumpet it must be because those thinking women like what I say and are perceptive enough to know that I wrote it.

Anyway, when I was asked to present *Film 73* every week I said yes. It was still only an opt-out programme and therefore a part-time job, so I was able to continue with my newspaper and magazine work. Even though it meant I was often working seven days a week I felt this was a wise course. Television programmes, especially opt-out programmes, came and went. If in the near future the BBC decided to kill off Film Whatever Year, maybe another little opt-out would be offered to me and that would be nice. But it wasn't worth giving up a column on the *Guardian* on the off chance.

Chapter Nineteen

NOT LONG AFTER I had been installed as full-time presenter I had an offer from Granada Television. Granada ran a film review show called *Cinema*, presented formerly by Michael Parkinson and at that time by Clive James. But Clive had decided to return full time to writing books and journalism. What Granada wanted to know was, would I be interested in replacing him? On the face of it this had two distinct advantages over *Film 73*: *Cinema* was shown on the full ITV network and it paid better. The latter was not surprising; in those days practically everything paid better than the BBC. So was I interested? Certainly, I said; after all, it was only a matter of doing exactly what I did for *Film 73* but getting more money for it. Wasn't it?

Well, yes and no, said Granada, or its representative. The thing was that Granada was controlled by Sidney (or Lord) Bernstein and his brother and they also owned a cinema chain. What they emphatically did not want was someone on their TV channel rubbishing a film that would open the same week in their cinemas. So the brief for *Cinema* was this: the presenter would pick the film he liked best that week and spend the first half of the programme saying how good it was. For the sake of argument, let us assume that the favoured movie was *Hello, Dolly*. Lots of nice things would be said about it up to the commercial break, after which, *Hello, Dolly* having set the theme, the second half of the programme would be devoted to old Hollywood musicals, which were never again likely to be seen in the Bernsteins'

Pre-match practice in the 1970s – when I could still bat a bit.

Ready to bat in a charity match in the 1980s. Ian Botham was bowling for the opposition, hence the anxious look.

The start of another, slightly windswept, Cannes Film Festival.

With director Mike Leigh, one of the 'usual suspects' whose films are invariably invited to Cannes.

Interviewing Quentin Tarantino, whose *Pulp Fiction* was about to win the Palme d'Or in 1994.

Not my favourite man – Arnie Schwarzenegger publicising something or other at the Hotel du Cap.

Michelle Pfeiffer, who says she looks like a duck. What do you reckon?

Two mixed Spices – Baby and Scary – in Cannes in 1996 to announce their forthcoming epic *Spiceworld: The Movie* (Ginger, Sporty and Posh are just out of shot). Nice girls but better at the day job than acting.

In Hollywood with George Clooney just before *Batman and Robin* failed to make him the superstar everyone knew he was going to be.

Pierce Brosnan, who took an easier route to superstardom by playing James Bond.

Nigel Hawthorne, who should have won the Oscar for *The Madness of King George*.

Anthony Hopkins, who has managed the rare feat of being both a Hollywood star and a first-rate actor.

Ewan McGregor, the only star I know who, bless him, turns up regularly at movie premieres with his mum, his dad and his granny.

Cannes again, with Kenneth Branagh who, as actor, producer and director, is constantly underrated in his own country.

Richard Attenborough, my co-host on Sky's *Millennium Movies* show.

Alongside David Attenborough as we took part in a TV trailer hyping the glory of the BBC.

To judge from our expressions, David Puttnam and I must have been discussing the current state of the British film industry.

Alan Parker, still a mate even though he duped me over *A Turnip Head's Guide to the British Cinema*.

With Diana, Samantha and Emma after receiving the CBE from the Queen.

Receiving my BAFTA in 1980.

Elisabeth Murdoch welcoming me to Sky in 1998.

My brother Rick, sister Valerie, Mum, Dad and me a couple of months before my father died.

As the photographer said, ''Ere Barry, who's that bird you're with?' Actually, it's my daughter Samantha.

Samantha again, this time with Emma, after I'd received an Hon. D. Litt. from their alma mater, the University of East Anglia. That's the only hat I've ever worn that suits me.

Diana and me in the garden, in the hammock, and mercifully far from all that show biz nonsense.

The family – Emma, Diana, Samantha (holding Charlie), Harry and, in the yellow car, Bertie.

cinemas or, at that time, on Granada. Here, the presenter had carte blanche to be as witty and excoriating as he liked. He could pick the worst musicals ever made and kick the remaining daylights out of them. Now I had never really watched *Cinema*, so I was not aware of this formula. In fact, I hardly ever watched any film programme other than my own, on the grounds that I had enough to do trying to make my show better each week than it had been the week before without worrying about what other people were doing. But I can't imagine that garnering an easy reputation as a savage wit by torturing cinematic corpses had appealed either to Parky or Clive and it certainly didn't appeal to me. So I politely declined the offer and this turned out to be a shrewd move because within a few years *Cinema* had vanished for ever.

Meanwhile, at the BBC, I and the film programme continued to thrive, though with the occasional blip. One such blip occurred when Malcolm Walker, then head of our department, came up with the idea that Esther Rantzen should be asked to present the show. When it was pointed out that Esther, though an excellent broadcaster, knew little or nothing about the movies Walker replied, 'Oh, that's all right. We can employ Barry to write the script for her.' Barry was asked how this appealed to him and replied, 'Fuck off' and no more was heard of that suggestion.

Another, and potentially more serious, blip occurred one week when, happily, I wasn't there, being away on an assignment for one of the newspapers for which I wrote. The producer, Pat Ingram, wasn't there either, some kind of virus or lurgy having struck her down. In her absence Don Bennetts, our Australian studio director, took over as stand-in producer and decided for reasons which even he could never adequately explain to open the programme with a review of an Ingmar Bergman movie in Swedish and with German subtitles. On BBC2 he might – just – have got away with it; on the more mainstream BBC1, no chance. Paul Fox was spitting mad. Programmes had been axed for less and Paul's reaction, when conveyed to me, only reinforced my belief that, as it were, TV shows unlike puppies were for Christmas, not for ever, and that I'd be a fool to give up everything else and concentrate solely on the telly. In those days anyway my BBC contracts ran for three or six months with no guarantee of renewal.

Pat Ingram had taken over from Iain Johnstone who, newly married, had left the BBC and gone to Massachusetts to become a lecturer in media studies at Boston University. Since then he has had a successful career as freelance TV producer, journalist and critic and, along with John Cleese, writer of the screenplay for *Fierce Creatures*. But I have often wondered what would have happened if he had stayed with the BBC. At the time he launched my TV career Iain, along with Will Wyatt, was one of the young men to watch at Television Centre. Paul Fox, it was widely believed, was keeping a benevolent and avuncular eye on them. Will went on to become managing director, or whatever flashy, American-type title that translated into, at the end of his career, and my feeling is that Iain would have done equally well; certainly there is no reason why he shouldn't have become Controller of BBC1 at least. God knows there have been Controllers not half as intelligent or capable as he is.

Pat, my new producer, was a splendidly feisty and able woman with a strong belief that film should be taken seriously. In that we had no argument. In the early years the more precious critics in the national press would opine, snottily, that I was 'trivializing' the cinema, presumably because I made jokes about bad movies. But in this they were missing the point: I always took film seriously – what I refused to do was take it solemnly. Part of my job, I thought, was to try to share with my audience the enthusiasm I felt for good films and to point it in the direction of same. Maybe this is a bit arrogant, bearing in mind that all I was delivering was my own opinion, not a bunch of tablets brought down from the Mount. There can be no absolutes in criticism since anyone who slips his brain into gear while watching a movie is, almost by definition, a critic. Some part of that brain is, consciously or not, explaining to its owner why the entertainment being watched is good, or bad or, most likely, merely indifferent, and that being so what makes a professional critic's opinion more valid than anyone else's?

Simply this: the professional has, or should have, seen far more films than the rest of the audience and therefore has many more yardsticks by which to measure the quality of the product. This is no longer as true as it used to be given television's current propensity for having much of its film coverage presented by people whose main qualification for the job is that they look good on the box. In a similar way even the national newspapers are now inclined to appoint as film critics not those who can lay modest claim to being an expert in the subject but people who have gained reputations for being good, or anyway provocative, writers in other fields.

This approach to film reviewing is decidedly odd. No newspaper would appoint a theatre, opera or classical music critic simply because he or she can write a jolly funny column about family life or the battle of the sexes. Nor would a TV company ask someone to do one of those jobs (assuming, which these days is most improbable, that a TV company would even want critical coverage of the theatre, opera or classical music) for no better reason than that he or she looked pretty on screen. At its best, film, too, is a serious art form. Unfortunately, for most of the time it aspires to be nothing more than mass entertainment and the feeling seems to be that coverage of it should also be mass entertainment. If you want critical opinion offered by people who know more about the subject than you do, it is still to be found. But you have to search very hard for it.

With Pat Ingram as producer life was never less than interesting. The BBC's view of a film review programme, voiced by Malcolm Walker, was that it should be entertainment, Pat's that it should reflect more than just British pictures and Hollywood blockbusters and give due acknowledgement to films made by the rest of the world. My sympathies were with her but on reflection I suppose we were wrong, though for the best possible motives. 'Art' films were considered the domain of BBC2, which at that time and for some while afterwards had programmes (presented by the likes of Gavin Miller, who went on to make films of his own) which covered them. God knows what has happened to such programmes now. BBC1, on the other hand, catered for a mainstream audience which, like the cinema audience, too, was interested predominantly in English-language movies and had little interest in subtitled films, arguing that it didn't go to the cinema to read. The compromise, as I worked out over the years, was to emphasize the mainstream while always slipping in reviews of the best foreign-language films. But these were early days when the battle lines were still being drawn and Pat was in no mood for compromise. Every battle, she felt, had to be fought and valiantly she fought them all, although even I would urge her to back off and think about winning the war rather than simply the latest skirmish. Whether she would eventually have succeeded in giving the programme a more international look is an interesting question but, doughty fighter though she was, she had one weak flank – she was under contract, not on the staff, bad news if you're inclined to make waves. When her contract expired it was not renewed. She left the programme bloody but unbowed.

Barry Brown, an expatriate Australian, replaced her. Actually, this is an oversimplification. Barry was already the producer of a movie review programme on BBC2 called *Film Night*. It covered pretty much the same ground as *Film 75* the main difference being that it had two pre-senters, Tony Bilbow and Philip Jenkinson. It also had a full production team in place whereas *Film 75* now did not; all it had was me and Barry was lumbered with me. At first, I was by no means sure that either he or the rest of his team was at all happy with this situation. And I had my doubts, too.

When it was first mooted that *Film Night* and *Film 75* should shel-ter under the same umbrella, Barry and I were taken to lunch to talk things over by a BBC executive, Mike Hill. I already knew and liked Barry but I didn't then like his ideas. For a start, he suggested that I should accept a co-presenter. I said that if he wanted two presenters he should approach two other people and leave me out. Then he talked about changing *Film 75*'s theme music, the Billy Taylor piece 'I Wish I Knew How it Would Feel to be Free', which had been chosen by Iain Johnstone. Although my musical ear is not so much tin as solid brass even I knew that the Taylor piece was a winner, so I argued fiercely against changing it. To do him justice, Barry, too, liked the music; his talk about co-presenters and a new theme tune was prompted by the not unreasonable idea that under a new management my programme should have a new look. My instinct was the opposite: the show had been on the air for about three years and, even as an opt-out, was attracting around a million viewers. If it ain't broke, don't fix it. By the end of the lunch we had agreed to leave things much as they were.

Even so, I didn't feel particularly welcome when I first appeared in the *Film Night/Film 75* office to write that week's script. It was an odd sort of office anyway, a thin, curved thing constructed out of what had once been a corridor at the top of Television Centre. Barry could not have been nicer but the rest of the team, whom I came to know and like a lot, viewed me with what I thought to be suspicion, if not downright hostility. It was understandable; they had enough on their plates producing *Film Night*, with which they were happy and comfortable, but now they had another programme to put together as well and they weren't getting any more money for it.

Formal introductions were made and I decided that, outnumbered as I was, politeness should be my approach. For some weeks I was unfailingly polite to everybody until Judy Lindsay, then one of Barry's assistants and later, in her turn, to be my producer, said irritably, 'For Christ's sake, why are you always so bloody polite? Can't you unbend a bit?' But that came later. On that first day, as someone moved away to leave a desk and typewriter free for me and I settled down to write my script, Barry came up and asked solicitously whether I needed any help.

'No, thanks,' I said. 'I think I can manage on my own.'

He looked doubtful. It is in the nature of producers to doubt whether any presenter is capable of managing on his own, especially when it comes to writing a script. But when in the late afternoon I turned in the stuff and he realized that not only would he not be required to have it rewritten but that I positively refused to have anyone make a single alteration, except in the interests of accuracy, he seemed quite relieved.

Thereafter a smooth working pattern evolved. Tony and Jenks, the *Film Night* presenters, came to the office on one day, I on another, therefore there was no conflict of interests or unseemly vying for attention. And after a while the production team seemed quite happy to have two programmes, rather than one, to put on air. In fact, the doubling-up worked to their advantage when, a few years later, BBC2 dropped *Film Night* and the team, for better or worse, was left with just me. They were probably closer, socially, to Tony and Jenks than they ever were to me but we got along very well and at least they were left with a mainstream BBC1 programme to make.

My programme finally sidled on to the full BBC1 network in April 1976. It didn't exactly turn up accompanied by fanfares and a full blast of publicity hype; instead, after the summer break, it appeared once a fortnight on Sunday evenings, alternating in its slot with Melvyn Bragg's book programme, *Read All About It*. This was not a bad way to go. With such a modest start there was no particular pressure on the programme to be an immediate success and because it only cropped up once every two weeks we were not bothered by the TV critics. Thus I was able to continue my personal learning process without undue attention and actually doing television is – or was then – the only training you got.

Producers looking for new faces would light upon someone, maybe from newspapers, maybe from radio, and offer a brief contract. The chosen one would then be led to the deep end and thrown in while the producers stood around wondering with mild interest whether he or she would sink or swim. Those who struggled to the surface would be given another opportunity; those who went down like a rock would be left to rot at the bottom of the pool, never to be heard of again.

It was much the same in radio. Sometime in 1974 I had a phone call from Alistair Osborne, then deputy editor but soon to be editor of the *Today* programme on Radio 4. They were looking for new presenters, he said: would I like to try my luck? Well, I said doubtfully, I've done some radio but very little; I've certainly never presented anything. Never mind, he said, give it a go.

This was the time when Robert Robinson, who had been co-presenting the show with John Timpson for some years, had decided he had had enough and Osborne and company were casting around to find a successor. I was merely one of several people approached, among them Desmond Lynam and Melvyn Bragg. For a while poor John

Timpson rarely knew when he reported for work who would be sitting in the chair beside him and would remark with understandable bitterness that the Beeb was 'dragging traffic wardens in off the street to present the show with me'.

As the latest traffic warden my training and preparation for the job were as follows: one evening I went into the *Today* office in Broadcasting House and sat around watching while the team prepared items for the next morning's programme. Then I went to bed across the road in the Langham, a former hotel, now a hotel again, which then housed a BBC dormitory for late night and early morning workers. The next day at about 5 a.m. I turned up at the *Today* studio and watched John present the show with whoever that morning's traffic warden happened to be. And when it was over Alistair said, 'There you are – that's how it's done. Now come in on Saturday and present the programme by yourself.'

Which I did. And it went okay. No, actually it was crap but then the Saturday programme was always crap in those days. It was shorter, ninety minutes instead of two hours, and regarded by many of the producers as an excuse to do nothing very much. There was a feeling that, this being the weekend, there should be a lot of quirky items rather than hard news. In effect what that meant was that the Saturday show was full of all the pieces that had been rejected Monday through Friday. These were known generically as 'square carrots', the name deriving from the idea that the ideal Saturday item was an interview with a man who grew square carrots on an allotment in Clapham.

This, I thought, was not good enough. Whatever day of the week it was this was supposed to be a news and current affairs programme and the content should reflect that. Luckily, I encountered a few kindred spirits among the duty producers, and together we instituted a new regime under which I turned up at the office on Friday evening and spent a couple of hours interviewing politicians and similar self-important layabouts on important matters of the day. Then I wrote the script, after which we all had a jolly supper in an Italian restaurant around the corner and then I went to bed. Partly because I was now presenting *Today* on a regular basis but largely, I suspect, because I was a freelance and thus treated better than the staff, I was put up in a pleasant little hotel nearby where I had a bathroom of my own and tea was brought to me at half-past four in the morning.

I would then check in at the office, rewrite the script to accommodate anything new that had come in during the night and prepare for a couple of live interviews during the programme. I don't know whether anyone at the BBC noticed – and if they did they didn't mention it because giving praise is not in the Corporation's nature – but I knew, as did my collaborators, that the Saturday show rapidly became a bloody sight better than it had been before.

I did not, however, only do the Saturday shift. Two other mornings a week I would co-present, usually with John Timpson, though not always. Sometimes I would find myself sharing the job with Malcolm Billings and, once or twice, Melvyn Bragg. Oddly enough I never worked with Des Lynam, though he and I were for a while John's two regular co-presenters.

The first couple of times I worked with John he was pleasant enough but not particularly friendly. I didn't blame him; I was, after all, merely another passing traffic warden and as far as he knew would probably be gone for ever by next week. But when I kept turning up we developed an amiable relationship and I knew I was accepted the day he offered me a whisky from his private bottle after the show.

Nine o'clock in the morning might seem a bit early to be hitting the Scotch but John argued, very reasonably I thought, that he had been up and working for about five hours and as far as his body was concerned it was already at least lunchtime and surely a chap was entitled to a whisky at lunchtime. I could see no flaw in this argument and was happy to join him.

By now my average working week went roughly like this: Monday, collected from home soon after 4 a.m. and taken to *Today* studio; do programme and then see two, maybe three, films. Tuesday, see more films, then to Television Centre to write script for *Film 74/5*. Wednesday, do *Today* show then record film programme at Television Centre. Thursday, write *Guardian* column and *Flook* script. Friday, deliver *Guardian* column, go to *Daily Mail* for *Flook* conference with

Wally Fawkes then to *Today* for interviews/script writing. Saturday morning, *Today* programme. Saturday afternoon, sleep.

I had thought, as Robert Robinson had done before me, that *Today*, being an early morning programme, would provide the time and opportunity to do the work I wanted to do, specifically to write novels. By 9 a.m. I had earned my daily bread and could now surely indulge my ambitions with an easy conscience. But it didn't pan out that way. Work expanded to fill the time available and except in the summer of 1975 I was either too busy or too tired to pursue my own interests. In that gloriously hot summer, however, when the film programme was off the air, I did use the spare time to take my typewriter into the garden and, stripped to the waist, write a novel, a police procedural called *To Nick a Good Body*. However the book may have turned out, at least I got a great tan.

I did the *Today* programme, mostly three days a week, for nineteen months but then there was a change of editorship: Alistair Osborne went and Mike Chaney came in. By then, before Mike was appointed, Brian Redhead, former editor of the *Manchester Evening News*, had been signed to co-present with John. There was no longer any need for a regular traffic warden and I knew my time had come. Mike, bluff, burly and bearded, was and is a very nice man but he clearly had a problem. He had been introduced as a new broom and new brooms are expected to sweep things away. He could do a bit of that by adding muscle to the content of the programme and this he did. But that sort of change was not immediately obvious. He had to alter the style and appearance of the show, give it a fresh look. But having inherited two presenters, one on the staff (Timpson) and the other (Redhead) on long-term contract, he was stymied unless . . . Well, unless he changed the Saturday presenter whose contract was about to expire. So . . . 'Sorry, Barry. Great job and all that but . . .' 'That's okay, Mike, I understand.'

I think it was a mistake. Well, I would, wouldn't I? But I suspect Mike thinks it was, too. Not that it matters now nor really mattered then, apart from peripheral damage to the pride at having been sacked. It wasn't as if I would be obliged to scrape around to make a living; I had more than enough work on without the *Today* programme. In fact, the only thing I resent about leaving *Today* was that in his history of the show, *All Our Todays*, Paul Donovan quotes Mike as saying that because I was a very busy man I 'didn't like coming in to do interviews on a Friday'. That was wrong, Mike. That was very wrong.

Chapter Twenty

I WAS DRUNK ONCE in a television studio. In recent years I have been accused if not of being drunk then at least of having taken drink by TV critics who had sat up all night to watch my coverage, first on the BBC, then on Sky, of the Oscar ceremony. But this allegation, I suspect, merely reflected the condition of the critics themselves who, to judge by their copy, had been pissed out of their minds when they wrote it. These days, and this has been so for many years now, I do not drink at all before appearing on television. I had learned my lesson the hard way.

In the late 1970s the staff of the film programme had included a lad called Benny, who had been sent to us for three months on attachment from the BBC World Service at Bush House. Now, to his regret – and ours, because we all liked him – his attachment had come to an end. At that time we were recording on Fridays for Sunday broadcasts and Benny suggested that, to mark his going, we should all have lunch together that Friday in the restaurant at Television Centre. We would pay for our own food but Benny would provide the wine and this he did, most liberally. It was a splendid lunch – Benny kept moving around refilling our glasses and the conversation was lively and uninhibited both at table and later as we trooped down the corridor towards the studio.

Like everyone else I was, I thought, amusing, witty and articulate – until I sat in the studio, the lights went on, the floor manager counted down, the programme titles came up and I started to read the Autocue.

Total humiliation. I fumbled and slurred and fluffed my way through the opening link – and at the end of it there was silence. Nobody in the studio would look at me; nobody in the gallery knew what to say to me.

I have rarely felt so ashamed. I took a deep breath and stood up. 'Right,' I said, 'I am now going to walk round the building several times. While I'm doing that I would like someone to get me lots of strong black coffee.' And that's what happened. I walked round and round the sixth floor of the circular Television Centre, pausing for coffee every time I passed the studio, and then went to my dressing room and kept plunging my face into a basin of cold water.

This, however, could not go on indefinitely. We only had the studio for a limited time and the moment came when, ready or not, I had to go back in to rehearse and then record.

I did not tell Diana what had happened. ('Good day at the studio, darling?' – 'Yeah, not bad.') Well, I felt enough self-contempt; I had no need for her to tell me what an idiot I had been. It was a bad weekend, though, as I waited in dread for the programme to go out. But when it did it turned out to be probably the most sober show, in every sense, that I have ever done. Nobody watching it could possibly have guessed that I had had so much as a sip of alcohol. It was also probably the most boring show I have ever done and it taught me a lesson which I have never forgotten. For weeks, months, afterwards I was haunted by a single thought: what if it had been live and I hadn't had time to sober up? That would have been the end. I have known studio directors (not on my programme) so drunk they had to lie on the floor to burble their instructions but it's comparatively easy to cover for them. Covering for a man obviously drunk on screen, on the other hand, is impossible. The occasional inebriated guest might be forgiven; an inebriated presenter, never.

Talking of inebriated studio directors, though . . . There was one (again not on my programme) who had so overdone it during the course of the evening that he could not be trusted to get home by himself. He couldn't even stand up by himself. A taxi was needed. Unfortunately, the BBC made no provision for hiring taxis for staff members and this staff member could not afford the cab fare, having drunk all his money in the bar. What to do? Someone remembered that Alan Bennett, eminent playwright and former member of *Beyond the Fringe*, had been on a programme that night and, though the BBC would have provided him, as a guest, with transport, had found his own way home. Why not, it was suggested, summon a cab, for which the BBC would pay, in the name of Alan Bennett and throw the legless director into it? So it was done. A disgruntled taxi driver looked on as the drunk was dragged to his cab and laid out in the back. Where was he going? Nobody, least of all the studio director, knew. Drive to Battersea. It's somewhere in Battersea. He'll know when you get there. The door was slammed and the director's colleagues ran away. The cab, so it was later learned, drove aimlessly around for ages until the director finally identified his own home and, cursing and shouting, fell out, though not before being violently sick all over the back seat.

The driver was irate, so was the company for which he worked and the next day an edict went out to all its drivers: on no account was anyone ever again to pick up Alan Bennett.

One more drunk story. In 1976 and 1977 I was again alternating with Melvyn Bragg, this time on *Tonight* on BBC1. One week he would discuss literary topics, the next, in the same slot, I would talk about films. On one occasion my studio guest was the American director Sam Peckinpah, whose Second World War movie *Cross of Iron* was about to be released. Sam was a man with a notorious thirst which he had clearly done his considerable best to slake before shambling in. He was all right, though, articulate enough if a bit slushy on the sibilants, and the chat was going well until, as we started discussing the war in general, he leaned across, tapped me on the knee and said, 'Have you ever thought how the world might have been if Mr and Mrs Hitler hadn't fucked that night?'

Well, no, I hadn't actually, Sam, but now you mention it . . . Fortunately, this, too, was a recorded item and since the word 'fuck', now almost lingua franca on the air, was then taboo at the BBC we were able to edit his question out.

Another time – and this, too, is a drink-related tale – Harold Wilson, the former prime minister, had announced an initiative to help the ever-beleaguered British film industry and, together with David Lloyd, my producer on *Tonight*, I went to interview him at his house in Westminster. He was much as I had expected him to be – charming, dead crafty, forever lighting and relighting his pipe to give himself time to think of answers to any awkward questions that might arise.

When we had done, he said, 'Would you lads like a drink?' Well, yes, we would thank you, sherry would be nice. He poured them for us, then helped himself to a Scotch. As he poured his own drink he half-turned away from us, his body shielding the bottle and the glass from our gaze. Unfortunately for him, he was standing in front of a mirror and in that we could see that what he was providing himself with was a tumblerful of neat whisky.

He looked up and saw us watching him in the mirror. 'Oh, my word,' he said, chuckling, 'look what I've done, given myself far too much.' Carefully, he poured half the contents of the glass back into the bottle. A couple of minutes later he diverted our attention to something on the other side of the room but I wasn't falling for that one. I sneaked a quick look back in time to see him filling his glass to the brim again.

One night my guests were James Ferman, secretary of the British Board of Film Classification, and his Swedish counterpart. The topic: the difference between British and Swedish attitudes to film censorship. What it boiled down to was this: in Britain violence was acceptable, overt sexuality was not; in Sweden it was exactly the opposite – violence was banned, sex scenes were welcome. To illustrate the discussion we showed clips from two films – a scene from an American thriller starring James Mitchum, son of Robert, in which a prostitute was viciously beaten to death and another from a Swedish picture in which, in long shot, an attractive young couple were shown naked and making slow, gentle love to each other on the deck of a yacht. Sweden had turned down the Mitchum movie, Britain would have no truck with the Swedish one.

The next day the programme's editor received a reproachful letter from Mary Whitehouse, founder of the National Viewers' and

Listeners' Association and self-appointed guardian of all our morals. She wished to complain about one of the clips we had shown. Which one? Oh, come on – the sex scene, of course. Any respect I might have had for the woman – and it was never much – vanished at once. What she and her followers seemed to personify was the worst kind of English puritanism. Sex and bad language, against which they levelled their most vociferous protests, are among the least of the media's problems. Sex, though not much of a spectator sport, is simply a matter of two people being very nice to each other, while cuss words are all around us all the time. No child ever had to learn to swear by going to the movies; the words were already familiar from the playground. Violence, gratuitous violence of which films are too often guilty, is another and much more worrying matter. No sex scene in any movie has made me want to rape somebody but an Arnold Schwarzenegger picture once evoked in me a strong urge to thump a teenage nerd whom I overheard on the way out shouting, 'That's the greates' movie I ever seen!'

Hugh Carleton Greene, when he was Director-General of the BBC, had the most sensible approach to Mary Whitehouse: he simply ignored her. His successors, on the other hand, cravenly listened to her every moan. The second most sensible approach came from the late, great Willie Rushton, who propounded the idea of an anti-NVLA. Its members, of whom I was invited to be one, would, he said, inundate television companies every night with furious protests on the lines of, 'I have watched your programmes assiduously throughout the evening and am bitterly disappointed. Never once did I hear a four-letter word, see a full-frontal nude or watch people having sex. This is not what I pay my licence fee for. I cannot complain too strongly.' Willie's theory was that if he could persuade enough people to call in regularly the TV companies, ever terrified of public opinion, would fill their programmes with naked people having it away and cursing like troopers. I think he was probably right but, alas, like so many good ideas his was still-born.

Chapter Twenty-One

THE NICEST PERK that came my way as a result of the curious celebrity that attaches to anyone who appears regularly on TV was membership of the Lord's Taverners. This is an excellent organization that has raised millions of pounds for charity, notably by arranging pro-am cricket matches, and I was invited to join one morning on the *Today* programme. The eight o'clock news had just come on and the man I had been interviewing (whose name, shamefully, I have forgotten) said, 'I have a question for you from Eric Morecambe. It's this, "Why isn't Barry Norman, the biggest cricket nut in the country, a member of the Lord's Taverners?"'

The answer was simple: I never thought they'd have me. Taverners' teams regularly included several people who had played in Test matches. What would they want with a village opening batsman and off-spin bowler? Surely, given their choice, they wouldn't let me in the same ground, let alone the same team. But if Eric Morecambe, who apart from being the funniest comedian in the land was also president or chairman of the Taverners, wanted me, I was there, for he was right – I was and still am a cricket nut.

But I owe more to Eric than my introduction to the Taverners. It was thanks to him (and, of course, his partner Ernie Wise) that on the night of 25 December 1977, an estimated 28,835,000 people – or more than half the entire population of the United Kingdom – were privileged to watch me on television. To be strictly accurate, I should point out that none of these people (with the possible exception of my own family and even that's doubtful) had actually tuned in to watch me. Eric and Ernie were the real attraction because this was their Christmas night special and in that era the Morecambe and Wise Christmas show was just about compulsory viewing.

My participation came about when their producer Ernest Maxin phoned me at home and said, 'The boys want you in the show. Are you game?'

Eric and Ernie wanted *me*? I couldn't believe it. 'Doing what?' I asked.

'Oh, it's a musical number from *South Pacific*, singing and dancing and that.'

I couldn't sing, I couldn't dance. I have absolutely no sense of rhythm whatsoever but, bloody hell, this was Morecambe and Wise calling; they were the very best and if the very best want you, you don't say no. So I said yes and turned up for the first of the two rehearsals that had been arranged, albeit with severe misgivings.

There were eight of us – Richard Baker, Michael Aspel, Peter Woods, Richard Whitmore, Eddie Waring, Philip Jenkinson, Frank Bough and me – all BBC presenters or newsreaders and, dressed in white American sailor suits, we formed a most unlikely chorus line to sing 'There is Nothing Like a Dame'. For me the singing was difficult enough. When I open my mouth and lungs to burst into song what emerges has no recognisable connection with music whatsoever. Many times when I have been singing happily to myself in the bath, the entire family has gathered round to hammer on the door and beg me to stop that awful noise. Well, I thought, I could overcome that by simply mouthing the words on camera, not making any sound at all, confident that with the other seven singing away nobody would notice.

But then there was the dancing and, on top of that, Ernest Maxin wanted us to give the impression that we were doing spectacular acrobatics. Bough, Aspel and Whitmore were supposed to do somersaults, Phil Jenkinson and I a couple of dramatic handsprings. Excuse me? Handsprings? *Me*?

Of course, we didn't actually do those things. We ran up with our arms outspread, looking as if we were about to do them and then Maxin cut to professional acrobats leaping, cartwheeling and somersaulting backwards and forwards across the stage. The editing was so immaculate that the biggest audience I have ever had – just about the biggest audience anyone in Britain has ever had – was firmly convinced that it had seen me doing a couple of perfect handsprings.

Before that show I was, I suppose, already reasonably well-known but for a few days after it I was truly famous. Virtually every second person I met said, 'Hey, saw you on the Morecambe and Wise show. Great stuff. How did you *do* that?'

At first I dutifully explained how it was really done and then I got bored with all the repetition and, merely to amuse myself, came up with an alternative explanation. 'Well,' I said, 'the trick is, you've got to get the height. So you have this springboard and you leap off that and if you jump high enough you can twist around and do anything you like.'

People actually believed me, which I thought was quite funny until the thought occurred that some idiot might go away, get himself a springboard, jump into the air and break his neck.

Eric and Ernie were unquestionably the funniest double act this country has ever produced and like all the best comedians took their work very seriously. While we were recording the *South Pacific* routine, and it took less than an hour, there were no jokes, no larking about. The boys – everyone called them 'the boys' – could hardly have been more friendly but this was their show, their reputations depended on it, and we'd all better try our damnedest or else. In fact Eric, as I learned later, was not at all sure that the scene would work and had to be constantly reassured by Ernest Maxin. But it did work; it worked so well that it's included in practically every Morecambe and Wise compilation shown on TV. Even now I still get tiny royalty cheques every year and they are tiny because my fee was only £100 in the first place. But who cares about that? I'd have paid them to let me be in their show.

This was the only time I worked with Eric and Ernie, although a year or so later, when they'd left the BBC for ITV, I bumped into Eric and he invited me to be on their Christmas programme again. I wanted to, of course I did, but for contractual reasons the BBC wouldn't let me.

Of the two, Eric was the one I knew better, largely because of the Taverners. I never knew him well but he was always a pleasure to be with because there was a quality about him that made you feel, when in his company, that life was an altogether more cheerful business than you had supposed.

Once, when I was playing for the Taverners at Peterborough, I took Samantha with me and at tea-time she and I went into the marquee and sat at a table together, just the two of us. A few minutes later Eric wandered in on his own. 'Mind if I join you?' he asked. Naturally, we didn't mind at all; Mamf indeed was thrilled. She was only seventeen and delighted to have him sit with us, but she was also a little shy.

Eric and I chatted for a bit, with Samantha listening but saying nothing and then he leaned across the table to her and said, 'Are you married?' She blushed and laughed. 'No,' she said.

'I am,' Eric said. 'Story of my life, that is. Every time I meet a pretty girl either she's married or I am.' She loved him for that ever after.

When he died I think the whole country went into mourning. I certainly did. Nobody has ever come along to replace him and I think of him still with great fondness, not only because of the Christmas show but also – and that brings us back to where we came in – because of cricket and the Taverners.

Cricket is my greatest passion, even greater than the cinema. My grandfather introduced me to it just before the end of the war. I had never played the game, nor seen it played. There wasn't much cricket going on at the time, although there was a little, some of it at Lord's. But it never occurred to anyone to take me there, nor did it occur to me to ask. So for a long time all I knew about it was what my grandfather told me and his enthusiasm was such that I was immediately infected. He was a lifelong Surrey supporter and would tell me tales of the glorious deeds of men with unaspirated names like 'Ayward, 'Ick and 'Obbs. Now I think back on it, he must have been a brilliant raconteur to make me so besotted with the most complicated ball game ever invented without my having the faintest idea what it looked like.

I soon learned, though. I read every cricket book I could find, so when at last on a glorious August day in 1945 I saw my first game – England v. Australia in a Victory Test Match at Lord's – I was ready. Thanks to Granddad and my book learning I knew it all – in theory anyway.

I went with my 15-year-old cousin Gerry and a school friend of his, a rather arrogant youth who really didn't want to be bothered with a kid like me. But I knew something about him that he didn't know I knew. His father was still away in the army and his mother, as I had heard tell around my grandparents' house, was well known for putting herself about among American army officers.

We sat in the free seats near the old Tavern with our sandwiches and bottles of Tizer and Gerry's friend had brought his in a khaki haversack with the initials US on it.

'Where did you get that?' I asked, disingenuously, because I was perfectly aware what US stood for.

'It's my father's,' he said. 'Those are his initials.'

'Really? What's his name then?'

'Ugene Smith,' he said. For a moment I felt a malicious glee. Come on – nobody spells Eugene with a capital U. But I said nothing and now I'm glad I kept silent for it occurs to me that maybe he wasn't really cocky, maybe he was just an unhappy kid, another casualty of war. There had been something defiant in the way he stared at me when he came up with that preposterous name, as if he didn't expect me to believe him and was challenging me to call him a liar. He had accepted the haversack from one of his American 'uncles' just as he had, no doubt, been obliged to accept the 'uncles' themselves but that's not to say he liked the situation and what was being done to his father or wasn't emotionally upset by it.

Soon, though, the extramarital activities of Mrs Ugene Smith faded from my mind, for the cricket had started and it was just as magical as I had imagined it would be. I think you have to be born to cricket; it's either in you or it isn't. You can explain it to the uninitiated as much as you like but no matter how intelligent your listener, unless the seeds of cricket are in him he will never understand and certainly he will never grow to love it. It's not just the mechanics of the game that are complicated; it's the psychology and the cunning of it.

Americans, with their obsession with winning and doing everything fast, can never hope to comprehend a game in which, after five days, a draw might still be the best possible result; although they might be beguiled by the statistics. Americans love statistics and so does cricket. But there, too, cricket's statistics, like every other aspect of the game, are special. I'm never impressed when, in America, I'm told that a quarterback has thrown the ball 147 miles in the course of the season and may even have been responsible for several touchdowns. But – and I quote from the 1949 *Wisden* – a line that reads: 'R. W. V. Robins . . . 105 overs, 15 maidens, 342 runs, 12 wickets, average 28.50', fills me with joy, not only because Walter Robins, captain of Middlesex and England, was the most celebrated cricketer who ever attended my old school but because I can imagine the thought and subtle variations that went on throughout every over. Cricket is chess played with human pieces. It's also the most deliciously devious way of wasting time ever invented by man.

On that lovely day in 1945 I saw Cyril Washbrook score 112, with Keith Miller bowling, Bill Edrich make 73 and Wally Hammond score 83. We stayed, Gerry and I and Ugene's son, till stumps were drawn and I knew then that Lord's was, as it has remained, one of my favourite places in the world.

Once, many years later, I was actually asked to play there. It was the fortieth anniversary of the Taverners, on whose cricket committee I then served, and a match had been arranged between us and the Marylebone Cricket Club to celebrate the occasion. Although our club had been first mooted over a pint or two in front of the Tavern, Lord's was by no means our home. We played on several other first class grounds but rarely, and never before in my experience, at Lord's itself. So this anniversary match was to be a milestone in our history.

At the cricket committee meeting a week or so before the game our chairman, Derek Ufton, the former Kent wicketkeeper and Charlton Athletic and England centre half, announced the team – and I was in it. Now I had no illusions about this; every playing member of the committee was in the team and most of them – Mike Denness, the former Kent and England captain, for example, and John Price, who played for Middlesex and England – had every right to be. But I was getting on for sixty, for God's sake; I was still bowling okay, putting the ball pretty well in the right place and turning it from off, but for years I'd been batting from an increasingly suspect memory and, worst of all, my fielding had deserted me. My reflexes were shot and as Derek read out the team I had a vivid mental image of what the game at Lord's would be like.

We would play on the pitch nearest the Tavern and I would be fielding miles away, underneath Father Time, the famous weather vane then still in his original location. The MCC batsmen, most of them former Test players, would keep hitting the ball in my direction – because, as every cricketer knows, the ball always, unerringly, seeks out the weakest fielder – and I would either be unable to stop it or would be incapable of reaching the wicket with my throw. I absolutely knew that if I turned out in this game only humiliation would await me. And so I found myself saying, 'Well, thanks very much but I've been thinking about retiring for some time and I reckon this is the right moment.'

Derek was very nice about it and even tried to persuade me to change my mind. But I hadn't missed the involuntary look of relief that crossed his face as he heard my announcement and realized that he could now choose a real cricketer to take my place.

So I never played at Lord's; I didn't even go to the game – it would have been too painful; and, indeed, I have never played cricket since that day. I thought I would miss it but curiously enough I haven't. If the anniversary match had come a year or two earlier I'd have insisted on turning out. But now I'd reached a time when I still liked bowling, didn't care too much whether I batted or not but actively dreaded fielding and because of that I hadn't really enjoyed any of the games I played that year.

Even so, was it craven of me to chicken out the way I did? Yes, probably. I suppose I could claim that I did it for the good of the team but sod the team. I did it because I knew beyond doubt that I could only make a fool of myself and the prospect of doing that in one of my favourite places in the world was too awful to contemplate. So I took the invitation for the fact; I was at least asked to play at Lord's and not too many people can say that.

Besides, I have a few splendid memories to keep me warm. One week in particular I will never forget. On the Sunday we played at Arundel, one of the prettiest grounds in the country, hard by the cathedral. The Taverners versus the Duchess of Norfolk's XI, captained by the great Colin Cowdrey, hero of Kent and England. And I got him out, caught for about thirteen as he misread my devilishly flighted off-spin. If Colin had made fifty or so he would probably have got himself out deliberately but never, not even in a charity match, would he have given his wicket away for thirteen.

On the following Saturday we played at Scarborough and I caught and bowled Mike Denness, also of Kent and England, for eight. Admittedly, he hit the ball back at me with such ferocity that if I hadn't caught it I'd have ended up with a navel the size of a small melon but I did catch it. And to add to my bliss – dismissing two former England captains in one week – my own skipper that day, Brian Close, ran up to congratulate me, saying in tones of genuine admiration, 'My, Ah wouldn't ha' put my hands behind a ball like that on a cold day like this!' Brian Close – the hardest man who ever played for England. Now there was praise . . .

Then, too, though I missed out on Lords I did play on several other first class grounds, including the Oval, where I scored one not out – a push off my legs, as I remember, and a wild scamper to the other end. And in its own way that was a great occasion. The first real Test match I ever saw was at the Oval in 1947, England versus South Africa, and four years later I was there again and so were England and South Africa. The film director, Basil Dearden, had two spare tickets that day and gave them to my father. It was the only time Dad ever took me to cricket.

We sat opposite the pavilion and brought our own sandwiches as almost everybody did in those days. Basil Dearden's wife, Melissa, seemed to me to be very beautiful but though she tried to draw me out

I was too overwhelmed to talk to her. Well, I was a shy kid and I couldn't find much to say to her husband either. So I sat there and watched the cricket, the most memorable aspect of which was Len Hutton, playing his hundredth Test innings, being given out for obstructing the field. He top-edged a ball from Athol Rowan high above his head and, as Russell Endean the wicketkeeper jogged up to catch it, took a wild swipe at it with his bat, explaining later that he hadn't noticed the 'keeper and thought the ball was going to fall on his stumps. It didn't matter, though, because England won.

But on that day, many years later, when I ran down the pavilion steps to bat for the Lord's Taverners I glanced up and found myself staring at exactly the spot where my father and I had sat in 1951. Could I have imagined then that one day I, too, would bat at the Oval? Well, of course I couldn't. What a bloody silly question. I might have dreamed about it and probably did but I would also have reckoned it was a total impossibility. And yet it happened and the fact that it came about not because I was a particularly good cricketer but because I was a sort of 'celebrity' is neither here nor there.

It's a pity, though, that Dad wasn't around to see my one not out. The only other time he had come with me to the Oval, on this occasion as my guest, was during the England–Australia Test in 1975. The cricket writer, David Frith, and I had books published that day and our publisher, another cricket nut, had decided that the Oval was the place to hold the celebration party.

Dad got gloriously pissed, so pissed that he seized upon an elderly member of the Surrey ground staff and introduced him to everybody as Godfrey Evans, the former England wicketkeeper. I knew Godfrey Evans, who wasn't even at the party, and kept telling my father that this little, wizened old man was not him. But he wouldn't listen and, what was worse, he plied the willing groundsman with so much free booze that in the end the bloke began to believe that he actually was Godfrey Evans.

Dad would drag him up to some unsuspecting bystander and say, 'This is Godfrey Evans.'

The bystander would look down suspiciously at the small, drunken, bewhiskered mess and say, 'Really?'

'Oh, yes,' the mess would reply. 'That's me – Godfrey Evans.'

'Great party, son,' Dad said as he fell into his car to be driven home. 'I especially enjoyed meeting Godfrey Evans. Wonderful bloke.'

One more Oval story. It doesn't have anything to do with cricket but it says a little about the devious workings of the pressman's mind. When Samantha was seventeen or so there was a party at the Oval to launch the publishing firm Pavilion Books with which Michael Parkinson and Tim Rice were associated. I was invited and asked to bring a guest. Diana and Emma being interested neither in celebrity events nor cricket were not at all keen but Mamf said she would like to go with me, so I took her.

It was a biggish party, lots of famous names there, but rather to my surprise Mamf and I were the ones who attracted most attention. The photographers, about a dozen of them, clustered eagerly around, shouting their instructions . . . 'Bit closer together, please' . . . 'Barry, will you put your arm around her?' . . . 'Could you look at each other and smile?' The usual stuff.

'Gosh, Dad,' Mamf whispered to me, 'you're more famous than I thought.' I shrugged modestly.

The photographers finished taking their snaps and withdrew to huddle together. A couple of minutes later, one of them whom I knew well from my Fleet Street days, came over to me as I stood by myself, Mamf being engaged in conversation elsewhere.

'Here, Barry,' he said, 'what's the name of that girl you're with?'

'Samantha.'

'Yeah, but who is she?'

'My daughter.'

His mouth fell open. 'You're kidding.'

'No, she's my daughter.'

'Oh, fucking hell,' he said. 'We thought she was your girlfriend.'

The next day none of the photographs was published. Not much interest in a happy snap of a father and daughter. A happy snap of an errant husband and father with a blonde, beautiful and illicit companion would, of course, have been another matter.

My own heroes were Bill Edrich and, almost inevitably, Denis

Compton. In those post-war years Denis was everyone's hero, unless
you came from Yorkshire in which case you probably couldn't see
beyond Len Hutton. Denis was a natural. He could play every shot
there ever was plus a few that never existed until he thought of them.
The only thing he notoriously couldn't do was judge a run. Those who
said that any call from Denis should merely be regarded as the opening
of lengthy negotiations were not kidding.

I was there when he ran his brother Leslie out for a duck in Leslie's
benefit match at Lord's. It was a typical Denis cockup – 'Yes, no, wait,
all right, come on.' Leslie never had a chance. He was out by miles with
the Sussex fielders chuckling happily and Denis trying to persuade
anyone who would listen that it wasn't his fault.

Years later when finally I met him I asked what Leslie had said to
him that day. 'I can tell you exactly,' he said. 'As he walked past me on
his way back to the pavilion, he said, "If you don't get a hundred today,
little brother, I'm going to fuckin' murder you."'

Naturally, Denis did get a hundred, a big one at that.

This first meeting between Denis and myself took place at the Savoy
Hotel where we were both guests at a Saints and Sinners dinner. I fancied myself as a Saint but Denis was there as a Sinner; his worst enemy
would never have accused him of being a Saint.

At the end of the evening Denis and his party joined the table where
I was sitting with, among others, David Gower. David, who was only a
lad at the time, was to captain the MCC the next day and later, when
I drove him back to his hotel near Lord's, he said, 'It's sad, isn't it, to see
Denis Compton all fat and red-faced like that?'

Well, maybe it was. But in my mind Denis was never fat or red-
faced; he was always the dashing Brylcreem boy who, in 1947, led the
charge when Middlesex habitually seemed to declare at 420 for six at
teatime on the first day. And anyway there was nothing sad about him
that night at the Savoy.

When he joined our table he came to sit next to me. Now if Marlon
Brando or Michelle Pfeiffer had chosen to sit beside me I'd have been
quite pleased. But for the great Denis Compton to do so was overwhelming and, even better, he not only knew who I was but said he

regularly watched and enjoyed my TV programme. He was a great movie buff, who wanted to talk about the film stars I knew, while what I wanted to talk about was cricket and in particular one story about him that had long intrigued me. It was, I was pretty sure, apocryphal because the way the story went was that in 1938, when he was twenty years old and playing in his first Test against Australia at Trent Bridge, he had to be woken up and told that it was his turn to go into bat.

'That's nonsense, isn't it?' I said.

'No,' he said, 'I'm afraid it's true.'

'But how could you do that? How could you fall asleep when you're just about to bat in your first Test against Australia?'

'Well,' he said, 'it was a warm day and Len had got a few and somebody else had got a few and I just nodded off.'

What he omitted to mention was that after he'd rubbed the sleep from his eyes he went in and scored 102.

Denis was simply a law unto himself, a cheerful, lovable maverick, who always enjoyed the good life, the food, the women, the booze. Indeed, it strikes me that in recent years when Graham Gooch was captain of England and physical fitness was the key note and everyone had to run five miles before breakfast Denis, even in his prime, would probably not have been selected. The single circumstance in which he might have been persuaded to run five miles on the day of a Test was if that was the only way he could get back from the night club before start of play. And even then he would have turned up in his dinner jacket and without his kit.

It was Denis Compton who caused me to end my exclusive deal with the BBC. In 1988 ITV were to celebrate his seventieth birthday with a special programme and when they asked him who he would like to present it he told them me. I was so thrilled that when my agent, Sue Freathy, broke the news I said, 'Yes, tell them yes' and I didn't even ask what kind of fee they were offering. Actually, I'd have done it for nothing.

But then the functionaries at the BBC stepped in. Under the terms of my contract I was allowed to work for other television companies but only with the BBC's permission. And they said no. It didn't matter how

much Sue and I argued that, as far as the BBC audience was concerned, I was associated simply with the movies and that a Denis
Compton tribute could hardly have been more removed from my specialist subject, they were adamant. My contract said I could only do it
with the Beeb's permission and the Beeb wasn't giving it, so sucks.

In the end Ian Wooldridge, an old mate from my *Daily Mail* days,
presented the programme and did it very well. But it rankled – indeed,
it rankled so much that when a couple of months later my contract
came up for renewal I insisted that, in future, I would be exclusive to
the BBC only in matters relating to films; if I wanted to do anything
else on any other channel I would be free to do it. The Beeb wasn't
happy and delegated Will Wyatt, who was an old friend of mine, to
take me to lunch and persuade me to change my mind. But in my
resentful – oh, all right, petulant – mood I wasn't to be moved even by
him.

So there was an impasse while the BBC grumpily chewed over my
demands. It's notoriously slow at finalizing contracts anyway. It quibbles
over this, won't accept that and always tries to knock as much as possible off whatever fee the presenter asks. So on this occasion, while Sue
was cheerfully engaged in confounding the Corporation's murky plots
and I was, technically, out of contract and therefore unemployed, I was
free to accept a mouth-watering offer from Channel 4.

In September the Olympic Games were to be held in Seoul and
Channel 4 wanted me and Elton Welsby to chair a live discussion programme every night while the event was on. I was to handle matters
from 11 p.m. until 1 a.m., at which point Elton would join me and I'd
stick around for another half-hour before leaving him to take things
through till seven o'clock in the morning.

I must have seemed an odd choice for such a job, certainly I was to
Mark Sharman, who was to be my producer. I was to work with him
again later on at Sky but in 1988, as indeed today, Mark had no interest in movies and was puzzled as to how he'd been landed with a film
critic to cover the Olympics. In fact, I was chosen by Bob Burrows, then
a top executive with ITV and formerly head of sport for BBC radio. And
he knew that I had often stood in as presenter of Radio 4's *Sport on 4*

programme on Saturday mornings. Presumably, too, he thought I must have done that quite well.

For someone like me, who reserves his hero worship exclusively for great writers and top-class sportsmen, the Olympic chat show was a dream assignment. According to *The Sun* I was paid £25,000 for the fortnight, a figure that was arrived at like this:

Sun reporter: 'How much you being paid then, Barry?'

Me: 'None of your business.'

Sun reporter: 'I know but I have to ask.'

Me: 'Maybe so but I don't have to tell you.'

He then went away and conjured £25,000 out of his imagination. In fact, I was paid considerably less, having accepted the first offer made to me. Sue sneered at it and said she could easily push it higher but I told her to accept because I wanted to do the job. As with the Morecambe and Wise show and the Compton tribute, the money didn't matter.

The regular studio guests we assembled each night included former Olympic champions like Steve Ovett and Alan Wells, Roger Black, the 400 metres runner who would have been competing at Seoul but for a leg injury, Harvey Smith, the gloriously bloody-minded show jumper, the former world boxing champions Jim Watt and Barry McGuigan and on one occasion Frank Bruno, whom I inadvertently upset.

As the women around the programme agreed, Frank was a great big, chuckling teddy bear and at the beginning of our chat that's how he seemed to me. I've always loved boxing, though I also despise myself for it. I know it's brutal, primitive, savage, whatever. And no matter how many reasons you give me for saying that it should be banned in civilized society I can add a couple more.

And yet I'm still fascinated by it. Many of those involved in it outside the ring are liars, crooks and cheats, the kind of people who give parasites a bad name, and there seems very little reason why some of them shouldn't be in prison. But for the boxers, whose skill, dedication and courage are so often ruthlessly exploited, I have nothing but admiration.

So I afforded Frank Bruno, cuddly and chuckling though he may have been, as much respect as I would have offered to any fighter. Apart from anything else the size of him inspired awe. His massive presence was such that you felt you would upset him at your peril.

I upset him.

I didn't mean to. This was a few months before his first fight with Mike Tyson, who was still a terrifying figure. Naturally I asked Frank what he thought about his prospects and, naturally, he was bullish. Nobody else was but I didn't like to tell him that. You didn't have to be a boxing expert to know that Frank, despite his size, power and heart, wasn't remotely in Tyson's class. So we chatted about the forthcoming fight and what it would mean to Frank if he won and became heavy-weight champion of the world and then I said: 'Yes, but what if you lose?'

All of a sudden he stopped being cuddly and chuckling. 'What do you mean, lose?'

'Well, you know. What will you do if you lose?'

He leaned menacingly towards me and Frank Bruno leaning men-acingly towards you is about as menacing as you want to experience. 'You're putting negative thoughts in my head,' he said in an angry rumble. 'I don't like that. I don't like people putting negative thoughts in my head.'

Wisely, I decided to offer no more negative thoughts.

Looking back I reckon those two weeks covering the Olympic Games from the Thames TV studios in Euston Road were the most enjoyable I have spent in television, though things didn't start too well. On the Friday night before the Olympics began there was a pre-Games programme in which the presenters of the various ITV/Channel 4 Olympic shows – about eight of us in all – took part.

That evening the car, ordered to pick me up from home, didn't arrive so I had to scramble frantically to the studio by train and Tube. Time was already tight when I got there and it became a lot tighter when the piece of film for which I was to write and record a voice-over commentary could not be found.

While people were rushing about trying to locate it Mark Sharman asked if I had my earpiece with me. What earpiece? Naked horror in Mark's eyes. 'The thing you stick in your ear when you're in the studio so I can talk to you from the gallery. You must use one on the film programme.'

'Nah,' I said. 'Never had one of those.'

'Oh, my God! Oh, my God!' Frantic phone calls were made, people took wax impressions of my ear and finally not one but two earpieces – one for each ear – were made and delivered. As it turned out I didn't use them much. Regular sports presenters are accustomed to hearing every word from the gallery while they are talking or interviewing someone but I couldn't be doing with that and came to an arrangement whereby my earpiece would only be switched on when Mark wanted to speak to me.

Meanwhile, Sue had at last come to agreement with the BBC, which meant that I was doing the day job – *Film 88* – as well as the Channel 4 stint. What's more on the Saturday the Olympics began Samantha got married – to Dr Piers Clifford, who is now a consultant cardiologist – with the result that, after the wedding, the reception and the trauma of handing over my daughter to the care of somebody else, I turned up for my Sunday night Olympic shift in a state of nervous and physical exhaustion and pretty well remained in that condition until the Games were over.

But it was an experience that I would not have missed. The only thing that clouds my memory of the time is that, sadly, Mamfie and Piers are now separated and on the verge of divorce. They, and all of us, are still on very good terms but, despite having two sons adored by all, matters did not work out between them. These things happen. What can you say?

Chapter Twenty-Two

IN THE LATE 1970s Lord Grade – Lew to those who knew him well – made a picture called *The Long Good Friday*. Or rather his film company made it; Lew wasn't personally involved in the production. It was first shown at the 1979 London Film Festival and impressed pretty well everyone as a cracking good British thriller, the story of a powerful London gangleader, played by Bob Hoskins, who can't understand who is messing up his plans for a Dockland development scheme, blowing up his pubs and killing his henchmen or why any of this is being done. It's an exciting, violent movie, confidently made and acted and most of the critics looked forward to its general release in the cinema.

Unfortunately, Lew had a temporary cash flow problem – nothing serious but irritating nevertheless – that involved another of his interests, the commercial television station ATV. And to solve it he decided to have *The Long Good Friday* cut and shorn of violence and bad language so that it could be shown as a TV movie and not distributed in the cinemas at all. When news of this became known the makers of the film – Hoskins, the producer Barry Hanson and the director John Mackenzie – kicked up a fuss and a number of critics supported them.

This was not a good time for the British film industry; money was tight, very few movies were being made and *The Long Good Friday* was incomparably better than any other indigenous thriller in recent years. That it should be seen only on television – and then in an emasculated form – seemed an appalling waste. So a few of us – Derek Malcolm, the film critic of the *Guardian*, was one and I was another – started independent campaigns to save it for the cinema. There was no collusion between us: we each acted spontaneously and without consultation. And the result of all this was that Handmade Films, a company whose directors included the former Beatle George Harrison, bought the cinema rights of the picture from Lew and organized nationwide distribution.

I was puzzled by George Harrison's involvement. I saw him at a party in honour of the film and he didn't seem at all comfortable among these movie people. He was, without doubt, the most famous person there but he stood by himself to one side, gloomily holding a glass of tepid white wine, and surveying the throng with no apparent enthusiasm.

'What are you doing here?' I said and he shrugged and said, 'I dunno, really. The movies aren't exactly my scene but we thought this was a good picture and we ought to back it.'

The party was held in a house in Regent's Park on the night *The Long Good Friday* had its première in the West End of London. And among the guests were those of us in the media who had striven to save the film from truncation and anonymity on TV. In fact, we turned out to be the guests of honour because Barry Hanson leapt up and delivered a gracious and elegant speech of thanks for our efforts and he was followed by John Mackenzie, who finished his own equally gracious and elegant address by saying, 'How about you, Bob? Do you want to say anything?'

'Yeah,' said Bob, 'all right.' And he sprang on to the dais and said, 'All I can say is, you done us fuckin' proud.' Not gracious or elegant perhaps but, we thought, from the heart.

I got to know Bob quite well at that time and he told me how some of the extras on *The Long Good Friday* were genuine villains with form and gangland connections. Which was why, when he got married around the time the film was wrapping production, he didn't tell anybody.

'Why not?' I said. 'Didn't you want them at your wedding?'

'Nah, it wasn't that. I'd have quite liked them to come, only they'd have insisted on giving us presents and I didn't want my house full of stuff that fell off the back of a lorry.'

Soon after the film opened to generous reviews and a healthy box office Bob was mysteriously approached by one of the gang-connected extras.

'Wotcha doin' tonight, Bob,' he asked.

'I dunno. Nothing. Why?'

The villain nodded. 'I'll pick you up at eight then.'

'Yeah, all right, but where we going?'

'You'll see.'

At eight o'clock the villain collected Bob from his home in north London and drove him to a pub south of the river. It was an unsavoury place, one that Bob had never heard of before, full of characters with bent noses and uncompromising stares.

'What are we doing here?' he asked his escort.

'Wait,' the man said. So they had a drink and waited and then, suddenly, Charlie Richardson was in their midst. By rights Charlie Richardson, a founder member of one of the most notorious criminal gangs in south London history, should have been in prison. Indeed, he had been in prison – until a week or so earlier when he had arbitrarily decided it was time to leave and, on the run, had begun a campaign of letter writing to the press to protest his innocence or anyway to complain about the severity of his sentence.

Now, huddled around with bodyguards, he was introduced to Bob. 'Good of you to come,' he said. 'Nice to meet you. Loved the film.'

'You've seen it then?'

'Oh, yes, and what I wanted to say was you done right by us, you really done us well.'

So Bob, the sort of screen equivalent of Charlie Richardson, thanked him for the compliment and they chatted awhile and then Bob said, 'Charlie, aren't you taking a bit of a risk? I mean – being on the run and coming into a pub. What if the police came in?'

'The police?' Charlie Richardson said. 'In here? They wouldn't bloody dare.'

A few years after this, in 1982, Bob was rehearsing for a play at the National Theatre and I went there to interview him. We talked for a while in his dressing room and the auditorium and then went out into the street behind the theatre for a few walking shots and the like. When we had finished that the camera and production crews went away to take some wallpaper footage, background for any voice-over commentary I wished to write, leaving Bob and me alone in the middle of the street.

'You fancy a drink?' he said.

'Well, I do actually, Bob, but it's gone three and the pubs are closed.' This, you understand, was in the days before the government, in its wisdom, decided that pubs could open all hours and those who so desired could be drunk pretty well twenty-four hours a day.

'That's all right,' he said. 'There's a place just down the road, a club I think. We can get a drink there.'

'Are you a member then?'

'Nah,' he said. 'But they'll let us in, won't they?'

So we tried it. The place down the road was in a row of high old houses that were already being demolished. It looked quite imposing with a heavy oak door upon which Bob knocked with great confidence.

After a minute or two the door was opened, or anyway cautiously half-opened, and a young man looked out at us with suspicion. 'Yeah?' he said. 'What do you want?'

'We'd like to come in for a drink,' Bob said.

'We're closed,' he said.

'Yeah, I know,' Bob said, 'but you'll let *us* in, won't you?' He winked a couple of times and nudged me with his elbow. 'You'll let *us* in.'

Now Bob was dressed in his rehearsing-at-the-National outfit, which is to say a dark blue fisherman's knit sweater, faded jeans and scruffy sneakers, while I was dressed in my being-on-TV outfit, which is to say the cashmere overcoat, the designer suit and shirt and the silk tie. Dead sprauncy, I was, though I say it myself.

Doubtfully the young man looked at me, looked at Bob, then looked back at me and said, 'Well, all right then', and he let us in.

He led us through a dining room where a smattering of apparently

affluent but tough-looking men was still sitting around enjoying post-
prandial brandies and cigars but he didn't invite us to sit at one of the
many unoccupied tables. Instead he led us through to a smaller, empty
room and there he took our orders for drinks and discreetly left us.

Bob and I talked for a while and then he said, 'Fancy another?' and
I did so we called the young man again and summoned up a second
round.

A little later I said, 'I think we'd better get back to the crew, Bob', so
once more the young man was recalled and I asked how much we
owed him.

'Nothing,' he said.

'What?'

'Nothing. It's on the house.'

'Well, that's very kind of you,' I said. 'Are you sure?'

'I'm sure,' he said and led us back through the dining room and to
the street and I thought: well, this is great. I must go out with Bob again.
You get into places that are either private clubs or officially closed,
drink what you want and don't pay a penny.

A couple of weeks later I was presenting the pilot for a projected television series at the BBC studios in Bristol. The programme was about
modern living; not a bad idea but it never got beyond the pilot stage.
Bob Hoskins was one of my interviewees.

We met in the make-up department where Bob was persuading one
of the women to give him a haircut. Actors often do that, I've noticed.
They drop into make-up to have the slap applied and say, 'Oh, and
while you're about it, darling, you couldn't give us a bit of a trim could
you?' I suppose it saves them money but, more than that, it saves them
the time and bother of making an appointment with a hair salon.

I dropped into the chair next to Bob and said I just wanted the
usual base and powder, no haircut, thanks, and he said, 'Here, you
remember that club we went to behind the National?'

I said I did; I remembered it well.

'Only I went back there a few days later,' he said. 'The same young
bloke let me in and he said, "Who was that geezer you was with last
week? I know him, don't I?" I said, "Yeah, you've probably seen him on

TV" and he said, "No, I *know* him, don't I?" So I said, "I'm telling you – he reviews the films on television" and the geezer said, "Oh, fuckin' hell. I though he was a face and you was his minder."'

It's a terrible admission but I was strangely chuffed. That was the only time in my life that I've been mistaken for a high-ranking member of the London underworld and – God knows what this says about me – I felt rather flattered.

At that time, in fact, I was engaged in nothing more nefarious than presenting the BBC's flagship arts programme, *Omnibus*, which I had joined a few months earlier. Big mistake, really. Or it could have been.

The previous year the British Academy of Film and Television Arts had given me the Richard Dimbleby Award for my contribution to factual television and a by-product of that was that I began to reassess where I was heading. I still enjoyed the film programme enormously but – and I'm beginning to sound like some pretentious movie star here – I felt I needed a new challenge. Where I was there was no way I could top the BAFTA award and a career change seemed a good idea about now. By chance the offer of a career change came along.

The BBC had decided to revive *Omnibus*, which had been off the air for a few years, and I was asked to present it. Both Sue Freathy and I thought this might be the right move at the right time. So it could have been, except that things didn't quite work out as promised.

Christopher Martin, the editor of *Omnibus* and an experienced, respected producer of BBC arts programmes, told me when I was considering the offer that he had in mind a new kind of show, much livelier than the original *Omnibus* and taking its style from me. I liked that. Unfortunately, the press did not. On ITV there was already in existence a new kind of lively arts programme in *The South Bank Show*, presented by Melvyn Bragg. Arts programmes were rare on ITV – still are, come to that – and the newspapers felt (rightly, because it was good) that *The South Bank Show* should be cosseted. So far, no problem. I agreed with them but I also believed that there was certainly room for two lively arts programmes on television.

The trouble was that the BBC made a crass mistake: it scheduled my programme to be shown at the same time as *The South Bank Show*, arguing that its allotted Sunday night slot was where *Omnibus* had traditionally sat and where it should therefore sit again. This was regarded by the press as a sinister move by the Beeb to use its many resources to kill off the upstart show on ITV and suddenly I found myself regarded as one of the chief villains in a dark conspiracy. Of course, it was nothing of the kind – it was just a cockup, as so many alleged conspiracies are. If the BBC had only unbent and said, oh, yes, you're quite right, it's daft to have the two main arts programmes on TV in direct competition with each other, so we'll move to another night instead, *Omnibus* would probably have been welcomed. But it is not in the nature of large corporations to unbend, so the Beeb stuck stubbornly to its original decision, thus apparently confirming the conspiracy theory, and poor old *Omnibus* was hated and vilified before it even got on the air.

It was a position from which we could not possibly win unless the very first programme was so outstandingly good that the critics would, however grudgingly, be forced to change their minds. But first programmes are never very good – every series takes time to settle down and gain confidence in itself – and ours was no exception. Actually, the first show was rather poor. Christopher had gathered a production team of more than thirty people, nearly all of whom were steeped in the middle-class, middle-aged, middle-brow tradition of BBC arts programmes and though they tried to make the opening show different and lively they didn't really know how. One way and another it was a bit of a mess. The reviews were scathing and inevitably, because I was at the sharp end, much of the abuse was directed at me, even though I had had very little control over the contents of the programme.

On Monday mornings it was Christopher's practice to hold a postmortem, a team meeting at which the previous night's offering would be discussed. Not a good idea, because it gave carte blanche to the disaffected producers – those whose items had not made it into the programme – to sneer at the work of the chosen few. On that first Monday morning very little except sneering went on and, with people still reeling from the savage reviews, confidence was non-existent. In truth, I reeled rather less than the others because, unlike them, I had worked in Fleet Street, I had read the jibes in the weeks leading up to the first show, knew the workings of journalism and was not at all surprised at the hostile welcome we had received.

For a couple of weeks after that, and largely because the items had already been recorded, lip service was still paid to the idea of a different, lively arts programme but the reviews did not improve, hardly anyone's heart was in it and by the third show vestiges of the old *Omnibus* had begun to creep in. Never from the start had the programme taken its style from me and now, as Peter Fiddick pointed out quite correctly in the *Guardian*, that style – expressed in the links and comments I wrote – was actually working against the rest of the contents.

As the critical flak kept flying in my direction I had some much-needed consolation from Jonathan Miller, who had come into the studio for an interview. He asked how the show was going and I said, all right, but the reviews have been terrible.

'You don't know what bad reviews are,' he said. 'You should have seen what was written about me when I was presenting *Monitor*.' He was talking about a BBC arts programme that he had edited as well as presented as far back as 1965.

'I expect you've got over that by now, though, haven't you?' I said.

'Yes,' he said, 'except that there are still one or two critics who I hope will die very painful deaths.' This made me feel a lot better because I'd been feeling rather guilty about wishing very painful deaths on a number of people myself. Even today I would probably still wish them the same, if I could only remember who they were.

Pretty soon there was a collective loss of bottle, a rejection of the idea of anything new and lively, and the old *Omnibus* was firmly back in place – middle-class, middle-aged and middle-brow – and if that was the kind of arts programme you wanted it was pretty good. But it was no use to me. In a fifty-minute show I was actively involved in perhaps one recorded item and one, or maybe two, live discussions. Otherwise I was simply a presenter, introducing reports put together by other people, and that's a job anyone can do. So I decided to cut my losses. In spring, after the initial run, I told Christopher that I would honour my contract and stay on until the end of the year but after that I was out of there. It was an amicable parting. I liked Christopher a lot. We sometimes lunched or dined together and went to films, plays and Lord's together but professionally our minds ran on parallel lines, never to meet.

At Christmas I left. By then the programme had settled down nicely into the sort of safe format which, I suspect, Christopher had always secretly wanted. For me it had been a strange year, not a particularly unhappy one but not one I would wish to repeat. In the course of it I had learned a great deal about branches of the arts of which I had previously been ignorant and there had been a few programmes – especially my last, a documentary on the producer David Puttnam, who had won the Oscar that year for *Chariots of Fire* – of which I was justifiably proud. But there had been many others which I was only too happy to forget.

What, though, was I to do next? Back in the spring when I handed in my resignation I had nowhere to go because I had given up all other commitments to concentrate fully on *Omnibus*. Unemployment faced me yet again as it had in 1971 but this time I was not particularly worried; I was pretty sure that radio would have me back and that I could easily supplement my income by writing for newspapers and magazines. Television wasn't even in my thoughts, although in fact it was to television that I returned.

Because of my defection to *Omnibus*, *Film 82* had started off without a regular presenter and various people, among them Tina Brown, later to cut a regal figure in New York's magazine world, had been tried out as my potential successor. The writer and journalist Miles Kington was the best of them but he didn't particularly like television so, come the summer, the chair of the film programme was still unoccupied.

Barry Brown, the producer, was wondering where to turn next when he heard – not from me, because I hadn't made the news public – that I was leaving *Omnibus*. Come back, he said.

The idea had not occurred to me, yet Barry's invitation had a strong appeal. What I had missed over the last few months was the feeling of being at least a kind of expert in something. I now knew a lot more than I had before about a number of things – music and the visual arts, for example – but I was far from being an expert in any of them. Films, though, I did know about even if my knowledge of that year's movies was a bit skimpy. And what, I now realized, I had missed even more was something *Omnibus* had promised but hadn't delivered – a programme built around me and my opinions, a programme in which, within the bounds of libel and decency, I could say whatever I wanted. So I accepted.

After the summer break Iain Johnstone presented *Film* 82 until the end of the year and in January 1983 I returned very happily to my old job.

Chapter Twenty-Three

SOON AFTER THE film programme had been installed, weekly, on the BBC1 network I was, I can see now, pretty well established on television, although the odd scraps of diary I have kept from time to time hardly reflect that. Every year I intend to keep a diary and some years I actually make a start, filling in the entries assiduously until well into February but then, I don't know, I lose interest, or something more urgent comes up. All of my fragmented diaries are like cliffhangers, ending breathlessly on the brink of something momentous which I have now entirely forgotten. But they each have one thing in common – a gloomy pessimism about the future, a conviction that any day now I shall be revealed as the imposter I am, stripped of stripes and decorations and ignominiously drummed out. The one consolation is that most of the worthwhile people I know have a similar fear. I remember Harry Secombe telling me, at the height of his popularity, that his abiding nightmare was of angry men beating on his door and shouting, 'There's been a terrible mistake. None of this was meant for you. We want it all back.'

In my case this trepidation manifested itself in a desire, maybe even a need, to take on all manner of different jobs to prove my versatility, if only to myself: interviews for *Tonight*, radio shows, TV documentary series – for a few years I was doing them all. In the late 1970s, for instance, Roger Macdonald, a producer with whom I had worked on the *Today* programme, phoned me in California where I was making a

TV documentary. Did I, he asked, know anything at all about transport? Absolutely nothing, I said. Great, he said, you're just the man I want, and revealed that he was about to launch on Radio 4 a current affairs programme called *Going Places*, which would take a sharp, critical look at all forms of transport in Britain. To present it he needed somebody just like me, a regular user of planes, trains and automobiles who was ignorant of the workings of airlines, railways and car companies but wondered, irascibly, why none of them was as efficient as it should be. The idea appealed and the programme was a great success. At that time, as ever, transport in Britain was in a terrible state and we happily waded in to British Airways, British Rail and the national car manufacturer, British Leyland, infuriating all of them and causing so many complaints to the Controller of Radio 4 that we knew we must be doing it right.

Later on I was the first chairman of *The News Quiz* on Radio 4 and, on the same channel, helped to launch another current affairs programme, this time about travel and leisure, called *Breakaway*. Later still, I had a call from Trevor Taylor, another producer with whom I had worked on *Today*. Much as Roger Macdonald had done he asked, 'What do you know about computers?' That was easy: I had never even set eyes on a computer and told him so. Great, he said, again much as Roger had done. I was just the man he needed. He was about to produce, once more for Radio 4, a programme called *The Chip Shop*, another current affairs programme that would investigate and explain the way the computer industry worked. This was in the mid-1980s when hardly anyone above teenage, myself included, knew anything about computers at all and, as with *Going Places*, a man-in-the-street approach was needed. *The Chip Shop*'s appeal was to adults who felt they really should know something about this important new technology but were too embarrassed to ask. I, however, was being paid to be embarrassed and to ask and as I learned, so did the audience. Over the next year we developed something like a cult following but, what with trips to Silicon Valley in San Francisco, we used up nearly all Radio 4's further education budget and for reasons of cost the programme was not recommissioned.

I enjoyed all this work. I may have ended every week exhausted and frazzled round the edges but I was never bored. What's more, no matter what other commitments I may have had, I always tried to make time to write novels.

When I was a kid my ambition was to play cricket or football, or both, for England. But when it became apparent that this was unlikely to happen, on account of the fact that I had no particular talent for either game – though, God knows, this doesn't seem to have stopped other people – my goals changed and I wanted, above all, to be a novelist. And I suppose I am one. I've now written ten novels, a fact which seems quite well known to borrowers from public libraries, though less so, alas, to people who actually buy books.

My first novel, a thriller called *The Matter of Mandrake*, was published in 1967, while I was on the *Daily Mail*, and for a moment it looked as if all my dreams were to be realized. While the book was still going from one unimpressed publisher to another my father read it. By then he had decided that he might as well work for television after all and was directing episodes of *The Saint*, starring Roger Moore, and they had often discussed the possibility of making a film together. To my delight Dad decided that *Mandrake* could well be the vehicle they were looking for and handed the cumbersome manuscript to Roger saying, 'Read this. There's a part in it for you.'

To my even greater delight Roger actually took it with him on holiday to Monte Carlo, read it and came back saying, 'Fine, Les, let's do it.' And suddenly it was all happening – Roger was to star, Dad to direct and I to write at least the first draft screenplay. Dad's agent started putting out feelers to see who might back this obviously thrilling enterprise, I began work on the script and for a while had wondrous visions of becoming a novelist whose books were automatically turned into films. And then Lew Grade, who had first call on Roger's services, came back from America with a contract to make another umpteen *Saint* episodes and the dream faded away. The book was eventually published – both here and in America – but by then it was too late. Roger was no longer in the market to play the reluctant amateur spy of my story because he was about to embark on a lucrative career as James

Bond. But it was nice of him to consider doing it and in 1978, when he was making *Moonraker* in Rio de Janeiro, I was able to show my gratitude in a small way. They were filming on Sugar Loaf Mountain and, as I prepared to do an interview with Roger, Cubby Broccoli, the producer, took me aside. At the time Roger and Broccoli were having a financial dispute (practically everyone who played James Bond had financial disputes with Broccoli) and, to the producer's dismay, there was a strong rumour that unless he was given a salary hike Roger wouldn't make any more 007 movies.

'Ask him,' Broccoli said, 'ask him if he's gonna make the next one. I have to know.'

I thought it over. I didn't feel I owed Cubby anything, especially as his then partner Harry Saltzman had rather disdainfully turned me down when, Sean Connery having given up the Bond role, I very decently offered to play it myself. (I always felt that Saltzman didn't have to laugh quite so heartily, especially as he then went on to cast George Lazenby in the role.) So I went to Roger and warned him of the question I was about to ask, thus giving him time to compose one of those typically bland, utterly non-committal answers which have been the despair of all his interviewers. He duly delivered such an answer and when he and I had finished Cubby descended on me again. 'Well,' he said cagerly, 'what did that asshole of an actor have to say?'

I told him what the asshole of an actor had said and he went away cursing, Bond having outwitted yet another opponent.

I followed *The Matter of Mandrake* with another thriller, *The Hounds of Sparta*, featuring the same protagonist, and my publishers, W. H. Allen, were keen that I should continue along the same path. Maybe I should have done but I had a different idea, a comedy about Fleet Street called *A Series of Defeats*, and I wrote that instead. W. H. Allen were not interested and neither, for some years, was anybody else. While that book, too, was doing the unsympathetic rounds I, with a lot of help from my friend John Poole, wrote *End Product*. It was inspired by the racial tension that was apparent everywhere during the early 1970s and presented an apocalyptic view of a future in which white people were farming black people for food. Yes, to eat them.

Well, you had to read the book to understand. Ian Chapman, of Collins, was eager to publish it but unfortunately Billy Collins, the head of the firm, thought it was inflammatory – though anyone could see it was meant to be a cautionary tale – and refused to touch it. Ian took it to him twice but he wouldn't be moved, so for a few years that seemed to be it. I was the author of two novels – count them, two.

But then my literary agent, Mike Shaw, put me in touch with a splendidly laidback firm called Quartet, which was run by a group of young men, refugees from more conventional publishing outfits, headed by the amiably eccentric William Miller. They had offices above a kebab house or something similar in Goodge Street but in my experience no deals were ever made there. It was William's practice to take potential authors to the nearest pub and engage them in ferocious games of table football, which he always won. This wasn't surprising; in my case because he was much better at the game anyway and in every case because the nervous author was wondering whether his book was ever going to be mentioned. The first time this happened we must have been playing for well over half an hour before I asked him diffidently whether he had managed to read *End Product* yet.

He looked up from the table, slightly irritated that his concentration had been disturbed. 'What? Oh, *End Product*. Yes. We're going to publish it.'

This was news to me – welcome news, of course, but surprising in the circumstances. 'And, er, *A Series of Defeats*?' I said. 'What about that?'

'Well, we're going to publish that, too,' he said, frowning slightly as if I should already know these things and he couldn't quite understand why I was bothering him with them when all he wanted to do was play table football. In the end, Quartet published four of my novels, one of which, another comedy called *Have a Nice Day*, was responsible for the most humbling experience of my life.

The publicity department had arranged for me to go on the rubber chicken circuit, that round of literary lunches at which the author stands up when the coffee is served and tells the paying guests how wonderful his book is. The first of these was in Glasgow where, though

I say it myself, I was a sensation. It was a fairly spicy novel and I told some fairly spicy stories, which went down a treat with the punters, who then proceeded to buy around a hundred copies of the book. I had, I felt, cracked it. Literary lunches? A doddle. Roll on the next one.

The next one was in Oxford, arranged by Blackwell's, the book shop, and took place in the Randolph Hotel. I arrived oozing confidence, knowing my speech was a cracker, guaranteed to wow the pants off any audience. It was only when I got into the dining room that the doubts began. I had gone down well in Glasgow because there I was the main speaker; here I was not. Here the main speaker was Sir Douglas Bader, the legless war hero; I was merely one of the supporting acts and this became apparent as we took our places at the top table and I looked out over a sea of elderly female faces, each topped it seemed to me by a blue hat, and heard the enthusiastic applause when Bader appeared. Right then the realization swept over me that I might as well be dead. And I was right.

My speech, the same one I had delivered so successfully in Glasgow, was a disaster. My jokes, even the innocuous ones, were (to steal a phrase from Billy Connolly) slightly less welcome than a fart in a space suit, while anything even a touch risqué invoked the sharply indrawn breath of disapproval. These women had not the slightest interest in me; they had never heard of me; they had no idea, before I stood up, that I had written a book and on the whole would have preferred it if I hadn't. All they wanted to do was worship Douglas Bader, so they fidgeted irritably throughout my increasingly halting speech and I sat down to a thunderous lack of applause. But at least, I thought as I grabbed deperately for a glass of port, that's over; things can't possibly get worse.

So they did.

After the meal we, the authors, sat at little tables in the foyer of the hotel while the lunchers queued to buy our books and ask us to sign them. The queue for Bader's book went right through the foyer and out into the street; the queue for mine consisted of precisely six people.

Fortunately, I was able to escape after I'd signed the six volumes, saying truthfully that I was to be interviewed at Radio Oxford, otherwise

I would have had to sit there, staring into space, until Bader had finished.

   This happened a long time ago and I have spoken at much more successful literary lunches since but that's the one I shall always remember. An experience like that leaves a scar that never heals.

Chapter Twenty-Four

IN 1977 BRIAN COWGILL, then Controller of BBC1, had a hole to fill in his summer schedules and asked Barry Brown and me to make five, fifty-minute documentaries on film-related subjects. The idea we and the rest of the team came up with was *The Hollywood Greats*, five profiles of stars from the so-called Golden Age of movies, the likes of Clark Gable, Spencer Tracy and Gary Cooper. These were not to be eulogies but warts and all portraits and so they turned out, with the result that when they were shown we were accused by the press of having chosen late greats only because you can't libel the dead.

Actually, that thought had never occurred to us. Our first idea had been to make the programmes about living stars but this proved to be impossible, largely because we had very little time and, come to that, very little money. The stars we originally approached were either too busy, not interested, working in widely different parts of the world (which would have involved us in a lot of expensive travel) or unable to fit into our timescale. Fred Astaire turned us down; Robert Mitchum's agent kept promising us a definite maybe and never delivered and so on. So we moved to Plan B, the advantage being that nearly all the people we wanted to talk to, people who had known the late stars, could be found in Los Angeles, New York or London. And since we had only six weeks to do the interviews and groundwork for all five programmes, that was a bonus. An additional, and unexpected, bonus was that because the stars we were discussing were dead their friends were much more candid about them. If, for instance, Spencer Tracy had still been alive people, hopeful that he might invite them round for dinner, would have said of him that he was a great actor and a wonderful man. But because he was dead and a dinner invitation was out of the question they would say that he was a great actor and a wonderful man but also that he could be a ferocious drunk, given to hitting people and smashing shop windows. I thought that such details, mentioned though not stressed, made the subjects much more interesting but fans, even journalists, obviously don't like to be told that their idols, like most of us, stand on feet of clay. When in the next series Joan Crawford was revealed, not from what I said but from the comments of her friends, acquaintances and colleagues, to have been a considerable bitch I was greatly vilified by journalists to whom she seemed to have been some kind of icon. One writer indeed declared that my programme had offended him so much that he had given away his television set, which I thought was a bit extreme. Had he never heard of the on/off button?

During that first trip to Hollywood we stayed at a place called the Casa Real Motel on Sunset Strip, a modest establishment with plastic grass around its tiny, grubby swimming pool, and known to us as the 'Karzy'. It wasn't exactly a toilet but it wasn't much better. From our windows we could watch the hookers parading up and down on the street outside. Their services, we were informed by a local expert, could be procured for $100 or, if you were strapped for cash and could stay awake that long, for $40 after 3 a.m.

One night our cameraman, John Goodyer, woke up to find a large black man crawling across his floor towards the wardrobe. For a moment John lay there, understandably petrified. What should he do, he wondered, and decided that nothing was the sensible answer. But then the intruder reached towards the jacket in one of whose pockets John kept his wallet and honest British indignation kicked in.

John sat up and switched on the light. 'What do you think you're doing?' he asked, adding, 'If you leave now I won't have seen you.'

This could have been a dangerous move but fortunately the burglar (for such he presumably was) was a man of bluster rather than violence. He apologized for the intrusion and said he was looking for a girl he knew whose room this had formerly been. John wisely refrained from asking why he thought she might have been in the wardrobe and again invited him to leave.

'Do you have any hookers in here?' the burglar asked. Rightly affronted, John said he had not and invited him to see for himself. The burglar looked around, nodded approval at the obvious absence of hookers, advised John against having any dealings with such women and asked, 'Is there anything else I can do for you?'

John said there wasn't. 'Right,' said the burglar and bade him goodnight. 'Mind if I use the door this time?' he asked.

'Be my guest,' said John and they parted.

The actor Robert Wagner was much impressed when we told him where we were staying. 'Down there among all the hookers?' he said. 'Gee, how are you guys making out?'

For some reason – economy, if you really want to know – we stayed at the Karzy again the following year and this time Margaret Sharp, our producer, swiftly realized that the room next to hers was occupied by one of the ladies of the night. She discovered this because her neighbour not only had a constant stream of visitors at strange hours but also owned a small, yappy dog which barked loudly with every coming and going. After a few days Margaret was haggard from lack of sleep at which point our English lighting man, or electrician, John Collins, took a hand.

Hammering on the hooker's door in the middle of the morning, when she herself was sleeping to recover from the exertions of the night, he confronted her with an ultimatum. He did not mind how she earned her living, he told her, for he was a reasonable man, but he did object to the dog and how it was disturbing the much-needed rest of his producer. Therefore, he was obliged to give her the following instruction: 'Get rid of the bleedin' dog,' he said, 'or either it or you are going to end up floating in that swimming pool.'

The hooker moved out that day.

Many of the people we interviewed for the series had been big stars in their time but now, old and retired, they were pleased to see us because they were lonely and largely ignored by contemporary Hollywood.

George Raft, aged eighty-three, was one of these. In his time he had been one of the biggest stars in the business, though noted more for the films he turned down – *The Maltese Falcon*, *Casablanca* and *Double Indemnity* – than those he actually made. But now he lived in modest comfort in a small apartment in Century City, just off Santa Monica Boulevard. And he had a grievance. Well, he had several actually – one with the Inland Revenue Service, which had caught up with him after many years and taken nearly all his money away. But the bigger grievance was with Britain, from which he had been barred and thereby denied employment as the front man for a gambling casino in the West End of London. The reason he had been barred, ejected from the country actually, was that he was believed to have Mafia connections. Everyone in America knew he had Mafia connections but he denied it strenuously. Happily, he didn't blame us for his treatment in Britain and was in fact very hospitable.

He offered coffee and cookies in his living room, which was decorated with plastic flowers, then as the time for the interview approached he asked Barry Brown and me to advise him on what to wear. We followed him into his bedroom and watched as he selected an outfit. Above the bed was a sign that read, 'If you can get it up, I can get it in' and next to that was what appeared to be a garish abstract painting.

'Waddya think of my picture?' he asked me.

'Er, very nice,' I said politely, though in truth it was an amateurish daub.

'No, no,' he said impatiently, 'look at it – look at it properly.'

I did. On close examination I realized that the top line consisted of the letters f and u and the bottom of c and k.

'Oh yes,' I said. 'Now I see.'

'Pretty good, huh?' he said. 'My girlfriend painted that for me.'

'Must be a nice lady,' I said. He agreed that she was and then told me that the previous night he had gone to a restaurant where he had been greeted fervently by a middle-aged actress. 'She was all over me, damn near fucked me right there in the restaurant.' He sounded sort of wistful when he said that.

The Hollywood Greats and its successors were very well received by the audience; over the next few years we made twenty-five programmes and if the BBC had shown a little more initiative I could have become famous in America and probably several other countries as well. The five series I did attracted attention among television executives in America where indigenous TV profiles of movie stars were little more than animated fanzine articles, strongly suggesting that the subjects could walk across their swimming pools without getting the soles of their feet wet. My approach, being quite unlike that, was thought to have a good deal of potential. Why then was it not sold – to the USA, to Canada, Australia, New Zealand or anywhere else?

Well, in the ever-stringent interests of economy, the BBC had acquired the rights to show the film clips and the interviews I did for each programme only twice and then only in Britain. If, on the other hand, they had secured worldwide clearance . . . Ah, but there you go. Like the poets tell us there are no words sadder than 'it might have been'.

In the event, the only time I came close to getting wide exposure on American television was a few years later when I made a ten-part series called *Talking Pictures*, which followed the development of Hollywood from 1927, the year talkies were introduced, until the mid-1980s. This time the BBC was in partnership with Turner Television in America and international rights were secured up front. Ironically, however, the series was shown in the USA but I was not. The Turner people, who had had nothing to do with the actual making of the programmes, were horrified by the often critical note I had adopted. Hey, who does this Limey think he is, criticizing Hollywood? So I, my voice and my comments were expunged from the screen and replaced by a much blander script presented by Burt Reynolds. On the whole that was the bit that hurt most of all. I mean, come on. To be replaced was bad enough but to be replaced by Burt Reynolds who, in movie terms, was yesterday's man was a bit thick. Couldn't they at least have tried for Clint Eastwood?

Not that any of the above ruined my life exactly, nice though it might have been to be world famous and even fabulously wealthy. The documentaries were hard work but great fun to make and thanks to them and covering the Oscars I've been to Hollywood more times than I can remember. A most amusing place it is, too, so long as you don't have to live there, a happy hunting ground for third-rate minds with boundless ambition, impenetrable hides and an unquenchable thirst for money. Of course, some very gifted people work there, too, but like everywhere else they are in the minority. The rest are driven by self-promotion and the profit motive. What struck me first about the place was that there you are what you earn and what you own. It doesn't matter what you do, still less how well you do it; all that counts is how much you make for doing it. You could turn out an endless stream of braindead movies (as so many of them do) but if your income is in seven figures and you live in a big house with a swimming pool you are perforce a solid citizen, respected and welcomed everywhere, while your more talented, more serious-minded but less affluent colleagues are directed to the tradesmen's entrance. That remains as true today as it was then but it's no longer quite so surprising because much the same now applies in this country. Hollywood may have invented the idea that fame, however acquired, is an end in itself but you only have to glance at the tabloids to see that Britain has embraced the notion with indecent enthusiasm.

Covering the Oscars was the job I disliked most. I have never, I should add, attended the ceremony itself but then I have never wanted to. If you're up for an award I'm sure it's a thrilling evening but if you are not it is – and I have this on much good authority – a considerable bore, basically a television spectacular broken up into twenty-minute sections of programme, each followed by five minutes spells of inactivity while the commercials are broadcast. In this manner the whole thing limps along to fill three and a half hours on a good night; sometimes it's even longer. If during this marathon anyone needs to go to the lavatory or has a fierce desire to sink a quick one in the bar his/her seat is immediately filled by a flunkey in full evening dress because God forbid that the Oscar ceremony should appear to be attended by anything less than a full house. It is at once the very pinnacle and the very nadir of Hollywood glitz and Hollywood bullshit.

AMPAS, the American Academy of Motion Picture Arts and Sciences, organizes the event but ABC television controls it, broadcasting the ceremony live in the USA and elsewhere and also providing a ninety-minute edited package to subscribers all over the world. Except in the interview room backstage nobody else's television cameras are allowed in the auditorium.

When I first started covering the Awards in the early 1980s the BBC merely bought the ninety-minute package for showing the following night. My job was to top and tail the edited programme while clad in dinner jacket to create the illusion that I had been present at the ceremony. What I actually did was to drive to the Dorothy Chandler Pavilion or the Shrine Auditorium in downtown Los Angeles a good two hours before anyone turned up, stand in front of a giant statue of Oscar and predict what was likely to happen. Then I would return to my hotel and watch the show on TV before – and this was the bit I hated most – taking my place outside the venue for the most popular celebration party of the evening and waiting for the winners and other nominees to turn up so that I could interview them. When that was done I would hastily compose a summing up and assessment of the results and record that to camera.

Doesn't sound all that bad, I suppose, and in the early days it wasn't because then the Governors' Ball (these being the governors of AMPAS, not California) was held at the Beverly Hilton Hotel in Beverly Hills and it was expected of all the nominees, winners and losers alike, that they should attend if only briefly. In those days the Oscars were not nearly as popular as they were to become and it was possible to get all the international TV camera crews into the foyer and lobby of the hotel. My job then was to stand beside the BBC camera while Tom Brook, the film programme's invaluable American correspondent, scurried around and dragged Oscar winners over to talk to me. With practically everyone worth interviewing assembled in the same place the work was over well before midnight.

But then, as TV channels proliferated throughout the world, interest in the Oscars became ever more feverish and the events around the ceremony itself changed. Now the Governors' Ball was held close to the auditorium, which meant that only the ABC cameras were present, and it became a matter of second guessing which of many other parties would be the best attended by the nominees. At first that wasn't difficult, the party of choice being the bash hosted by the celebrated literary agent Swifty Lazar at Spago, an upmarket pizza house just off Sunset Strip. But now the goalposts had been moved. Where before the camera crews had at least been indoors at the Beverly Hilton, now they stood in the street and it rapidly became clear to me that this kind of doorstepping was a young person's job. I found myself surrounded by eager, bright-eyed, very young American reporters with sixty-four teeth and Europeans, Indians and Asians, no less eager, bright-eyed and young but, compared with their transatlantic colleagues, dentally challenged. I'm too old for this lark, I said to myself, and that feeling was underlined one cold, drizzly night when, on his way into the party, Norman Jewison, the Canadian director whom I knew well, looked at me with obvious pity as I stood on the steps outside and said, 'Barry, what the hell are you doing here?'

Miserably, I had been asking myself the same question and it was no comfort to know that my discontent was due to nothing more than a dented ego. I tried to convince myself that it was good for my soul once a year to get down into the gutter (almost literally) and scrabble for interviews but I knew it was a lie. The fact was it was a job I was stuck with. 'Why do I have to do this?' I would complain to my producer, Bruce Thompson. 'Why can't somebody else do it?'

'Because the stars know you,' he said. 'They won't talk to anybody else.'

Matters became even worse in the mid-1990s. By now Oscar hype was such that 1 billion people were said to watch the ceremony worldwide. Yeah, right. There were then about 5½ billion people in the world and nobody will ever convince me that, say, two out of every eleven Chinese were sitting up, glued to their sets wondering who would be named best sound editor. But the BBC bought into the razzamatazz and also bought the rights to show the Oscar ceremony live. God knows why. It went out in Britain at about 2.30 a.m. when a quarter of a million people might be watching, if we were lucky, and for me

Oscar coverage became even more unpleasant. My job now was to watch the show as it went out and fill in the commercial breaks by chatting to whatever guests we could assemble. But where were we to watch it? Where were we to sit? Clearly, we weren't allowed into the auditorium and because this was a typical shoestring BBC operation with a minimal budget we couldn't afford a decent studio. For the first two years Bruce managed to blag us a bit of space at film company parties, first one given by Miramax, then at a thrash hosted by Columbia. The conditions both times were nerve-racking: there was a constant, rising hubbub of sound all around us as the party guests became increasingly loaded; some people had to be deterred from wandering in and out of shot and others had to be hauled back as they ambled up to engage me in conversation while I was addressing the camera. And when all that was finished I had to rush off and stand outside Morton's restaurant in Beverly Hills, where the trendy *Vanity Fair* party was held (Swifty Lazar now being dead and the Spago binge no longer so important), and accost the winners and nominees as they made their way in. By this time Oscar frenzy was such that the TV cameras were arrayed three or four deep and stretched for about fifty yards. The third year was much the same except that Bruce, realizing the futility of trying to do a decent programme from a table by the lavatory in a crowded restaurant, managed to hire us a studio about the size of a broom cupboard, which was better except that communication between studio and gallery constantly broke down with the result that I kept missing my cues.

In truth my 'celebrity' was often useful. One year Mel Gibson, strolling past with two Oscars for *Braveheart*, saw me shivering in the line-up and said, 'Oh, hello, Barry. How are you?' and came over for a chat. And another time Bruce spotted Anthony Hopkins wandering into Morton's and yelled, 'Hey, Tony! Come over here and talk to Barry!' And he did, prefacing our interview with, 'Hello, love, how's your mum?'

This, of course, gave me tremendous kudos among the American interviewers flanking me. That Sir An-tho-ny Hopkins, who had met both my parents, should enquire solicitously after the health of my mother clearly indicated that I was a person of importance and that was gratifying but so what? Other, younger, reporters who didn't personally know either Gibson or Hopkins managed to get a word with them and if their conversations were not perhaps as informal as ours it didn't matter. In the end what every programme needed was only a soundbite, not a leisurely chat.

For me things improved later when I left the BBC and joined Sky, which had now taken over the Oscar rights. Again God knows why because the audience on a satellite channel in the small hours of the morning was even tinier than it was on the Beeb. A question of prestige, I suppose. But at least Sky covered the event properly. It organized a party of its own, a particularly lavish one in the second year at the Four Seasons Hotel in Beverly Hills. Kenneth Turan, the *Los Angeles Times*'s film critic, and Elle McPherson, the Australian model and occasional actress, were brought in to talk to me during the commercial breaks. Now Oscar coverage became a four-and-a-half-hour marathon of live television because before the ceremony began I presented another, hour-long, programme, setting the scene and chatting over film matters generally with the likes of Gary Oldman, Martin Landau and Vinnie Jones, the former hard man of football now transformed into a most unlikely movie star. By the time the award for best picture was announced I was exhausted but at least I didn't have to rush off and stand outside Morton's or any other restaurant. Sky had a small team of people to do that and they did it very well.

But in my third and final year at Sky things had changed. Elisabeth Murdoch, daughter of Rupert, had left the company and nobody else among the higher executives had any interest in movies apart from showing as many as possible on their designated film channels. Even less did they have any interest in spending more money than was absolutely necessary. So while the Oscars were again broadcast live by Sky, they were broadcast without me. No lavish Beverly Hills party, no guests, no pre-Oscar programme – just the Academy Awards with the commercial breaks filled in by such commercials as Sky could rustle up.

I watched the programme at home while recovering from a bout of vertigo – no, not a fear of heights, though I have that, too – but an infection of the inner ear that makes you throw up and roll about like a cartoon drunk.

When I first fell over – in the garden, on a wet night – Diana thought I had had a stroke and rushed me to an all-night clinic where the duty doctor, who seemed to know roughly as much about medicine as I did, assumed I *was* drunk, no doubt regarding my mud-covered suit as conclusive evidence. The fact that in the middle of the consultation I had to stagger out, holding the wall for support, to vomit in the lavatory probably didn't help either. He said my blood pressure was high. I reckon his would have been, too, if he had found himself suddenly subject to extreme dizzy spells and falling fits. It was not until the following day, when I saw my own doctor, that the vertigo was properly diagnosed and treated.

Anyway, still slightly dizzy, I watched the Oscars from a couch in my sitting room and was then driven into the Sky studios at Isleworth to pontificate on the results. Apart from the lack of sleep and the slight possibility that I might (a) fall off the chair or (b) throw up all over the newscaster I found this a more agreeable way of covering the Academy Awards. I missed my annual reunion with my sister, Val, and those of her three children who might be in and around Los Angeles at the time but otherwise being in London rather than Beverly Hills for the Oscars caused me no distress whatsoever.

As far as Oscar is concerned I've been there, done that and though I never got the T-shirt – if, indeed, they ever handed any out – I acquired a lot of impressive-looking badges which informed envious onlookers that I was an accredited person.

From an artistic point of view it's a nonsense event anyway. Financially? Oh, yeah, it's worth a bundle, adding around $30 million (or more) to the box-office take of the best picture and possibly doubling the asking fee of individual winners. Thus it's easy to see why Hollywood loves Oscar so much – what he's about is money and Hollywood does love money. But when it comes to acknowledging merit, the Academy Awards too often get it wrong. Tom Hanks as best actor for *Forrest Gump* rather than Nigel Hawthorne for *The Madness of King George*; Helen Hunt as best actress for *As Good As It Gets* instead of Judi Dench for *Mrs Brown*; James Cameron (*Titanic*) for best director and not Curtis Hanson (*L.A. Confidential*)? Oh, please! This is a mickey-taker, right? Well, no it's not and I only wish it were.

Oscar is at his most interesting at the nomination stage when quite often – actually, more often than not – they do get it right and the best five films, performances, screenplays etc. are recognized. The nominations are decided by people's peer groups: actors vote for actors, directors for directors, cinematographers for cinematographers and so on. Only the nominations for best film are open to all the Academy members. But after that it's just a crapshoot with everyone, no matter how old, senile or inactive, free to vote in every category to decide who wins what.

I once went to an Academy members' viewing of a film at Twentieth Century Fox studios. The film had already been nominated; tonight's audience would help decide its fate. I was hanging around the lot when the members arrived, some in their own cars, some in coaches. But however they turned up this was the most ancient group of people I had ever seen outside an old folks' home. Most of them tried to disguise their age – the women with plastered make-up, eyelashes a foot long and stiletto heels at the end of varicosed legs, the men with open-necked safari suits, casually ruffled toupees and gold medallions nestling in chests full of white hair. In Hollywood the second worst sin is to be old; the very worst is to look old. But, no matter what desperate measures they took to hide the fact, these people *were* old – by God, they were old – and it was obvious that none of them could possibly have been employed in the film industry for many years.

Fox provided them with dinner and as much alcohol as they wanted in the commissary, then took them into the studio's private cinema where I joined them and where within fifteen minutes 75 per cent of the audience was sound asleep. When they awoke as the final credits rolled they probably felt they'd had a good evening and maybe voted wholeheartedly for the film hardly any of them had seen.

Nowadays, though special screenings are still arranged, individual video tapes of nominated films, performances and the like are sent to each of the 5,000 or so Academy members but who is to say whether anybody actually watches all, or any, of them? Especially among the elderly and inactive I suspect it's much more likely that some kind of consensus prevails along the lines of, 'I see that Tom Hanks has been nominated. Good ol' boy, Tom. And then there's this Nigel whatsis-name. Who the hell is he? Never heard of him. I'll vote for Tom.'

Humphrey Bogart once suggested that the only way to determine who was best actor was to have each of the five nominees play Hamlet and the one who did it best would get the award. Even that would hardly have been perfect but it would have been preferable to the exist-ing system under which, in the best picture category for instance, voters must decide whether a drama is better than a comedy is better than a musical is better than a western is better than a fantasy. Which do you like more – chalk or cheese? Well, if I wanted to write on a blackboard I expect I'd go for the chalk but if I were hungry the cheese would get my vote. In Oscar voting, however, no such options are available. Here's a bit of chalk and here's a bit of cheese – which is better? Go for it.

The ceremony itself is often much enlivened by the behaviour of the winners – Jack Palance (*City Slickers*, 1992) doing one-handed press-ups on stage, Tom Hanks (*Philadelphia*, 1994) 'outing' his former teacher as gay, whether the man wished to be outed or not, and ending with 'God bless America', James Cameron (*Titanic*, 1998) declaring himself to be 'King of the World', Gwynneth Paltrow (*Shakespeare in Love*, 1999) extending her thanks to include cousins long deceased and creating a new record for the number of tears shed by a single indi-vidual at an Oscar ceremony. These are moments to cherish and I do cherish them. But for the most part the awards themselves are not to be taken seriously by thoughtful observers of the cinema.

Then, too, the frenzy whipped up by the competing production companies, the dirty tricks, the whispering campaigns directed against rival films, lend a sour note to what should be a festive occasion. Because none of this politicking is done in the name of art – it's done in the name of money.

And yet . . . This year (2002) the Academy did rather redeem itself.

It gave a much-deserved special award to Sidney Poitier, who in 1963 had become the only Afro-American to win the best actor award for his performance in *Lilies of the Field*. And then it delivered a double whammy – best actress to Halle Berry (*Monster's Ball*) and best actor to Denzel Washington (*Training Day*), two black winners in one night, Berry being the first black actress ever to be so honoured.

This was a remarkable breakthrough. Black performers had been deserving of the top acting prizes before – Washington himself for *Malcolm X* in 1992 and Angela Bassett for *What's Love Got To Do With It?* in 1993, among them – but hitherto all they had ever won was a couple of handfuls, if that, of supporting awards. The Academy would deny strenuously that it ever practised a colour bar but until 2002 the results suggested otherwise.

It has been whispered, meanly, that this year's Oscars had something to do with the events of 11 September 2001 and a desire to prove that regardless of caste, colour or creed America is one nation. It has also been said that others were more deserving of the awards than Washington and Berry but that is simply healthy argument and, anyway, it happens every year. In any event both allegations are unworthy because they serve only to cheapen the winners' achievements. I believe the real importance of the 2002 Academy Awards is their revelation that, at last, Oscar has come to realize that talent has nothing to do with colour. The fact that on the evening itself Berry positively shattered Paltrow's record for tear-shedding only added to the general joy.

Nevertheless, I still believe that the Academy Awards would be more worthy of respect if they stopped at the nomination stage, when both chalk and cheese are given their due and nobody has to choose between them.

Chapter Twenty-Five

O N THE OTHER hand I did enjoy the Cannes Film Festival. Well, most of the time. Sometimes, though, this can also be a bit of a nonsense; juries consisting of earnest intellectuals and, far worse, would-be intellectuals have given the top prize, the Palme D'Or, to some very bizarre films as well as handing out acting awards to people who have never acted before and may quite possibly never act again.

But it has a couple of huge advantages over the Oscars. In the first place, all the films are judged equally, there being no such category as 'Best Foreign Language Film' since nearly all the pictures in competition arc in a foreign language – to the French anyway. And, secondly, prizes at Cannes having very little box office value in the world market, possible financial gain hardly comes into it. The juries are truly looking for the best film, the one with the greatest artistic value, and argument and dissension arise because, of course, one man's work of art is another man's turkey.

Then, too, Cannes juries can be much bolder than the Oscar voters, as, for instance, when they gave the Palme D'Or to films like Martin Scorsese's *Taxi Driver*, Steven Soderbergh's *sex, lies and videotape* and Quentin Tarantino's *Pulp Fiction*. And men like Scorsese for *After Hours* and David Lynch for *Mulholland Drive*, who have never been honoured by the American Academy, have won best director prizes at Cannes.

I first covered the festival in the early 1970s when the film programme was still shown only in London and the south-east and had no kind of reputation beyond that narrow area. Consequently we had hardly any invitations to the Cannes films and none at all to the parties. Don Bennetts, our Australian director, took the latter as a challenge. We would find out where the parties were being held, he said, and simply gatecrash them. This was an idea that was better in theory than in practice. One evening we heard of a particularly lavish, black tie thrash that was taking place at the Carlton Hotel and to which invitations were as coveted as gold dust. We, of course, had no invitations. No problem, said Don, I'll get us in and he led us confidently, about six of us, to the door of the ballroom. Even at the time I thought this was a touch optimistic; one gatecrasher, possibly two, might sneak in but to try to usher half a dozen people in jeans and sneakers past the dinner-jacketed security men was pushing it a bit. Even so Don almost managed it. 'Invitations, please,' said the jobsworth on the door. Don shook his head wearily. 'We don't *need* invitations,' he said, as if explaining something to a child. 'I happen to be a personal friend of the host.'

Now another dinner-jacketed person joined the jobsworth. 'You're what?' he said.

'A personal friend of the host,' said Don, with just a touch of hauteur.

'Well, I'm the host,' said the newcomer, 'and I've never seen you before in my life. Get out.' And so we went, with the words 'And stay out!' ringing in our ears. Sometimes, though, Don was successful – up to a point, anyway. Another evening he managed to talk us on to a yacht where a party was being held in celebration of a Swedish film showing in competition. We were much impressed that he had got us there but then he had us thrown out by getting into an altercation with a young Swedish PR woman. How it started is a mystery but it pretty well ended with the girl crying indignantly, 'You pushed my bosoms!' and Don replying, with equal indignation, 'Me? I never touched your tired old tits!' Which of them was right didn't really matter because large, blond Swedish persons had assembled to show us politely but firmly to the gangplank.

Another year we didn't have enough money to take a camera crew but employed a stills photographer instead, with the result that our coverage of the world's most prestigious film festival consisted of film clips, snapshots and a sort of essay written and delivered by me, mostly in voice-over, from our London studio. Nobody could possibly get away with anything like that now. Indeed, I don't know how we got away with it then.

I didn't go to Cannes at all for a few years in the late seventies and early eighties because during May, when the festival takes place, I was always in America gathering material for *The Hollywood Greats* and its successors. So it was not until 1984 that I started covering the event regularly.

The first Cannes Film Festival should have taken place in the summer of 1939 as a kind of antidote to the Venice Film Festival which, under the aegis of Mussolini, was inclined to hand its prizes to Fascist movies. Unfortunately, Hitler had other plans for Europe in 1939 and Cannes did not get under way until 1946. Journalists I know, who have been attending it for forty years, tell me wistfully that in those earliest days it was a small, almost intimate, affair. You wanted to interview Brigitte Bardot? No problem. There she was strolling along La Croisette, taking the air. You just walked up, introduced yourself and bingo.

Or perhaps a photographer wanted a sexy picture. Again no problem. Saucy, bare-breasted starlets would be playing with a beachball by the water's edge, simply longing for someone to point a camera at them.

But by the mid-1980s Cannes, now the centre of media attraction for two weeks each May, had shed its slightly raffish air and become respectable. For most of the year it's just a pretty, rich little town on the French Riviera. At film festival time, however, it's like a village on steroids, gross and bulging with about 35,000 visitors. The streets, especially La Croisette, the long promenade that runs along the beachfront, are crammed and almost impassable. Every few yards some white-painted human statue stands motionless for minutes on end, its unblinking eyes staring out to sea, while a small but critical crowd waits to spot any unintended movement and tosses coins into a bag at the statue's feet. It seems an odd way to earn a living but I suppose it's show business of a sort.

Pretty, roller-skating girls in halters and tiny shorts weave between the pedestrians handing out leaflets advertising a film, a bar, a restaurant, whatever. Men and women, sweating profusely in gaudy monster outfits, trudge disconsolately around, publicizing the latest horror/fantasy/comic book epic and small planes fly constantly overhead, trailing banners proclaiming some forthcoming movie.

Meanwhile in the Palais du Festival – otherwise known as 'the Bunker' – a huge, ugly concrete edifice purpose-built to house the various festivals and conferences that converge on Cannes throughout the year, that day's competition film is being shown to the critics. But to prove that Cannes, or at least part of it, is about money as well as art the less lofty-minded can go downstairs into the basement where, if such is their taste, they can watch extracts from porno movies, available for sale on film or video.

And while all this is going on the wheelers and dealers of the movie industry are meeting, bargaining and haggling on the terrace of the Carlton Hotel or in the bar at the Majestic. In either place even a coffee will cost an arm and a leg, while the average person would have to take out a second mortgage to treat a couple of business acquaintances to lunch. It was at the Carlton in 1986 that the Israeli producer Menahem Golan agreed to back Jean-Luc Godard's film of *King Lear* and drew up the contract on a paper napkin.

In the evening, again at the Palais, comes the gala première of the competition film, a strictly black tie affair attended by oppressive security. Now the crowd in the street is enormous, its numbers swelled by tourists come to town to catch a glimpse of the famous as, in their finery, they make their self-consciously unselfconscious way up the red-carpeted stairs into the cinema. Occasionally these proceedings are enlived by some kind of stunt. One year somebody threw a custard pie at Jean-Luc Godard; another year a couple of movie musclemen, Jean-Claude Van Damme and Dolf Lundgren, staged what purported to be an angry fight at the top of the steps.

Television coverage of the festival increased year by year until it seemed to me that practically everybody who had received a camcorder for Christmas was turning up at Cannes claiming to be an independent TV producer. The stars more than the films are the attraction for the television cameras but, year by year, as the crowds of media people as well as rubberneckers swell, the stars become ever more inaccessible. Nowadays nobody of any fame whatsoever would be foolhardy enough to stroll along La Croisette alone or even accompanied by bodyguards. The only time the screen idols appear in public is for the gala pre-mières and then they will make the journey of little more than a hundred yards from the Majestic Hotel to the red carpet by limo. And that can take up to half an hour, such is the density of the crowds and the number of star-filled limos jamming the street.

Most years I would spend ten days at Cannes and, enjoyable though it always was, that was quite long enough because we would all come home exhausted, not from excessive high-living but from sheer exercise. If you are planning to visit the film festival the first thing you must have is full media accreditation, for without it you will get in nowhere. And the second thing you must have is a really comfortable pair of shoes because you will walk everywhere. Yes, you can hire a car or, yes, you can take a taxi but the congestion is such that if a man in a car and a man on a zimmerframe set out at the same time for the same destination my money would always be on the zimmerframe.

By the early 1990s Bruce Thompson and I had got Cannes pretty well sussed. Every year all the people we wanted to talk to, film publicists and the like who helped us arrange our interviews, were to be found in the same offices in the same buildings along La Croisette. Not only did this mean that one hard afternoon's walking and talking would pretty well establish our schedule for the next ten days but the familiarity of the same faces in the same places created a cosy village atmosphere. Home from home was what it was.

Bruce had become the seventh and last of my producers on the film programme, the line of succession going from Iain Johnstone, to Pat Ingram, to Barry Brown, to Margaret Sharp, to Jane Lush, to Judy Lindsay and finally Bruce. In all of them I was extremely fortunate. Each had come to this area of television from different directions: Iain had been a journalist, Pat had worked in current affairs, Barry in show business in Australia, Margaret and Jane had climbed up from secretarial jobs in TV, Judy had been a stewardess with BOAC (one of her pilots having been the egregious Norman, now Lord, Tebbitt) and Bruce had arrived at production via banking, cinema projection and film editing and studio directing at the Beeb. By the time each of them became producer they had acquired the skill and know-how which come with experience and that made life easier for me. We would confer about which particular film clip would best illustrate the script but otherwise I left the visual aspects of the programme to them while I got on with the verbals.

It is no reflection on any of his predecessors to say that Bruce had the greatest impact on the programme. Before he moved out of the cutting rooms to take on the job of studio directing that task had been undertaken by a series of high-flying graduate trainees, who were seconded to us for three or six months as part of their indoctrination into the BBC's methods. For several years this training scheme – only possible perhaps within a publicly-funded broadcasting company – whereby bright kids (usually Oxbridge graduates) were passed around from one department to another was the envy of the world and produced a flow of top-rate people not only for the BBC but for ITV as well.

The only problem was that most of our graduate trainees, anxious to make their own no doubt brilliant programmes, regarded studio directing as a chore, something that each of them had to do once every three or four weeks but which offered no opportunity for creative imagination. Therefore they brought no creative imagination to bear. It was Bruce, assigned to direction full-time, who realized what should have been obvious to us all – that the better the programme looked, the more people would enjoy it – and he introduced a sharpness and vivacity that hitherto had been lacking from the visual presentation. Previously, the show had been rather static – clip, me, clip, me and so on. What Bruce did was to give it fluidity and pace by the judicious use of eye-catching graphics and sharp cutting. Just as I tried to write a programme that I would want to listen to, he sought to make one that he would like to watch – and he succeeded. When, in his turn, he became the producer he made sure that the studio directors followed his precepts.

Anyway, one year in Cannes we had a stroke of luck. On a 'we're told he's okay' recommendation from the BBC's Paris office, Bruce had hired a local cameraman to cover the Cannes festival for us. What immediately became apparent was that he was certainly not okay; he seemed to be about nineteen and with only a minimal idea of how a video camera worked and just about the first thing he did was to annoy Clint Eastwood – whom I was interviewing – by leaping up and down behind his tripod and making exasperated Gallic noises.

Bruce fired him at once, contacted the French agency Capa, which was covering the festival with a whole team of cameramen, came to an agreement with them and returned having secured the services of Alexandre Aufort, a handsome/sophisticated/cynical Parisian with an American wife and a splendid command of English. Quite apart from being an excellent cameraman Alexandre had produced and presented his own programmes and, to our delight, he shared Bruce's and my insistence on doing things fast and, wherever possible, only once. I had a piece to camera to deliver? Right. I wrote it, learned it, rehearsed it in my own time then stepped in front of the camera and did it. So long as I didn't fluff (and, immodestly, I must say fluffing was rare) or a truck/police car/ambulance/barking dog/helicopter didn't appear at the crucial moment that was it. One take and move on. Alexandre, Bruce and I formed a mutual admiration society and from then on whenever we went to Cannes we made sure Alexandre would be working with us.

By now the programme (and I) were well known to the denizens of Hollywood so getting interviews with the biggest stars around was no problem; we had all the accreditation we needed to get in anywhere; and we were invited to all the parties, most of which we shunned.

Early evening cocktail parties, yes, we went to them; they made a pleasing end to the working day and provided a good opportunity to schmooze and catch up with people I might not have seen since last year's Cannes. But the late night parties – whether in hotels or on yachts – were best avoided. For a start they were always overcrowded, mostly by freeloaders who hadn't been invited in the first place, which meant it was almost impossible to get a glass of wine, let alone something to eat. Secondly, when the eager publicity people said, 'You've got to come – Sharon Stone will be there, and Robert De Niro. Steven Spielberg has promised to look in and we're pretty sure Brad Pitt will put in an appearance', you knew beyond question that not one of them would show up; indeed no actor or film maker you had ever heard of would show up and you would spend the entire time surrounded by people you'd spent the rest of the fortnight trying desperately to avoid.

One year I interviewed Dirk Bogarde at his house in Grasse, in the hills above Cannes, and asked why we never saw him at the festival. 'Because,' he said, 'it's always full of all the people I'd hoped were dead.' This was perhaps a little harsh but on those rare occasions when I was misguided enough to find myself trapped in one of the over-crowded, overhyped late night parties I knew exactly how he felt.

In any event, Cannes parties always have to be approached with a certain amount of caution. One year Victor Davis, then of the *Daily Express*, had attended the grand première of a slightly scandalous French film in which orgies figured largely. He hadn't liked it. Afterwards, resplendent in dinner jacket and clutching his invitation to the celebration dinner, he was accosted by one of the producers who made the mistake of asking what he had thought of the movie, where-upon Vic made the mistake of telling him. 'Disgusting,' he said. 'Obscene. I hated every minute of it.' The producer snatched the invitation away and tore it up.

To a large extent the success of Cannes depends on how many well-known Americans are there. The numbers vary, partly because Hollywood has an ambivalent attitude towards the festival; on the one hand it's the biggest event of its kind in the world and there is a lot of easy publicity to be grabbed by taking part; on the other hand the studios cannot face the potential humiliation of entering their megabucks epics in competition only to see the prizes awarded to films made for tuppence-ha'penny by first-time directors from North Korea or Outer Mongolia. So a few years ago they hit upon a cunning wheeze: they would set up camp in the luxurious Hotel du Cap at Antibes, show selected reels from their forthcoming blockbusters and simply hijack the festival. The world's media, after all, were assembled down the road in Cannes; an easy matter to drive them out by coach or taxi to the Cap, give them a coffee and a croissant, show them twenty minutes of film and set up brief interviews with the star of the movie. This way the film companies acquired international publicity at very little cost without running the risk of their highly expensive pictures being booed out of town.

Happily, however, it didn't always work. In 1998 Bruce Willis turned up with fifty minutes or so of *Armageddon*, an apocalpytic yarn about a comet threatening to destroy Earth. This footage was to be shown at a cinema in Cannes, by invitation only, to an audience of international critics and journalists. At the appointed hour we duly assembled, took our seats and waited. And waited. People as lofty as Bruce Willis cannot be expected to turn up on time. Punctuality is for peasants. A good twenty minutes went by before Willis, the director Michael Bey and various acolytes made their grand entrance and the screening began. All went well for a bit. This was not an inspired film but it seemed workmanlike enough until they showed us the great emotional climax – the scene in which the noble Willis, having landed on the comet, is about to blow up both himself and it to save the world but before doing so is somehow linked by satellite with his daughter, Liv Tyler, back on Earth. This is the last time they will ever talk to each other; she will never see her daddy again. Tear-jerking stuff and it duly evoked tears – of mirth. The audience burst into a spontaneous howl of joy, crying with laughter, rocking in their seats.

Willis was furious. 'I didn't realize we'd made a comedy,' he said in a brief and surly speech from the stage. Nor was his mood any better the next day when people were taken to the Hotel du Cap to interview him. Instead of making light of yesterday's mild disaster, perhaps admitting that the scene might have looked odd when taken out of context but insisting that it would be terrific in the finished film – in other words, showing a sense of humour, which would have endeared him to all – he behaved as if those of us who had laughed at his big emotional moment were guilty of *lèse-majesté* at the very least. He cut the interviews down to a point where some people were only allowed two minutes in his presence, went off for a long and leisurely lunch, insisted that critics didn't matter because nobody read them anyway, so sucks boo, and generally behaved like a spoilt little boy who had been told that, no, he couldn't have any sweeties because they would spoil his appetite. It was wonderful; all of us who went to the Cap that day agreed that Willis was a fairly considerable plonker.

Arnold Schwarzenegger, who is quite as fond of himself as Willis appears to be, was also made to look an ass at Cannes. It was 1993 when Schwarzenegger, under the aegis of Columbia-TriStar, was beating the drum at the Hotel du Cap on behalf of a piece of junk called *The Last Action Hero*. Only fleeting glimpses of it were available to be seen but, as usual, Schwarzenegger was putting himself about among the media.

One of the best and most talked about films in competition that year was Mike Leigh's *Naked*, which won prizes for Leigh as best director and David Thewlis as best actor. That was the film, that was the première, which Schwarzenegger selected for his grand entrance at Cannes. Perfect choice; he emerged dramatically from his limo outside the Palais du Festival, waved to the crowd and the photographers and made his regal progress into the screening, letting the world know that though he might be publicizing a mere popcorn movie up at the Cap he was a man of artistic sensitivity who appreciated serious cinema. It was a miserable thing to do because he distracted attention from Leigh and his cast, whose big night this should have been, and took it all for himself. But even then he might have been forgiven if he had actually stayed to watch the film but he didn't. As soon as the lights went down in the auditorium he sneaked out of the Palais by a back exit where the limo was waiting to return him to the Cap and dinner.

Columbia-TriStar had high hopes of *The Last Action Hero*. It was to be their big, fat blockbuster of the year and, to prove their faith in the product and the star, not only Mark Cantor, head of production for Columbia, but also Peter Guber, head of practically everything, turned up for the publicity shindig. This culminated with a dinner in the

Eden Roc restaurant at the Hotel du Cap, to which Columbia staff and a few media persons were invited. The sole purpose of this function, it rapidly became clear, was to flatter the hell out of Schwarzenegger. Just before the meal began I caught sight of Guber and Cantor in earnest consultation, comparing notes about the speeches they were to make. Which of them said to the other, 'Let's get in there and kiss arse', I don't know but in the light of the fulsome rubbish they were to deliver I'm sure one of them must have said it. It was cringe-making stuff whose import was that Schwarzenegger was the greatest star, actor, human being, philanthropist, benefactor, you name it, the world had ever seen and Schwarzenegger loved every moment of it. He probably agreed with every moment of it.

The nadir of all this drivel came when Cantor remarked that the instruction on the invitation read, 'Lounge suit'. Yeah? So?

'Well, what's a lounge suit?' he said. 'I'm just a kid from New York. What do I know from lounge suits?' This witty sally evoked almost helpless mirth from the assembled Columbia sycophants, while the feeling among the non-partisans was: Well, yes but you're also head of production for one of the world's biggest film studios and you're telling us you don't know what a lounge suit is?

That apparently was, indeed, what he was telling us because he said, 'Tell you what, whatever Arnie's wearing – that's a lounge suit. Arnie, stand up.' Arnie stood up, smirking. Arnie was wearing a sports jacket, a T-shirt and chinos. 'That's a lounge suit!' cried the fatuous Cantor. My, how we laughed. Well, some of us – those employed by Columbia – laughed; the rest of us just wanted to get the hell out of there.

Sylvester Stallone, one of Schwarzenegger's partners in the Planet Hollywood restaurant chain, was also at the Hotel du Cap that year to launch *Cliffhanger*, a decent enough action adventure story that briefly revived his sagging career. I interviewed Schwarzenegger one week, Stallone the next. Stallone was far better value – amusing, self-deprecatory, witty, much more intelligent than his loose-lipped, muscle-bound screen image would have you assume. When we had finished our chat I said, 'Why don't you have a word with your friend

Mr Schwarzenegger and tell him how to give a decent interview?'

'What!' said Stallone. ' You didn't get a good interview with Arnie? But he's supposed to be the world's greatest expert at dealing with the media.'

'Maybe,' I said, 'but he doesn't seem to have any humour at all.'

Stallone put his arm round my shoulder and said confidentially, 'I'll give you the answer – German. Name me one funny German comedian. I'll be in my room.'

Actually, Schwarzenegger is Austrian but I suppose the same stereotype covers both nationalities.

Chapter Twenty-Six

THAT BUSINESS OF Bruce Willis being late for his film show in Cannes – it was not in the least unusual. Hollywood movie people are almost invariably late for appointments with the media, almost as a matter of policy.

In 1990 Bruce Thompson and I went to Hollywood to interview Francis Ford Coppola about his film, *The Godfather: Part III*, which I had liked. It was not as good as its predecessors (both of which were superb) but it was well made and played. I had never met Coppola but I admired his early work in particular and our idea was to devote an entire programme to the director and his films. Paramount, the distributors, ever keen on publicity, were eager to help. A date and a time were set and a pretty location was found in the garden of the Bel Air Hotel, immaculate flowers and shrubs and a softly tinkling fountain in the background. Bruce and I, who had flown from London the previous day, were there, jet-lagged but punctual. Coppola, however, was not.

Time passed, one of the Paramount publicity men, Leslie Pound, went away to find out what was happening and came back, looking pale. 'Francis says he can't make it,' he said.

'Oh, Christ!' said Bruce. At the time he was comparatively new to this kind of dealing with Hollywood people and took Leslie's pronouncement at face value. He could imagine us flying home empty-handed with a dirty great hole where next week's programme ought to be. I, however, had been there before. 'Don't worry,' I said. 'He'll make it. They always make it. It's just a game they play.'

More time passed, more phone calls were made; Francis wasn't budging; Leslie and his PR colleague, John Wrench, kept huddling together, whispering and shaking their heads; Bruce took to pacing up and down and frowning a lot. 'Fear not, Bruce,' I said. 'It'll happen. Trust me.'

Finally, an explanation was offered: Francis couldn't make it because he had to baby-sit for his granddaughter. No way could he get to the Bel Air Hotel but – and this was the bit I'd been waiting for – if we could go to him . . .

So, of course, we did. We went to his southern California pied-à-terre, possibly the smallest and ugliest house in Beverly Hills, a tiny, scruffy back yard and a swimming pool not much bigger than the average bath tub. As an attractive location for filming it was Coronation Street to the Bel Air's Buckingham Palace. Leslie and John escorted us to the house, introduced us to Coppola and then scarpered, never to be seen again. Charitably, I assume they'd simply forgotten their promise to buy lunch for Bruce and me at the Bel Air. Never mind, though, Les – we're still up for it. Any time.

Meanwhile, Coppola, of course, wasn't baby-sitting at all. To nobody's surprise his daughter was there, looking after the child herself, leaving her father with nothing to do but the thing he had always intended to do in the first place – be interviewed by me.

So what was all that other nonsense about? The failure to turn up on time, the refusal to come to us, the insistence that we should go to him? I believe it's simply a ploy Hollywood people use to prove to everyone – not least I suspect themselves – that they, not the interviewers, are the important ones. The irritating thing is that I have no quarrel with that. If they would only arrive punctually, I'd be perfectly happy to have them announce in a loud, clear voice, 'I am more important than you are'. For then I could say, 'Fine, great. Now we've got that cleared up can we get on with the job?'

Another one who kept me waiting – this time for an hour and a half – was Warren Beatty but I'd expected that because he is a notoriously bad timekeeper. On this occasion he had arranged the location – a film editing suite in a building on Broadway – and had insisted that his favourite cameraman should be employed to light him. The reason for the latter immediately became clear: the camera that would be filming Beatty had on it a tiny light which would shine on his eyes, making them look particularly bright and clear. Because we had plenty of time to spare I was able to sit in Beatty's chair and try the light for myself. How he was able to bear it I have no idea because I couldn't see a damn thing.

Though we knew he would be late I did think ninety minutes or so was a bit over the top until he and his entourage turned up and his publicity woman whispered excitedly to me, 'You should feel very flattered. This is the least late he has ever been.' She sounded as if she meant it, too.

We had provided a make-up woman but Beatty airily declined her services, saying, 'I don't need any of that' and, indeed, he didn't because he was already plastered with the stuff. He turned out to be charming and personable and, off-camera and off the record, an excellent and saucy raconteur. But when the camera was turned on and the little light was shining in his sparkling eyes he was practically anal-retentive. It was almost impossible to get any unequivocal statement from him at all. Every question was regarded as a sort of thinly disguised bear trap to be circumvented as non-committally as possible. I swear that if I had said, 'It's a lovely day, Warren', he would have got up to check for himself before agreeing with me. When it was over his PR girl came whispering to me again. 'Gee, that was a great interview,' she said and sounded as if she meant that, too. God knows what his other interviews must have been like.

Robert De Niro kept me waiting for an hour. This was at the Savoy Hotel in London and I hadn't wanted to interview him in the first place. Friends of mine, newspaper and magazine journalists who had enjoyed this dubious privilege, had all declared that he was the most boring, monosyllabic interviewee in the world. I was not disappointed or disillusioned to learn that. Many movie stars are dull and boring, and, since, when you come right down to it they are only people, there's no reason why they shouldn't be. So I had never even attempted to interview De Niro but had simply contented myself with admiring his work, which I did most strongly. But when *GoodFellas* was about to open in London and the girl from Warner Brothers phoned in a state of great excitement to say that De Niro was in town for one day, had promised to give one TV interview and had said he would give it to me, I thought, 'Well, it's his idea, not mine, so presumably he's actually got something to say.'

As ever Bruce, crew and I turned up on time and by the appointed hour we were ready to start; but also as ever the Hollywood star was not. He was in his room one floor up and directly above us and there he stayed. After a very long while I enquired of the PR girl whether De Niro had perhaps got lost on the hazardous journey down one flight of stairs and, if not, why wasn't he here yet? She said she would find out, made a phone call and reported that the great man was waiting for his shirt to come back from the laundry. Now if someone had asked me how many shirts I thought Robert De Niro owned I would certainly have said, 'More than one' but in this, apparently, I would have been wrong. He arrived, eventually, wearing his newly laundered shirt, a rather drab thing in dull autumn colours and with a Hawaiian pattern, the sort of shirt I wouldn't wish to wear even on a deserted beach.

At once I realized that this was not going to be one of my greater triumphs. Grudgingly and without making eye contact De Niro allowed himself to be introduced to Bruce and me but showed no interest in meeting the crew. Unusual, that. Actors usually suck up to camera crews, knowing that how good they look on screen depends to a large extent on the cameraman's good will. De Niro, however, was mostly interested in finding a place where he could leave his newspaper and be confident that nobody would take it away and it was only when this had been accomplished that the interview began.

It was exactly as I had been warned. When he was not evasive he was monosyllabic; he directed many of his answers not to me or even the camera but to far corners of the room, sometimes to places over his own shoulder. It was a curiously unprofessional performance that left me annoyed, dissatisfied and wondering precisely what planet he had come from and why he had bothered to leave it. But that was before I made him angry.

I didn't mean to make him angry, though I wasn't unhappy when I did. After all, he had made me angry so why shouldn't I return the favour? What upset him, however, was essentially this: in the research I had done while preparing for the interview I had come across a recurring story, repeated in one magazine after another, that had puzzled me a lot. According to this story, some three years earlier, when the film *Big* was about to be made, De Niro had gone to the producers begging to be allowed to play the main character, an 11-year-old boy who wakes up one morning to find himself occupying the body of a 35-year-old man. And the producers had turned him away, declaring that he was box office poison and they wanted a real star for their film. The 'real star' they had chosen was Tom Hanks who, in 1987, was not even a household name in his own household. I kept reading this story and not believing it because it simply didn't make any sense to me. So I asked De Niro to explain it and he thought I was trying to stir up trouble, dig the dirt, whatever. But I wasn't; I was genuinely seeking enlightenment.

Grudgingly, haltingly, slowly, confiding sometimes in me, sometimes in the camera, sometimes in a distant part of the room where his newspaper lurked, De Niro told me his version. The producers, he said, had approached him to play the part (not the other way round) and he had been interested. But then they began discussing the details – when, where, how much and the like – and when it became clear that they were not going to reach agreement De Niro had walked away. Immediately after that the story the magazines had printed so faithfully and gullibly began to circulate. De Niro's account made far more sense: at the time *Big* was made he was an established star and an Oscar winner, Hanks was neither of those things. I believed, and still believe, what De Niro told me and would have thought it was in his professional interests to have it made public. He, though, did not agree.

As the interview ground to a weary halt I thanked him politely, though not sincerely, and reached across to shake his hand. He wasn't playing. Keeping his hands to himself he got up muttering, 'You hadda get that one in, didn't you?'

This was a bit much. He'd kept me waiting, wasted my time with a lousy interview and now he was upbraiding me for trying to do him a favour. 'What are you talking about?' I said. By then I was really cross.

He pushed his chair aside and went out into the corridor and I followed him. 'What is your problem?' I asked. He rounded on me. 'You know what my problem is!' We were standing very close, almost nose to nose, snarling at each other. For the moment there was nobody else around and it occurred to me that this face-off could lead to fisticuffs in which case I would be in serious trouble, De Niro being younger, fitter and much tougher than me. But I stood my ground as he revealed that I was a disappointment to him: he'd been told I was a straight-up sort of guy yet here I was trying to make trouble by resurrecting the *Big* story and, no, he wouldn't have it that all I was trying to do was get to the truth.

In the end I said, 'Look, if you don't want me to use that stuff in the programme, I won't.' It had been the most interesting part of the interview but it took so long to get to the point that I knew we wouldn't have time to use it anyway. This placated him immediately. 'You mean it?'

'Sure,' I said.

''Preciate that.' And now it was he who offered to shake hands. So we did and we parted without, I suspect, much affection on either side and without either of us looking forward to another meeting. I had, in fact, enjoyed the row far more than the interview but that afternoon, as I wrote my review of *GoodFellas*, I found myself describing De Niro as one of the best screen actors on the planet, which he was and, when he puts his mind to it, still is and that is true whichever planet we are talking about, his or ours.

My worst experience punctuality-wise, to coin a phrase, was with Madonna. It was 1992 and she, then about as big a show biz phenomenon as you could find anywhere, was trying to resurrect a film career that had never really got off the ground with a dire thriller called *Body of Evidence* and this she had come to Europe to publicize. To Europe, you notice – not to Britain. She had been so badly mauled by the British press that she refused to set foot in Britain and in that she had my sympathy. On the other hand she did want publicity and so we at

Film 92 were asked if we wished to go to Paris and interview her. None of us had met her, all of us were curious and I, in particular, wanted to ask why she had associated herself with what is known in the technical language of the trade as 'a piece of shit' like *Body of Evidence.*

So it was arranged. We hired a two-camera crew and a room was made available for us in the Ritz Hotel, a place soon to be gloriously associated with political sleaze, brown envelopes stuffed with money and the satisfying downfall of the Tory Party.

I spent the morning of the interview up to my knees in mud and water helping the local wildlife association to publicize its attempt – eventually successful I'm happy to say – to return the otter to Hertfordshire's rivers. A BBC car picked me up and took me to Heathrow and I arrived at my hotel in Paris – not the Ritz; we couldn't afford to stay there – to learn that the interview had already been put back half an hour. Now it was to take place at 6 p.m. Well, I didn't mind that. I got to the Ritz comfortably before six to find Bruce and his assistant, Helen Cook, waiting and the cameras and lighting already set up. Just one minor inconvenience – Madonna wouldn't be there at six after all; she would be there at 6.30.

She wasn't.

At seven o'clock an excited young French PR flunkey came dashing in to say that Madonna and company hadn't turned up yet. I said I had noticed that. But, he said, 'Zey are on zeir way!' At 7.15 and 7.30 zey were still on zeir way and it wasn't until 7.40 that an American PR woman, oozing self-satisfaction and attended by the young Frenchman and another flunkey, breezed in to announce, 'We're running late.' And at this point I rather lost it. I am myself almost pathologically punctual; so is Diana and, come to that, so is Bruce. Being on time – or apologizing sincerely for not being on time – I regard as small but important courtesies and I tried to communicate this belief to the smug American woman.

'Why are you running late?' I said. 'You've kept us waiting here for an hour and forty minutes without a word of explanation or apology. That's a disgraceful way to treat people.'

She reacted as if I'd slapped her; so did the young French flunkey.

'Gee,' said the woman, adding memorably, 'I'm not sure I wanna bring my artiste into all this hostility.' And she flounced away. Bruce heaved a deep sigh and went after her while the French flunkey, looking at me in amazement, said, 'But Madonna is a *star* . . .' as if that explained everything. And in a way it did and that was the problem. Madonna was a star and therefore she and her retinue could behave as inconsiderately as they wished while everyone else must wait, uncomplaining and humble.

Bruce came back after a few minutes saying things didn't look too good but by then I'd decided I didn't feel humble and I didn't want to talk to Madonna any more either because I was so angry that I knew I would be rude to her and would regret it later. Nor was I consoled by learning the reason for the delay – that Madonna had been the guest on a sycophantic French TV show and had been so carried away by the adoring, uncritical atmosphere that she had simply stayed there, confident that others who wished to talk to her would still be hanging around when she deigned to give them her attention.

Yeah, I know – mine was an unprofessional attitude but I don't regret it and if necessary I would do it again. Being a star is all very well but it wouldn't hurt any if stars could remember to behave like human beings, too. Many of them, of course, do. Many of them – and I mention this lest you begin to think I'm a querulous sort of person who falls out with everybody – are genuinely nice people and these I like a great deal.

Tom Hanks, for example. Just before *Forrest Gump* was released I was in Hollywood and said I would like to interview Hanks. This was arranged and a meeting was set up in a hotel in Santa Monica. Unfortunately, some dozy public relations person at the studio sent Hanks to the wrong hotel. An embarrassing experience for anybody, not least a superstar (which by then he was), to turn up and be told that no, nobody was waiting for him and no, nobody was even expecting him.

A lesser man (me, for instance) might well have murmured, 'Sod it' and gone home. But not Hanks. He phoned the studio, waited patiently until he was connected with someone who knew what was going on, found out where he was supposed to be and turned up, very late but hugely apologetic, at the appointed place.

Quite often the problem, when trying to arrange a face-to-face meeting with the lofty and elite of the movie industry, is created not by the lofty and elite themselves but by their overprotective assistants. On two occasions I have conducted lengthy interviews with Martin Scorsese, one of the very best directors of the last thirty years. Both times I was told, 'Marty's very busy. You just have an hour, okay?' Well, yeah, okay, if you say so . . . But both times Scorsese turned up (punctually), discovered that I wasn't interested in gossip but just wanted to talk about films, a subject on which he is even more passionate than I, and became so involved in the conversation that when, after an hour, his assistant came in claiming that he was needed urgently on the phone, he waved her away, saying, 'No, it's fine. This is good' and stayed for at least another thirty minutes.

But then Scorsese is a total movie anorak. A few years ago an American magazine asked a number of leading film makers to list the ten pictures that had most influenced them. The story goes that, dutifully, all – except Scorsese – named their ten. He, however, did not respond so a reporter was sent to extract the required information personally and was obliged to stop him when he had got to 127. True or false? I asked him. 'Yeah, it's true,' he said. 'But, you know, how can you choose just ten? There are so many great movies.'

In the film business, as probably in everything else, the best and most approachable people are those who are confident of their own abilities. Steven Spielberg is one such. Not only is he a brilliant director (*ET: The Extra-Terrestrial* and *Schindler's List* are enough to prove that) but he also has the rare gift of being totally in tune with public taste. I asked him once whether, when deciding which story to film, he picked the one he thought the audience would most like to see. 'No,' he said, and I believed him implicitly, 'I pick the one I would most like to see.'

Spielberg has his own studio, Amblin – now also the headquarters of Dreamworks SKG – in the grounds of Universal Studios. Universal provided it for him as a thank-you because '*ET* made us more than enough money in Bolivia alone to pay for it'. The Amblin complex is built like an old-style Spanish hacienda and practically everyone in Hollywood wants to work there. This is not surprising because Spielberg has set up a crèche for his employees' children (which, in the evening, can be turned into a gymnasium), kennels with plenty of fenced-in ground for his employees' dogs, a games room, a private cinema and a state-of-the-art kitchen complete with resident chef to provide his employees with lunch. Who wouldn't want to work in a place like that?

Once when I went to interview him there Bruce and I were met with the message that Steven was in bed with mild 'flu, was terribly sorry but would like to postpone our meeting until the following day. We said we understood perfectly and wished him a speedy recovery but had to go back to London the next day. This was passed on to Spielberg, who promptly got out of his sickbed and came into the studio to do the interview, despite the fact that already he was just about the most powerful player in Hollywood. But then if you are the most powerful player in Hollywood you don't have to prove anything to anybody.

Another time, when we were discussing his most recent film *Amistad*, he said, 'I always think of you as the $65 million man because every time you come to see me I've just made a picture that cost at least $65 million.'

'I know,' I said, 'but why does none of that money ever stick to me?' He smiled at me, a trifle smugly but also with sympathy. 'Because,' he said, 'you're at the wrong end of the business.' Tell me about it.

Michelle Pfeiffer, too, I remember with affection. I was to interview her in California about a film called *Frankie and Johnny*, in which she co-starred with Al Pacino and which, for various reasons, was to receive an unusually belated release in Europe. The team and I got there early and were standing around outside the hotel, chatting, with plenty of time to spare, when I heard a deferential clearing of the throat behind me and turned to find myself face to face with Pfeiffer, quite the most beautiful woman in the cinema. She had arrived all by herself – and, believe me, major stars hardly ever do that – and apologized for being a little early. Graciously, we forgave her.

The resulting interview, however, was not one of my most acclaimed. Pfeiffer was contractually obliged to help publicize *Frankie and Johnny*, even though it had been made a year earlier and much had happened in her life since then. She answered my questions about the film politely and thoughtfully but without much zest and our chat wasn't really going anywhere until, in desperation really, I asked her to explain why she had once said she thought she looked like a duck. Anyone who has ever seen even a still photograph of Michelle Pfeiffer would have been moved to ask the same question because, if ducks truly looked like her, courts the world over would be constantly filled with men charged with bestiality.

Amused by this change of tack she immediately became more animated and the conversation developed, I suppose, into a discussion of how gorgeous she was and the fact that we were sitting so close together that my knees were touching hers made me even more conscious of how gorgeous she was. Anyway, what the hell, I don't apologize. The interview was rather fun and the audience seemed to find it so. But one pompous young critic didn't. My attitude towards Pfeiffer, he said, made him feel ashamed to be a man. Had he known more about his alleged specialist subject he would have realized that we used only those parts of the interview that showed Pfeiffer at her best and liveliest – how I, the interviewer, appeared being of secondary consideration. But he was only a television critic. What did he know?

I have fond memories, too, of David Lean, probably the greatest of British directors. In 1988, around the time of his eightieth birthday, he came into the studio for a chat. We were looking for about a five-minute piece to slot into the next week's programme but as it transpired he stayed there, talking to me on camera, for the best part of an hour and afterwards, as I recorded the show for that night, he asked Bruce if he might stay and watch because he had never been in the gallery of a TV studio before.

The next week David Lean *was* the programme and that interview turned out to be the most popular I ever did. It was repeated at least four times, the last time being on the night he died in 1991. I was in the middle of recording the show that afternoon when Bruce burst in to tell

me that David Lean had died a few hours earlier. Did I want to write a
quick obituary to slip into the programme? No, I said, let's scrub the
programme amd repeat the 1988 interview; I'll top and tail it to bring
it up to date. And that's what we did. It was a big success.

Since the beginning of my television career I have made it a rule never
to become too close to the people whose work I have to review. This
has not been difficult to accomplish because, on the whole, the people
whose work I have to review have shown no great inclination to
become too close to me. This suits me very well because no actor,
writer or director whose latest work I feel obliged to savage can claim to
have been betrayed by a friend. With a vast number of people in the
film industry I have a very friendly acquaintanceship but nothing more
intimate than that. There are, of course, a few exceptions. Richard
(Lord) Attenborough, for example, is a kind and generous man for
whom I have great affection and respect.

The popular image of him, put about by journalists who have probably never met him, is of a show biz 'luvvie' forever dissolving into tears.
In fact, he has a core of steel and is driven by boundless determination.
Anyone who could, as he did, spend twenty years trying to get his film
Gandhi made is certainly no softie. As for the tear-stained luvvie image,
well, yes he does call people 'love' and 'darling' but, as he once told me,
that's simply because he can never remember anyone's name. As for
the weeping, he has a perfectly good explanation for that, too. 'I'm just
an emotional person,' he said. 'I can't help it. If someone walks up to
me in the street and says "Hello" I'm quite likely to burst into tears.'

David (now Lord) Puttnam, producer of *Chariots of Fire* and *The
Killing Fields*, I would regard as a friend; so, too, Alan (now Sir Alan)
Parker, head of the British Film Council and director of such films as
Midnight Express, Mississippi Burning and *The Commitments*. I have
got along well with both of them since the very early days of their
careers, though I did fall out once with Parker.

He is, as I have often said, a perfectly balanced man, having a chip
on each shoulder, the words 'film critic' being notched somewhere on
both chips. In 1985 he made a documentary for television called *The*

Turnip Head's Guide to the British Cinema and asked me to appear on it, interviewed by himself, in my guise as film critic. Knowing precisely how contemptuous he felt about film critics generally I told him to get lost but he was persistent. 'No, no,' he said. 'I want you there to show what good critics are like.'

Foolishly, I agreed, only to discover when the programme was shown that (a) I had never been photographed so unflatteringly in my life (and Alan is far too good a director for that to have happened by accident) and (b) only the bits of the interview in which I said dumb things were used. I was so angry that I refused to talk to him for a whole year, not that he knew that because, as it happened, we didn't meet at all that year. But then I thought, 'Life's too short for this and anyway I like him, warts and all', and friendly relations were resumed.

There are, too, a number of actors for whom I have a particular fondness, Judi (Dame Judi) Dench being one. I had met her only once, and then socially, before she came into my studio for an interview early in 1998, just after she had been nominated for an Oscar for her performance in *Mrs Brown*. All of us felt a little trepidation for even then she was the *grande dame* of English acting and none of us knew what to expect. What we certainly did not expect was a remarkably likeable and modest woman who turned out to be utterly starstruck. She didn't care whether or not she won the Oscar, she said, and it was impossible not to believe her; she was simply thrilled at the prospect of being in the same audience as the likes of Jack Nicholson, Dustin Hoffman, Anthony Hopkins and Robert Duvall. The fact that she could act the pants off most of them didn't seem to occur to her. Indeed, she was so starstruck that she even claimed to be impressed by the fact that she was being interviewed by me.

She didn't win the Oscar that year (shame!) but a month or so later she received the best actress award from the British Academy of Film and Television Arts. I was at the next table that night and as Judi's name was announced and she went up to receive her prize I looked across and saw her husband, Michael Williams (later, alas, to die of cancer), sitting there with tears of sheer joy rolling down his cheeks. Michael was himself a fine actor but his wife was even better and he knew it but not for one moment did he resent it. Instead he took the greatest possible pleasure in her achievements.

Talking of Oscar nominations . . . The first time I met Ralph Fiennes, an actor for whom I have much regard both personally and professionally, was early in 1993, a few days before the Oscar nominations. Like many actors he is a very shy man who had never before, I think, been interviewed on television. Bruce and I did our best to make him feel at ease and just before the interview started we explained that, though we were sure he would be nominated for his performance in *Schindler's List*, we wanted to cover ourselves either way. Since our programme would not go out until after the Oscar nominations I would therefore ask him two questions. The first was on the lines of, 'How do you feel about winning an Oscar nomination?' and the second was, 'How do you feel about not winning an Oscar nomination?' Only the appropriate Q & A, of course, would be used.

Ralph agreed happily to this and the interview got under way. It was going very well, too, until after about fifteen minutes I said, 'Now how do you feel about winning an Oscar nomination?'

His face lit up in delight. 'What!' he said. 'Have I really got one? How do you know? When did they tell you? Gosh, how wonderful!'

I had to explain. 'No, Ralph,' I said. 'This is make-believe. It's what we agreed on earlier. Don't you remember?'

He looked quite crestfallen. 'Oh, yes,' he said. 'I'd forgotten.'

It turned out all right, though. He did get a nomination.

On the subject of forgetful actors, Eddie Izzard came to the studio to talk about *The Velvet Goldmine*, or some such film in which he had appeared, and midway through our chat announced that his next project was to produce a movie. About what, I asked.

'Er, well, it's about a highwayman.'

'Good, yes, any particular highwayman?'

'Yes, well, quite a famous one actually.'

A pause. 'Who would that be, Eddie?' I asked.

'Umm. He's *very* famous in fact. Well, you know.'

'No, I don't, Eddie,' I said. 'It's your film, not mine.'

'Oh, God,' he said. 'This is embarrassing. Look, very famous.

Highwayman. Eighteenth century, I dunno, maybe seventeenth century. Give me the name of a highwayman, for God's sake. '

'Dick Turpin?' I suggested.

'Yes! That's him. Dick Turpin.'

As far as I know the film has yet to be made and given the fact that the prospective producer couldn't remember who it was supposed to be about I'm not entirely surprised.

Chapter Twenty-Seven

M Y FATHER WAS always a heavy smoker: three, maybe four, packs a day – John Players, unfiltered, until the later years when he switched to Silk Cut – and all that tobacco, pleasurable and consoling to him though it may have been, was bound to take its toll. In his mid-sixties his voice began to fade and he developed a small lump on his neck. He didn't complain about it but he kept fingering it and it was obviously bothering him, so it was arranged that he should consult a specialist at the Ear, Nose and Throat Hospital in Golden Square.

My mother and I went with him and I remember the three of us in a small room – Dad sitting on the surgical bed against the wall, Mum and I on chairs – each smoking a cigarette while we waited for the Old Man to be called into the consultant's office. It may well have been the last cigarette Dad smoked because the diagnosis was much as we had feared it would be: cancer of the larynx. I don't recall him smoking again after he came out to tell us the bad news but by then, of course, it was far too late to achieve anything by giving up.

A week or so later I drove him to the Royal Marsden Hospital in Fulham Road. The specialist we saw that day suggested a course of radiotherapy and asked whether Dad would have it privately or on the National Health.

'Privately,' Dad said.

'Are you a member of a health scheme?'

'No. I'll pay for it myself.'

'Take my advice,' said the specialist. 'Don't. The treatment we give you on the National Health will be just as good as any you pay for.'

And he was right. The treatment was immediate and efficient but it was typical of my father to offer to pay for it. He wasn't asking for any special privileges that might be accorded to private patients; he just didn't want to be a burden on the state, goodness knows why. He had earned good money and therefore paid high taxes for most of his life; he was as entitled as anyone to whatever benefits the welfare state might have to bestow but to him it seemed like getting something for nothing.

The radiation therapy sent the cancer into remission for about three years but then it returned and this time there was no option but surgery, the removal of the larynx.

Once again I went with him to the hospital, this time in Gray's Inn Road, and stayed with him throughout the day. He didn't want the operation; indeed, when he was first told he should have it, he had refused. It was only when the doctor pointed out that there was no easy alternative, no swift merciful death, but instead a lingering and painful one, that he reluctantly agreed.

That day when I hung around the hot, drab little hospital room while Dad went off for various tests, then came back and waited until it was time for someone else to prod him and take a blood sample and check him over, was one of the worst I can remember. The operation was set for the following morning and I knew when I left him that I would never hear his voice again, at least not as I had always known it.

I'm never sure what word to use when describing someone coping well with illness. 'Brave' isn't quite right – brave is what you are when you do something dangerous that you don't have to do. And yet there was certainly courage in the way my father faced cancer and other painful illnesses that followed. Of course, he endured them – he had no alternative; the courage lay in the uncomplaining manner in which he endured them. There were many times when he was clearly in pain or at least great discomfort but you would never have known it from anything he said.

When he recovered from the laryngectomy he could not for some while make any kind of sound at all. He communicated with his visitors by scribbling on bits of paper – 'Good to see you. Thanks for coming' or 'How you?', that sort of thing. A few days after the operation an old friend dropped in to see him. Dad gave him the 'How you?' note. On the back his visitor scrawled, 'Fine thanks. How you?' Furiously Dad grabbed the pad from him and scribbled, 'I'm not deaf, you bloody fool!' It was that sort of bellicose spirit that pulled him through, that made him learn, just as his friend Jack Hawkins, who suffered an identical operation, had done, to speak from, as it were the stomach, producing what Dad called his 'Dalek' voice. It was a strange sound; the echo of his own voice was still there and his words were perfectly comprehensible but he spoke now in a monotone – the decibel level never varied and there was no inflexion. And yet the strength of his personality was so unimpaired that many times after we'd had one of our political arguments (he on the right, I on the left) I could have sworn that he had been shouting at me.

The same quality of bloody-mindedness made him determine, once he had mastered the Dalek voice, to return to film making and around 1978 he directed several episodes of *The Return of the Saint* for television virtually without benefit of voice. It was the producer Bob Baker who gave him the opportunity and Dad was always grateful to him, as well as to the star of the series, Ian Ogilvy, and most of the actors and crew for their support but it was very hard for him and when he had proved to his own satisfaction that, handicapped or not, he could still do it he pretty well retired.

But he wasn't happy doing nothing. He knew, I am sure, that years earlier he had prematurely pulled the plug on his own film making career (and perhaps the unhappiness of that knowledge had made him particularly susceptible to cancer) and now, many years later, he did not simply want to fade away. He tried his hand at writing novels, at setting up film deals (and this in a period, the early 1980s, when the British industry was going down the toilet) and with his adaptation of one of my novels, *A Series of Defeats*, he came close to persuading the BBC to turn it into a TV series. Whether I could have helped him more I'm not sure. I could, and did, tell him where I thought he might improve his novels but I knew less about screenwriting than he did and besides my feeling, rightly or wrongly, was that for the sake of his own pride and self-esteem it was better that he should do things himself and without the aid of his apparently successful son.

Not too long after Dad had finally given up directing television I attended, as I always did, Lew Grade's pre-Christmas lunch to which he invited his favourite media critics and correspondents. Over the years Lew and I had our altercations, especially over my reaction to *Champions*, the story of the crocked jockey, Bob Champion, and the equally crocked racehorse Aldaniti who, together, won the Grand National. I didn't like the film at all; Lew, whose company had made it, liked it very much. Sharp letters were exchanged about the critical nature of my review but Lew was never one to hold a grudge and I was still invited to his Christmas lunches. This particular year he asked after my father. I told him how Dad hated the fact that he was no longer actively involved in the industry that had dominated his life. Lew was sympathetic and asked me to pass on his regards. Very nice of him. Even nicer was the fact that a couple of weeks later Dad received an offer of a monthly retainer to read and assess screenplays for Lew's film company. The letter was sent by Lew himself and both he and Dad honoured the agreement until the company passed into other hands. It was an act of great kindness on Lew's part. The next time we met I thanked him for it but after that he never discussed the matter with me again; it was an arrangement between him and my father, nothing to do with me and certainly not an attempt to influence my opinion of Lew's films. Even later, when he was so hurt by my response to *Champions*, he made no mention (as a lesser man would have done) of the fact that he was employing my father.

Lew was a man of great honour, as were his brothers Leslie Grade and Lord Bernard Delfont. For many years they were among the most powerful people in British show business – practically every branch of it – and just about the only ones whose word I could trust implicitly. To my knowledge none of them ever told me a lie and if you have the slightest experience of show business anywhere you will know how rare that is.

A Thursday in February 1993 a week before Dad's eighty-second birthday. I was at home, working on a novel, when John Vasey, our family doctor, phoned. It was about my father. Could I get down to the surgery? Yes, of course – but why? John would say nothing more but by then he had no need to. I knew at once that Dad was dead.

What had happened, I learned later, was that he had left home for an appointment with John. 'Shan't be long,' he said to my mother as he got into his car to drive the hundred yards or so to the surgery. There he collected a prescription and started off towards the chemist shop in the village. He had not gone far when, presumably, he felt unwell because he had pulled into the kerbside, applied the brake and – as the postmortem established – died almost immediately, causing an enormous traffic jam that stretched back a mile or so. I think that would have amused him greatly.

John came with me when I went to break the news to my mother. I told her as gently as I could and her immediate reaction was a stricken wail of, 'What's going to happen to me now?' At the time I thought this a chillingly selfish reaction. Her husband of sixty-two years was suddenly dead, for God's sake, and without a word of sorrow from her. But, as I realized afterwards, there was grief in that apparently self-centred outburst – an acknowledgement of her reliance on him, her need of him, his importance to her. She was nearly eighty-five years old, physically – though not mentally – frail and now half of her was gone. They may at times have quarrelled bitterly during their last years together but like many long-married couples they seemed to have blended into one being called Bet'n'Les or Mum'n'Dad, two equal parts of a whole. Her memories of him until her own death were never uncritical – I think they'd run out of uncritical when they were making her – but they were fond and amused and she derived much comfort from the belief that his spirit still hung around the house that she refused to leave until she had to.

I would say that he loved her more than she loved him but I couldn't really swear to it. My mother was demonstrative only in her love for her children but that is not to say that she felt no other love. She had a quality of reserve and a sort of self-protective coldness that, like her charm, she could switch on or off at will. I have inherited these char-acteristics (and probably use them much as she did to keep fools and bores at bay) and consequently know that a lack of any overt show of emotion does not mean that emotion doesn't exist. That my father loved my mother was obvious; how much she loved him was something known only to them. But he would not have stayed with her through six decades if all the love had been on his side.

I still miss the Old Man. Sometimes when watching a film on TV I find myself thinking, 'What d'you make of that then, Dad?' They say – or anyway somebody said – that no man really grows up until his father dies. I think that's nonsense. I'd done all the growing up I was ever going to do while Dad was still alive. Maybe if you're comparatively young, twenty- or thirtysomething perhaps, your father's death does make a difference. But I was nearly sixty and had been running my own life, with no little assistance from Diana, for a very long time. So now, with him gone, I was nominally the head of the family – big deal. With Christine's help, my brother Rick, who is a Chartered Accountant and far more practical than I am, had long been looking after the details, the nitty-gritty, of our parents' affairs and he carried on doing that until Mum died and there were no more parental affairs to be looked after.

I miss my mother, too. I miss her outspokenness, her fierce inde-pendence and that streak of larceny, which never left her. A year or so before she died she had to go to the local hospital for a checkup. Diana took her. Normally on these occasions Mum insisted on using her own wheelchair but this time, surprisingly, she instructed Dee to leave it behind. She'd use one of the hospital's chairs, she said. So she did. Diana wheeled her into the waiting room and sat with her until it was time for her appointment, this interval being enlivened by my mother's comments, loudly and clearly delivered, on her fellow patients who, she seemed to think, were all either stone deaf or braindead.

'Look at these poor old sods,' she said, though many of the old sods were younger than her. 'And that woman over there – look at her, the size of her! Fancy letting yourself go like that!'

Mum's appointment over, Dee wheeled her back to the exit, helped her into the car and was about to return the wheelchair to its rightful place when the reason for Mum's decision to leave her own chair at home at last became clear.

'Put it in the boot,' she hissed. 'The wheelchair – put it in the boot!'

'What – you mean, steal it?' Diana said, horrified. 'I can't do that, Betty – I'm a magistrate!'

'Go on, they won't miss it. Take it to your house, then Barry won't have to lug my wheelchair about when I come to visit you.'

Diana stoutly refused. Mum was very disappointed in her, no doubt thinking this was typical: wouldn't even nick a rotten wheelchair to please her poor old mother-in-law.

So, yes, I miss her. The world is a much more predictable place without her, no doubt more law-abiding, too. And if I miss Dad more it's because he enjoyed life to the end; for Mum death came as a release from an existence which she found increasingly irksome and for which she could no longer see much purpose. Because she, I believe, finally embraced death and he did not his was the sadder loss.

Chapter Twenty-Eight

I T HAD NOT been a great day. The morning's film had been dull, the afternoon's not much better and now in the early evening I was trudging through Soho on my way to Mr Young's viewing theatre in D'Arblay Street to watch what would probably turn out to be another piece of rubbish. This may sound like a cynical attitude but actually it was just realistic. In my view about 70 per cent of films, like 70 per cent of everything else – plays, TV, books, music, whatever – range from the tolerable down to the execrable. Of the other 30 per cent most are good, some are very good and one or two are nuggets of pure gold. If you are a professional critic the best you can do is accept the odds, reconcile yourself to the fact that disappointment probably awaits you but always approach the next film with optimism. Without that optimism you're in the wrong job.

In such a mood of hope, though not necessarily expectation, I passed a trio of young blokes leaning on a parked car and as I went by one of them said, 'And why not!', whereupon the other two fell into uncontrollable mirth. I had the vague impression that somehow I was the subject, or maybe the butt, of the first bloke's apparent witticism but since I could see nothing particularly funny either in what he had said or the way he had said it I was kind of puzzled.

At Mr Young's I was talking to an old friend before the screening began when I became aware of a small, plump man staring fixedly at me from across the room. He was pink with excitement and seemed to be bouncing up and down and his gaze never left me. On the principle that film critics, like everyone else, include their share of lunatics I ignored him until suddenly he came across to me and, even pinker and bouncing ever more obviously, took a deep breath and said, 'And why not!' before giggling hysterically.

I said, 'What?'

He said, 'And why not!'

I said, 'Yes, I heard you. What's that supposed to mean?'

He said, 'It's what you always say.'

I said, 'No, to my knowledge it's what I never say.'

He looked crestfallen. 'But it's what Rory Bremner says you always say.' And gradually the mystery was solved. Apparently on his television programme the previous night Rory Bremner, while impersonating me, had used the phrase 'And why not?' several times and such is the power of TV – or perhaps of Rory's personal magnetism – the whole country seemed to believe that this was what I said all the time.

Now people asking for my autograph wanted me to write 'And why not?' as well as my signature and the presenters of various television programmes on which I happened to be appearing at the time, either because I had a book out or was about to start a new series, would say, 'About this catch phrase of yours – And why not? – when did you first start using it?'

Useless to tell them that I had never used it, that it was entirely Rory's invention. I defied people to find a single programme in which I had ever uttered the words but they wouldn't listen. Wherever I went people murmured 'And why not?' at me. It was very irritating and I went around complaining bitterly that I had been lumbered against my will with this meaningless phrase until one day I got a note from Rory. It said, 'Invent your own bloody catch phrase in future.'

It was only then that I realized he had done me a favour. Comedians struggle for years to find a few words which immediately bring them to the public mind – Bruce Forsyth's 'Nice to see yer, to see yer nice', for instance, or Max Bygraves's 'I wanna tell you a story' (though I understand that was bestowed upon him by Mike Yarwood in much the same way as 'And why not?' was gifted to me). I'm not a comedian but the principle is the same: a catch phrase is a sign of familiarity, a confirmation that people know who you are. It probably has nothing to do with whether the public likes you but at least it indicates that you haven't spent all those years doing whatever it is you do without anybody taking the slightest bit of notice.

For much the same reason I was happy to be pilloried on *Spitting Image*. I didn't like the grotesque puppet (and I still can't figure out why, unlike me, it had a huge wart on its forehead) but then I wasn't supposed to. The point is that the producers went to the trouble and expense of making the damn thing and they wouldn't have done that if the audience was likely to say, 'Who's that supposed to be then?'

If you are doing any job in the public eye what you need is acceptance, which is not at all the same thing as fame. Acceptance means recognition as somebody who, whether you agree with him/her or not, can be trusted to know what he/she is talking about and to deliver his/her opinions honestly. You have to work for that. Fame is much easier; fame is simply a matter of being there, on screen, as often as possible.

When I first started working for television in the 1970s it was probably a much more amateurish business than it is now. The people who presented programmes were chosen not for their looks but because of what they could bring to the subject under discussion – journalistic know-how, writing or interviewing skills, informed opinions and the like. They were television presenters only by chance, as a by-product of whatever else they did. In America it was different. There the presenters were all good-looking – bright eyes, gleaming teeth, glossy hair, gym-honed bodies. They were professionals; television was what they did, all they did. News, current affairs and entertainment programmes were presented by a thirtysomething all-American boy next door accompanied by a little sister figure, usually blonde but sometimes oriental and always as cute as French knickers. Occasionally the newscasts were given apparent gravitas by the addition of a handsome, silver-haired avuncular person, straight from Central Casting. What was obvious about nearly all these people was that (a) they brought nothing to the programmes except their own presence and (b) many of them seemed hardly to understand what they were reading from the Autocue. Over the years more black and Hispanic presenters were introduced but otherwise nothing changed.

The news, good or bad, was delivered by people who looked like the patron saints of toothpaste. 'And that's how World War Three broke out last night.' Gleaming smile. 'Cindy Lou?' – 'Gee, thanks, Chuck.' Another gleaming smile. 'Well, Chuck, in Burbank last night little Wayne Jerkowski got his head caught in a rain barrel . . .' We, working for the BBC, used to watch all this with horrified delight and say, 'Thank God it's not like that at home.'

But that was in the days when British television was the best (or, in the words of the critic Milton Shulman, the least worst) in the world and before every idea that came out of America was eagerly adopted over here. Good God, we even have ambulance-chasing lawyers advertising on the box now, just as America has had for decades.

Meanwhile, our television, generally, is dominated by young, pretty people, whose only ambition ever was to be on television. Some of them, of course, are very good and some are not. But that was always the case and always will be. Essentially, though, they are there because they look nice on television; what they have to say is a secondary consideration. What you actually do no longer seems to matter very much; what is important is how famous you can become for doing it. Ten, twenty years ago people were derided for being famous for being famous; now fame for its own sake is the Holy Grail.

Well, television, like society, changes and in my time it has changed dramatically. The old Reithian idea that TV should inform, educate and entertain (probably in that order) is now regarded as arrogant. Why, we are asked, should people be told what they ought to watch? Why can't they watch what they want? So now, for the most part, they are given what they want and if it turns out to be the most undemanding kind of light entertainment, well, that, too, is merely following the American pattern.

Beyond that, TV has become the people's medium. In shows like *Big Brother* and various survival programmes the 'stars' are, for want of a better phrase, ordinary people, the equivalent of John Timpson's traf-

fic wardens dragged in off the street. I can't imagine the cinema or theatre handing over leading roles to men or women who just drifted in
saying they rather fancied being on stage or screen but television does,
increasingly. The excuse for this is that it reflects real life but, of course,
it doesn't. As soon as you point a television camera at someone real life
stops and play-acting begins. Whether this makes for more entertaining
programmes is also open to doubt since real life, though often stranger
than fiction, can also be a lot more boring. On the other hand, such
telly is cheap to make.

That changes have happened, in television as in every other branch
of life, is both beyond question and inevitable. The clock ticks forward
and only a fool would try to stop it. The sensible course is to accept the
changes, study them and wonder why they came about. Perhaps they
merely reflect the fact that a new generation is in charge; perhaps they
are a reaction against the intellectual Establishment that introduced
television in this country and controlled it for so long; perhaps they are
no more than a dumbing down, a pandering to the lowest common
denominator. Just as likely, in an age when league tables seem to be
quite as important for schools and hospitals as for football clubs, they
are the result of a wild scrabbling about for improved ratings, underlaid
by the great H. L. Mencken's dictum that 'nobody ever went broke by
underestimating the intelligence of the American public' and for
'American' read any nationality you like.

Whatever the reason the name of the game is celebrity. And
celebrity, whether you are a presenter or an actor in a soap opera, has
precious little to do with ability: it has to do with visibility, ubiquity and
just being there.

Well, you might say – and I wouldn't necessarily disagree with you –
'And why not?'

I wouldn't say that myself, of course, because, I repeat, it's not a
phrase I use. On the other hand if, thanks to Rory Bremner, everyone
thinks that's what I say, who am I to argue? If you've got it, flaunt it and
that goes for catch phrases as much as anything else. Hence the title of
this book.

And why not?

Chapter Twenty-Nine

I LEFT THE BBC in the summer of 1998. I wasn't unhappy there at the time but I was certainly less happy than I had been. Everyone was. Something had happened to the BBC – John Birt had happened. He had been brought in a few years earlier as Director-General, charged with making the organization more efficient and cost effective and in that I'm sure he succeeded. But his greatest achievement – and it took some doing – was to assume control of the broadcasting organization for which everyone in the country, and many people outside it, wanted to work and within six months make the entire workforce fearful and unsettled.

The confident security which in my time there had made the BBC innovative and admired throughout the world seemed to vanish overnight. There were redundancies and downsizing; staff members who retired or left for other jobs were replaced by people on contract, often short-term contract, and it's difficult to build a career, or a life, like that. If you are on a contract, three months, six months or even a year, and that's your only source of income, you can never be sure what the future holds. You think twice about getting married, more than twice about taking out a mortgage or starting a family. Your main consideration is making sure that your contract is renewed and that means you play for safety and never put your head above the trench.

In the 1970s and 1980s BBC staffers who were not too busy would have long lunches together or meet in the bar after work. Some of them, of course, were just loafing about, for there was a lot of dead wood around, but mostly they used these occasions as brainstorming sessions. Emboldened by a couple of drinks, they would mention ideas which, otherwise, they would think too outlandish to bring up. And quite often they would find a kindred spirit who would say, 'That sounds good. Let's get together and try to develop it.' My documentary series *Talking Pictures* came about like that when Judy Lindsay suggested it one evening in the bar.

Safe in the knowledge that, come what may, their jobs would still be there people were not afraid to grab an idea out of left field and persuade the BBC to run with it. If it worked, fine, and those whose idea it was had done themselves a power of good; if it didn't, well, back to the drawing board.

If you are on a short-term contract you're much less likely to do that. A safe idea, one that has been seen to work before, you would probably put forward. But anything at all daring, or just unusual, you would keep to yourself because the last thing you would want is to be earmarked as the guy who caused the BBC to waste money on something that did not take flight. What you want most of all is to stay employed, so you work hard and simply do as you are told.

The evidence of that is to be seen every day in the BBC schedules – a plethora of cookery programmes, gardening programmes, makeover programmes, quiz shows and game shows. There is very little on the BBC right now that you can't find replicated on the commercial channels because the bottom line is cost and ratings. Margaret Thatcher was to blame for the latter. It was she who voiced the notion that a public service broadcaster was perhaps an unnecessary expense to the nation if it couldn't attract the same kind of audiences as the commercial channels. But that, surely, is to miss the point: a public service broadcaster should offer not a carbon copy of what's available elsewhere but an alternative and that, in its glory days when it provided the least-worst television in the world, was what the BBC did and what, for the most part, it no longer does. Now it seems to devote its energies to competing with ITV in the ratings game and that inevitably means minority audiences are being short-changed.

Not, to be honest, that this affected me too much. I only worked for BBC television three days a week. On Mondays I went into the office to revise my script, rehearse and record the programme and then see a film in the BBC's viewing theatre; on Tuesdays I saw three films in private cinemas in and around Soho; on Wednesdays I returned to the office to write next week's script and see another film. Also, to be fair, there was never any interference with what I was doing. Phil Edmonds, the splendid England cricketer and equally splendid eccentric, who believes – or certainly did believe – that the world is virtually run by the CIA and similar organizations, once demanded to know who told me what to write about the movies. When I replied that nobody did, he nodded wisely and said, 'I understand, Barry. You can't say.'

But it was never like that. One of the great attractions of the film programme was that it was among the few places on television where, subject to the laws of libel, the presenter was free to say precisely what he or she believed. Even when the BBC started making films for cinema release, I was never under any pressure to say nice things about them, which was just as well because some of them didn't deserve to have nice things said about them.

Nor, in truth, was there much attempt at interference from the film industry. In the early days, yes. In the early days film publicity was in the hands of middle-aged men who hated television because they had seen it steal the cinema's audience and thus endanger their own industry. In their opinion a TV show dealing with the movies should act as an unofficial branch of the Wardour Street publicity machine and restrict its comments to such remarks as, 'And here's another wonderful film for you to see.'

But neither *Film Night* on BBC2 nor *Film 71* and onwards on BBC1 did that. Instead both programmes were honestly critical and there came a point when Wardour Street, or parts of it, rebelled. First, United Artists, angry at having several of its releases panned, hit on *Film Night* and refused to provide any clips for future shows. Barry Brown, naturally indignant, told me he was going to break the story to the newspapers and enlist their support. I, who had worked and indeed was still working in Fleet Street, advised him against it. 'Newspapers hate television as much as the film industry does,' I said. 'They won't be on your side.' And they weren't. TV was disliked by newspapers, even those which had invested in it, because the commercial channels deprived them of advertising revenue and also because every channel provided news and current affairs much more quickly than the papers could and that was a threat to their circulations.

So the press offered Barry precious little sympathy and, thus emboldened, MGM decided that I should not be given clips to show either. Having learned from Barry's experience I adopted a more low-key response; I went to see MGM films, reviewed them fairly and then told the audience, 'I'm afraid I can't show you a clip because the studio won't let me. I don't know why. It's not that bad . . .' The Wardour Street rebellion did not, in fact, last long because the publicity people swiftly realized that a film represented by a clip or two was able to make a case for itself, no matter how unfriendly the review, whereas a film visually represented by nothing more than a poster was not.

Apart from that brief hiatus I had no further trouble with the film industry until several years later when a visiting bigwig from Hollywood happened to be in town and watched a programme in which I slated his studio's projected summer blockbuster. Furiously, he summoned the head of the company's London publicity department and said, 'Why don't you do something about that guy? Can't you buy him off?' The PR man said it didn't work like that, not over here anyway. But he did his best to please the boss. At the next meeting of the film distributors' association he suggested that I should be banned from reviewing any films at all. Happily, his colleagues refused to take him seriously. I know this happened because a friend of mine, who was at the meeting, told me about it. As a matter of fact, the PR man who put forward this desperate idea was also a friend of mine – still is, indeed – and to this day he doesn't know that I know what he tried to do. Not that I hold it against him: he was only doing his job.

For the most part then I soldiered on happily enough, neither molested nor otherwise interfered with by anybody either inside or outside the BBC, for more than twenty-five years. But around the mid-1990s the atmosphere changed noticeably. A new, more remote kind of executive had moved in to toe the Birtean line. Management was now all-powerful and didn't seem to care much about the people who actually made the programmes. The last Controller of BBC1 while I was there was Peter Salmon, whom I met once at a party in Television Centre soon after his appointment. We talked amiably for perhaps three minutes but thereafter I neither saw nor spoke to him again. Well, no doubt he was a busy man and since BBC1 was not particularly distinguished at the time I daresay he had problems of his own. But the lack of contact with or reaction from those at the top leads to a feeling of isolation. In the past I had always had easy access to the Controllers of BBC1. I didn't bother them much, nor did they bother me. But we would meet and chat from time to time. Now this had stopped.

The BBC, which had once proudly been about making programmes, now seemed to be predominantly about management. In my time in Fleet Street I had often felt that newspaper owners would be much happier if they didn't have to employ awkward people like journalists. In the same way now the BBC seemed to regard programme makers as a nuisance who got in the way of saving money and making economies. I was not, I know, alone in the belief that nobody much cared what you did so long as you didn't make waves.

At the beginning of 1998 with my contract coming to an end there began the always lengthy business of negotiating a new one. Eventually, the BBC came up with an offer, financially quite handsome but in other respects not what I wanted. With the nation deciding by common accord that the new millennium would begin on day one of the year 2000, rather than day one of the year 2001, Peter Salmon wanted my weekly review programme to continue until the late spring of 1999, whereafter it would be dropped while I prepared a series of programmes to be shown at the end of the year and to feature my choice of the 100 best films of the twentieth century. Not a bad idea but I didn't fancy it much, partly because I enjoyed the review programme, partly because I had already published my 100 best films in a book and had no desire to go over the same ground again, albeit in a different medium.

Salmon's decision was not conveyed to me personally, or even

through my agent Sue Freathy, but by way of Bruce Thompson, my
producer, and this only added to the sense of isolation, of working in a
vacuum, or of trying to punch custard. After all, any changes were
going to affect me and it didn't seem too outrageous to expect to be
consulted. I'm a reasonable bloke; I'd have been prepared to talk things
over, listen to arguments. So would it have killed someone to pick up
the phone and discuss the matter with me? Or was that against company policy?

I wouldn't say I was disgruntled but I wasn't exactly gruntled either
and I began to think that maybe the best course would be to work out
my existing contract and then retire. I was nearly sixty-five and several
of my friends had retired happily much earlier than that. But while I
was in that mood I had an offer from Sky. In fact, Sky had sounded me
out a few times over the last five years but always when I was in mid-
contract with the BBC. This time I was more receptive.

The instigator of the approach was Elisabeth Murdoch, Rupert's
bright young daughter, who was about to revitalize Sky's movie channels and who felt that my kind of film review show would be an
important part of the shake-up. The financial offer was considerably
better than the BBC's and yet, believe this or not as you wish, it wasn't
the money that attracted me. Far more appealing was the care that had
been put into preparing the package. Sky, guided by Sue, had taken
considerable trouble to discover my interests and the proposal included
whatever car I wanted plus a dress allowance and, most telling of all,
two season tickets to the football club of my choice and tickets to any
Test match I wished to see in England. None of these perks, or anything like them, had ever been offered by the BBC, though in fairness
I should add that I had never asked for such things.

I said I would think about it and, while I was doing so, Sue, as was
her duty as an agent, told the BBC that another company had made me
an offer. There was no response. Maybe they didn't care; that's perfectly
possible. Maybe they thought I was trying some bluff, playing two bid-
ders against each other but I had never adopted any such policy before
and I don't suppose anyone would seriously have believed I was trying
it on then but you never know.

Time went by until it was clear that I would have to make a decision soon. The BBC, having made its bid, had collapsed into exhausted silence. It wouldn't have been so bad – well, let's be honest, it would have been disappointing – if someone had said, 'Look, we think it would be a good move for you to go to Sky. The best of luck in your new career', but even that didn't happen. Nobody tried to approach me in any way.

Sky and Liz Murdoch, meanwhile, were flatteringly eager that I should join them so in the end I had lunch with Liz and her right-hand man, Bruce Steinberg, and told them I would accept their offer so long as they understood that if Twentieth Century Fox produced a film that I thought was a stinker – always a possibility, if not an inevitability – I would be free to say so. I was adamant about this because Rupert Murdoch, who owns practically everything including Sky, also owned Fox and I didn't want any interference.

'Of course,' said Liz. 'No problem.'

So it was agreed. I told Sue, she told the BBC and then, and only then, did anyone bother to contact me. I had a message from Alan Yentob, Director of Television, to say that he would like to meet me urgently for a drink and a talk. We met at a hospital in West London where Alan's mother was seriously ill and from there went to a bar in a nearby hotel. I was touched that with all the personal worries he had he could still find time for this other problem. He asked me to reconsider; he said the BBC did value me and wanted me to stay. But it was too late; I had given my word to Liz Murdoch and I wasn't going back on it.

And that was the last time, before and after I left, that anybody in the loftier echelons of the BBC had anything whatsoever to do with me. I felt a bit like the woman in the joke who is abducted by a gorilla, is rescued and then mopes around saying, 'He doesn't write, he doesn't call . . .' When finally I walked away from Television Centre it was as if I had never been there in the first place.

Diana was very cross; I was not. I was actually quite amused that such an organization, whose *raison d'être* was to communicate with people, should behave in such a way. It was rather like being in the playground and suddenly ostracized by schoolmates who said, 'We don't like you any more and we're not going to talk to you, so there.'

That year I was awarded the CBE for services to film and television, something that pleased me enormously. In the same Birthday Honours List John Birt was given a knighthood. I must admit I didn't congratulate him on his honour but then he didn't congratulate me on mine. Nobody did, except the people I worked with.

After the last programme I recorded that summer Bruce Thompson, knowing that nothing else was being done, arranged a small party for me, attended by the production staff and the regular studio team. That was very touching. I liked these people and knew I would miss them. But I also knew that I would not miss the BBC and that was sad because I had had a wonderful time there, a career that was unexpected and richly rewarding in every way. I had worked and made friends with a lot of talented and amusing people and I'd been given the opportunity, denied to probably 99 per cent of the world's population, to earn my living doing what I wanted to do. Like so many of my colleagues I had been genuinely proud to work for what, most of the time I was there, was universally regarded as the finest broadcasting outfit in the world.

But I knew the time had come to move on and maybe my leaving did a little good. Soon after I left I was followed through the Exit door by Desmond Lynam and Harry Enfield. Not exactly a mass exodus but enough to persuade the BBC that in future it might be a good idea to pay more attention to and take a little more care of its presenters and stars. And that, I believe, is now being done.

My going attracted quite a lot of press coverage, most of it fairly complimentary, and journalists were eager to know whether the Beeb had given me a going away present of any kind, in recognition of my twenty-six-year stint. 'Your chair, for instance,' they said. 'The one you always sat in in the studio. Did they give you that?'

'No,' I said. 'No, they didn't.' I wouldn't have wanted it anyway. It was only the last of several chairs I had used over the years, wasn't particularly comfortable and, though this wasn't apparent on screen, had actually become very shabby.

But one day, soon after I left, I was lounging around at home when a young woman from the *Sunday Mirror* appeared at the door. 'We've got your chair for you!' she announced excitedly. 'We bought it from the BBC and we want you to accept it as a gift from us.'

Now a photographer and a driver appeared, lugging the chair itself. Would I, they asked, please let them take a picture of me sitting in it? How could I refuse? The house was in a mess – grandchildren were present; need I say more? – but it was a sunny day so they photographed me sitting in the chair in my front garden.

Diana provided coffee, I answered the reporter's questions and she and the photographer went away, justifiably pleased with their good deed.

I still have the chair. It resides, grey and battered, in the guest bedroom and the only thing that mars the story slightly is that it's the wrong chair.

I had never set eyes on it before the people from the *Sunday Mirror* carried it down my path.

Chapter Thirty

I MET RUPERT MURDOCH, owner of Sky, *bête noire* of the rest of the British media and one of the corporate Lords of the Universe, only twice. The first occasion was on Oscar night, 1998, when I was still with the BBC and had not yet decided to leave. *Titanic* had won pretty nearly everything that evening and Bruce and I, along with about fifty other camera crews, were outside the venue for Twentieth Century Fox's celebration party, waiting to interview anyone who came by. None of us was having much luck. There was no sign of Kate Winslet or Leonardo Di Caprio, though James Cameron, the director, was poncing about, waving Oscars. But he was refusing to talk to anybody having earlier proclaimed himself King of the World.

Then a limo drew up and a smallish, elderly, grey-haired man got out. 'Hey,' said Bruce, 'that's Rupert Murdoch. Do you want to talk to him?'

'Might as well,' I said and Bruce sprang into action with his customary cry. 'Oi, Rupert!' he yelled. 'Come over here and talk to Barry!' Even I thought this was a touch on the informal side, since neither of us knew the man, but the said Rupert trotted obediently across and talked amiably about the film and what its success meant to Fox. The interview, needless to say, didn't make it into the BBC's Oscar coverage.

The second meeting was soon after I had joined Sky and took place at a lavish but rain-sodden party in the old Battersea power station, where the company was launching its new digital service. There Liz

Murdoch came over and said, 'I want you to meet my Dad.' Dad seemed to have no objection and again we chatted happily enough, though neither of us mentioned Oscar night, which he had probably forgotten anyway.

Those to whom Murdoch is the Devil incarnate may be interested to know that I could detect no sign of horns, while as to the presence or otherwise of cloven hooves I have no knowledge because he was decently shod. The point of all this – such as it is – is that while there are many aspects of Murdoch's power and the way it is used that make me decidedly uneasy, I can have no complaints about the way he and his television company treated me. To those journalists who still ask indignantly how I could have taken 'Murdoch's shilling' I have two answers: one, that it was actually a lot more than a shilling and, two, that although in an ideal world I would work only for people with whose views I agreed, this is a long way from being an ideal world. I didn't agree with a lot that the *Daily Mail* or the BBC did but neither in those places, nor at Sky, was I ever asked to do anything that went against my beliefs or conscience. And that's pretty much all you can ask.

So what about Sky? Well, I had suggested a two-year contract but Liz Murdoch thought three years would be better and that's what we settled on. Nice to be wanted so much, although when I signed the deal it was not without trepidation. Sky had a staff of bright, ambitious young people but it didn't actually make many television programmes, so they were all pretty inexperienced and that worried me.

My kind of review programme, constructed around my script, may look pretty simple to make but a great deal of technical skill, know-how and knowledge of both the film and TV industries goes into the production of it and it seemed unlikely that there was anyone at Sky who was quite up to that speed. Liz had asked whether there was anybody at the BBC I wished to bring over with me and there was – Bruce Thompson. But I didn't think he would come. He had been at the BBC for a long time and was, or certainly should have been, one of the most valued members of staff. For that reason I had not personally asked him to join me; I felt he would be giving up too much.

Fortunately for me, however, the BBC cocked it up. Bruce's first self-appointed task when it was known that I was leaving and that, whatever happened in the future, the existing *Film 98* setup would be disbanded, was to scurry around making sure that every member of his team had a job to go to. That done he then presented himself to Those in Authority and said, 'Now what about me? What am I going to do?'

Those in Authority hadn't a clue. Well, they said vaguely, you're on the staff, lots of things you can do. You could do daytime cookery programmes, or a travel spot, or . . . This to the man who, for several years, had produced the best film programme on TV. Bruce was furious and, happily for me, he was still furious when Sky phoned and asked if he might consider joining me. Yes! he said and then, to the delight of both of us, Liz Ekberg, who had been an associate producer on the film programme for a long time, said she would like to come, too.

For me it could not have been better. Bruce, Liz and I had always worked together pretty seamlessly. All right, there was the odd tantrum – invariably thrown by me – but they knew me well enough to take no notice of my occasional sulks and outbursts of ill temper and they were certainly not intimidated by such bad behaviour. Other people were and frankly I intended them to be. For one thing I had not knocked around Fleet Street and television studios for more than forty years without realizing that being Mr Nice Guy doesn't always work. People take advantage, slack off and cut corners. But if I can report for duty as fully prepared as possible I see no reason why everyone else shouldn't. In short, I do not suffer fools gladly. Bruce and Liz understood me well and knew my tantrums were never directed at them and I valued them highly.

I could not have asked for a better team with which to launch *Barry Norman's Film Night* on the Sky Premier channel. We didn't talk much about the programme; we had no need to. We were so familiar with each other's work patterns that we conversed in a sort of shorthand . . .

'Barry, about Pete Postlethwaite . . .'

'Yeah, bring him in.'

'Next week then?'

'Fine.'

So the studio interview would be arranged and no further discussion was needed. For Pete Postlethwaite you could substitute the names of Richard Attenborough, the cinematographer Freddie Francis, Ridley Scott, Ewan McGregor, Cate Blanchett, John Madden, director of *Mrs Brown* and *Shakespeare in Love*, and several others. Both Bruce and Liz knew that wherever possible I would only interview people whose work I admired and that saved an awful lot of time and argument. Occasionally, as on the abortive trip to Paris to see Madonna, other considerations – a combination of extreme celebrity, availability and topicality – came into play but generally speaking our attitude was: why give free publicity to a film that was worthless no matter how famous its maker or its star?

Moving into Sky was, therefore, a much easier process than I probably had any right to expect. By the time I started work in September 1998, Bruce and Liz had assembled a small but enthusiastic team, including Marcus Shepherd and Paddy Taylor as assistant producers and trainee studio directors, and Chris Smith, as energetic if occasionally erratic researcher and, as it turned out, future film maker. Bruce was in overall command with Liz as his right-hand person and regular studio director. Because she is small, blonde and slight – bossy, too, though that is not immediately apparent – Liz initially had some difficulty in establishing her authority.

'You the director then?' said a senior technician, doubtfully, the first day she turned up in the gallery in that capacity. 'Directors are pretty young these days, aren't they?'

'No,' said Liz, 'I am not young. I am merely short' and quelled him with a glance, whereafter she had no more trouble. In its time Liz's glance has also quelled both Bruce and me, so I rather felt for the man.

The most publicized thing Sky did in the first year I was there was to announce a project to find the 100 best, or most popular, films of the century. Which was a little ironic, considering that this was exactly what I had not wanted to do at the BBC. But the difference was that this list would not be drawn up by me but by a poll of Sky's viewers. The idea was launched, quite lavishly, at the Dorchester Hotel in

London, where I immediately predicted what the winner would be – *Star Wars*. You didn't have to be a genius to work that out; *Star Wars*, recently reissued, had been quite the most popular film of the last thirty years and since I am convinced that vast numbers of young cinemagoers believe it was the first movie ever made it was bound to come out on top. Channel 4 later conducted a similar poll of its viewers with exactly the same result.

The Sky viewers' list was announced, in reverse order, on a special programme where I had Richard Attenborough alongside me to discuss the voting as we went along. That night we had an audience of invited guests, who included Kate Winslet, Noel Gallagher and Freddie Francis, whom I publicly congratulated on reaching his ninetieth birthday. Freddie was not at all pleased. At the time he was a mere stripling of eighty-two, who had just finished working as cinematographer on David Lynch's film *The Straight Story* and was naturally alarmed that if the rumour that he was ninety got about people might stop offering him jobs on the grounds that he was a bit old.

Working for Sky was very similar to working for the BBC, except that I only turned up at the studios in Isleworth once a week. I would do most of my film viewing on Wednesdays, rehearse and record the script and see another film on Thursdays, then write the next week's script at home on Fridays. Other films were slotted in as and when.

In the beginning I was worried that the shorter time-slot available on a commercial channel would affect the programme's quality. A BBC half hour is twenty-nine and a half minutes (the other thirty seconds being taken up by opening and closing credits); a commercial half hour is about five minutes shorter, on account of the adverts. But, in fact, thanks to Bruce and Liz the production values were quite as sharp as they had ever been at Television Centre and the need for shorter, crisper reviews made me think harder about the script. Essentially, again on the basis that if it ain't broke, don't fix it, the format remained the same but because of the necessarily leaner look I reckon the show was even better at Sky than it had been at the BBC and, immodestly perhaps, I think it had been pretty damn good there.

Again nobody interfered, despite the fact that for a lot of the time I

was happily slagging off films which would later turn up, heavily promoted as not-to-be-missed masterpieces, on Sky's movie channels.

The only thing I was sorry about was that we had to leave the Billy
Taylor theme music behind. The BBC owned the rights to use it and
weren't letting them go but that music had been associated with me for
a very long time and I missed it. On the other hand Sky – and Bruce –
argued quite reasonably that having a different tune up front would at
least show that we hadn't just transferred *Film 98* in its entirety to
another channel.

All in all, I had no regrets about leaving the BBC and still have
none. But at the same time I always knew that my spell at Sky, agreeable though it was, represented a sort of coda to my career. I knew, and
I'm sure Bruce and Liz did, too, that it couldn't last, nor did I really
want it to. While Elisabeth Murdoch was there, running all the movie
channels, *Film Night* enjoyed a privileged position. But when she left,
to have a baby and set up her own independent production outfit, and
economies began to be introduced throughout the company we were
affected as much as anyone else.

From our point of view the most notable budget cut was the decision not to send me and a production team to cover the Oscars in
2001 but there were other signs of serious belt-tightening, too. When
Chris Smith left to make his film, he was not replaced. And there was
no money around for the comparatively cheap pre-Oscar special, which
Bruce and I had suggested, in 2001.

Sky is essentially a television provider rather than a television maker.
Most of its programmes are bought in, not produced in-house, and
since it is cheaper to buy programmes than to make them, economies
tend to be applied first to production. Our budget being cut back did
not mean that the programme was no longer appreciated; despite the
fact that most of the people now running the company had little interest in films I think they were pleased with it and rather proud of it. But
it was costing more money than Sky liked to spend and the omens were
not good.

Yes, we were still going to cover the Cannes Film Festival because
Cannes, unlike the Oscars, provides lots of material that can be used

throughout the year, but otherwise our spending was restricted and so . . .

Flash forward to 24 April 2001. In an interview with Brian Viner in the *Independent* I announced my retirement from weekly film reviewing.

Compared with the bang with which my departure from the BBC was announced, I suppose this was a bit of a whimper but then Sky was, in truth, a backwater. Compared with terrestrial TV few people watch it. Besides, for most of the time I was there my programme was only on the Sky Premier channel – a subscription service within a subscription service – and the audience was miniscule.

But though I lost the viewers I did not, I'm happy to say, lose much, if any, stature within the industry. The people I respected still seemed anxious for my good opinion of their work and with rare exceptions – and exceptions occurred even when I was with the BBC – I was able to interview whomsoever I wanted. The difference, however, was that except when people came into the studio the lengthy interviews I used to be able to arrange were things of the past. But then that is now true of other film programmes as well. The increase in TV stations and channels has handed power over to the film publicists.

Television's demand for material, any kind of material, simply to fill the time is voracious and no material comes cheaper than (free) film clips from current movies and (free) interviews with the stars and makers of such movies.

So now the press, or more accurately media, junket is the publicist's tool of choice. This is a Hollywood invention to ensure maximum coverage of a film with the minimum of effort. Stars and directors are installed in separate rooms in a hotel. Each room contains two camera crews, provided by the film company, and TV interviewers are wheeled in one by one, on a sort of conveyor belt, to do their stuff. Since these 'in-depth' interviews often last no more than five minutes, what they comprise is exactly what the publicists want – lightweight chitchat rather than a serious discussion of the merits, or otherwise, of the film under review.

When attending these junkets I refused to talk to anybody for less than the maximum time allotted, usually fifteen minutes, but even so it was an unsatisfactory system. With every film there are a few basic questions that have to be asked, simply to set things up, and even in fifteen minutes there is not enough time to ask much more than those basic questions. The result is that all the interviews on whatever channel are very much the same. This was not so when it was possible to arrange individual and more leisurely meetings.

The first junket I ever attended was at a hotel in Beverly Hills. The movie being launched was *Wyatt Earp* and I went along because I happened to be in Hollywood making a programme for *Film 94*. This was an opportunity to pick up some useful material and, besides, I was eager to see how these things worked.

The stars of the film, Kevin Costner and Dennis Quaid, were there, along with several members of the supporting cast and the director, Lawrence Kasdan. It was a big hotel, the Four Seasons, and Warner Brothers had occupied a lot of it. Something like a dozen actors, plus Kasdan, were set up, along with camera crews, in their separate rooms, outside each of which four or five chairs were lined along the wall in the corridor. Here the interviewers sat while they waited for their summons to the presence. Any moment you expected a white-coated receptionist to put her head round the door and say, 'The dentist will see you now'.

It was a clinical, impersonal way to approach what should be a relaxed and intimate process, although I have to say the hospitality was good – a lot better than it was later at the London junkets. In Beverly Hills a large suite was set aside where the interviewers were assembled to wait, waiting in fact to be asked to wait in the corridors. In the morning, to while away the time, a full breakfast was provided – bagels, pastries, coffee and soft drinks, scrambled eggs and bacon – and at lunchtime hot and cold buffets were on offer. In London the coffee and the soft drinks plus a few croissants were as much as you could expect.

The *Wyatt Earp* junket was a big one that went on for a couple of days with a seemingly endless stream of television interviewers from all over America drifting in and out. But what kind of people were these?

Well, I'll give you an example. When I'd reached the second stage of waiting to see Costner (on a chair in the corridor) I found myself sitting next to a film critic from some mid-American TV station.

'Hi,' he said, 'how you getting on?' I said I was getting on fine, although in truth I was already rather bored.

Then . . . 'How many autographs have you collected?' he asked. What? Autographs? You don't collect autographs from the people you're interviewing; you don't want to approach them as a supplicant. Ideally, you should pay them the compliment of treating them as your equals. 'None,' I said.

He looked at me pityingly. 'I got 'em all,' he said, 'all except Costner's and I'm waiting for that now.'

Oh, right. A fine, impartial critic he must have been, charging in like a groupie, brandishing his autograph book. *Wyatt Earp* could have turned out to be the worst film ever made (actually, it was rather good) but I bet you'd never know it from that bloke's review.

'Got it!' he said, when he came out, beaming. 'I'm finished now. Good to meet you.'

The publicity people bade him a particularly fond farewell. Why wouldn't they? He was exactly the kind of interviewer they loved and I wager there wasn't a movie junket in the entire United States to which he wasn't invited. As I watched him go the 'Only in America . . .' line came into my mind but, as I was later to discover, autograph-hunting interviewers were not unknown in London either.

I always said that I would give up the weekly show as soon as it ceased to be fun. In fact, thanks to Bruce and Liz, it was still fun but during my last year at Sky it had become less so and the indications were that with the introduction of conveyor-belt interviews and tight publicity control it would soon cease to be amusing or enjoyable at all.

That was the reason I gave for calling a halt but it wasn't entirely my choice. I had been dickering for some time about whether I would sign a new contract if one were offered. My instinct was not to do so. But on the other hand another year, which is as long as I would have wanted, would, I think, have been welcomed by Bruce and Liz.

In March 2001 Paul Taylor, who took over the running of Sky's movie section after Liz Murdoch left, and his number two, Frances Naylor, asked Sue Freathy to meet them and discuss the future. At the same time I had a call from Mark Sharman, now Sky's Director of Broadcasting and Production, asking me to go and see him a few days before the other meeting. Bruce and Liz regarded this as encouraging; a new contract was surely about to be offered. Would I accept it? Yes, I thought, as I made my way to Mark's office, I probably would, though not with great enthusiasm.

The conversation started with Mark telling me how, if he didn't lose a couple of pounds in weight over the next few days, he would have to contribute seventy-five quid to some kind of Sky executives' weight-watchers club and then drifted comfortably into reminiscences about journalists and TV people we had both known and the enjoyable time we had spent together doing our 1988 Olympic talk show for Channel 4. After that he started on a lengthy explanation of how Sky was embarking on a programme of interactive digital expansion or some such highly technical grown-up stuff which I didn't understand and frankly didn't want to understand. And when he'd finished that he said, suddenly and without further preamble, 'So you won't be surprised to learn that I won't be commissioning the programme again after the summer.'

Well, actually, Mark, yes I was surprised. I'm not saying I was heartbroken because I certainly wasn't. But nothing in the previous conversation had prepared me for this so I was surprised all right. On the other hand I didn't argue with him. There was nothing to argue about. In many ways what he had said suited both of us. We chatted some more and then he walked me to the lift. On the whole, it had been an agreeable session and I was still fond of Mark. Indeed, I think it had probably been harder for him than it was for me because I believe he has for me, as I for him, a personal affection and professional respect.

What I felt, as I walked back to the office to break the news to Bruce and Liz, was both sadness and relief. My mind had been made up for me: I wouldn't have to do the programme again after June and I was happy with that. But the downside was that Bruce and Liz would also be out of work. They had come to Sky with me and it was pretty certain that they would leave, like it or not, with me.

Why should that be so? They made up the best team I have ever worked with; they're intelligent, talented, hard working and super-efficient. But with my programme gone and not to be replaced Sky, which, as I have said, makes very few programmes, except where news and sport are concerned, had nothing to offer them.

Sport, news and movies are Sky's main *raisons d'être*, not necessarily in that order, although movies always come third. News coverage, of course, has to be produced in-house but, for the most part, covering sport is hardly the same as making television programmes, since all it involves is pointing cameras at events that are taking place anyway. Around the events themselves are built studio discussion programmes but these are fairly cheap and cheap is what television companies like. What it boiled down to is that I was too expensive for Sky. As Paul Taylor said, for the price of each *Film Night* he could buy the rights to show another film. A good film? Didn't matter. A movie, any movie, would fill two hours of screen time while our programme, however good, only filled thirty minutes.

Bruce and Liz were, I think, as philosophical about the matter as I was. There was no reflection on anyone's ability. Sky was simply cutting back on personnel and saving money and that's just the way it is with big business.

My leaving of Sky was an altogether happier business than my departure from the BBC. I recorded my last programme in June 2001. All very professional, all very efficient. A hire car had been sent to bring me to the office where I arrived about mid-morning, rejigged my script, as I always did, handed over my suit and shirt to be pressed by Elsa, the ever-solicitous wardrobe mistress, did the rehearsal and lunched with the production team in the canteen.

Then I went to my dressing room to change into what was popularly known as my 'party frock', dropped into make-up for a bit of slap (base and powder) and then to the studio. The recording went well. No hitches, no fluffs, only a couple of retakes and those for technical reasons. I thanked everybody in the studio and that was it.

Well, not quite. Afterwards in a private room near the studio there was a party – wine, beer, soft drinks, sandwiches, assorted finger food. Just like the BBC really, except that this time it had not been left to Bruce to arrange it. This time it had been laid on by Paul Taylor. Officially. On behalf of Sky. Somehow it made a difference, a big difference.

The next day I went on a family holiday in Spain and when I returned Mark Sharman and Paul Taylor took me to dinner in Chelsea. They did it, Mark said, just to say thank you. No big deal, no presentations, no gold watch. We had an excellent meal in an excellent restaurant and parted on the best of terms and with warm expressions of mutual regard. If you're going to leave a company, that's as good a way as any.

Chapter Thirty-One

FOR TWENTY YEARS, both at the BBC and Sky, my programme was off the air for most of the summer. A combination of long days and the holiday period means that audiences are smaller in the summertime, so every channel rests its regular programmes and fills the schedules with repeats.

Things were no different in 2001. My last programme went out in mid-June, whereafter I went on holiday. When I returned I pottered about, as I had always done, writing my weekly column for the *Radio Times* and other bits and pieces here and there. I was a guest on a few radio and TV programmes and, all in all, nothing much seemed to have changed. Mid-August, I thought, would be the crucial point; that's when I would start pawing the ground like an old war horse and wondering why, for the first time in decades, I didn't have to go and see films and write scripts. That's when the withdrawal symptoms would reveal themselves.

But it didn't happen. August came and went, so did September – by which time I would normally have been back on the air – and I didn't miss television at all. I was still reviewing films but in print rather than on TV and – this was the best of it – for the first time in nearly thirty years I could pick and choose the movies I wanted to see. Like what? Well, like anything by the Coen brothers (*The Man Who Wasn't There*), Martin Scorsese, the Stevens Spielberg and Soderbergh, Robert Altman (*Gosford Park*), David Lynch (*Mulholland Drive*, though frankly I haven't the faintest idea what it was about and I'm pretty sure David Lynch hasn't either) and several others. I'm talking here about masters of their craft. First-time directors you have to be wary about. Might be okay, might not. What I no longer have to go and see and now wouldn't go and see at gunpoint are things like *American Pie* in which a horny teenage boy had sex with something his mother had cooked for dessert. I mean, come on, I don't much enjoy watching people have sex with each other on screen. I certainly don't want to see a horny teenage kid raping an apple pie.

When I gave up the day job my old sparring partner Michael Winner, blithely ignoring my reasons for having done so, suggested in some newspaper that this was a sort of old fart's syndrome – I was going to stop watching films because films weren't as good as they used to be in my youth. Dear old Michael – he entirely missed the point, of course.

People are always complaining to me, 'Ah, they don't make 'em like that any more' but it's not true. The best films today are as good as – and technically far better than – any that were made before. The worst films . . . ah, now that's a different matter. The worst films were always bad but now they are bad in a more cynical way. They pander to an audience of twelve- to twenty-four-year-olds, mostly male and mostly governed by raging testosterone. Dialogue is kept to a minimum because it holds up the action. Ditto characterization and the building of it. As for wit, no, let's not bother with wit. The audience won't appreciate it and anyway it's very hard to achieve. Crude and shocking will do because they'll get the laughs we want.

It's not that I have a blanket aversion to comic book, gross-out or deliberately dumb movies. Whatever the subject matter the only criterion is this: is it well done? If it is, I will support it. But most of the time it's not well done. That was probably always true but now there is a new and worrying kind of bad film – the bad film which has had vast amounts of money thrown at it in every department except, almost deliberately it seems, the screenplay.

It's not good enough. Even the lightest of entertainment should be imbued with a certain amount of intelligence because the audience, no matter what Hollywood might think, is also imbued with a certain amount of intelligence. Of course, there are many film makers who still believe that but too many others do not. People don't go to the movies to think, the argument runs: they go to laugh, or be thrilled or scared, and, yes, that's true. But the very best films that thrill or scare or amuse you also ask you to put your brain into gear. A film that urges me to leave my brain at home with the baby-sitter doesn't exactly have my full sympathy.

John Malkovich, not among my favourite actors but one who consistently tries to appear in intelligent movies, said recently that people get the cinema they deserve and that's true, too. But since the vast majority of the audience is very young, the cinema they deserve – and no doubt want – is unlikely to appeal to anyone much over twenty-five. Yes, most weeks there are also more thoughtful films to be found but you have to look hard for them.

Sometimes over the years, when I had been particularly harsh about something aimed at an audience with an IQ roughly the same as David Beckham's boot size, people would say, 'Ah, but it wasn't made for you. Maybe you should get a fifteen-year-old to review films like that.' Well, it's a point, I suppose, but it wouldn't have a lot to do with film criticism. A critic is there to say whether or not a film is good of its type and I doubt whether a fifteen-year-old would have enough experience to do that with any conviction.

It's an odd business, criticism. Almost by definition all critics are parasites; they could not exist unless someone else had first created something for them to pick at. But parasites can be useful; they can clean the wounds and that, in part, is what critics should do. They should also be imbued with such a love of the medium at its best as to strive to maintain standards, to be familiar with the best and the worst of each genre. But to do that they have to be fairly knowledgeable; it's not just a matter of passing opinions but of passing opinions formed by experience and honestly held.

A long time ago the director Lindsay Anderson sounded off about 'these dreadful film programmes' on television. By coincidence, or maybe not, this happened soon after he and I had had a verbal punch-up on the box about his film *O Lucky Man!*, which I hadn't liked very much. He got a lot of support in the press but I was strangely cheered. If programmes like mine were getting under the skin of those who made the movies, then we were doing our job.

I always believed that my first obligation was to the audience – not to pander to it, but to be honest with it. To do that, of course, one had to be honest about each individual film. If, when writing a review, I thought of a good joke I would put it in. But if, on rereading, I felt the joke unfairly belittled the film I would take it out. It wasn't wasted; another movie was bound to come along that thoroughly deserved to be belittled.

Mind you, whether the audience was always paying attention is open to doubt. In 1975 I reviewed David Cronenberg's film *Shivers* (or *The Parasite Murders*, as it was also known). It was about slimy parasites that invaded people's private parts and turned them into venereally diseased sex maniacs. I hated it and said so as vehemently as I could. And what happened?

For days afterwards people came up to me saying things like, 'That was a rotten film you sent us to, that *Shivers*.'

'*I* sent you to it? Did you listen to my review?'

'Yes. You said it was disgusting and made you feel sick.'

'And?'

'And it was disgusting and it did make me feel sick.'

'So why did you go and see it?'

'Well, I thought I'd better check it out for myself because it couldn't be as bad as you said.'

'And was it?'

'Yes.'

About the same time I gave a considerable pasting to a British comedy called *The Confessions of a Window Cleaner* but because we were nothing if not fair we showed a couple of the better clips. The next morning the driver taking me to Broadcasting House for the *Today* show said, 'Saw your programme last night. That *Confessions of a Window Cleaner*, that looks a good film.' He hadn't listened to a word I said, just watched the clips. My golden prose had been wasted on him – a bit deflating, though it did serve as a sharp antidote to self-satisfaction.

If all this leads you to suppose that people don't take much notice of critics, you could be right, in this country, anyway. In America it's different. There, for example, the success or failure of a Broadway show can depend almost entirely on the opinion of the *New York Times* drama critic. Here, I honestly don't know how much influence we have. British audiences are more sceptical than Americans, reminding themselves that a critic's view is only one person's opinion and not necessarily right. It's a much healthier attitude. What happens here, I think, is that people who read or listen to reviews find and follow a critic whose tastes more or less coincide with their own and ignore the rest.

Against that, of course, some films, action-packed Hollywood block-busters for instance, are pretty well critic-proof but then the people who like them probably don't bother with reviews anyway.

So, during all those years, did I do any good? Yes, I think I did. I probably didn't have much effect on the popularity of expensive mainstream movies and I certainly didn't stop bad films being made – but then nobody except perceptive audiences voting to stay at home can do that. But I've been told, often enough to believe it, that my opinion of foreign language films and 'art house' movies – those made with some ambition but without large budgets or star names – could make an appreciable difference to the size of audience they attracted. The distributor Pam Engels once said that my enthusiastic reception of *Cyrano de Bergerac*, starring Gerard Depardieu, had a lot to do with its success outside London. I was very proud of that, though I'm sure other critics' opinions were equally important.

The great joy of being a critic is when you come across a film which pleases you so much that you can't wait to share that pleasure with other people and urge them to see it, too. Sometimes this happens against the odds. One evening in 1984 I went along to see Sergio Leone's gangster epic, *Once Upon a Time in America*. I had already seen three films that day, I had had no lunch and I was desperate for a cup of tea. But when I got to the viewing theatre no such thing was on offer. Not even a glass of water. We were simply bundled into the screening room and told to our – or, anyway, my – horror that this thing was going to last for nearly four hours. Parched and starving I slumped into my seat thinking, 'This had better be bloody good'. And it was. Within thirty minutes I had forgotten my thirst and hunger and was totally absorbed in the story.

Over the last thirty years there have been many films like that. Off the top of my head I can think of *The Godfather, Chinatown, Jaws, Taxi Driver, Annie Hall, The Discreet Charm of the Bourgeoisie, Day for Night, Raging Bull, Chariots of Fire, ET: The Extra-Terrestrial, Ran, Gandhi, GoodFellas, The Silence of the Lambs, Unforgiven, Schindler's List, Reservoir Dogs, Pulp Fiction, Crouching Tiger, Hidden Dragon, The Gladiator* – and there I'll stop because I don't want to make this a book of lists but there are lots more. These are not necessarily great films or classics that people will still be watching in thirty years time but they are films that hit the spot, captured a mood, or reinvented a genre and generally thrilled and delighted. You may not agree with many, or any, of those I mentioned but that's all right; you'll have your own list.

The beauty of film is that it grips and enthrals far more people than any other art form and that's partly due to television, which increasingly fills great chunks of its schedules with movies and movie-related programmes. Given the added availability and comparative cheapness of DVD and video and these days any home with a TV set also doubles as a small private cinema.

My enthusiasm for the movies is shared by Samantha and Emma, both of whom also work as film reviewers, less so by Diana, who only really likes happy endings. But then she's a very gifted historical novelist, who puts some of her own characters through quite harrowing experiences and doesn't want to see the same kind of thing portrayed on screen, almost certainly less convincingly than she would have written it.

Give or take a few amicable differences of opinion she and I get along extremely well. She likes sailing (which I don't), dislikes cricket (which I love), has an aversion to glitzy premières and the mutual back-slapping of awards ceremonies and believes that all actors (with the exception of Kenneth Branagh) are overpraised, overpaid and should keep their opinions to themselves. In the matter of premières, awards ceremonies and the intellectual musings of actors I'm pretty well in agreement with her, although there are a few other actors, as well as Kenneth Branagh, to whom I am always happy to listen.

So, in an atmosphere of occasional but always amiable bickering, Diana and I have managed to raise two beautiful and clever daughters and, in Bertie, son of Emma, Harry and Charlie, the sons of Samantha, we have three perfect grandsons, who would have been four but for the death at the age of six months of Bertie's twin, Oliver. He, like his brother, was born prematurely and was never able to leave hospital. We didn't know him very long but we miss him still.

So now what? Well, I have a great sense of release at having got off the weekly treadmill. It was a marvellous treadmill to be on and having got on it more or less by accident I wouldn't have chosen any other. It was hard work and yet it never seemed like working. To me, work is something you have to do, whether you want to or not, to earn a living but ever since I left school I have been in the happy position of doing whatever appealed to me. Even so a regular job, however pleasurable, is a kind of treadmill in that it stops you doing other things that you might have wanted to do even more. In my time in newspapers, television and radio I have travelled a great deal, though not as much as I would have liked, seen a lot of cricket, though not as much as I would have liked and written several books, though not as many as I would have liked. Now, in my sixties and, to borrow Woody Allen's words, 'a third of the way through my life', I have the freedom to do all those and more. It's a good thought.

Things change, as David Mamet wrote (no doubt a lot of other people did, too), and so they should. Sometimes they change for the better, sometimes for the worse. Swings and roundabouts. For me, the most dramatic change of all came on the evening of 12 March 1971, when Walter Terry handed me a long white envelope and said, 'I'm sorry but I've got to give you one of these.'

At the time I thought it contained the equivalent of a poisoned chalice but in fact what was inside turned out to be a passport to a better, richer, fuller life than I could otherwise have known. Lucky or what?

Index

('BN' in entries refers to Barry Norman)

and literary lunches 274–5
and Lord's Taverners 244, 247, 249, 251, 252
and MacLean profile 221–5
in Madrid 138–9, 153
and marijuana 162, 204
in Milan 175–8
in Monaco 106–9
in Morecambe and Wise Christmas show 245–6
on movie stars 154–6
and near-drowning incident 41–2
and *The News Quiz* 271
as novelist (*for individual titles see under* novels by BN) ii, 165, 191, 197, 237, 272–6
and *Omnibus* 265–9
and *Open Night*, appearance on 209–10
and the Oscars ceremony 282–90
paternal grandparents of 22
and Paul Tanfield column 94, 103–11
at Pitman's College 63
on politicians 143–6
prostitutes and 83, 136–7, 138
redundancy of, from *Daily Mail* ix–xiv, 192–3
retirement of, announced 345
in Rhodesia 82–4
with *Rhodesia Herald* 82, 85
on Rhodesian blacks 83–4
in Rome 139, 168, 169, 170–1
and Ron (childhood friend) 8–9
in Russia 129–37
and shoplifting and petty thieving 8–9, 13
as show-business correspondent of *Mail* 111–91 *passim*
at Sky 342–4
Sky, joins 286
and Sky, last year at 347
and Sky, leaving 345, 349
and Sky, offer from 335
on society 105–6
on South African blacks 73
in South Africa 67, 70–84
Spitting Image puppet of 327
with *Star*, Johannesburg 68, 72–85
and *Talking Pictures* 281, 331
and Taunton, move to 26
threatens resignation from *Mail* over Sellers–Ekland wedding 115–16
and *Times*, television review for 193, 196, 199, 207, 208
and *Today* 234–8, 244

on today's worst films 347
and *Tonight* 241–2, 270
and *The Turnip Head's Guide to British Cinema* 315
on TV and presenters, changes in fashion of 326–9
and university, decision not to attend 58–9
and vertigo 287
and war years 21–2, 24–5
on Winner 66, 94, 218–21
Winner, fires 94
Norman, Diana ('Dee') (BN's wife) ii, 1–2, 3, 6, 18–19, 22–3, 41, 62, 96–9, 101–3, 115, 125–6, 147–52, 183–4
BN becomes engaged to 98
and BN's *Guardian* column 206
BN marries 398–9
BN meets 96–7
and BN's redundancy 192
and daughters, birth of 149
grandchildren of 357
Hertfordshire, moves to 147
as historical novelist 356
likes and dislikes of 356
and MacLean 221
and Social Democrats 145–6
Norman, Elizabeth (née Crafford) (BN's mother) 4, 11–23, 41
death of 20–3
and Leslie, meets 30
and Leslie, rows with 31
and Leslie's death, reaction to 322
marriage of 30–1
and Milland 16
and petty thieving 9, 13–17 *passim*
and wheelchair, intent to steal 324
Norman, Emma (BN's daughter) 2, 41, 183
birth of 149
and movies, enthusiasm for 356
Norman, Leslie (BN's father) 4, 24–5, 33–42, 43–4, 76, 147
and army life 48
as associate producer, Ealing 49
and Barlow 34, 35, 36–9 *passim*
and *Blossom Time* 33
and BN's novel 272
in Burma 43–6
and cancer 318–20
and *The Case of the Frightened Lady* 37
and cricket 251–2
and *The Cruel Sea* 50
death of 31, 322

POCKET
BOOKS

NOBODY'S PERFECT
Billy Wilder: A Personal Biography

Charlotte Chandler

'You must read *Nobody's Perfect*' *Sunday Times*

Wilder's movies are consistently mentioned among the greatest of all time. The titles are familiar, but the man behind the camera is not. For years, publishers tried to persuade Wilder to tell his life story, but only biographer Charlotte Chandler succeeded.

Billy Wilder agreed to let her tell his story. But he ended up telling it himself. Soon, Chandler was recording conversations with his many friends, including such legends as Ginger Rogers, Jimmy Stewart, Jack Lemmon, and Tony Curtis.

Nobody's Perfect is touching, revealing and as close to perfection as anyone will ever get to capturing in print the essence of Billy Wilder.

ISBN 0 7434 6098 7
PRICE £7.99

POCKET
BOOKS

THE MEASURE OF A MAN
A Memoir

Sidney Poitier

In this beautifully written, candid memoir, legendary
actor Sidney Poitier reveals the spiritual depth, passion
and intellectual fervour that has driven his remarkable
life. Crediting his childhood of poverty for equipping
him with the unflinching sense of self-worth and
family values, Poitier reflects upon his poineering
career. He shares his provocative thoughts on racism in
Hollywood, consumerism and the media, illness and
mortality, honouring a higher consciousness and
paying the price for artistic integrity.

The Measure of a Man is a powerful testament to the
rewards of being true to one's self, acting passionately
on one's convictions and boldly walking on the edge.

'A thoughtful and stimulating memoir'
Spectator

'Reflective, generous, humane, moving'
New York Times

ISBN 0 7434 0386 X
PRICE £6.99

SIMON &
SCHUSTER

ALEC GUINNESS
The Authorized Biography

Piers Paul Read

Sir Alec Guinness was one of the greatest actors of
the twentieth century. He gained a world-wide
reputation playing roles on the screen such as Fagin
in *Oliver Twist* and *The Man in the White Suit*.
His performance in *Bridge on the River Kwai*
won him an Oscar.

Yet Guinness remained an enigma to the general
public and a mystery even to his family and
closest friends. After his death in 2000, his widow
Merula asked Piers Paul Read, who had been a
friend of her husband, to write his biography. Given
full co-operation by the family and free access to Sir
Alec's papers, including his private and unpublished
diaries, Read has written a penetrating and perceptive
account of an intriguing and complex man.

ISBN 0 7432 0729 7
PRICE £20.00

**SIMON &
SCHUSTER**

This book and other **Simon & Schuster/Pocket** titles are available from your bookshop or can be ordered direct from the publisher.

0 7434 6098 7	**Nobody's Perfect**	**Charlotte Chandler** £7.99
0 7434 0386 X	**The Measure of a Man**	**Sidney Poitier** £6.99
0 7434 0729 7	**Alec Guinness**	**Piers Paul Read** £20.00

Please send cheque or postal order for the value of the book, free postage and packing within the UK; OVERSEAS including Republic of Ireland £1 per book.

OR: Please debit this amount from my VISA/ACCESS/MASTERCARD:

CARD NO: . . . .

EXPIRY DATE: . . . .

AMOUNT: £ . . . .

NAME: . . . .

ADDRESS: . . . .

. . . .

SIGNATURE: . . . .

Send orders to SIMON & SCHUSTER CASH SALES
PO Box 29, Douglas Isle of Man, IM99 1BQ
Tel: 01624 836000, Fax: 01624 670923
www.bookpost.co.uk
Please allow 14 days for delivery. Prices and availability subject to change without notice.